MW01029024

ALSO BY EDWIN FRANK

Snake Train: Poems, 1984–2013

STRANGER THAN FICTION

STRANGER
THAN

LIVES OF THE

FICTION

TWENTIETH-CENTURY NOVEL

EDWIN FRANK

FARRAR, STRAUS AND GIROUX
NEW YORK

Farrar, Straus and Giroux
120 Broadway, New York 10271

Illustration credits can be found on page 453.

Library of Congress Cataloging-in-Publication Data
Names: Frank, Edwin, 1960– author.
Title: Stranger than fiction : lives of the twentieth-century novel / Edwin Frank.
Description: First edition. | New York : Farrar, Straus and Giroux, 2024.
    Includes bibliographical references and index.
Identifiers: LCCN 2024017379 | ISBN 9780374270964 (hardcover)
Subjects: LCSH: Fiction—20th century—History and criticism. |
    LCGFT: Literary criticism.
Classification: LCC PN3503 .F67 2024 | DDC 809.3/04—dc23/eng/20240625
LC record available at https://lccn.loc.gov/2024017379

Our books may be purchased in bulk for promotional, educational, or business
use. Please contact your local bookseller or the Macmillan Corporate and
Premium Sales Department at 1-800-221-7945, extension 5442, or by email at
MacmillanSpecialMarkets@macmillan.com.

www.fsgbooks.com
Follow us on social media at @fsgbooks

10 9 8 7 6 5 4 3 2 1

To Emma and Gus, and to Phoebe

Our unfortunate times thus compel me, once again, to write in a new way.

—GUY DEBORD

CONTENTS

INTRODUCTION

This book began over the kitchen sink a long time ago. I was doing the dishes after dinner. A CD of Radiohead's album *Kid A* was playing, which got me thinking about a recently published book, *The Rest Is Noise*, by the classical music critic (and Radiohead fan) Alex Ross. Ross's book told the story of modern classical music in light of the twentieth century's political, social, and technological upheavals; it took a rarefied Western art form out of the shelter of the concert hall into streets and factories, cabarets and concentration camps. Connecting the music's challenging, refractory character to the delirium of modern times, Ross established classical music as a shaping presence in the cultural life of the century, which continued to enliven the work of, for example, Radiohead. Radiohead's lead singer had cut his artistic chops in a church choir, singing music that dated back to the Middle Ages—in the band's keening, staticky, doom-laden anthems you could make out the hosannas—while the record *Kid A* was, I remember the not very well-founded rumor to have been, a nod to Theodor Adorno, the twentieth-century German philosopher who had been an unyielding champion of modern music at its most abrasive, as well as an unrelenting scourge of popular music. This was another of Ross's achievements: to connect the music of the century past with the music of today.

Writing about art in a way that illuminates the art itself as well as the life of art in the world is tricky. Ross had pulled it off. Could the same thing be done with the novel? The situation of the novel was different from the situation of so-called modern music. Far from slipping into notoriety and obscurity over the course of the last century, the novel had attained an even greater centrality to literary culture than it enjoyed in the past. It stood now as the literary form of the time, prestigious, popular, taken as both a mainstay of cultured conversation and of democratic culture. At the end of the twentieth century, the American pragmatist philosopher Richard Rorty went so far as to anoint it the touchstone of contemporary ethical awareness. Without a doubt, the novel was central to a certain contemporary sensibility: where, for example, in the eighteenth and nineteenth centuries, educated English speakers would have turned to the ancients, to Shakespeare and the poets, and to the Bible for edification, in Rorty's account they now picked up *Lolita*. I grew up between the pages of novels, and the better part of my adult life has been spent there too. Reading novels and thinking about the novel, the kinds of forms it has taken at different times and places and the ways they might continue to speak to readers today, has also been one of the pleasures and puzzles of my job as the editor of the New York Review Books Classics series. (I have never had the least interest in writing a novel—but that is another story.) It was the novel by which we had come to take the measure of who we were and who our neighbors were and what, for better or worse, we were all capable of: good, evil, deception, irony, truth. In America after 9/11, the recent publication of Jonathan Franzen's *The Corrections*— a big novel about the latter days of the last century—came to seem a timely reassurance that a rattled superpower could still see its reflection in the mirror.

How had the novel come to occupy this position? Could the story be told? Perhaps, but an obvious problem emerged. Novels are set apart by language in a way that music is not, while the very attention they lavish on local customs and mores, which can make them so telling to those in the know, can also render them entirely inscrutable to those who are not. We distinguish French literature from English and English from American, and only so much news slips across those borders. At the start of the twentieth century, Virginia Woolf wondered quite seriously how English readers could be expected to make head or tail of the translations of Russian literature that were beginning to appear at the time—and were, she was quite aware, already radically reshaping ideas of what the novel could be—when, she pointed out, Americans could hardly be counted on to grasp what was really going on, what was really at stake, in an English book. Her puzzlement, now, may seem exaggerated and even quaint, but the reasons for it haven't gone away. The academic study of literature remains linked to university language departments, while our sentimental attachment to the novel draws on a sense of shared community. The novel, no matter how sophisticated, remains homey. No book is more densely located in language and place than *Ulysses.*

It would be hard then, I thought, to tell anything but the most summary story about the novel in the twentieth century, irrespective of languages and literatures. Perhaps it was impossible. Yet just as I was abandoning the idea, I glimpsed the outlines of this book. My thoughts turned again to the Russian novel, and the way it had made such an extraordinary impression on the literature of the world almost entirely in translation. "In translation" was the key, opening the way into the story of the novel, which was, as I suddenly saw it, a story of translation in the largest sense, not only from language to language and place to place but more broadly as the translation of lived reality into written form, something the expansive and adaptable form of the novel had from the start been uniquely open to, which the last century had provided the perfect—what?—petri dish in which it could further develop. On one hand, the twentieth century had been a century of staggering transformation—world war, revolution, women voting, empires falling, cities sprawling, expanded life spans and lives cut short, mass media, genocide, the threat of nuclear extinction, civil and human rights, and so on—a century to boggle the mind, which demanded and stretched and beggared description. On the other hand we had the novel, emerging from the nineteenth century as a robust presence with a tenacious worldly curiosity and a certain complacent self-regard, a form that was both ready to shake things up and asking to be shook up. Hadn't the two, as the phrase goes, been made for each other?

The story of an exploding form in an exploding world? I thought it might make an interesting book.

More than a decade later, and well into a new century, here it is. What kind of book is it? As is so often true, it's easier to start by saying what it isn't. It isn't a book about all the different kinds of novels written in the last century, which would be impossible for me and, I imagine, anyone to write. It is not a narrower survey, reviewing how key moments and developments of the last century found representation in the fiction of the times. It's not—or only incidentally—a book about authors, notable or neglected, and how over the course of their careers they responded to such developments. Nor is it a book about artistic movements. A term like *modernism* has the usefulness of any carrying case, but it is hopelessly overused by now: the endless academic arguments about whether it is a backpack or a steamer trunk, and what to fit in or leave behind, have come to seem like the interminable deliberations of someone determined never to get out the door.

So much for what the book doesn't do. What it does is establish a rough-and-ready category, the twentieth-century novel—a category of novels that have made it a point to puzzle over what they, the century and the novel, were doing together and how, in effect, they were to get along (a category that, it should be clear from the get-go, is by no means coextensive with every book written in the course of the century). Given that, the book then looks closely at some thirty novels by thirty different novelists, written over the course of rather more than a hundred years, in a number of languages, from places across the world. By "looks closely" I mean simply that it looks at the kinds of things these books show us in relation to the kind of show they make. This is how any work of art demands that we look at it: form is always another form of content. When we look closely at the novel in the twentieth century, we see an art form of extraordinary amplitude put under unprecedented ongoing stress, and we see too that certain novels—the ones I look at here, particularly—respond to that stress by radically reshaping the novel as a literary form. These are books in which the novel seeks to prove itself "equal," in the words of the poet

Charles Olson, "to the real itself"—the real being all those realities of
the bedroom and the abattoir that the novel in the nineteenth century
had tended to keep in the background but which, in the twentieth
century, it would place front and center along with all the previously
unimaginable, too often unspeakable news that the new century delivered time and again. There were these drastic realities to put into
words, to attest to, and along with them—no less urgent, no less real—
was, as the century went on, the ever-altering, ever more searching
sense of the different shapes that novels could now take.

The book begins not at the stroke of midnight on January 1, 1900,
but in 1864 with the publication of Dostoevsky's *Notes from Underground*, an unclassifiable work—neither novel nor novella, at once
confession and caricature—that would come to seem ever more ahead
of its time and would go on being written and rewritten time and time
again in the century to come by writers as different as Jean Rhys, Vladimir Nabokov, and Philip Roth. In many ways, the 1860s laid down the
fractured foundation of that century. The decade had been preceded
by the imperial and colonial establishment of the British Raj in India,
and it was immediately followed by the unification of Germany, which
would become a fiercely determined new contender for European and
world power. The 1860s also bring the Meiji Restoration, inaugurat-
ing the modernization of Japan; they see the end of serfdom in Russia
and, in the United States, after the first mass industrial war, the end of
slavery. They see the publication of Karl Marx's *Capital*. And 1860, I
realize as I write, precedes my own birth by precisely a hundred years.
I suppose this may stand as an indication of the provisional and essentially personal character of any timeline.

Such is the prologue to what follows, a book in three parts, the
first of which takes us from the last years of the nineteenth century
through the end of World War I. Here we meet writers who turn
sharply away from their nineteenth-century forebears, rejecting existing forms of the novel and pioneering new ones shaped by the expansion of education and literacy, the new authority of science, changing
social and sexual mores, the flow of books and people to and from
places that previously had been inaccessibly far apart. I look at *The
Island of Doctor Moreau*, by H. G. Wells, and *The Immoralist*, by André

Gide, two writers who could not be more unalike, yet whose shared impatience with social convention and hunger for new experience and understanding turn them into pioneers of the twentieth-century novel. Wells invents a new kind of fiction that questions everything imaginable, first and foremost the state of the world, and it turns out to be immensely popular with everyone everywhere; Gide, disdaining popularity, recasts the novel in the most rarefied and personal of forms, a move that is no less subversive and is increasingly influential in its own right. At the turn of the century, Colette's Claudine novels and Rudyard Kipling's *Kim* are bold tales of brash youth taking on the world at large, a world that is being remade around them, while Kafka's *Amerika* and Gertrude Stein's "Melanctha" refashion the paragraph and the sentence into suggestive new instruments of discovery. In Machado de Assis's *Posthumous Memoirs of Brás Cubas* and Natsume Sōseki's *Kokoro*, the European novel is consciously refashioned in light of non-European realities, and something like a world literature begins to take shape. These are all urgent, exploratory, impatient books, full of anticipation and worldly appetite, and between them they advance attitudes and a repertoire of novel gestures that will provide a model for novelists to come. What does come, largely unexpectedly, is the Great War, welcomed at first by many as the storm that will clear the nineteenth century's stagnant air, soon turning into a four-year deadlock of destruction. Part One ends with three novels—*The Magic Mountain*, *In Search of Lost Time*, and *Ulysses*—that still stand as towering monuments of the twentieth century but are also direct responses to that war, reports from the novel's front line.

After the war, the new century is no longer, in Wells's words, the unknown "shape of things to come," whether longed for or dreaded. For the novelists of the twenties it has become a present reality, and what to make of it becomes their task. Proust and Joyce provide models, but their work can seem as solipsistic as it is suggestive. Virginia Woolf, for example, takes *Ulysses* as an exercise in navel-gazing, even as she can't deny (or accept) its importance, and in *Mrs. Dalloway* she finds a way to step around that obstacle, arriving at a style of her own and offering a spirited vision of men and women in the postwar world. Also written in the shadow of Joyce, Ernest Hemingway's first book, *In Our Time*, like *Mrs. Dalloway*, is a study in individual style, its narrative as splintered as its characters' lives, its sentences stress tested. Robert Musil's *The Man Without Qualities*, first sketched at the start of the century, interminably underway by the 1920s, finally interrupted by the author's death in 1942, is a book that is a bit of everything: satire, essay, philosophical inquiry, love story, and spiritual handbook, an attack on the novel as it exists and an effort to remake the novel as a lifesaving device. Italo Svevo's *Confessions of Zeno*, Jean Rhys's *Good Morning, Midnight*, and the great novels of D. H. Lawrence offer singular fictional points of view on the life chances of modern men and women. (The upended, provisional relations between the sexes is a theme in all these books.) A new world war, not at all unanticipated this time and even more devastating than the last, brings this period of astonishing invention to an end. In Hans Erich Nossack's *The End*, an account of the firebombing of Hamburg, and the two volumes of Vasily Grossman's monumental tale of the Battle of Stalingrad, the battle that turned the tide of war against the fascist Axis, the imaginative resources of fiction struggle both to engage with and fight clear of unbearable fact.

How does it all end up? At times I have thought of the twentieth-century novel as a fictional character in its own right and of this book as an old-fashioned picaresque, full of scrapes and capers, scares and narrow escapes, till at some point sightings of our protagonist become infrequent. She has no more news for us. There is no more news of him. They've gone missing once and for all. Something like that does happen, but before it does—in the long period of comparative peace and prosperity that, always under the threat of nuclear destruction, opens up the world after the war—the twentieth-century novel continues on its merry way. Great, flashy, scenery-chewing novels mark the moment, books that are at the same time marked with unsettling undertones of retrospection, reflection, and regret. Books like *Lolita*, Alejo Carpentier's *The Lost Steps*, Ralph Ellison's *Invisible Man*, García Márquez's *One Hundred Years of Solitude*, and George Perec's *Life A User's Manual* seek both to live up to and even outdo the spectacular precedent of the century's early masterpieces while also trying

to reckon with the scandal of the century's history. That history becomes the overt subject of Elsa Morante's no less prodigious *History*,
while more concentrated books like Anna Banti's *Artemisia*, Chinua
Achebe's *Things Fall Apart*, and Marguerite Yourcenar's *Memoirs of
Hadrian* look beyond the brutal and startling emergencies of modern times to recognize haunting specters of ages past. V. S. Naipaul's
The Enigma of Arrival, written after the defeat and demoralization
of the United States in the Vietnam War and a few years before the
collapse of the USSR—the end of what the historian Eric Hobsbawm
would designate the short twentieth century—examines the life of
a nameless, uprooted mid-twentieth-century writer born of a South
Asian family in the West Indies, resident in England, as if from an infinite remove. That life, spanning the whole of the ever more traveled
and commercialized twentieth-century world, is presented as only
one more episode in the endless coming and going of peoples and
worlds, the traffic of oblivion, and the book arrives at its moment of
truth before a funeral pyre.

Why these books? Well, I hope the roll call above gives some sense
of why I think they are telling. They are books with common concerns and with some common literary reference points—*The Arabian
Nights*, Flaubert, the Russians prominent among them—but they
can hardly be said to constitute a company or a tradition. My own
formulation, the twentieth-century novel, is perhaps best taken as a
useful fiction for considering how fiction responded to a century of
fact, and though the books gathered and juxtaposed here could be
seen to constitute a constellation, it is the limit of constellations, I am
all too aware, to exist only in the beholder's eye. Some of these books
are what passes for canonical, but that is not what interests me about
them, any more than setting up some sort of counter-canon of outcast
texts. I am interested not in what books prove, one way or another
(and in the end it is surely nothing), but in their life on the ground
and on the page, which is what I have tried to bring out. The selection is personal, too. I have written about books that move me, always
keeping in mind Randall Jarrell's affectionate jibe about a novel being
a long story with something wrong with it. Literature makes its own
demand on our attention, and the power of literature—to respond to

the times, to transform our perceptions and our lives, to be itself—is not only my subject but also something that all the books here struggle to engage and bring to light. Late in the writing of the book it came to me that I could be said to see the novel as prophetic in form. It embarrassed me a bit, since I certainly don't want to suggest that fiction should trade in portent and rebuke, and the books assembled here are neither finger-pointing nor finger-wagging. What I do mean is that literature is meant to open eyes.

The book covers a fair amount of ground. It also leaves a great deal out. I think of all the other books and other authors I would have liked to include, among them Rabindranath Tagore, Willa Cather, Mikhail Sholokhov, John Dos Passos, Louis Aragon, Louis-Ferdinand Céline, Andrei Platonov, Daniel O. Fagunwa, Naguib Mahfouz, Jun'ichirō Tanizaki, Janet Lewis, Qian Zhongshu, John Cowper Powys, Giorgio Bassani, Marguerite Duras, Ingeborg Bachmann, Julio Cortázar, Joseph Heller, and so on and so on, and perhaps above all Joseph Conrad, whose unparalleled tetralogy—*Heart of Darkness, Nostromo, The Secret Agent,* and *Under Western Eyes*—invented the twentieth-century political novel, in which politics is a disease from which no recovery can be hoped. (In acknowledgment of omissions, I've provided a roundup of further reading at the end of the book.) I think of all the other things there are to say and how the case I make is by necessity a limited instance of the story I seek to tell. The books I write about are, for example, all written in major European languages (Sōseki's *Kokoro* is the one exception), and this is hardly representative of the novel's spread throughout the world or even in Europe itself. This book isn't and doesn't pretend to be comprehensive even within its own terms, and I hope it retains something of the casual quality of the thought experiment with which it first began.

Finally, a word about the manner of presentation. Broadly conceived, this is an essay in literary history, a work of descriptive criticism as practiced by such working critics as Clement Greenberg, Randall Jarrell, Pauline Kael, Elizabeth Hardwick, and Greil Marcus, but also by scholars like Eric Auerbach, Sydney Freedberg, Tony Tanner (in his great *Prefaces to Shakespeare*), and T. J. Clark. I suppose the models who mean most to me are three subjects of this book,

Henry James, Virginia Woolf, and D. H. Lawrence, whose criticism is as alert and as astonishing as any of their writing. All these critics are also artful writers, and their criticism arrives at its insights by sticking close to the work at hand while also seeking (struggling) to find words of its own to describe the work and the feelings and thoughts it evokes and contends with. It is, I'm sure, by tracking a novel's turns of event and turns of phrase, its varied voices and points of view, stepping up to it and away from it, keeping an eye on it, paging through it (since the experience of reading a book, and a novel perhaps most of all, is inseparable from its presence in hand) that one begins to discern how it goes about making sense and how it matters and might continue to matter. The critic's sense of a book is always partial and provisional, but so long as it doesn't set out to substitute an interpretation or explanation for the book itself—well, then it may provide a glimpse of both the book in action and the action of reading the book—that hoped-for moment of encounter.

STRANGER THAN FICTION

PROLOGUE: THE ELLIPSIS

FYODOR DOSTOEVSKY'S *NOTES FROM UNDERGROUND*

It is the beginning of 1864. Fyodor Dostoevsky is in Moscow writing the first twentieth-century novel.

He doesn't know it, of course. (He never will.) What he knows is that he is in a fix. The only way to get out of it is to finish the work at hand.

Dostoevsky was forty-two, unhappily married, childless. He was short, slight, high-strung, with pale, thin hair and a long, scraggly beard. He wrote manically, deep into the night, over endless cups of coffee, cigars, and cigarettes. He was always on deadline and always running behind. He suffered regularly from epileptic fits that left him debilitated for days.

He'd already made a name for himself as a novelist to watch and as an influential critic and editor. In 1861 he and his doggedly supportive older brother, Mikhail, had started a monthly magazine called *Time*, and it had developed a following. Tsar Alexander II had ascended the throne in 1855, and the early years of his reign were a time of openness to new ideas, leading, in 1861, to the emancipation of the serfs. Periodicals like *Time*, known as "thick magazines" as they could run to hundreds of pages, played an important role in nineteenth-century Russia's intellectual and cultural life and had been especially influential during this period of transition.

Politically, the Dostoevsky brothers were proponents of what was called *pochvennichestvo*, from the Russian word for soil, *poch*. Back to the soil. Dostoevsky felt that the way to reform Russian society—and few doubted that the tsar's vast, unwieldy, politically regressive, economically underdeveloped empire needed some kind of reform—was to cultivate native Russian virtues and institutions, not to chase after Western fashions such as constitutionalism and capitalism. This belief aligned Dostoevsky with Slavophiles and conservatives, as well as with certain socialists, who were united in seeing modern, moneyed Europe as spiritually bankrupt. It set him completely apart, however, from the increasingly influential young radical utopian materialists—in many ways precursors to the Bolsheviks—sometimes characterized as nihilists.

The Dostoevsky brothers had positioned *Time* as a scourge of materialism and Europeanism that could serve as an honest broker in the dispute among patriotic "true" Russians, whether on the left or right, about where the country should go. It was a tricky balancing act, and in 1863 it came to a confused, almost comic end—disastrous for the brothers' fortunes. That year in Warsaw there was an uprising of Polish nationalists against tsarist rule. *Time* had run a piece on the uprising, arguing that the Polish rebellion had an essentially European character. Given *Time*'s Slavophile sympathies, this was intended as a condemnation; the government censor—missing the right note of jingoistic outrage and mistaking subtlety for subterfuge—saw it instead as a seditious endorsement. *Time* was immediately shut down. In general, the government was turning away from the policy of reform, which had only prompted demands for further reform: the Poles were up in arms, the peasants restive. The closure of *Time* was part of a wider crackdown not just on dissent but on open discussion.

The previous year, the radical periodical *The Contemporary* had been shuttered for some months, then permitted to resume publication. Swamped by debt after the sudden demise of *Time*, Mikhail Dostoevsky hoped for a similar outcome. Instead, the authorities eventually gave him the go-ahead to begin an entirely new magazine. This was hardly a blessing. *Time* had an established reputation and a subscriber base that allowed it to turn a profit. All the work that had gone into it would have to be done again. The new magazine—to be called *Epoch*—would have to be launched with a bang.

While this was going on, Fyodor had run off to Europe in pursuit of a young woman.

Apollonia (Polina) Suslova, who was in her twenties, had contributed a few articles to *Time* before becoming Dostoevsky's mistress. At first she had been wildly in love with the middle-aged married writer. Soon, however, she was furious at his unwillingness to make their relationship public. He didn't want to hurt his wife. Polina set off for Europe, and Dostoevsky pursued her to Italy. She led him on and put him off while he gambled away his own money and money borrowed from her or from Mikhail. When the affair came to its inevitable end and Dostoevsky returned to Russia, his wife, Maria Dmitrievna, was in the last throes of tuberculosis. "At every instant she sees death before her eyes," Dostoevsky wrote to his brother. He began to suffer one violent epileptic attack after another.

Meanwhile, *Epoch* was demanding his attention. New fiction was needed for the first issue: he had commissioned a story by the celebrated Ivan Turgenev; then, largely for lack of anything by anyone else, he decided to contribute something of his own. Dostoevsky wasn't sure just what form his contribution would take—a story, perhaps the start of a full-scale novel; one way or another, the work was "going badly." "I have messed up something," he wrote Mikhail, who had problems of his own: his young son died shortly after. Dostoevsky missed a February deadline, but then in March 1864 the work was done, sent to the censor, and approved for publication. When Dostoevsky received the printed magazine, he was shocked to discover that the censor had cut "the very idea of" his story. The thing has been left completely incomprehensible, he complained.

Desperation and uncertainty surrounded the composition and publication of *Notes from Underground* from the start. That uncertainty would take on a life of its own in pages of frantic, baffled, scabrous, satiric, prophetic intensity. Uncertainty of the most matter-of-fact sort is evident in the note that preceded the first section of the work in *Epoch*:

> Both the author of these notes and the "Notes" themselves are, it stands to reason, fictitious. And yet, individuals like the penner of such notes not only *can*, but even *must* exist in our society . . . In this excerpt the individual presents himself, his point of view, and, as it were, wishes to clarify the reasons for which he has appeared—and necessarily so—in our midst.

The reader can only wonder, What is this? What's to come? Doesn't the writer know?

Here the uncertainty is all the more striking for being compounded with inevitability. (What goes without saying, any savvy reader knows, is precisely what doesn't.) The author sets himself apart from his character and then attributes to the character the same project—of proving that the character is a necessary manifestation of modern life—that the author claims as his own. How far apart, or close, are the two writers, fictional and actual, of these *Notes*, the very title of which is ambiguous? Notes—writing that is personal and provisional, anything but final—from Underground, a word with an unmistakable whiff of the grave, and, well, what could be more final than that?

The story begins, "I am a sick man . . ." It begins—and immediately breaks off with that ellipsis. Resumes: "I am an evil man. An unattractive man I am. I think my liver hurts." And so it goes, an unfurling, furious scribble, filling the columns of *Epoch*.

Who is this? Not Dostoevsky, we've already been alerted (though he too was, as he wrote, a sick man), but some unknown yet representative character, some writer who is writing about himself and demanding our attention. Writing is a solitary activity, but this writer makes a pretense of being in our presence. "A moment, please! Allow me to catch my breath . . ." The voice is nagging, needy, self-conscious, clowning, and hectoring. It is out of control, the voice of someone who accosts you on the street and won't let you go.

The voice is a pain, and like pain it threatens to go on and never stop. But what claim does this pain have to implicate us in its existence? If we continue to read, isn't that claim somehow borne out? So now there is a question in the air, or rather in our heads, into which, by a strange and distinctly disagreeable act of ventriloquism, the voice has slipped, occupying our thoughts: Why are you putting up with this? Who am I? Who are you? If you're reading this, perhaps you're sick too? Perhaps this is your pain?

Everything happens fast. The sentences are hard to focus on or follow. The subject keeps changing and yet somehow is always the same. The reader is ambushed, stunned.

Now the writer introduces himself, assumes a form: he is an educated man; a vain man, "guilty that I'm the most intelligent of all those who surround me"; a middle-aged man; a single man; "an intelligent person of the nineteenth century." He is a forty-year-old former functionary from low down in the civil service who retired early to live on a meager inheritance in a seedy apartment in an outlying district of St. Petersburg, the "most abstract and calculated city on the whole earthly sphere." He is, in other words, a nonentity: "I wanted to become an insect many times. But even that wasn't afforded to me."

And now, with swelling voice, he introduces a new character, us. "Ladies and Gentlemen," he says, taking the spotlight. We, like him, are people of the nineteenth century, though unlike him in every other way. We are respectable, normal people, subscribing to well-founded beliefs. "There's no doubt in your mind," he tells us. What do we believe? In progress, reason, science, in pursuing our own best interests, in maintaining and managing ourselves with the understanding and skill with which a trained mechanic operates a machine. We believe—or so the writer says—in the perfectibility of man and the inevitability of utopia, the crystal palace in which, with motives as transparent as our deeds are good, we will all at last come to live in perfect harmony.

We believe that two times two equals four.

And here the writer, Dostoevsky, introduces a memorable image:

> For two times two as four is no longer life, ladies and gentlemen, but the beginning of death [. . .] Let us suppose that man does nothing but seek out this two times two as four, he swims across oceans, sacrifices his life in this seeking-out, but to seek it out, to truly find it—oh Lordy, he's somehow afraid of that. For he feels that, once he's found it, then there'll be nothing left to seek out [. . .] But two times two as four really is an unbearable thing. In my opinion, two times two as four is nothing but impudence—yessir. Two times two as four stands there with its hands at its sides, it's in your way, it's spitting in your direction. I agree that two times two as four is a superlative thing; but if we're just going to heap praise on everything, then I say that two times two as five can also be a most sumptuous little thing sometimes.

By this time it has become impossible to say what kind of writing this is: confession, tract, polemic, rant, philosophy, literature, or, as the writer now tells us, anything but literature? And it seems to be about everything and nothing: the nineteenth century, politics, progress, literature, life. Well, it's all lies, the writer now blurts out. These pages could never be published, after all; and even if someone were to offer to publish them, he would never allow it. What we are reading does not and could not exist.

And then Dostoevsky ends by playing the oldest, tawdriest trick in the book of writerly tricks: promising a story, one that will explain everything—next time.

Maria Dmitrievna died on April 16. Dostoevsky kept watch over her body that night, notebook in hand. It is an occasion for thought. "Masha is lying on the table. Will I meet Masha again?" And he continues:

"I" is the stumbling block . . . The highest use a man can make of his individuality . . . is to seemingly eliminate that I . . . And this indeed is the greatest happiness . . . This is the paradise of Christ . . . the final goal of humanity . . . In my judgement it is completely senseless to attain such a great goal if upon attaining it everything is extinguished and disappears . . . Consequently, there is a future, heavenly life.

And much more in this vein, pages and pages of diary writing, with no further mention of Masha, though after a few entries we read "2 x 2 = 4 is fact, not science."

A letter from some months later contains an epitaph for the marriage: "Despite being positively unhappy together (because of her strange, suspicious, and unhealthy fantastic character)—we could not cease loving each other; the unhappier we were, the more we became attached to each other. No matter how strange, that is how it was."

Devastated, Dostoevsky continues to work on his book, the promised second part of which is due. He has only the sketchiest idea of where he is going. "I write and write . . . Mere verbiage, chatter, with an extremely bizarre tone, brutal and violent. It may displease." At the same time, he insists to his brother, "It's absolutely necessary that it be successful; it is necessary for me."

Readers would have to wait until the July 1864 issue of *Epoch* to meet the writer of *Notes from Underground* again. The second part would seem to stand in a classically symmetrical relation to the first. If the first part ended with the claim that it was all lies, it also promised that the truth behind both parts, the cause of the effect, would be revealed in the second. Now, no longer protesting and disclaiming, the writer reappears as a more or less conventional first-person narrator, recounting a story from his youth.

The story may be conventional in form, but its content is shocking. Once upon a time, the narrator tells us, he was a devotee of the true, the good, the beautiful—and here's what happened. Having gotten a minor job in the government bureaucracy, he decided to crash the birthday party of a former classmate whose riches and popularity he envied. He makes a scene at the party, humiliating himself. His companions ditch him and head to a whorehouse; he follows and picks out a girl, Liza, fresh from the country and new to the job. They have sex, after which he earnestly warns her about the perils of her life and offers to help her mend her ways. Weeks later she shows up at his apartment. He is appalled. He mocks and vilifies her. Thinking back on the scene, he accuses himself: "Power, power was what I needed back then, games too, I needed to bring forth your tears, your humiliations, and your hysterics . . . How I hated her and how I was attracted to her in that moment! One feeling overpowered the other." So he comes on to her. She is confused, then welcoming, loving; fifteen minutes later he wants her to leave. What he wants her to feel, in fact, is raped, though when she is at the door, he slips her some money before abruptly turning away. After which, crushed with guilt, he rushes out after her into the snowy night. But she is gone. Only the five-ruble note he tried to give her remains.

"Brutal and violent" this record of resentment, degradation, and violation is, and though not much of a story, it does seem like a page ripped out of real life. Ripped out of literature, too, ripped out and defaced, since this is nothing if not a send-up of those staple sentimental stories about earnest young men redeeming fallen women. The writer himself used to crave the fix of that kind of fiction ("You speak somehow . . . as if you were reading a book," Liza says to him questioningly), at least until his real, irredeemable character was exposed.

Not that he asks forgiveness: "I'm really not justifying myself . . ." In fact he thinks that what he's done—and his willingness to tell us just what he's done—ugly as it is, gives him a certain authority: "In my life, I have only taken to an extreme that which you didn't even dare to take halfway, you took your own cowardice for prudence too, you used it to console yourselves, deceive yourselves. It is thus that I may still perhaps turn out 'more alive' than you." Having presented himself as a nonentity in the first part, he now exposes himself as a monster. That is his peculiar authority, his proof of authenticity, but does it give him the right to address us as he does? To judge us?

At which point the book breaks off. Breaks off and resumes, ending (as it began) with a note from Dostoevsky: "In point of fact, the 'notes' of this paradoxalist do not end here. He could not restrain himself and continued on. But it also seems to us that we might as well stop here."

He couldn't resist and went on writing. This is fiction, we have been told, but not literature. The fictional narrator, in fact, has a horror of literature: "I've at least been ashamed the whole time I was writing this *narration*: as such, this is no kind of literature, but a corrective punishment." He generalizes the point: "For we don't even know where the *living* now lives—and what is it, what is it called? Leave us alone, without books, and we'll immediately get all tangled up and lost."

If literature is a problem throughout *Notes*, reality is even more so. Reality is associated with violent disruption. Why does the narrator decide to crash his classmate's party, unwanted though he is? Because, "[If I don't go], I'd then taunt myself for the rest of my life: 'Alright then, you lost your nerve, *reality* made you lose your nerve and you lost your nerve.'" Going, he thinks, will result in "some radical rupture in my life," though he adds sardonically, "It's out of habit, perhaps, but for my whole life, at any external event, even the smallest of occurrences, it always seemed to me that some radical break in my life was impending, at that very moment." And after his humiliation, what is his first thought? "So, there it is, there I've finally had my encounter with reality."

Reality is associated with disruption, but also with compulsion: this is real writing, not literature, because it can't be helped. Reality is also associated with pain, not to mention sickness. And though *Notes* may at times seem forbiddingly abstract, near hermetic in its hysteria, it is in fact very much connected to the real life of its own time. The book is almost topical.

The realities are global—those of a time and place that is ever more aware of what's going on in the wider world, that is besieged by news and new ideas. The writer mentions the American Civil War and the Schleswig-Holstein conflict, and of course the Crystal Palace, the celebrated centerpiece of the great 1851 World's Fair in London in which Victorian England held up its power and prosperity for the admiration of the world. (Dostoevsky had visited the London fair of 1862 and left in horror.) Darwin comes up. *On the Origin of Species* had been published in 1859. The prospect of test-tube babies even makes an appearance.

The realities are also distinctly Russian. The writer identifies himself as a member of a particular Russian generation, the one that came of age in the 1840s—this is Dostoevsky's own generation—and the second part of the book is set in the 1840s. The great inspiration to this generation was Vissarion Belinsky, an immensely influential literary and social critic—he started off as a high-minded romantic and ended up as a politically committed realist—and Dostoevsky's first critical champion. This manic monologuist—Dostoevsky described his voice emerging as a continual scream—once stopped a guest from leaving his house in the early hours of the morning with the words "But we haven't even gotten to God yet!"

The writer of *Notes*, who offers himself to a poor prostitute as her savior and then proceeds to rape her, is, among other things, a bitter caricature of the generation of the 1840s, with its sentimental and revolutionary dreams. And yet by identifying the writer as a resident of St. Petersburg, Dostoevsky places him in a different, more vertiginous, Russian historical perspective. Petersburg, built from scratch in a frozen Baltic swamp on the command and under the supervision of Peter the Great, is, like Versailles—or for that matter ancient Nineveh—both an assertion of absolute power and an expression of idealism. Petersburg, known as Russia's "window on the west," opened the prospect of a transformed empire, enlightened and prosperous, that would emerge in the future, and yet it remained inseparable from Russia's despotic and murderous past.

Petersburg's vast avenues, dwarfing statues, and looming government buildings are reflected in its shimmering canals or engulfed in freezing fog or by the wet snow that falls throughout the second part of *Notes*. The city had a hallucinatory aspect. At the center of Russian reality was a mirage.

Could literature help people penetrate the mirage? In Russia it had become the main forum for investigating the country's unrealized potential and sometimes deadly realities. Literature, you could say, was another kind of spying in a country full of spies, even as notable, good writers might find employment as government censors. Under the tutelage of reaction, Russian writers had learned how to play the stops of their language. Pushkin's verse novel *Eugene Onegin*; the wild prose of Gogol's *Dead Souls* (subtitled "an epic poem"); Lermontov's *A Hero of Our Time*, a novel in the form of a bundle of stories; Turgenev's *Fathers and Children*; Chernyshevsky's fictional tract *What Is to Be Done*: these are bold, innovative books that sought out new forms—some found abroad, some very much homemade—to give imaginative currency to the life-and-death issues of the day.

Notes from Underground is certainly a conscious contribution to this ongoing, distinctively Russian exploration of Russian fact and fiction. Readers, familiar with Dostoevsky's politics at the time, would have recognized it as a riposte to the revolutionary fantasies of *What Is to Be Done?* (published not long before *Notes*, and itself a response to *Fathers and Children*). In this enormously successful utopian novel, a cult book among the radical young, Nikolay Chernyshevsky, drawing inspiration from the 1851 Great Exhibition in London, envisioned an ideal future of material plenty and emotional harmony in the form of a crystal palace—the crystal palace that the Underground Man dismisses with disgust. Beyond that, however, the title of Dostoevsky's work connects it to Gogol's seminal *Dead Souls* and to Dostoevsky's own autobiographical (as everyone knew, though it was disguised as fiction) *Notes from the House of the Dead* of 1859, then his most successful work to date.

Indeed, some readers coming to the new book, this new set of notes, this new confrontation with death, might well have expected a continuation of the earlier, autobiographical work, a reading that the note at the head of *Notes* might have been intended to head off. Head it off, or invite it, or at least conjure up the possibility. Because everyone knew that Dostoesvky, like his character, was a member of the generation of the 1840s, a legendary one in fact. They knew that for many years he too had been counted among the living dead.

The Dostoevsky of the 1840s had been a rising young writer. His first novel, *Poor Folk*, had come out in 1846 and was a great success. An epistolary novel about the hopeless love between a hapless copy clerk and the pretty girl next door, *Poor Folk* makes the human cost of poverty heartbreakingly vivid and was immediately hailed by Belinsky, who admired the way Dostoevsky made the reader feel for his rather pathetic characters and feel, too, that things like this shouldn't be allowed to go on. Belinsky heaped praise on the young man, who did a brief star turn as Belinsky's protégé and the next big thing. Before too long, however, Dostoevsky's gaucherie, vanity, hypersensitivity—like the writer of *Notes from Underground* he was "extremely touchy . . . as suspicious and as quick to take offence as a hunchback or dwarf"— lost him most of the new friends he'd made.

He was in any case getting caught up in politics. Around the time *Poor Folk* made his name, Dostoevsky began to participate in a discussion group that met at the house of a radical young aristocrat, Mikhail Petrashevsky. In 1848, as nationalist and revolutionary uprisings challenged traditional dynastic powers throughout Europe, it was the Petrashevsky circle's fervent hope that reform, even revolution, might at last come to Russia. Their enthusiasm was matched by Nicholas I's alarm. The tsar even considered dispatching an army to defend Europe's threatened rulers. At home, his spies set to work, and the meetings at Petrashevsky's house were placed under surveillance.

The Petrashevsky circle was quite large, and over time it spawned various subgroups. Dostoevsky was a member of the so-called propaganda society, a covert groupuscule whose main mover was another radical young aristocrat, Nikolai Speshnev, a connoisseur of conspiracy who fascinated Dostoevsky. ("I am with him and belong to him," he told a friend. "I have . . . my own Mephistopheles.") The propaganda society had developed a plan to secretly assemble a printing press (access to printing presses was under government control) in order to publish seditious material: a pamphlet, for example, explaining in simple language that the tsar, in requiring peasants to serve in the army, was violating the commandment "Thou shalt not kill," which meant that it was right to kill him. Tracts of this sort would prepare the way for a popular uprising, and this, it was hoped, would find support from progressive elements in the army.

In April 1849 the authorities cracked down on the Petrashevsky circle. Dostoevsky was arrested in the middle of the night, along with some sixty other people. They were imprisoned in the Peter and Paul Fortress, the tsarist Bastille. Many of the prisoners were released, but the ringleaders, including Dostoevsky, Speshnev, and Petrashevsky, were interrogated repeatedly throughout the summer as the authorities sought to link the radical talk of the circle to revolutionary conspiracy. They suspected the existence of something like the propaganda society but were never able to prove it. The prisoners were under enormous psychological pressure, but the conditions they lived in were comparatively benign. Dostoevsky had access to magazines and books—he read *Jane Eyre*—was free to correspond with his brothers, and even wrote a story. He wasn't sure how his case would turn out, but he expected to be able to handle whatever happened.

On December 22, a bitterly cold day, Dostoevsky was awakened in darkness and driven in a carriage through crowded streets to the vast Semyonovsky Square. There he was reunited with his fellows from the Petrashevsky circle, all very excited to see one another. The men were led by an Orthodox priest to a raised platform and ordered to line up and remove their hats: they would learn what they had been found guilty of and the sentence that would be imposed. This was it: found guilty of conspiring against the government, they were condemned to go before the firing squad.

No one had expected it. It was impossible, Dostoevsky blurted out as he and his companions were ordered to strip and don the suits of cheap white sacking with white caps worn by men condemned to death. The priest called on them to repent. No one did. They were given a cross to kiss, and they kissed it. Three men, Petrashevsky among them, were escorted from the platfom to face the firing squad. Hoods were pulled down over their eyes—Petrashevsky, intransigent, pushed his back—and their arms were secured to stakes. The firing squad took aim. The other prisoners looked on from the platform, and there was a crowd in the square. Time passed, abruptly punctuated by a roll of the drum. The soldiers lowered their guns. A messenger from the tsar had arrived: the death sentence had been commuted; the prisoners were to be sentenced to hard labor in Siberia instead.

The death sentence had in fact been entirely for show—but the prisoners didn't know that. One of the men who had faced the firing squad went crazy for life. Dostoevsky, who had been next in line for execution, returned to his prison cell in a state of wild exultation. He wrote a letter to Mikhail:

> Life is life everywhere . . . There will be people around me, and to be a *man* among men . . . that is what life is, that is its purpose . . . Yes, this is the truth! The head that created, that lived by the superior life of art, that recognized and became used to the highest spiritual values, that head has already been lopped off my shoulders. What is left is the memories and the images that I have already created but not yet given form to. They will lacerate and torment me now, it is true! But I have, inside me, the same heart, the same flesh and blood that can still love and suffer and pity and remember—and this, after all, is life. On voit le soleil!

"On voit le soleil" quotes from Victor Hugo's novel *The Last Day of a Condemned Man*. No sooner is life restored than it turns to literature. There's no mistaking that the voice we hear in this letter is the one we hear at the end of *Notes from Underground*.

Notes from the House of the Dead is Dostoevsky's account of his years in prison camp. In Siberia, the convicts wear heavy fetters around their ankles (they are not designed to prevent escape; they are designed to inflict pain) and different uniforms to match their crimes. A sullen silence reigns. Everybody has a story to tell, but it is a mistake to tell it and even worse to pry. They talk in their sleep, though. "We are beaten folks," they explain. "The insides have been beaten out of us, that is why we call out of nights."

The camp is under the direction of a drunken, sadistic major who patrols the barracks at night, prods the prisoners awake, commands them to roll over. One day his pet poodle dies; he weeps inconsolably.

As a so-called "political," above all as a gentleman, Dostoevsky is despised by his fellow convicts. They "wouldn't mind murdering [you]," he's told, "and no wonder. You're a different sort of people, not like them." He can't write letters and is not allowed to receive them. (He doesn't know this. He believes that his family has given up on him.) He is allowed to read the Bible. The convicts' backbreaking labor is too much for him, and a sympathetic doctor gives him a pass to the infirmary. The patients wear gowns crusty with every kind of bodily discharge, including the blood of prisoners brought there, insensible with pain, to be patched up after running the gauntlet. What is the pain like? Dostoevsky wants to know. He cannot get a satisfactory description.

The prison camp depicted in *Notes from the House of the Dead* is a world where the inner life has been systematically destroyed. Spirit manifests itself only in explosions of destructive, and ultimately self-destructive, behavior. Dostoevsky looks at one prisoner—a particularly evil man—and sees only "a lump of flesh, with teeth and a stomach." We sense that he has come to see himself this way, too.

What does it mean to be human? In prison Dostoevsky learns that to be human is to be capable of doing anything, of getting used to anything. For every different personality, he remarks, there is a different crime. This is finally a point of human pride, he thinks. The infinity of human perversion proves the freedom of the human soul.

To describe the "inexhaustible stream of the strangest surprises, the greatest enormities" that Dostoevsky confronted in Siberia—that, you could say, he had already confronted when he stared at death in Semyonovsky Square—he had to invent a new kind of writing. Founded on fact, *The House of the Dead* is a strange hybrid, as much an ethnography and an allegory of Russian life as it is an autobiographical novel. Much of the book is devoted to describing his first days in the camp. (Days after that, we understand, are all the same. They become years—four years in full—and then the years fall away.) The book is the record of an initiation; it is an initiation, at least insofar as reading can assume the dimensions of reality, and that is the question Dostoevsky's new writing proposes. The tone is largely deadpan. The book is submitted as evidence, not as an explanation.

Tolstoy and Turgenev thought *The House of the Dead* was Dostoevsky's greatest work. It would have many successors in the twentieth century, from the terrible chronicles of the gassed trenches that would come out of World War I to the memoirs of the survivors of the world's prisons and death camps. *Literature or Life* is the question posed by the title of Jorge Semprún's memoir of Buchenwald. The title of Primo Levi's great book about his time in Auschwitz raises another question, *If This Is a Man*. One of Dostoevsky's convicts protests: "After all, I too am a man." And then he pauses: "What do you think, am I man or aren't I?"

And that too could just as well be the writer of *Notes from Underground* speaking. It has the sound of his bitter, self-wounding self-assertion.

Notes from the House of the Dead and *Notes from Underground* are related by more than their titles. They are related in conception, offering distinct but complementary takes on the same dilemmas of life and literature. In the earlier book we observe the prisoners' lives from the outside. They are without freedom, and they have no way out. In the latter we are drawn into a certain tormented state of mind, no less imprisoning than the prison camp of *The House of the Dead*. In *Notes from Underground* the writing explodes and implodes, and all the time the writer is trapped inside it, not only unable to get out, but unable to see what it is he has gotten himself into, an inside that is all inside out, just as his squalid living space, his hole, the hole he is in, is indistinguishable from the space of his self.

This collapsing of inner and outer space becomes explicit, part of Dostoevsky's artistic design, in the second part of the novel. The writer relaxes a bit, paints a comic, almost forgiving picture of his youthful self needing, after days of solitude, "to embrace all mankind immediately." Here we step back into the social world, into which the main characters of most nineteenth-century novels venture in order to meet the future and find their proper place, be it good or bad. And yet, having briefly raised the expectation of a story with a normal development and conclusion—a story of the day, like Turgenev's elegant *Fathers and Children*—Dostoevsky decisively frustrates it. *Notes from Underground* takes us back into the past and dumps us there like a dead body.

For the reader, in other words, there is no more possibility of escape than there is for the writer. Even more than *House of the Dead*, *Notes* exists to make us confront an intractable reality, one that demands our attention but does not respond to it. The book doesn't describe this reality so much as impose it upon us.

In this way, *Notes* introduces a conception of reality, and a relation of author and reader to it, that are quite different from reality as it had been previously represented in what, conventionally, we refer to as the nineteenth-century realist novel. How is it different? After all, Dostoevsky, whose first literary undertaking was a translation of Balzac's *Eugénie Grandet*, is as deeply engaged with the still-thriving tradition of the nineteenth-century novel as his near contemporary Flaubert is or as Henry James will be. And yet *Notes from Underground* represents as significant a shift in the history of the novel as does Karl Marx's adage "the philosophers have only interpreted the world; the point is to change it" in the history of philosophy.

Reviewing a novel that is roughly contemporary with Dostoevsky's *Notes*, Anthony Trollope's *Can You Forgive Her?* of 1865, the young Henry James witheringly begins, "This new novel of Mr. Trollope's has nothing new to teach us either about Mr. Trollope himself as a novelist, about English society as a theme for the novelist, or, failing information on these points, about the complex human heart." James's sally captures the conventional view of the day of what the novel should do quite exactly, and the criticism would have been all the more wounding since Trollope certainly shared its assumptions. That view, as described in Ian Watt's classic study *The Rise of the Novel*, had gradually taken shape, especially in England, over the course of the eighteenth century. Samuel Richardson's novels, the tragic *Clarissa* (1748) above all, had introduced a new emotional realism to the genre. Their epistolary form allowed the novelist to put his pen in the hand of his characters, who are set free to track the motions of their minds and hearts, in which the reader may become as absorbed as they are. (*Clarissa* was in a sense the first cult novel; the cult was international and huge.) The comic fiction of Henry Fielding, by contrast, demonstrates what Watt calls a realism of assessment, as Fielding sizes up his characters' deeds and motivations with a shrewd, worldly eye, the better to entertain but also to educate the reader in the ways of the world. Toward the end of the century, these two forms of realism come together, Watt argues, in Sterne's *Tristram Shandy* (a triumph of rococo whimsy, as authorially playful as its characters are silly and moody, that was another international hit) and, especially, in the work of Jane Austen. In the very title of *Sense and Sensibility*, the perils and possibilities of two distinct ways of perceiving and responding to the world are presented for our consideration (and amusement): one (sense) alert to the world at large and to the consequences of our actions; the other (sensibility), which attends to the world of feelings. There are, in other words, claims that the world, or society, makes on us and claims made by the self, and within the capacious and welcoming confines of the great nineteenth-century novels that follow from Austen, claims of both sorts must find accommodation. Indeed—it is implicitly suggested—it is simple common sense to recognize that only by integrating these two views can a proper—realistic—relation to reality as a whole will emerge, whereas clinging exclusively to one or the other way of seeing things will lead to disappointing, if not tragic, results. Yet the seemingly simple imperative of responding to the summons of common sense turns out to be much harder than anyone would imagine, or so the nineteenth-century novel works to show. The problem is of infinite interest, in fact—and significant risk. If Emma Woodhouse finds her Mr. Knightley, Emma Bovary finds death.

Description or imitation is of course central to the power of the nineteenth-century novel, but its vaunted realism doesn't stem from its many realistic effects, persuasive and pleasurable though they are, so much as it does from the judgment it displays in assembling such features of the common human predicament for our consideration. Character and situation, expressed and explored through a reliable interplay of dialogue and description conducted under narrative oversight: that's the form the novel settled into in the nineteenth century, and which the vast majority of novels take to this day.

Dialogue and description are of essence to the nineteenth-century novel, especially as it develops in the metropolitan centers of London and Paris. So too of course are plot and story. People often say that a novel needs to tell a good story, but in fact the stories told by novels are for the most part commonplace (and unremarkable and unmemorable compared with the wondrous or thigh-slapping stories of, say, *The Decameron* or *The Arabian Nights*). There is nothing unusual or unlikely about the stories of either Emma Woodhouse or Emma Bovary, and it's just that ordinariness that recommends them to our attention. These are not books of marvels, but books about things we know something about.

Ordinary though it may be, the story must still be made to enthrall, and to this end the nineteenth-century novel resorts to plotting, the elaboration, that is, of how the story unfolds until it is fully told. Plot is distinct from story—the Russian formalist critic Yuri Tynianov drew a sharp analytic distinction between them in the 1920s, and E. M. Forster, in his *Aspects of the Novel*, also emphasizes their difference— and plot, even more than the interaction of dialogue and description, works in complicated ways. Plot paces the story, its convolutions both revealing and obscuring it; it tantalizes and leads readers on until they yield themselves to the author, unable to "put the book down." Plot has a seductive dimension, in other words, and this side of it is just what makes Marianne Dashwood's sensibility, in Austen's novel, thrill to novels. Plot, however, is equally a sign that the book as a whole is under authorial and perhaps even providential control: the continuities will be maintained, and everything will at last come round, at least if the novel is any good. And plot finally engages the reader as the judge of whether in fact it is any good. The plot of a nineteenth-century novel is in a way analogous to the developing representative politics of the nineteenth century, or for that matter to a well-run railway system. The novelist must find a place in his pages for all his characters, with all their various motives, and keep things under control (even as they threaten to break apart). And all the time, the novelist is also working to obtain the reader's vote of confidence.

None of these things are on offer in *Notes from Underground*, where there is no plot, just a travesty of one, and hardly any story to speak of. To the contrary, as the writer might squawkingly interject. Emerging from a state of comprehensive crisis—personal, professional, financial, political, national, philosophical, religious, and certainly literary—*Notes* resembles nothing so much as a swept-up heap of broken glass. The book gives voice to views that Dostoevsky shares (for example, the essential and necessary perversity of the human will) but also to ones that he does not (the writer mocks the back-to-the-soil program Dostoevsky had espoused). It is a send-up of conventional romantic literary themes (the redemption of the fallen woman) that flirts with a certain Christian sentimentality of its own. (Perhaps what would redeem the writer is love?) It is a psychological study and a caricature of a generational type. It is an attack on the bien-pensant bourgeoisie, an attack on utopian radicals, an attack on idealism, an attack on literature, an attack on Russia, an attack on "our unfortunate nineteenth century." ("Just take a look around: blood flows in rivers and in such gleeful fashion, like champagne. That's the whole of the nineteenth century for you.") It is a howl of dismay, a mere personal gripe, and an expression of defeat. It is an essay in paradox: this hopeless man gives voice to unmistakable truths; this man who gives voice to unmistakable truths knows nothing, is hopeless. Formally not much of a story, it retains something of story while also being a polemic, a satire, a philosophical meditation, a case study.

The thing is, it is all these things (and more) but none of them definitively or conclusively. "This is a form, nothing but an empty form [. . .] I don't want to be restricted in any way [. . .] Whatever occurs to me I shall put down . . ." the writer says, and what he writes does not make sense of his crisis (which is somehow everybody's crisis) so much as enact it helter-skelter. Embodiment is what he is after, in "real flesh and blood" (and it is hardly coincidental that slaughter holds such a grip on his imagination). The writer may be despicable, combining all the attributes, as he says, of an antihero, yet his voice retains an impersonal power and an authority of its own. And whose voice finally is it anyway? The voice is supremely equivocal: Dostoevsky's or not; ours (as we are repeatedly told) or not (as we are also told); public address or interior monologue; the voice, variously, of the 1840s, of the 1860s, of Russia, of "our unhappy nineteenth century." Supremely equivocal and not just unreliable, radically unreliable. But real.

This is the voice of the twentieth-century novel.

Notes stands as a precursor in part because the kind of political and social problems that Russia faced in the nineteenth century, which seemed at that point distinctively Russian, become general, indeed global, in the century to come. Like the writer of *Notes*, like Dostoevsky on Semyonovsky Square, the writers of the twentieth century are ambushed by history. They exist in a world where the dynamic balance between self and society that the nineteenth-century novel sought to maintain can no longer be maintained, even as a fiction.

Influential twentieth-century novelists, from Proust and Mann to David Foster Wallace, have written about the importance of Dostoevsky to their work, and *Notes* in particular echoes with uncanny frequency through the novels of the twentieth century. (So much so that I suspect that many of the echoes are in fact indirect: an echo of an echo.) Consider, in any case: the book introduces an archetype; the anonymous writer of *Notes* becomes the Underground Man, as much a modern myth, Dostoevsky's American biographer Joseph Frank has rightly said, as Faust, Hamlet, Don Juan, or Sherlock Holmes. The shadow of this mythic character can be detected in the protagonist of Knut Hamsun's *Hunger*, Jean Rhys's lost women, Gombrowicz's *Ferdydurke*, Bellow's *Dangling Man*, Ellison's *Invisible Man*, and Bernhard's *The Loser*, among many others. The book introduces a setting: call it the infinitesimal, infinitely squalid retreat in the midst of the inconceivably spreading urban wasteland. In Kafka's novels and stories this setting becomes the world. Flann O'Brien relocates it to

Dublin; Kōbō Abe's *Woman in the Dunes* to postnuclear Japan. *Notes* introduces several remarkably robust motifs: "There's great pleasure even in a toothache"; "I wanted to become an insect many times. But even that wasn't afforded to me." (Kafka writes a story about a man who, in a sense, succeeds); the anthill; "2 x 2 = 5." The book introduces a tone: it can be seen (André Gide will argue this) as the precursor of stream of consciousness; it also resonates behind the rhythms, at once propulsive and splintered, of writers as different as Andrey Bely, Faulkner, Céline, Kerouac, and Saramago. The underground shows up all over the place. Nabokov professed to despise Dostoevsky, but the notes Charles Kinbote attaches to *Pale Fire* are for all that a take on *Notes*. *Portnoy's Complaint* rewrites the book as Catskill schtick.

"I am a sick man . . ." The defining moment of the story might be said to be the ellipsis with which, after that first outburst, it breaks off. The ellipsis that could mean anything: the ellipsis that is a sign of hesitation, of something that has been taken out (as, Dostoevsky lamented, the censor had taken out the crucial lines of his book, although he never sought to restore them), of something deliberately left unsaid, of lacking words to say what one means, of having nothing to say. A sign of expectation, of interruption (it carries a trace of violence), of exhaustion (it marks a void). "But enough," the book ends; "I don't want to write anything else from 'Underground.'" But of course he goes on, as his voice goes on repeating itself. Here it is, still going on, at the end of Beckett's *The Unnamable*:

> perhaps they have carried me to the threshold of my story, before the door that opens on my story, that would surprise me, if it opens, it will be I, it will be the silence, where I am, I don't know, I'll never know, in the silence you don't know, you must go on, I can't go on, I'll go on.

As for *Notes from Underground* itself, Dostoevsky was hopeful that on appearance of the second part, the work would make a strong impression, though he fretted that it might be a bad one: the work was not good enough. But apart from passing mentions in letters from friends, there is no trace of contemporary response to the book. Dostoevsky was still in touch with Apollonia Suslova, the amour fou who'd helped to bring the book about, who was in Paris now, frequenting Russian émigré circles. People were talking about his "scandalous novella," she wrote. They deplored the cynical turn his work had taken. She herself hadn't bothered to read it.

PART I

BREAKING THE VESSELS

I. THE VIVISECTOR

H. G. WELLS'S *THE ISLAND OF DOCTOR MOREAU*

Dostoevsky's Russia is a disturbed and disturbing place, and to sound the depths of that spreading disturbance, Dostoevsky imagines a profoundly disturbed man. But how did this unlikely character become a representative figure for the fiction of the next century? After all, Dostoevsky's Russia is a very different place from Victorian England, Belle Époque Paris, the Austro-Hungarian Empire of Franz Joseph I, Wilhelmine Germany, or America in the Gilded Age—times and places that were and remain bywords for ostentation and complacency. Public scandals like the Dreyfus affair and the Wilde case may provide alarming evidence of rot within, but for the Western world, the end of the nineteenth century is a time of prosperity and, allowing for the occasional anarchist attentat or financial crash, success.

The novel partakes in that success. It has done well for itself over the years, establishing itself so thoroughly that even to this day, when we think of the form of the novel, it is the great novels of the nineteenth century that come to mind. The novel is ubiquitous, and novelists like Scott and Balzac, Dickens and Dumas, George Sand and Jules Verne are international figures of unquestioned brilliance. The novel is also a thriving business. Novels are being written and published not only throughout the Western world but wherever the increasing literacy and disposable income that the form requires to flourish are to be found: in Japan, for example, as we shall see.

If the market for the novel is robust and growing, so too is critical awareness of the form. Its gathering influence has long been an object

of critical alarm to the guardians of public decency, and English novelists in particular are forced to cater to the supposed sensitivities
of their readers, as determined by the lending libraries through which
their books mostly reach their audience. Nothing remotely untoward
or discomfiting should stain the product! Novelists, at the same time,
and partly in reaction to such strictures, are becoming more solici-
tous of their art and honor as artists. Here, for the decisive turn, we
need to go back to the mid-nineteenth century and Flaubert and his
Madame Bovary. Madame Bovary is nothing special. She is not unusually wicked. She is hardly a heroine of the liberated self. She is
a misguided reader of cheap romantic novels, and Flaubert's book
is as much about the art of the novel and his art—a proof piece, of
sorts—as it is about her. Emma Bovary is solidly present as a person,
but she is also a pretext for her creator to display how perfectly chosen his words are, how carefully paced his sentences, things we are
made alive to quite as much as to what those words and sentences
describe. She provides a pretext, too, for a no less marked display of
unsentimentality—what will be called Flaubert's realism. Disdaining
the uplifting moral and emotional resolution typical of the novel as
Emma, among other readers, knows and craves it, Flaubert offers in
its place the steely polish of his novelistic technique. He is deft at handling what has come to be called free indirect discourse, the technical
name given to the novelist's common practice of moving in and out of
the thoughts of characters as needed to move the story along, creating
a sense of both transparency and intimacy, the sense of a common
world. For Flaubert, though, it will serve instead as an index of individual isolation: he may enter the minds of his characters, but only to
cordon them off by virtue of their point of view.

Perhaps the most celebrated scene in *Madame Bovary* is the one
in which Emma yields to her first lover, the aristocrat Rodolphe. The
two are alone in a room on the upper floor of the municipal building
of Charleroix. Rodolphe has arranged for them go there in order to
enjoy a better view of the county fair that is going on below—and
with a view to something else as well. Anticipating cinematic mon-
tage, Flaubert cuts back and forth between the scene on high and the
scene on the ground, and the very different things going on at these

different levels. This would seem to emphasize the omniscience of the novelist; it certainly does make us aware of being in his hands. But the true effect of Flaubert's manipulations is to make readers keenly aware of how inevitably limited is anyone's point of view. In this brilliant staging, novelistic omniscience is ironically deployed to instill a cruel consciousness of being in the know—we see what is going on, we think, unlike the people in the book—but also of knowing that, all things considered, you never really know. All we ever know is what we think we know, and that in the end may well be nothing.

Flaubert is a great stylist, and as a stylist he will exercise an immense influence on the novelists of the century to come. With Flaubert's example in mind, Ford Madox Ford and Joseph Conrad, who collaborated on a couple of novels, would prepare passages of description in French before turning them into English: only in that way could they get them right. Gertrude Stein, James Joyce, Ernest Hemingway—absent Flaubert, their work would be unrecognizable. He is a great and transformative stylist, but he is an even greater pessimist, and in this respect he remains a very nineteenth-century figure. In his books the balance between self and society holds, even if as nothing more than a deadlock in the unflinching eye of the artist. Here we can contrast him with Henry James, who knew Flaubert as a young man and was to some degree his disciple. From Flaubert, James learns to be hyperscrupulous about points of view, but in James's work this attention carries an entirely different charge. What concerns him is not just the given and infrangible limits of our perception and understanding but also the zone of our responsibility, and for him novelists are called on to respect their characters' points of view in the same way that we as people, as human beings and moral agents, are called on to observe and to promote the freedom and individuality that makes each of us distinct. Thus in *The Portrait of a Lady*, from 1881, James depicts Isabel Archer's quest to fashion herself as person—to assume an active, public face that she recognizes as hers, on her own free terms, that classic challenge of the nineteenth-century novel. Freely she makes the terrible mistake of marrying the wrong man, a man with a demonic contempt for freedom. Having made that mistake, she must learn to abide the consequences and suffer her private grief; so she does, and

James leaves the reader uncertain as to whether she has sentenced herself to a life of submission or attained the more complex freedom of self-awareness and responsibility for her actions. It is within that uncertainty, however, that real life takes place. In his preface to the novel, James deploys the metaphor of a balance to describe what he was out to do: put Isabel's consciousness in one scale; put those of the people around her in the other. Keep adding weight on each side while the tension mounts. And the effect? Proud of his artistic accomplishment, James writes, "The girl hovers inextinguishable."

Flaubert's pessimism; the tragic optimism of *Portrait of a Lady*, maybe the most beautifully calibrated of nineteenth-century novels: by the start of the twentieth century the novel had developed not only an audience but an extraordinary range. The nineteenth-century novel was something remarkable; the nineteenth century was soon to be over. What would happen now? (The notion of measuring historical eras in centuries becomes prevalent only in the nineteenth century, and the presumption that each century will come with its own specific story—very strong at the end of the century—may itself be seen as reflecting the growing influence of the nineteenth-century novel.) Dostoevsky, translations of whose work were at this point beginning to spread around the expanding world of the novel, had shown a Russia in which inner and outer worlds were flying apart. What kinds of other worlds, and novels, might there be?

This is the question that H. G. Wells, James's younger contemporary and, for a while, friend—their falling-out will be part of our story—puts to the broad public at the threshold of the twentieth century. Wells, more than any other writer I can think of, writes out of the conviction that the new century demands a new vision of humanity and a new novel to go with it, and he provides it. He writes in a spirit of continual experimentation: what kind of effect will this kind of story have? It is a formula designed to attract and involve a new popular audience. It is at the same time the product of an acute authorial self-awareness. Wells's career is nothing so much as an ongoing staging of H. G. Wells as all-round prophet and big-time producer of the twentieth-century novel. That, some hundred years later, he has come to be taken for granted—and as something of a lightweight—at once reflects and fails to register the extraordinary impact this angry, ambitious, brilliantly innovative young man's work would have, not only on the novel but in the new technologies of film and radio, whose transformative effects Wells was among the first to appreciate.

Experiment in Autobiography is what Wells called his life story, published in 1934 and presented as a kind of massive dossier, a pile of lab notes, about his private and public adventures. The book is first of all the story of a social outsider. Wells, born in 1866, came from the lowest rung of the bourgeois social ladder, and his family lived in terror of slipping off it. Sarah, his mother, was a lady's maid in a great house; his father, Joe, was a gardener, and they were both, in their son's view, closer to the feudal past than to the modern world. In 1855, however, Joe persuaded Sarah that they should strike out on their own: the couple purchased a china shop on the high street of Brompton, a small town to the southwest of London that an expanding rail system would eventually transform into a suburban bedroom community. For the next twenty-five years, Sarah stood at the counter and tried to make a go of the shop—to no avail. Joe, by contrast, shook the dust off his feet and took up cricket—he was a talented player at a moment when sport was becoming a public attraction—until an injury ended that career, and he was reduced to selling sporting equipment and, ultimately, faced bankruptcy. Eventually Sarah went back to being a maid; Joe to gardening.

Atlas House was the impossibly grand title of the small edifice that housed the shop, the family's cramped living quarters, and, in Wells's memory, a whole world of disappointment: "exhausting, impossible, Atlas House"—"that dismal insanitary hole . . . in which I was born," he writes in his autobiography. He could neither forget nor forgive the dim prospects and dimity curtains he had been born to, the "needy shabby home" packed with secondhand furniture, because "furniture shops that catered to democracy had still to appear in the middle nineteenth century." His narrative revisits the rooms of the house like the scene of a crime.

Escaping all this, upsetting all this, transforming all this—that was the only thing to do, but how? Wells's elder brothers had apprenticed at a draper's shop, and he was to follow in their footsteps. It was, he would say, this "scheme of things that marched me off before I was 15 to what was plainly a dreary and a hopeless life." At the draper's, he did his best to do his worst, and he was duly dismissed, after which he had a piece of good luck. An excellent student, he received a scholarship to study at the Normal (later Imperial) College of Science in London, one of the new state institutions (by contrast to the private corporations of Oxford and Cambridge) that were being founded not just in the UK but throughout Europe to develop the sorts of expertise required by modern states. Wells, hoping to be a scientist, eagerly attended the lectures of Sir Thomas Huxley, one of the first popular scientific gurus and a fanatical proponent of the theory of evolution (he was known as "Darwin's bulldog"). Wells's interest in science soon waned, however. It was too technical. He preferred to immerse himself in Blake and attend left-wing political meetings. Before long, he had lost his scholarship and acquired a wife and was teaching correspondence courses and writing textbooks. One day, playing soccer, he crushed his kidney; around the same time, he was diagnosed with TB. Wells in his autobiography goes so far as to provide a numbered list of the failures that by this point had beset him. All things considered, he concludes, they left him with nothing to do but die.

And yet he was saved—by a piece of popular fiction. On vacation the following year, he picked up *When a Man's Single*, by J. M. Barrie (later the author of *Peter Pan*), a novel that features a character who makes it big by writing humorous pieces for the popular press. Wells took the story as a career tip, and before long he was publishing all sorts of different articles all over the place, and there were lots of places to publish. By the 1890s, some two thousand journals were in circulation in England—"the first school generation educated under the Education Act of 1871 was demanding cheap reading matter," Wells explains—catering to "new classes" with "distinctive needs and curiosities. They did not understand and enjoy the conventions and phrases of Trollope or Jane Austen." Wells was a member of this new class, and Frank Harris, an influential editor of the time (his racy, completely unreliable memoirs are still read), who was looking for brisk, brash, amusing, surprising, opinionated, rousing, smart writing, whether about science, politics, the latest novel, the theater, or daily life, saw that Wells could give it to him.

Wells shed his wife and found a placid partner, Jane, willing to countenance the innumerable affairs and liaisons he now commenced and would pursue all his life. He found an agent, A. P. Watt, the inventor of the modern literary agency. Quite suddenly the miserable child of Atlas House was doing pretty well by himself.

Soon he was not just coming up in the world, he was a celebrity.

Wells dug up the draft of a story about time travel he'd begun in college and brought it to W. E. Henley, another pioneering editor of the time. Henley urged him to finish it. Serialized between January and May 1895, "The Time Traveller's Story" caused a sensation—"H. G. Wells . . . is a man of genius" a critic declared even as the story was still appearing in installments. When the book, *The Time Machine: An Invention*, came out shortly after, the sensation only grew. Before long, Wells would be approached about turning his tale into a theme park attraction.

The Time Machine could not have been more timely—a new kind of story written for the century to come that also captures and holds up to the light the complacency and anxiety of the century that is on its way out. The words of the title alone make for a potent concentrate. Time: the bourgeoisie banked on time: time yielded interest; time secured progress. In place of the aging dynasties of yore, they had the "century"—that convenient, newly minted unit, larger than a lifetime but conformable to the memory of the nuclear family and designed to connect past and future in the developing narrative of human history. Time was the element of history, and history was the vessel of hope. But time was a treacherous element, too. There was the deep geological time Charles Lyall had uncovered, in which not only humanity but divinity threatened to sink from sight; there was talk of time as a fourth dimension (Wells's novel begins with a discussion of this still new and trendy concept), the nature of which we can hardly begin to imagine. As to the machine: here again we have one of the triumphant symbols of the new order, something that has vastly expanded human control over nature and yet, like time, may hold surprises.

The book begins by convening a group of contemporary experts and worthies—the Editor, the Medical Man, the Psychologist, the Journalist—who are to hear the Time Traveller's tale and pass judgment on its credibility. You could see them as the collective spirit of the nineteenth-century novel, and Wells's description of the time machine itself—as a delicate, frail, puzzling thing put together from wire and ivory and whatnot, trembling slightly—brings to mind the scale in which James weighs Isabel Archer's fate, though this machine is about to throw absolutely everything out of whack. Far in the future, in the year 802,701, to be precise, humanity has split into two species: the delicate, childish, pacific Eloi, who live on the Edenic surface of the earth; and the hairy, savage, sly, resourceful Morlocks underground, apparently oppressed and subservient until the reader discovers that the pampered Eloi are the Morlocks' livestock and prey. This future is both a deceptive evocation of a socialist utopia (what the Time Traveller takes it for at first) and an inverted image of Wells's and his readers' late-nineteenth-century present, seemingly stable and orderly yet riven by class and driven by exploitation, and here we encounter in a new form the specter of the underground. Civilization is just another form of cannibalism, the only law is the Darwinian imperative of species survival and things will not turn out well. Moving on, the Traveller arrives at the end of earthly time— and discovers a drowning beach prowled by massive predatory crustaceans under a dying sun. There is no trace of humanity, whatever that may have been.

Like Dostoevsky toiling on his *Notes*, Wells was desperate for success. To a friend he wrote, *The Time Machine* is "my trump card and if it does not come off very much I shall know my place for the rest of my career"—which is to say Atlas House. Eager to follow up on the triumph of this book, he hatched a plan to bring out a bunch of books, each different in conception and execution, with a bunch of different publishers, all in a single year.

His immediate impulse was to take things to an extreme. Cannibalism is on the table right at the start of his next book, *The Island of Doctor Moreau*, which finds three survivors of a shipwreck thrown together in an unprovisioned lifeboat. The narrator, Edward Prendick, is a gentleman whose passion for butterfly hunting has led him on this ill-fated voyage to the South Seas, and he is out of his element. His more vigorous companions fight and fall overboard, which leaves him no better off, but then he is picked up by a small, seedy transport ship carrying a caged puma, a lot of rabbits, and two passengers— a young doctor, Montgomery, and his swarthy, strange-looking serving man. The captain of the boat is an angry drunk who takes a dislike to prissy Prendick, and when they arrive at the remote island that is Montgomery's destination, he insists that Prendick disembark too. But Montgomery's boss, a "massive white-haired man in dirty blue flannels," refuses to let him land. Once again Prendick finds himself adrift in a dinghy.

One way or another, Prendick is adrift throughout these opening chapters of *The Island of Doctor Moreau*, slipping in and out of consciousness, uncertain of what is going on, caught in a bad dream. As is the reader. Wells's chapters are short and savage, marked off with sensational titles—"The Man Who Was Going Nowhere," "The Thing in the Forest"—that he hoped would be suitable for serialization, except that this book was just too raw: editors refused to take it. The sensationalism goes deeper, however, than mere showiness. Wells's short, stabbing sentences rely on sensation: sights, tastes, smells, sounds imposing themselves without context or explanation. Prendick "saw with no more interest than if it were a picture a sail coming towards me over the skyline," recollects "some stuff being poured in between my teeth," wakes to see "a youngish man with flaxen hair, a bristly straw-coloured moustache, and a dropping nether lip," who speaks "with a slobbering articulation, with the ghost of a lisp." (This is Montgomery.) Prendick's own hands are "a dirty skin purse full of loose bones." Meanwhile, the air is full of noises: "a snarling growl and the voice of a human being together," yelping dogs, Montgomery howling *"Damn that howling!"*

What is going on? Wells exploits Prendick's predicament, and ours, with undisguised glee. Prendick, full of ideas about how things should be, does nothing but get things wrong. He has been mugged by reality—or rather mangled by a novel. Not a well-bred, leisurely Victorian novel, the kind that takes its time and takes time to read, of the sort that Prendick, when not chasing butterflies, might savor; not the kind of book that exists to remind the privileged reader, as self-consciously literary novels do to this day, that he has and has had, by virtue of long education if nothing else, the privilege of time. No, a relentless popular novel, a novel designed for impact, of the most unconventional and unaccommodating darkness.

Prendick is again reprieved. The tall white-haired man with a "fine forehead" relents and allows him on the island. He is Dr. Moreau. Prendick dimly remembers the case of a scientist in London whose experiments with vivisection came to light after a flayed dog escaped his laboratory. An outraged public "howled" the man out of England. (The mob and the dog are equally animal, and Prendick is more appalled by their reaction than by the dog's pain. He "follows the science" of his day, which took vivisection seriously, as did Wells.) Wasn't that a Dr. Moreau? Prendick wonders. It was, and now on his little island the good doctor pursues his studies unhindered. He is "itching to get to work" on the magnificent female puma, whose ear-splitting shrieks resound in the background for much of the rest of the book.

Moreau is a scientist, and he is a kind of artist, too, sculpting in flesh. What interests him, he declares, is to "find out the extreme limit of plasticity in a living shape"—extremism is the order of the day—and his hypothesis is that it is effectively unlimited, which is to say that with the right technique, any living thing can be transformed into any other living thing, or rather into a human being. As he says, "the great difference between man and monkey is the larynx," and for years now Moreau has been blending boatloads of beasts—apes, dogs, deer, sheep, hyenas, wolves, bears, foxes, leopards, pigs, Wells keeps adding to the list as the story continues, in a sort of perverse echo of the story of Noah's Ark—into something like men. Montgomery's strange servant, M'ling, is "a bear tainted with dog and ox," and, like him, Moreau's manifold creations walk on two legs and even speak, sort of, though they are reluctant to, since speaking, like the fetters in Dostoevsky's *House of the Dead*, causes them physical pain. Moreau benignly remarks that "a mind truly opened to what science has to teach must see that [pain] is a very little thing."

Moreau has made progress, but he is dissatisfied. "They revert," he laments. "As soon as my hand is taken from them the beast begins to creep back." He has set up these backsliders, these failed experiments, in a pathetic little community of their own on the other side of the island. He has given them laws and established rites that they do their best to observe. If they do not, he threatens to return them to the terrible "house of pain" from which they first came. Ape Man, the highest of animal kind, stands over the little community as the so-called Sayer of the Law, leading them in prayerful recitation—"Not to go on all-Fours, that is the Law . . . Not to suck up Drink; that is the Law . . ." Again and again, they repeat the refrain "Are we not men?"

Moreau is a scientist and an artist, a colonialist handing down the law to "lesser breeds," a man of God ministering to lost souls, a teacher drilling in lessons, a politician and a tyrant, a would-be God who, as it turns out, is about to lose control of his ugly Eden. His creations will soon get the better of him and his henchman, leaving Prendick stranded again "among the Beast people," though holding, as he nervously assures us, "something like a pre-eminence among them." The poor man is sorely tried. There are males, and especially females, who attempt "public outrages on the institution of monogamy," while the Ape Man treats him to an unceasing stream of philosophical gibberish that he terms "big thinks," his words progressively disintegrating into "lumps of sound." Finally, a boat washes ashore; Prendick is able to make his way back to London. But his experiences have changed him, and the city crowds strike him as indistinguishable from the inhabitants of the island of Dr. Moreau.

Moreau is as compound a character as his own creations. Wells, as will be true of many of the writers in this book, reaches back to the early years of the novel or beyond for imaginative models, and Moreau's prototypes include Homer's Circe, who turns men into swine, Shakespeare's Prospero with his feral servant Caliban, Milton's depraved forest spirit Comus, Goethe's overweening Faust, and Mary Shelley's Dr. Frankenstein. The figure he most resembles, however, is the biggest monster-magician of all, Jehovah. Scientific Wells may be, but there is a prophetic furor to his attack on the pious certitudes of bourgeois existence, and he projects himself in Moreau as a counter- or anticreator. Wells wants to do harm to our self-regard. Are we not men, the beast creatures drone, and yes, indeed, they are not-men. But shouldn't the same question be asked of Montgomery, Moreau, Prendick, and all of us? Wells wants us to recognize that there is no virtue or insight or understanding that sets us apart from the rest of the animal world (except perhaps for humanity's greater capacity for inhumanity); that men are not men, in any of the exalted senses of that appelation, but beasts. We are mechanical assemblages of muscle and organ, behavioral bundles, and what we call knowledge or deem good or bad are nothing more than our usual way with things, which the power of circumstance or some greater power can easily alter or thwart. In any case, neither our sentiments, our convictions, our so-cial niceties, nor that prize possession, language, confer any distinc-tion upon us. Meaning is grunting. There is no difference between the best people and the beast people.

The Island of Doctor Moreau was not a success. *The Times* of London condemned it as a "book that should be kept out of the way of young people and avoided by all who have good taste, good feeling, or feeble nerves." That didn't get in the way of Wells's literary career, however. The books that came in rapid succession after *Moreau*, among them *The Invisible Man* and *The War of the Worlds*, cemented his fame and carried it around the world. More conceptual than Jules Verne's adventures, they not only laid the foundation of modern science fic-tion, they have become part of modern mythology. On top of that, they establish a mythology of the modern. The modern, for Wells, is the moment of crisis when we recognize both the mind's power to see through the false certitudes of the past and equally the mind's perilous blindness to the future. Modern science had opened up an unknown world, and terrifying though that may be, it was also exciting, infinitely more exciting than the vocations and equivocations of Trollope's novels. We lived in the midst of a terrifying excitement—the excitement of science, the excitement of economic growth, the excitement of political change, the excitement of men and women and sex, so long hampered by convention—the excitement of the century to come, which would be full of nothing but excitement. This is what literature had to convey, and Wells did convey it, as countless readers and admirers, among them George Orwell, Jorge Luis Borges, and Saul Bellow, testified.

And Wells would be along for the ride until his death, shortly after the Second World War. Indefatigably productive and involved in everything, a public intellectual and campaigner for multiple causes, the man who would dub World War I "the war to end all wars" and who, after the war, would be a proponent of world government, Wells was no less restless and questing as a writer. His early masterpieces—he called them scientific romances—were followed by autobiographical and activist novels. *Kipps*, *Love and Mr. Lewisham*, and *The History of Mr. Polly* are about young men on the make and the challenges society presents to them, while *Tono-Bungay*, about a vast pharmaceutical scam, offers an image of twentieth-century capitalism sinking into commercialized decadence that, as the critic Edward Mendelson has pointed out, looks forward to a novel like Thomas Pynchon's *The Crying of Lot 49*. *Ann Veronica*, from 1909, has a suffragette for its heroine, and the book ends with her openly taking a married man for a lover. The book was inspired by one of Wells's lovers, and this points to another aspect of his accomplishment, less noted than his engagement with public issues. He is one of the first novelists to make his personal history, whether his deprived childhood or his later love affairs, undisguisedly central to his work. His fiction is as confessional as it is conceptual, though quite unmarked by any sentiment of contrition. It

exists as a kind of ongoing speculative report on the state of humanity, the state of the world, and the state of H. G. Wells.

Wells sets out to excite his readers, but he also wants to influence them.
He wants to influence how they think; he wants to influence them to
buy his book. For him popularity is a badge of honor, just as it is for a
politician. And here we come back to Henry James, with whom Wells
had a quarrel that—*Experiment in Autobiography* makes clear—
continued to rankle well after James's death. The quarrel is telling and
helps to further illuminate the peculiar new resources Wells brings
to the novel and the hold that his work will have on the twentieth-
century novel.

James was the first serious critic of the novel in English, the first
to see a critical knowledge of the novel's history and a distinct consciousness of its formal construction as crucial equipment for the
working novelist, and throughout his life he maintained an active
interest in new fiction. His taste wasn't limited to the kind of novel
he wrote: he admired Stevenson, encouraged younger writers like
Rudyard Kipling and Stephen Crane, and he could not fail to be
impressed by Wells's energy and invention. In 1914 he sat down to
write a survey of new developments in fiction for *The Times Literary
Supplement*, and Wells, along with Conrad and Arnold Bennett, was
among the writers he discussed. About Wells, James says perceptively
and appreciatively,

> It is literally Mr. Wells's own mind, and the experience of his
> own mind, incessant and extraordinarily various, extraordi-
> narily reflective . . . of whatever he may expose it to, that forms
> the reservoir tapped by him.

But then James goes on to rebuke Wells—he is talking about a love
scene in the novel *Marriage*—for simply manipulating his characters in the interest of all the things he has to say and points he has to
make, leaving them, in the reader's eye, as James sees it, at least, without actual motivation, without, he is basically saying, any interior

from which to emerge and encounter each other in a believable way. James writes, "If the participants have *not* been shown us on the way to the encounter, nor the question of it made beautifully to tremble for us in the air, its happiest connections fail and we but stare at it mystified." That "tremble in the air" recalls Isabel Archer's "hovering inextinguishable" and the nineteenth-century ideal of balance, but really what he is accusing Wells of is of not respecting point of view. That, as I said, is for James not just a matter of the novel's psychological verisimilitude but of its moral seriousness.

Wells, angry at having his artistry questioned, was having nothing of it, and the two writers' friendship never recovered. Revisiting the quarrel in *Experiment*, Wells flatly dismisses James as a fussy old man, a snobby and déclassé American abroad who has an overelaborate style. Wells had been present at the disastrous staging of James's play *Guy Domville* in 1895; he was also aware that for all of James's self-appointed critical authority, his late novels had found no popular audience at all, to Wells an obvious mark against them. His attack is taunting and personal, but it also carries a sociological and political edge. He presents himself as a radical writer whose gift is precisely to show the socially determined, constructed nature of character that James takes as given, and this, Wells argues, requires the novelist to get "the frame . . . into the picture." The art James summons to evoke inwardness is art in the service of a bourgeois illusion of individuality. Wells, moving his characters like chess pieces, not only entertains but instructs in the nature of the game they are caught up in. Wells is the morally serious artist, digging down to the roots of things. "There cannot be pictures without backgrounds," he insists, "and the source of the shifting reflected light on the face has to be shown." James he views as nothing more than a buffer of surfaces.

This is a ridiculously reductive reading of James—Wells's suggestion that Jamesian interiority is akin to a wallet or a purse could not be further from James's sense of individuality as infinitely imperiled, from within as much as without—and as for Wells's allegations about James's social anxieties, well, it takes one to know one. It is, however, a clear statement of Wells's own aspirations and clear evidence of the aesthetic sophistication, if not subtlety, of his fiction. With his dictum of "get the frame into the picture" Wells is insisting on the speculative and instrumental nature of his endeavor, which does not reflect reality, but rather calls on us to recognize it—which more than anything may be to recognize how little we know of it—to question it and to change it. And, he is saying, the form of the novel is as much in question as its content. Novels are based on convention, and such conventions like any conventions are open to change. Complacency can attach itself to this sort of radicalism quite as easily as it can to conservatism, and while Wells is not free of complacency, his best work, especially the early science fiction, is full of a sense of terrifying exposure. That is certainly the case with *Moreau*, and one of the reasons why it begets not only countless adaptations and spin-offs, such as *Jurassic Park*, but also helps to shape *Heart of Darkness* and *Animal Farm*.

Wells was an enormously successful, insistently controversial, and unabashedly commercial writer at the start of an era that would be defined by ever-growing commercialism as much as by the growth of scientific knowledge. Supremely accessible but also supremely ingenious, he invented a new kind of fiction and a new audience for fiction, by which I mean that in establishing a new genre, he also helped (with the assistance of Sherlock Holmes) to establish genre fiction, or genre in fiction, on a new footing, giving it a new mass appeal in the literary marketplace but also a new prominence in the larger imagination of literature. Wells's argument against James is an argument about the nature and responsibilities of literature, and though his understanding of the older writer, who was long since dead when Wells wrote his autobiography, is crude, he is not wrong to see James as a nostalgist for the balance of the nineteenth-century novel, whose measured effects are, to Wells's mind, so many evasions of social (and cosmic!) realities and political tasks of immense, terrifying urgency. These are matters that fiction must take up, Wells insists, and so, with dread and glee, popular, speculative fiction would. So too would a new, self-consciously highbrow literature, quite disdainful of popularity, emerging around the same time and epitomized, as we will see in the next chapter, by the work of Wells's near contemporary André Gide. The tension beween so-called low and high modes of fiction, between formulaic (which is what we mean when we refer dismissively to genre) and self-proclaimedly innovative modes of fiction (often no less formulaic), will be ever present (and often generative) throughout the century to come. That fiction should split into these modes is as much a manifestation of the collapse of the old balanced order as the breakdown of narrative in *Notes from Underground*, and the one thing that will unite both the low and the high mode will be their common disdain for balance.

Or should that be their appetite for vertigo? When Wells says "get the frame into the picture," he raises a question. Once the frame has entered the picture, a new frame has to be conceived of around that picture, and so on. Where does it end? This conundrum is present everywhere in his immense *Experiment*, which bears the quaint subtitle *Discoveries and Conclusions of a Very Ordinary Brain (since 1866)*. Wells's brain will travel to Russia to see Lenin's brain—well before Lenin was dead. Wells will describe his brain having a quickie in the hall (it is a versatile brain), but he cannot get around the problem that the brain, for all its busy researches, never gets outside the frame of the self, or the self out of the frame of the brain. Proclaiming the brain as the basis of lived experience doesn't in the end explain anything about ourselves or our world, and Wells's pretense that it does is nothing more than a materialist provocation. Nonetheless, it goes, as much as *Moreau*, to the heart of a dark vision of humanity as inescapably determined by material factors—from brain to outer space to the outermost limits of time where you can be sure you will find no trace of your precious self at all—and so inexorably bereft of understanding. You could say that at the center of Wells's work is a vision of a looming, unknowable, infinite, shelterless outside. We are locked within this inhuman space, and no matter how hard we try, and we must try, it will not in the end be given to us to understand it. The author bears witness to that predicament and to the fact that there is no escape from it, any more than there finally was from the miseries and indignities of his childhood in Atlas House.

2. THE ABYSS

ANDRÉ GIDE'S *THE IMMORALIST*

H. G. Wells came from the lowest, iciest rung of the bourgeois social ladder. André Gide, three years his junior, was born securely perched at its top. Gide's father was a distinguished jurist; his mother's family had money from textiles. The couple lived in a book-lined apartment off the Jardin du Luxembourg in Paris and summered in a sixteenth-century chateau on a 370-acre Norman estate. Young Gide whiled away childhood hours fishing from a turret above the moat. "Nothing could be more bourgeois than the society my family moved in," he would write, as if this were all very ordinary and dull. Dull, perhaps, but his family was rich enough to leave him free to do pretty much whatever he wanted all through his life.

Except, of course, for the span of childhood. Childhood passed under the vigilant gaze of his Protestant mother, proud of her Huguenot ancestors, some of whom had died for their faith, and possessed of a relentless work ethic and sense of moral purpose. It weighed on her only child. He had symptoms and problems. He required professional attention. Gide appeared to be a slow learner; he didn't socialize well. Once, he was caught playing with himself in class; and when he was ten, his father died of tuberculosis of the spine, after which the boy suffered from migraines and anorexia.

Even so, he attended a succession of the best private and public schools in Paris, and at eighteen he entered the prestigious Lycée Henri IV. This formation, as the French say, left him an experienced reader of Latin and Greek, steeped in French literature and classical and modern philosophy, with an inexhaustible curiosity about foreign literatures. (Fluent in German, he taught himself English, loved Blake and Browning, and translated Conrad.) He was also an excellent pianist, practicing regularly and performing privately, and he liked to brag that he could have had a concert career. And he was connected. When still a teenager Gide became a regular at the celebrated Tuesday salons of the great poet Mallarmé, where he met a wide range of writers and artists, among them Anatole France, Oscar Wilde, Gauguin, and Debussy. When he published his first book at the age of twenty-one, he received a warm note of appreciation from Mallarmé.

"Mallarmé for poetry, Maeterlinck for drama," Gide wrote to his friend Paul Valéry around that time, "and—though beside those two I feel rather quite puny—I will add myself for the novel." This was perhaps a little premature: Gide had many things to find out about himself. At twenty-three, still a virgin, he and his friend Paul Laurens, an aspiring painter in the same plight, decided to travel to North Africa to put an end to the embarrassing state of affairs. The two young men settled in the Algerian town of Biskra, on the edge of the Sahara, Laurens unpacking his brushes, Gide the piano, which accompanied him on his travels, and then they found an Arab girl who could instruct them on what they wanted to know. A few days later, however, Gide took a walk in the desert with a young Arab porter; the boy threw himself down on the ground suggestively, and Gide, after a long minute of hesitation, took up the offer and was left overjoyed. A few days later, however, his mother showed up. Laurens had written his family to say that Gide had coughed up blood. She was there to take him home.

Back in Europe, Gide fell into a state of "estrangement." He was close to suicide. He traveled; he finished a new novel; he decided to return to North Africa. There he happened to run into Oscar Wilde, in the company of Lord Alfred Douglas, and the understanding Wilde set the young French writer up with a young Arab musician. Some twenty years later—I am quoting from the autobiography Gide wrote in middle age—he makes a point of recording the five orgasms he experiences in the boy's arms, adding that on returning to his hotel room, he continued repeatedly to bring himself to a climax. "I realize," he adds, "that a certain numerical precision I am bringing into this may make you smile; it would be easy to omit this or modify it for the sake of plausibility. However, I am not out for plausibility, but truth, and is it not when the truth is most improbable that it most needs telling?" He had discovered his true sexual nature, and no other truth seemed as important.

He was that, and yet that was not all he was. Gide was, had been from an early age, intensely spiritual. He had been brought up reading the Bible, a central part of Protestant religious observance, and he would remain a reader of the Bible. He had been brought up, too, to think of himself, his soul, as personally answerable to God, which required that he engage in rigorous self-scrutiny, the better that he bring all his thoughts before God—who knew them, and how wanting they were, anyhow. All this was very much part of him, and if later he stepped decisively away from Christian belief, he still continued to think along these lines.

Gide's youthful devotion to God found a further outlet in his devotion to his cousin Madeleine, two years his elder and deeply pious herself. They read and prayed together, and they had a bond in their common knowledge and grief over a terrible and shameful secret: Madeleine's mother was an adulteress. Gide's first book, the one Mallarmé admired, was effectively a love letter to Madeleine, to whom Gide had proposed marriage. She refused him, and his mother thought it was a bad idea, too. Gide remained determined even so.

Not long after he returned from his second, decisive trip to North Africa, his mother died. Gide was devastated, all the more so because he was so relieved:

> I felt myself sink into an overwhelming abyss of love, sorrow, and liberty . . . like a kite whose string has been suddenly cut, like a boat broken loose from its moorings, like a drifting wreck at the mercy of wind and tide. There was nothing now I could attach myself to but my love for my cousin . . . I believed I could give her my whole self and did so without any reservation altogether. Shortly after we became engaged.

This, coming a few pages after the orgasm count, is the end of Gide's autobiography—not unlike Jane Eyre's "Reader, I married him." Soon Gide and Madeleine were married, and Gide would cruise the city streets and country roads, at home and abroad, for years to come. He liked to carry toys and candy to give to the adolescent boys who attracted him. He would remain married, too, which would not be all that surprising, except the marriage was not simply a matter of convention or camouflage, but, for both Gide and Madeleine, an obsession. It was happy enough to begin with. Madeleine was the first, trusted reader of his work, and in early years the couple traveled together while carrying on an intense and extensive correspondence when they were apart. It seems hard to believe, yet it appears to have taken years for Madeleine to develop the least suspicion of Gide's homosexuality. Eventually she did, however, and from that point on, she stopped reading his work, even as Gide left his manuscripts and journal lying around to tempt her attention. When, in 1917, he fell violently and briefly in love (perhaps for the only time in his life: he was sexually, but not emotionally, needy) with the son of a Protestant pastor, a friend of Gide's who, on going off to World War I, had entrusted the teenager to the great writer's care, Madeleine retaliated: she unpacked the letters Gide had written her over twenty years and burned them.

"Our child is dead," Gide said to her, accusing her of destroying his best work. But the marriage was not destroyed. Madeleine retreated to the country once and for all, where Gide visited, as did friends. Madeleine said very little, devoting herself to charity and sharing housework with the servants. The old house gleamed. When she died, in 1938, Gide published a selection of entries from his journal about her. "*Et Nunc Manet in Te*," it was called, a citation from Virgil, meaning "Let them remain in you." He was setting up his journal as her headstone. The marriage was never consummated.

Scenes from this marriage fill Gide's fiction; it and his homosexuality, itself a central fact of the marriage, defined his interests and concerns as a man and as a writer and drove him to remake the novel. Those interests and concerns could hardly find an outlet in the nineteenth-century novel, even if, by the end of the century, French novelists enjoyed a lot of latitude in talking about sex. Gide wasn't interested, however, in chronicling or describing sexual behavior; he was interested in what it meant to be homosexual, what it meant to him, and this was something that could not be openly discussed, certainly not when he was young. (It was not very long after Wilde set him up with the young musician that Wilde was sent to prison.) Gide was interested in himself, endlessly interested, and that self was hardly the sort of thing whose claims, sexual or otherwise, could be balanced with those of society. It was set apart from others and in many ways from itself. (In his autobiography, Gide recounts a harrowing moment when, still very much a child, he cried out to his mother, "I'm not like other people!" and he could not be consoled.) The self was torn within and without—that was what it meant to have a self— and torn as it was, it led people to tear at others, as, for example, Gide and Madeleine did. What interested him was the self in extremis, in his view the self's true state. Even at the start of his career, he felt that each book of his should have a distinct and specific form of its own—its own self, in effect—that would bring out the extremity all the more clearly. He frequently protested that he had no imagination. He had only the one subject, himself, yet it was nothing if not protean. In Gide, the self steps to the center of the stage and pursues its own shadow.

Newly married, Gide brought out the book he had been working on in North Africa, dedicating it to Madeleine—a book he would later describe as "a manual of escape." *Fruits of the Earth* it is called. Earth, not the spirit, which is to say it was not really Madeleine's sort of thing. "Families, I hate you" is the line for which this slender book, a hymn to the senses that tells the most minimal of stories and hardly has characters, would become famous. It didn't make much of an impression when it came out in 1897, but after World War I, when young men returned disillusioned from the front, it had a great vogue. Introducing a subsequent edition, Gide remarks waspishly of his paean to freedom: "To this [book], it is customary to confine me."

Fruits of the Earth consists largely of a series of passionate addresses and exhortations to a young man called Nathanael. Once upon a time, the mysterious narrator tells Nathanael, he was the respectable, studious sort; now, however, he has cast all that off to voyage the world, to savor the transient moment, to engage in the endless process of being himself. He advises Nathanael to do the same, saying that once he has, he will—he must—cast the book aside, having established his own truth. It is true that Gide's own book, like many self-consciously innovative and poetic narratives that the twentieth century would produce, has held up badly. The freedom it celebrates seems more like the diversions of a life of inordinate privilege, and in places it sounds a bit like a high-minded tourist brochure. "Perpetual novelty" reads one entry in its entirety; another, "The whole past of the world completely absorbed in the present moment." Here and there capitals light up like a neon sign: "Life for us had a WILD AND SUDDEN FLAVOR."

Gide sent the manuscript of the book to Wilde, and when the two men met, Wilde complimented him on it. Nonetheless, as Wilde was climbing into his carriage to leave, he turned back to Gide with a last word of advice: "Listen, dear," he said, and *dear* was in English, "Promise me one thing. *Fruits of the Earth* is good, very good. But dear, promise me: never ever write *I* again."

The Immoralist, Gide's next book, doesn't exactly heed Wilde's advice. It too is a summons and a confession, and in the first person, but it is as austere in its working as the earlier book was effusive. Unlike *Fruits of the Earth*, it has a story to tell, a raw and unsettling one. It will sound familiar. Young Michel is a classical archaeologist of significant promise. His father dies, and quite abruptly he marries Marceline, his cousin. The new couple set off for North Africa, where they intend to honeymoon and where Michel will also do research, but no sooner do they get there than he begins to spit up blood. It appears he has tuberculosis; he is told he may well die. In the oasis town of Biskra, Marceline nurses him back to health. One day he looks at himself in the mirror and shaves off his self-serious Victorian beard. He has a revelation that the meaning of life is, simply, to live.

Michel and Marceline decide to return to France. On the way back through Italy they consummate their marriage, conceiving a child. Michel lectures at the Sorbonne, but he takes no pleasure in it. He decides to move to the country and tend to the estate he has there, but his efforts at reform are frustrated by his stubborn peasant tenants. Nothing satisfies him. Marceline, meanwhile, has fallen ill, and as the baby grows within her, she grows ever more ill. At last she miscarries.

Marceline is dying, but perhaps a different climate will allow her to recover. In chilly Switzerland her condition does improve, yet Michel hates Switzerland. He proposes they go south. In Italy, Marceline's health rapidly worsens while Michel leaves her alone in their hotel to go prowl the docks. They proceed to North Africa, where he goes out to pick up a woman. Late at night he returns:

> —What was that noise? . . . I didn't recognize her cough . . . Could that be Marceline? . . . I put on the light . . .
>
> She was half sitting up on her bed; was clutching at the bars of the bed with one of her thin arms to hold herself up; her sheets, her hands, her nightgown glistened with a stream of blood; her face was smeared with it; her eyes were staring, hideously wide; and no cry of agony would have horrified me so much as her silence . . . I didn't know what to do; I wanted to run for help . . . Her hand clung to me desperately, holding me; ah, she thought I wanted to leave her now, that was it! She said: "Oh, can't you wait a little longer?" Then she saw I wanted to speak to her. "Don't say anything," she added, "everything's all right." . . .
>
> Toward dawn she vomited blood again.

This is the end of the story that Michel, who, still in North Africa, has summoned a group of close friends from France to hear. They are a band of successful young men, pillars of the establishment in the making, who as students had vowed to be there for one another at times of need. Michel's story is framed by and contained within a letter one of them is sending to France, in which he wonders if Michel, once so promising, can still "render service to society." It is the same framing device as in Wells's *Time Machine*, and like the Time Traveller, Michel has gone to a place from which there is no coming back.

The Immoralist tells a shocking story, a story of renewed life ending with a brutality little short of murder; a story of a man who stands to be condemned, as the title would seem to indicate. Yet it is his story, and he tells it unapologetically. There is, for example, the profound joy that, sick in Biskra, Michel feels in the company of the poor Arab boys Marceline has taken on as objects of her charity. His last words to his friends, his last words in the book, concern the sister of the boy he has taken on as a servant, herself a prostitute, with whom he has dallied a bit. (Such contrition as he may feel after Marceline's death hasn't led him to change his ways.) "Each time I see her," he tells his friends, "she laughs and claims that I prefer the boy to her. She claims he's what keeps me here more than anything else. There may be some truth in what she says . . ."

After the grim story, a wink and a word to the wise. Gide's good friend, the very Catholic poet Francis Jammes, who had admired *Fruits of the Earth*, was not just shocked but repulsed. He dismissed Michel as a "lamentable madman who doesn't even have the conviction of his vices, sadistic and pederastic in vain." As to the title's Nietzschean implication that the immoral may perhaps constitute an alternate morality of greater vitality (the French word *morale* takes in physical vitality as well as morality)—well, it has to be said, as Gide himself did say, that if he had summoned that specter, he had also gone out of his way to call it into question. Michel is hardly a figure of satanic majesty or libertine passion. He is a selfish, unfeeling man caught in a miserable marriage.

The book doesn't make an example of Michel, nor does it make him out to be exemplary, but it does presume that we will find his predicament, if not Michel himself, familiar. And yet why should we? This was the question Jammes posed, as did other of Gide's friends, not seeing (or suspecting, but being unwilling to say) what Gide could not and would not say (indeed, he explicitly and repeatedly denied it): that Michel's predicament made sense to Gide because it was his own.

Without this knowledge, the book presents us with an evidently representative figure—the title proclaims it, the immoralist—and then does its best to dodge the question of who, exactly, the correlate of this figure is. It seems to set out to make a point, and then it doesn't, and in an introduction to a later edition of the book Gide makes a point of saying that it has no point. "I have tried to prove nothing, just to paint my picture well," he writes, saying next to nothing.

Cultivating inscrutability in this way, *The Immoralist* finds a real form, troubled and troubling, to explore the real predicament of being a gay man in a society where being a gay man is impermissible and punishable. The book is very carefully shaped. The story of Michel's restoration to health (and moral collapse) and Marceline's physical collapse (and spiritual exaltation?) are juxtaposed with classical symmetry, a symmetry that suggests a kind of balance, a clarity of understanding, which, however, is not to be found. Instead, this shapely plot feels like a setup, while Michel and Marceline, shocking and pathetic as their story is, emerge from it less as tragic figures than as failed types and images of each other, tortured sinner and saint whose alliterative names underscore a fundamental likeness and weakness. The Nietzschean title also evokes a very different tradition of classical judgment and restraint, which the book's sentences bear out—"I had sought and found what makes me what I am: a kind of persistence in the worst," Michel crisply affirms—which stands in ever starker contrast to the book's gaps, exaggeration, and drive toward violent release. Release is what this tight little package of repressed feeling, of chaos, both demands and cannot find.

The book is Michel's confession, though one delivered without contrition, and we of course know that it is also Gide's confession, a retelling, still veiled, of his North African revelation, a prediction, scarily prescient, of the course his marriage would take. It is a book searching to find a way to say things it cannot say, and a hundred years later, even if we know nothing of Gide's life, its tortured, evasive sexual subtext seems fairly transparent; what strikes us as odd is how opaque it seems to have been to the author's friends and family and even to himself. It can hardly be read as a gay manifesto. It sternly rules out any kind of practical or sentimental resolution. That, after all, would be the sort of thing you'd find in a nineteenth-century novel, where characters are provided with backgrounds that make them recognizable to themselves and others. The immoralist is condemned and self-condemned to be an isolato.

The Immoralist is a confession, but it gives nothing away. Michel, showing himself to us, is not to be seen. Beginning with his bizarre and unmotivated marriage, Michel sheds contexts—his profession, Paris, the countryside, and, in the end, his wife—becoming unrecognizable even to himself. He is left in the desert with nothing but the desert of that unrecognizable but implacable self, as abstract and absolute as the Old Testament God, for company. Meursault in Camus's *The Stranger* will be his lineal descendant.

Gide did not need to make money from his writing, and he despised the thought of doing so. "For us, followers of Mallarmé, the very idea that literature might 'bring in' money was a shameful one . . . We were not to be bought." Gide could afford his principles, but no writer likes to be without readers, and though at the turn of the century he already cut a figure in the literary world, he was not insensitive to the fact that he didn't have many. He requested that his publisher print only three hundred copies of *The Immoralist*, because printing more would only set him up for disappointment. The three hundred copies did in fact sell out within a year, but another fifteen years would go by before the reprint was exhausted.

The Immoralist feels like a novel, but Gide didn't call it a novel. He called it a récit—a tale, in effect, which in French indicates a book driven more by voice than by character and incident. Gide made a point of not attaching the word *novel* to his fictions in later years, either—he wasn't writing anything so conventional—and the one and only book he would give that name was *The Counterfeiters*, which appeared in 1925. Coming out after *In Search of Lost Time* and *Ulysses* had transformed perceptions of the novel—something I'll discuss later—*The Counterfeiters* was among other things a bid to establish an international reputation. Gide, after all, had been publishing for much longer than Proust or Joyce, and though *The Counterfeiters* is nothing like their books, it succeeded in doing just that. *The Counterfeiters* has the range of characters and social reach and variety of events of a nineteenth-century novel (and it is set at the turn of the century), but it is also marked throughout by Gide's highly individual sense of form. The story revolves around the struggle of two young men to arrive at self-understanding and self-expression in a world that is, as the title indicates, full of false values and temptations, sexual and otherwise, to which of course they will at points succumb. It is about that struggle, but equally it is about the struggle of an older novelist, Édouard, who is related to one of the young men and is a sympathetic observer of both, to write a novel called—*The Counterfeiters*. Édouard's notes for his novel, his efforts to find a proper form for the story he wants to tell, are part of Gide's novel, at the end of which Gide's own notes about his own struggle to write his own *The Counterfeiters* appear in turn. Is his *Counterfeiters* Édouard's *Counterfeiters*? No, of course not, but in another sense, yes. They are and aren't the same; identity is both secured and evaded. The crucial point here is the parallel established between self-fashioning and authorial independence and integrity, Gide's central concern throughout his career. He was freeing the novel from the shackles of convention, putting the question of its form in play, just as his young men seek to find their way among the fads of their day.

As early as 1895, Gide had written a book, *Paludes* ("Marshlands"), about someone writing a book called *Paludes*, and in an entry in his journals from 1893 he admits his special love for works of art in which the work as a whole finds a reflection of itself in some part of the work. He gives the example of the play within a play in *Hamlet*, the picture within the picture in *Las Meninas*. But these are not quite what he is after, he adds. What draws him most of all is an effect that he compares "with the device of heraldry that consists in setting in the escutcheon a smaller one 'en abyme,' at the heart-point."

Thanks to Gide, *mise en abyme* has entered the critical and philosophical lexicon as a byword for metafictional elaboration. Mise en abyme is an exercise in fascination, mirror mirroring mirror to hypnotic effect, but for Gide, never shy of contradiction, it is also a serious thing, not so much a matter of aesthetic play with conventions of

representation as evidence of writerly self-awareness and moral discipline. "The heart is deceitful above all things and desperately wicked,"
the Bible says. "Who can know it?" For Gide, this abyss at the heart-
point stands as an image of the vertiginous and interminable labor of
self-reflection—and for the threat that the more it goes on, the more
it may go astray: that heart-point is vanishingly small. Mise en abyme
is not for Gide a device, heraldic or aesthetic (though the heraldic
source of the term does point us to an image of the writer as knight
errant, an aristocrat of the spirit). For him the abyss is the real thing;
everything else is make-believe. He understood salvation and damna-
tion, but he certainly would have had no patience for safe spaces. At
the heart of his work is the risk that it may not work out, just as the
good Protestant knows that it is not by his works but by God's grace
that he can be saved, and nothing on earth can assure him that he is.

Here mise en abyme should be paired with another term that Gide
donated to the vocabulary of the twentieth century, the *acte gratuit*,
or gratuitous act. Influenced by Dostoevsky, Gide imagined a character, a swaggering bisexual adventurer called Lafcadio, who, at the
end of Gide's novel (this one called a sotie, or diversion) *The Vatican
Cellars*, kills an upstanding bourgeois citizen for no good reason, for
no reason at all, by pushing him off a train (in other words, hurling
him into the abyss). This, Lafcadio exults, is the perfect crime, free of
motivation, a pure act, and in that it can be compared to—Gide wants
us to compare it to—God's gift of grace or original act of creation.
Well, this murder is a travesty of that, Gide is perfectly aware, but I
think it's fair to say that he is nonetheless offering it to us as a model
of good writing: good writing surprises us into suspending moral certainty, leaving us in free fall between goodness and badness, spiritual
life or death—leaving us, that is, where we are, in a world where, as
Dostoevsky had it, if there is no God, everything is permitted.

The great French Catholic novelist Georges Bernanos, a generation younger than Gide, presents a fantastical portrait of Gide in his
novel *Monsieur Ouine*. It is a denunciation, but also a recognition
of the power of Gide's example. Monsieur Ouine is an enormously
fat, sweaty old professor of languages who has, in the novel, an unhealthy interest in a fatherless teenage boy. Ouine is hideous but also

seductive, sly, endlessly intelligent, a spellbinding shape-shifter with a strange radiance, even if it is only the radiance of his rotting away. He is, one of Bernanos's characters says, "the most dangerous man he'd ever met," with a gift for making anything he talks about fascinating while draining it of meaning. Another character says, "The way he talks, you'd think he was a priest." At the novel's end, the boy has succeeded in standing up for himself, and Monsieur Ouine is dying. His demise is operatic. "His closed eyes and thin mouth with its pinched lips all seemed to trace the same ironic expression on his austere face," Bernanos writes, and Gide is clearly recognizable in that description, while Ouine goes on and on, the entranced, dispassionate observer of his own demise. "I can now see to the bottom of my own depths, there is nothing stopping my gaze, no obstacle is in the way. And there is nothing there. Remember that word: Nothing." "I'm hungry . . . I'm raging with hunger. I'm dying with hunger," the obese man says, and, finally, "My child, I am going back into myself forever."

Mise en abyme: Wells's assertion that the picture must also include the frame is interestingly close to Gide's formulation. Close, yet far apart: Wells is looking to context to reframe how we see things, and he is, as I have said, eager to address a broad audience. Gide by contrast envisions a lone reader being drawn endlessly into the unresolvable enigma of the picture, a black hole. Different visions correspond with the two men's distinct but no less seminal contributions to the twentieth-century novel and its audience. Wells's speculative fiction, reflecting his impatience with social strictures and conventional understandings, assigns the novel a new topicality and finds a new mass readership for it. Gide is no less frustrated by and impatient with the way things are, but his response is to cultivate the readership of a select few. Gide writes for people who think of themselves as outsiders to conventional social groups; people who feel, as Gide had cried out to his mother, that they are "not like other people" and that society has cast them out. These people, as much as Wells's people, have a strong conviction that they are nothing like the characters out of a novel by the likes of Trollope, and they have no interest in reading novels of that sort. They want to read things as unlikely and unusual and self-aware as they take themselves to be—books that, like them, set themselves apart. Of course, in an era of widening literacy that is the backdrop to the novel's advance across the world, there are plenty of people who feel just this way. The self-selected audience of the select is big enough.

As a writer, Gide stands as a champion of the self before society, all the more persuasively because he is profoundly aware of how complicated and contradictory the claims of the self may be. He does not sentimentalize the self or any ideas of its freedom and fulfillment. And so his work becomes the distillation of a literary genre that, as much as science fiction, only fully takes shape in the twentieth century: the highbrow or literary novel.

Wells and Gide may seem like opposites, petty and grand bourgeois, heterosexual and homosexual, popular and mandarin panjandrum, but on second thought they bear a curious resemblance to each other. Both are public figures; for both of them sex is a cause; both of them, coming up in the world at the end of the nineteenth century, are in a sense monuments to the moment when Victorian conventions are being challenged but a Victorian sense of moral purpose still motivates the challenge. Because as writers and public figures, Wells and Gide, for all their questioning of moralism, are very much old-fashioned moralists, determined to reshape the attitudes of their contemporaries for, as they see it, the better—even as their work is shot through with the random violence and considered brutality that they, certainly Wells, could feel coming. Bernanos paints a picture of Gide as a predator, of himself along with others, and there is some truth to that picture. For many people, however, he figured as an indispensable liberator.

Gide certainly had a very long and productive and public career—he died in 1951 at the age of eighty-one, and he kept writing and publishing almost until the end of his life. He was the model of the modern public intellectual, and he had an international following. First and foremost a writer of fiction, an artist, he also wrote a great deal of criticism and commentary as well as his scandalizing autobiography. Then there was his journal, which he had begun as a teenager and continued to keep through the years. He kept it religiously, and with this devotee of the self, the cliché is to the point. Everyone knew he was keeping it (curiously, strikingly, many of Gide's closest friends maintained parallel journals of their friendships with him), and in 1939 the journal came out in the canonical Bibliothèque de la Pléiade, making Gide the first living author to receive that honor and, too, acknowledging the journal, the record of his private life (paradoxically, from the start, meant for publication) as the center of his work and achievement. The journal was where he had articulated his crucial concept of mise en abyme, and the journal was the generative abyss from which the one novel and countless other narrative experiments emerged and into which they flowed back.

Gide also became increasingly politically active. As a young man, he represented the district where he had his country house in Normandy. During the First World War, he worked in war relief, and after, when Walther Rathenau—the industrialist who became the finance minister of the Weimar Republic only to fall prey to a right-wing assassin—visited Paris, he made sure to confer with Gide about the state of the world. In the twenties and thirties, Gide also wrote two important and controversial travelogues, *Travels in the Congo* and *Return from the USSR*. In the first he chronicled the abuses of French colonialism and in the second the false promise of Stalinism. Since Gide had been a prominent Communist sympathizer, his depiction of the Soviet state as a new form of tyranny caused deep anger on the left, even as his books continued to be on the index of works proscribed by the Catholic Church.

Gide was also a central figure in French publishing. He helped found and, rich as he was, bankroll and edit the most important French literary journal of the new century, *La Nouvelle Revue Française (NRF)*, out of which grew the new publishing house of Gallimard, which, as the publisher of Proust and the surrealists, influenced literary taste throughout the world between the two world wars.

Gide was an agent and symbol of intellectual and political liberation and of sexual liberation, too, in his autobiography, in *If It Die*, and in *Corydon*, a Greek-style dialogue that was his apology for Greek love. (Gide's vision of homosexuality as a vigorous and virile and improving relation between younger and older men, like that of Achilles and Patroclus, made him the face of an open, unblushing homosexuality, losing him friends and losing, it was thought, the chance of winning the Nobel Prize. When in 1937 it went to Gide's close friend Roger Martin du Gard for his family chronicle *The Thibaults*, it was widely belived that this was a vicarious recognition of a writer who could not be openly acknowledged. There was some irony in the fact that Martin du Gard was also gay, just in the closet.)

Gide became Gide, his long, austere, monkish shaved head, with its penetrating gaze, and his wide, sensual lips identifiable all around the world as a symbol of discernment and seriousness. In France, the surrealists and, later, the existentialists acknowledged his example and his influence. He, in turn, encouraged them, as throughout his career he would support promising new writers. In England, he was translated by Dorothy Bussy, a member of the Bloomsbury circle, who wrote, under a pseudonym, her lesbian novella *Olivia by Olivia*, a very Gidean title. In 1943, with World War II raging, Klaus Mann, the son of Thomas Mann and a novelist himself (as well as a flamboyantly gay man), wrote a study of Gide's work called *André Gide and the Crisis of Modern Thought*. "Why devote, just now, a whole book to [Gide]?" he asks in his preface. He goes on to explain:

> His grace and his gravity, his conscientiousness and his pride, his subtleties, his moral fervor, and his adventurous spirit— Everything he stands for is now mortally challenged. The barbarians mean to exterminate the human type represented by men like Gide.

The author of *The Immoralist* had become a moral exemplar. In 1947, with the war now won, Gide received the Nobel Prize.

3. SHUTTER TIME

ALFRED KUBIN'S *THE OTHER SIDE* AND
FRANZ KAFKA'S *AMERIKA*

Wells and Gide are self-conscious writers and self-consciously activist writers: they have that in common. This is a time for change, they insist, on the page and in the world, and they push those changes on their readers. For others, however, change, even if welcome, inspires a sense of terror. D. H. Lawrence's *Women in Love* (1920), set in the first decade of the century, recounts a conversation between Gudrun, one of the novel's two boldly unconventional heroines, and her German lover:

> As for the future, that they never mentioned except one laughed out some mocking dream of the destruction of the world by a ridiculous catastrophe of man's invention . . . Or else, Loerke's dream of fear, the world went cold, and snow fell everywhere, and only white creatures, polar-bears, white foxes, and men like awful white snow-birds, persisted in icy cruelty.

The Spanish writer Arturo Barea, in his memoir *The Forging of a Rebel*, writes that when he was a child in Madrid, "many people believed that the end of the world would come after the end of the nineteenth century," and he describes his fearful aunt refusing to "to come out and see Halley's Comet." Both of these books were published after World War I, and so could be seen as enjoying the benefit of hindsight, yet there is a feeling of being at the end of things that emerges at the beginning of the new century. Like the sense of youthful vitality (the subject of my next chapter) that grows up alongside it, this reflects a larger new sensitivity to the presence and passage of time, as if time had taken on a wayward life of its own. The mystery of time is the subject of *The Time Machine*, as we have seen, and it will also motivate Proust's *In Search of Lost Time*. A novel that captures this distinctively fin de siècle sense of being both blasted out into time and bogged down in it is *The Other Side*, by Alfred Kubin.

Kubin, like Wells, was a product of the new social state of the late nineteenth century—with its expanded public provisions for popular education and welfare—and not a very happy one. He was born in 1877 in Bohemia, then part of the Austro-Hungarian Empire, and his mother died when he was a child, leaving his father, a land surveyor in the Austrian civil service, to bring him up. The father was a severe man, frightening to his son, and Kubin, a poor student, undisciplined, and without initiative, disappointed him. Apprenticed to a distant relative who owned a photo studio, the boy mooned over early photographs of Europe's old cities, their streets emptied by slow shutter time, and he was soon dismissed. Still a teenager, in 1896 he tried to commit suicide on his mother's grave.

He liked to draw, and a small inheritance allowed his father to send him to art school in Munich. Kubin felt at home in the city's bohemian circles, and in 1901 he had his first show—at the Paul Cassirer gallery in Berlin, alongside another artist whose work was just beginning to attract attention: Vincent van Gogh.

Kubin was a clumsy draftsman, but he used his clumsiness to effect. Working in pen and ink, in shadowy tones of black and white and gray rubbed into heavy surveyor's paper that he got from his father, he depicted a weird, scary world of his own. A great black ape clasps a stark-white naked woman to his chest, drawing her so close that her breasts appear to be his. With his hand he strokes her sex while engulfing her head with his open mouth. A lady in a fashionable riding outfit sits sidesaddle on a rocking horse that has blades for runners, rocking back and forth on a field of mutilated men. A muscular young man kneels to perform cunnilingus on a corpse.

The images are horrific and erotic, catnip for an era—the era of Freud's *Interpretation of Dreams*, of Otto Weininger's notorious treatise *Sex and Character*—gripped, like that naked white woman, by sexual obsession, an era caught between the stifling proprieties of the bourgeois home and a swarming public sexual marketplace kept well supplied by the ongoing migration of country people to overflowing cities. A review of a 1903 show—Kubin was pleased by it—praised him for "conveying ideas and moods of uncanny reality that will burn themselves into your brain as with hot punches." Another critic called the work "a true cry for help."

For Kubin, however, the vision began to fade. He made muddy paintings. He married. His wife was sickly, and the couple retreated to a house in the country. He paid the bills by working as an illustrator, and he felt as lost as he had as a teenager. He wrote to a friend: "I don't believe I am an artist any longer; perhaps I am a writer, perhaps a philosopher, perhaps something else—a thing or something else again, or I am nothing at all."

One day he picked up some leftover illustrations he'd drawn for Gustav Meyrink's *The Golem*, a book Meyrink wouldn't finish for some years, and began to compose a story to go along with them. Soon he was writing compulsively, and in almost no time at all, he completed *The Other Side*.

The Other Side starts with a knock on the door. The narrator, a successful illustrator, happily married, answers it to find a stranger who explains that he comes as an emissary of one of the narrator's old high school friends, Patera, whom the narrator remembers as an exceptionally gifted and charismatic youth. Patera, the visitor reports, is now fantastically rich, and he has just bought a vast tract of land in Central Asia that he intends to turn into a private kingdom of his own, called Dreamland, to which the narrator and his wife are now invited, all expenses paid. Though a little taken aback, it's an invitation they can't resist. No one ever can, the emissary remarks, and, by the way, no one ever comes back.

This could be the beginning of one of the popular adventure stories of Kubin's day—say H. Rider Haggard's *She*—but that is not the kind of story *The Other Side* turns out to be. Husband and wife make their way to Dreamland—a journey that begins in style but ends with the couple dumped unceremoniously into a goods train—and settle down in Pearl, the country's capital city. At this point Kubin's book is suddenly transformed—a kind of shape-shifting on the page that will occur with increasing frequency—into a satire. "By and large things here were much the same as in central Europe," the narrator writes, "and yet, on the other hand, so very different." Dreamland does bear a pronounced resemblance to the Austro-Hungarian Empire under the interminable reign of Emperor Franz Joseph I, the double kaiserlich and königlich dominion that Robert Musil will dub Kakania ("Shitland") and Stefan Zweig "the world of yesterday." Everyone dresses in out-of-date fashions; only old, valueless currencies circulate; and no one knows how much money he has anyway. All religions are represented among the population; none is observed. Time is passed gossiping or playing chess in cafés. "The barometer," we are told, "[is] permanently set on 'dull and cloudy' . . . There [are] no glaringly modern buildings . . . [Patera had] had old buildings sent from all parts of Europe." Patera himself remains inaccessible behind the dysfunctional bureaucracy that regulates daily life, but the idea of him is reassuring: "Behind all this confusion, is the presence of a *strong hand*."

Dreamland, Shitland: Patera's private dominion resembles not just the throwback empire that was Austria-Hungary but some of the great new attractions of Kubin's day and of the incipient century. Dreamland was the name of the great pleasure resort that opened at Coney Island in 1904, and though Kubin may not have known about it, Patera's claim to fame at the start of the book is as a new style entrepreneur. Pearl has a fictional parallel in L. Frank Baum's Emerald City, and Dreamland is a harbinger of Disneyland, and now *The Other Side*, having begun as an adventure and morphed into a satire, turns into a wild ride. Things become unpredictable and scary. Genres multiply, overlap, and dissolve into each other like figures and reflections caught in a revolving door. There are transcriptions of dreams—at one point the narrator finds himself naked in the city streets, while the city itself is strangely alive, full of sexual fantasies, odd inconsequential adventures, dead ends. There is an ethnography of the inhabitants of Dreamland before Patera laid claim to it, and the book also has a religious side: when the narrator does finally meet Patera—the "father"—the go-getter he had been told of turns out to be a figure in agony, a Gnostic demiurge who has lost control of his creation.

This proliferation of narratives and of kinds of narrative is counterpointed by the story of the narrator's marriage: the couple is increasingly estranged—they don't really know why—and then the wife, now a chronic invalid, dies. The novel has no more use for her. Meanwhile, this crumbling story of a crumbling marriage is accompanied by a literal crumbling of material reality—even jewels crumble—as public order collapses, wild beasts spring out of the ground, and people engage in orgies of sex and bloodshed. The apocalypse is not far behind, complete with four horses, but world politics go on as usual: an American fat cat, Hercules Bell, enters the story, smoking "propaganda cigars," building a railway, starting a newspaper, intent on bringing Patera down. The Russians attack. In the end, the book falls back on the most banal ending of all: none of this happened; the narrator has had a nervous collapse. Dreamland is just a dream.

The Other Side is like a narrative demolition derby—improvisation, fantasy, confession, prophecy, allegory, nightmare, and a bit of a joke, though who the joke is on is an open question. Is it the unpracticed author who is no more in control of his imagined world than his mysterious, tormented, oddly pathetic Patera, or is it the reader, lured into and swept up by this curious production? It's a minor book, a one-off. Kubin abandoned writing after finishing it and resumed his lucrative career as an illustrator. Yet minor though the book is, it made its mark, surprising traces of it turning up in fiction all through the twentieth century. Kafka read it (his journal records a meeting with Kubin in Prague—the two men discussed constipation remedies), and the offices of the law that Joseph K battles so helplessly in *The Trial* are very much modeled on Dreamland's impenetrable bureaucracy. Ernst Jünger, who made his name after World War I as the author of *Storm of Steel*, an exultant tale of the savagery of the war, was another admirer. Writing in the 1920s, Jünger praised Kubin's novel as a powerful example of magic realism, a term that had recently been coined by the art critic Franz Roh to describe how piercingly strange the world appeared in paintings executed in the sharp-focus style of the Neue Sachlichkeit (the "New Objectivity"). Jünger is much more of a stylist, but his teasingly allegorical fictions, notably *On the Marble Cliffs*, a veiled account of Nazi misrule that he published in 1939, are clearly influenced by Kubin. And then, across some sixty years, *The Other Side* finds an echo in Gabriel García Márquez's *One Hundred Years of Solitude*. In García Márquez's Macondo, as in Pearl, there is a plague of insomnia, and in Macondo, as in Pearl, the approaching end of days is signaled by the returning jungle and a plague of ants. Did the Colombian writer know Kubin's book? It's certainly not impossible—Kafka was a central influence on him—but I haven't found any actual evidence of it. Perhaps what Kubin lighted on in *The Other Side* simply enters the bloodstream of the twentieth-century novel.

But what exactly did Kubin light on? A new genre? Not really. What he came up with is more like a not-quite genre, a poetry of neither fish nor fowl, of the junk collecting in the attic. In Kubin's book the shabby past, a misbegotten utopia, and a disastrous future all crowd together uncertainly, like strangers waiting at a bus stop, and whatever story there might be to link them never really materializes—and yet, to our surprise, the lack of that link somehow holds the imagination. When I say *The Other Side* is a "minor" book, I don't mean that it possesses the sort of purity of conception and perfection of execution that W. H. Auden, introducing his anthology *Nineteenth-Century British Minor Poets*, contrasts with the ambition and range but all too frequently dull prolixity of such great poets as Wordsworth or Victor Hugo. I mean minor more in the way that Gilles Deleuze and Félix Guattari speak of Robert Walser—and above all of Kafka—as minor writers, where minorness is proposed as a distinctive and defining category of twentieth-century literature. Walser is a writer for whom meaning lies in the overlooked, the cast out, and the equivocal. He disclaims any interest in the grand gesture, makes a point of his inadequacies, and shrinks from the "big thinks" of Wells's ape-men; and *The Other Side* can be read as a tacit rebuke to the destructive and boring nature of high ambition. This, however, is to make too much of Kubin, whose accidental inspiration—writing a story to illustrate the illustrations he made for another, as yet incomplete, story—is perhaps best described as letting contingency enter and drive a work, so managing to capture something of the terrible, ridiculous contingency of modern existence. Contingency or disposability, a sense that each and every one of us stands on the brink of obsolescence or oblivion: *The Other Side* is imbued with it, and remains memorable as a book that keeps slipping into its own cracks.

Kafka is not a minor writer, Deleuze and Guattari aside, if only by virtue of his influence. The Kafkaesque is everywhere in the literature of the twentieth century—in Nabokov, Borges, García Márquez, Ishiguro, and so on—and it is by now a cliché to call Kafka a prophet of the last century's totalitarian horrors. He's not at all a minor writer, yet even more than Kubin's his work carries the mark of the accidental. He himself wished for his work to be burned. It deserved nothing but oblivion. Max Brod felt otherwise, and we can only be grateful that he did. If some controversy still attaches to his sparing Kafka from the flames, that's surely not because of some niggling question of the rights and the wrongs of the matter, but because the idea of the work's finally being destroyed is so much in tune with the work itself. It's as if Brod deprived us of the real, right ending of Kafka's story—a story by Kafka. Even so, much of Kafka's work, and certainly the three novels, come to us unfinished, and his greatness as a writer, his authority, is inextricably bound up with his despairing but determined embrace of the sketchy, the provisional, the terminally inconclusive. Kubin stumbled on a novel, completed it too, and Kafka saw something there, but what Kubin stumbled on, Kafka took up and explored with obsessive deliberation. Left unfinished, Kafka's work takes on an aspect of the unfinishable, and so may be seen, in the theological terms that haunt all his work, as partaking of the eternal or, contrariwise, as sentenced to perdition. It would, in any case, be a fool who set out to complete *The Trial* or *The Castle*.

If Kafka's novels are unfinished, all of Kafka's work retains the mark of the moment of revelation in the fall of 1912 when he figured out what he was doing as a writer. Kafka was twenty-nine. For five years, while living with his family in their apartment in Prague, he had been working as a lawyer for an insurance company that handled claims for workers who'd been injured on the job. He was not happy. "Day before yesterday was blamed because of the factory," his diary records on March 8, 1912. "Then for an hour on sofa thought about jumping-out-the-window." March 10: "So deserted by myself, by everything. Noise in the next room." The next room was his parents' bedroom, from which snoring and muttering and other sounds penetrated his own jealously guarded space.

Kafka's father had come from a poor Jewish village in the country to set himself up as the successful owner of a fancy goods store in Prague. He was a big, coarse, angry man, perpetually anxious about business affairs. He didn't like his educated and equally high-strung son, who insisted on being served vegetarian meals, took no interest in the family's fortunes, and had literary pretensions that kept him up all night and left him exhausted every day. Jews in the Czech city, at that time still part of the Austro-Hungarian Empire, were chiefly German speaking, and Kafka was steeped in German and European literature.

He was writing, but he didn't feel the writing was going well. That summer, however, his friend Max Brod, a novelist, had taken it upon himself to introduce Kafka and his work to an enterprising new publisher in Leipzig—Ernst Rowohlt (Rowohlt and his sometime partner Kurt Wolff would play a role comparable to that of Gallimard in promoting the twentieth-century novel), and Rowohlt had declared that he would be interested in seeing a slim collection of Kafka's work. Kafka was having trouble putting it together, in spite of Brod's prodding. Brod had taken on Kafka as a kind of project, and Brod's house in Prague afforded Kafka a respite from his own miserable homelife.

It was at Brod's that late in the summer of 1912 Kafka met a young woman from Berlin who impressed him mainly by not impressing him much. ("Bony, empty face that wore its emptiness openly. Bare throat," he wrote in his diary after meeting her.) Nonetheless, by the end of their first evening together, he had already agreed that the two of them must visit Palestine. But Felice returned to Berlin, and in the next weeks Kafka's family situation grew more parlous than ever. His sister got engaged. His father celebrated a birthday. It was Yom Kippur. Kafka's sense that he was wasting his life, that he was no one, seems to have become acute. On September 20 he wrote Felice a letter: "In the likelihood that you no longer have even the remotest recollection of me, I am introducing myself once more: my name is Franz Kafka, and I am the person, etc."—the beginning of a correspondence that would, within days, become absolutely frantic and lead to an agonized engagement. Then, on the night of September 22, Kafka returned from the office and began to write. He wrote all night. By morning he had finished a new story, "The Judgment," which he would call Felice's story. He knew it was good. A week later, September 29, he was again writing through the nights in, as Brod's diary records, "an ecstasy." By October 1 this new work, "The Stoker," was also finished. Kafka read both stories to Brod on the sixth, and Brod, as much as Kafka, recognized them for the breakthrough they were.

"The Stoker" was in fact a new first chapter to a novel that Kafka had in mind and had been working on for some time, a novel about America, and he had done a good deal of research, attending lectures about life in the USA, taking careful note of a series of articles on the same subject in a local newspaper. He had thought of Ben Franklin's *Autobiography*, much loved by European readers, as a sort of model for his book, and he had taken his manuscript with him the previous summer when he went to Jungborn, a popular new health resort, for a rest cure. Jungborn saw nudity as curative, and Kafka found himself distracted by the sight of naked middle-aged men dashing through the fields.

So far the novel hadn't gone anywhere. In October and November, however, along with the new relationship and ongoing correspondence with Felice, it began to take shape. *The Man Who Disappeared*, as Kafka called the book (Brod would publish it as *Amerika*), is the story of a young man who has been sent to America, a Dreamland of

a sort, to make his fortune (he has a rich uncle there) and to extricate
him from an entanglement with a servant girl. That the son has been
exiled instead of the servant being dismissed is only one of the odd-
ities to emerge in the first chapter, in which our hero has just arrived
in New York, its harbor swarming with warships under a Statue of
Liberty that brandishes not a torch, but a sword.

Karl Rossmann is the young man's name, and he is to make a new
life in the New World, far from all his old mistakes, though in fact he
will encounter nothing but setbacks. At first his uncle Jakob, a senator,
provides for him, giving him a room, a desk, a piano, and English and
riding lessons, making introductions, urging him "to avoid all manner
of commitments . . . to absorb and examine everything . . . The first
days of a European in America were like a new birth . . ." But then, just
as abruptly, Uncle Jakob drops him, and Karl, suitcase and umbrella
in hand, hits the road. He meets up with Robinson and Delamarche,
an Irishman and a Frenchman, who sponge off him and rob him. He
finds work as an elevator boy—and is arbitrarily dismissed. Pursued
by the police, he is rescued by Delamarche, now the gigolo of an immensely fat opera singer, Brunelda. Karl, their servant, sleeps out on
the balcony. Later—the book, which by November Kafka again de-
spaired of, peters out in a succession of fragments—Karl sees a poster
for the Great Theater of Oklahoma, where "'All are welcome.' All,
even Karl," he thinks. He is employed there under "what had been
his nickname on his last jobs: 'Negro.'" (Not for nothing does Liberty
wield a sword in this brave new world.) Enrolled as Negro, Technical
Worker, he sets off by train for Oklahoma: "Only now did Karl begin
to grasp the size of America."

The book is one ongoing disaster, yet much of it is oddly cheery in
tone. Karl is a curious character, hardly a character at all, in fact. The
kind of character he is—like the young Franklin or David Copperfield,
another model Kafka had in mind, or one of Horatio Alger's heroes—is
supposed to grow up and make his fortune, perhaps at the cost of becoming a little more worldly-wise. Karl, by contrast, regresses. Every
challenge reveals him to be a child. Toward the end of the unfinished
book, Robinson says, "You're still just a baby, Rossmann. You've got a
lot to learn still. You've come to the right place for that." The servant

girl he seduced in the old country "actually undressed him, and laid him in her bed, as though she wanted to keep him all to herself from now on"—like a doll. Karl is always being picked up, taken in hand, taken by the hand, packed off. *Rossmann* means "horseman" in German, like a knight in a child's illustrated book—or a hobbyhorse.

America, in the novel, is a scene of epic and absurd hustle and bustle, all business and busyness. In the harbor, Karl already feels New York "looking at him with the hundred thousand windows of its skyscrapers." His uncle's thriving business is "a sort of commissioning and forwarding business, of a kind that Karl thought probably didn't even exist in Europe . . . People were criss-crossing the middle of the floor, in all directions, at great speed." Outside

> in the morning and the evening and in his dreams at night, the street was always full of swarming traffic. Seen from above, it appeared to be a swirling kaleidoscope of distorted human figures and the roofs of vehicles of all kinds, from which a new and amplified and wilder mixture of noise, dust and smells arose, and all this was held and penetrated by a mighty light, that was forever being scattered, carried off and eagerly returned by multitudes of objects, and that seemed so palpable to the confused eye that it was like a sheet of glass spread out over the street that was being continually and violently smashed.

America, the New World, the promised land, is in fact a vast demolition site, and Karl is permanently out of place in it. Naive, eager to please, terminally modest and deferential, he cannot withstand the unremitting and unforgiving positivity of America. He is hopelessly conditional, much too young for the modern world. "At times I believe I know nothing at all, and everything I might possibly know would still be too little for America."

Kafka may have been uncertain of his vocation as a writer, but by the end of 1912 (which would see him turning from *The Man Who Disappeared* to *The Metamorphosis*) he was writing to Felice, "Dearest, I really should have gone on writing all night. It would have been my duty," and, some weeks later, "Dearest, it is 3:30 AM. I have spent too much and yet too little time on my novel." It was a new kind of writing he was after. He and even more his friend Brod were active participants in Prague's literary circles, where innovation was very much the order of the day, so it's interesting that what makes *Amerika* feel so new is its use—odd, even disconcerting in a book about the New World—of distinctly old, even dated forms. Franklin and Dickens were inspirations, but in writing it, Kafka also drew on the Yiddish theater, which he had been enthusiastically attending for some time, a kind of entertainment that assimilated Jews such as Kafka considered provincial and primitive, a throwback. This however is the source of the book's slapstick violence and stark sets. And it is a picaresque novel, one of the simplest and oldest of written narrative forms.

An old form is a familiar form, one that makes the reader feel he is on safe ground. Or so in principle, but not in Kafka. Kafka uses old forms in a startling way, to make things look unfamiliar—"making them strange," to use a formulation that the Russian writer Viktor Shklovsky developed contemporaneously with Kafka—in such a way that the forms themselves come to look no less unfamiliar. Why are we being shown this in this particular way? the reader wonders. Kafka's work is shot through with that basic disjunction.

Consider, for example, his use of allegory, that handsome antique mirror in which everything is revealed to be what it means. Starting with America, symbol of the modern, Kafka's novel is full of allegorical symbols, symbols that seem clear but turn out to be unclear. In Karl's eyes, the Statue of Liberty takes the allegorical form of justice. And what is the sense of this symbolic swapping of symbols? the reader wonders. Is it a simple mistake on the part of Karl, or is some larger point being made about mistaking Liberty and Justice? (Has the author perhaps made a mistake?) Karl, hoping to rise in society, becomes an elevator boy, mixing up the real and the symbolic.

Then again, Karl's life is part of a story in which, as he himself recognizes, "his lift-boy work hadn't, as he'd hoped, turned out to be a prelude to some higher position, rather he had been pushed out of it into something still lower, and was even very close to going to prison." Here again, questions of justice and liberty and judgment arise—as they do throughout Kafka's work—in "The Judgment," *The Metamorphosis, The Trial,* and "In the Penal Colony," among other places—without it being clear whether Karl has any handle on them or Kafka has given us any real clue to what we are to make of his fate. In Kafka's work, symbolism becomes the ongoing pursuit of a meaning that has always moved on. (The symbol, left behind, has been evacuated of meaning.) Is the pursuit comic, tragic, pathetic, all of the above? But to try to define it is simply to engage in the same pursuit at another level. The pursuit is inescapable, and we are not even allowed to conclude that it is fruitless.

But always it is the movement of imagination and the writing that is so powerful, so persuasive. Kafka's sentences are all about movement, and it is at the level of the sentence, or even the clause, where he works his real magic. His sentences are at once relentless and jittery, breathless and deep-breathed. They run on (and though the run-on sentence is an accepted rhetorical device in German, Kafka runs away with it) and accumulate as they go by a process of both constant addition and constant qualification, slight nervous shifts of tone and implication, abrupt introductions of unforeseen elements that are then absorbed without comment, as if expected. The process may seem almost mechanical (almost a kind of procedure, like doing your accounts), yet at the same time it is unpredictable (sheer wayward inspiration), making those sentences an endless surprise, entertaining, disconcerting, effortless, tortured, suddenly funny, and wonderfully sad. The sentence itself is always displaying another side of itself.

Karl's progress, or lack thereof, through the ship at the beginning of *Amerika* (a book that starts with its main character turning back) is exemplary:

> Below deck, he found to his annoyance that a passage that would have considerably shortened the way for him was for the first time barred, probably something to do with the fact that all the passengers were disembarking, and so he was forced instead to make his way through numerous little rooms, along continually curving passages and down tiny flights of stairs,

one after another and then through an empty room with an abandoned desk in it until, eventually, only ever having gone this way once or twice previously, and then in the company of others, he found that he was totally and utterly lost.

What happens to Karl here is what happens to the reader throughout the book. Indeed this passage can be taken as a symbolic description of reading and interpreting literature—or life. There is even a desk, albeit an abandoned one!

Kafka's work has a purity of conception and of execution, a sublime single-mindedness that makes it stand out from that of his contemporaries and—as was quickly recognized all over the world when Brod brought the work out between the wars—in the whole of twentieth-century literature. What makes writing relevant, and how much relevance matters anyway, are tricky questions, but it's striking that Kafka is a writer who immediately seemed relevant and has gone on seeming relevant, in all sorts of different places too. There is something athletic about his writing, the poise of a surfer on a breaker, which makes it the perfect gauge of a century of crisis. Of course he was also very much a product of his particular time and place, and at the time he appeared to some of his contemporaries too much so. The Jewishness of Kafka's work, those slapstick touches from Yiddish theater, his use of parable, led another Prague novelist of his generation, Franz Werfel, to characterize Kafka's work as essentially provincial. It would, Werfel predicted, be utterly incomprehensible outside of his local context. Werfel would later have an enormous success with *The Forty Days of Musa Dagh* and, later yet, in Hollywood exile, with *The Song of Bernadette*, and when he made this remark, early in the second decade of the century, he was already seen, by Kafka among others, as a coming man. His assessment is not in a sense wrong. You can see how Kafka's stories, though original, would have seemed twitchy and esoteric, the product of a parochial Jewish world that was being left behind by history and first and foremost by educated and ambitious Jews like Werfel, an exercise in anxiety and nostalgia, almost a private language. But what Werfel didn't see, and even Brod saw only dimly, is the prophetic wit with which Kafka transformed the things the modern world was bent on casting aside—as archaic or primitive or parochial—into perfect embodiments of that world's own terror of the modern. Stripped of their original context, such things—old forms of storytelling, like parable and the picaresque tale—stood apart and alone with a potent new strangeness that allowed them to live on amidst the superficiality of the new and in the face of threatened extinction. Parable has a lost totemic force that Kafka imbues with a new force by deploying it—much as Picasso does African masks—formally.

But again, Kafka's ruined properties would never loom so large in the life of the twentieth-century novel if it were not for the pace of his sentences, which capture the sense of time—mental, emotional, historical—on the fly and set his work apart, making it, you could say, a genre of one. His sentences are always running under the relentless pressure of time, a relentlessness that also figures as the subject of the great breakthrough story, "The Judgment." In it the infirm old father, put out to pasture, obsolescence personified, suddenly swells with fury to curse his virile and enterprising, very modern son, the son who is a model son, expanding the family business, getting engaged to a nice girl, and so on. The father curses him, and the son, as if gripped by a primitive compulsion, rushes out the door to hurl himself off a bridge. What allows the father to pass judgment on the son? The usual answer would be that the son has not honored his father or honored the old ways. In this case, however, the reason—not that Kafka explains anything—seems to be quite different. The father's urge to curse and sudden power to curse issues from his weakness; already the son's shiny new world casts its shadow over the father's enfeebled being, and nothing the son does can deliver the father from doom, a doom the son's very being pronounces on him. And in that sense the father's arbitrary judgment, or curse, is just—it is a curse the son can be said to pronounce upon himself—and perhaps not so much the deed of either father or son as of the individual outraged by the murderous nature of the passage of time and the oncoming march of future generations. And here once again we are on the doorstep of the nineteenth-century novel, which sought to do justice to those realities, and here Kafka, like Gide and Wells but with a darker determination than their crusading spirit permitted them, is turning away. If there is justice—and there is no guarantee that there is—it must lie elsewhere than in the arrangements and accommodations of nineteenth-century and, even more, twentieth-century life and art. "At this moment," "The Judgment" ends (note the emphasis on the moment), "an unending stream of traffic was just going over the bridge." In this image (in which the cliché of a stream of traffic takes on a new, dizzying life as the stream flows over a bridge that passes over the flowing stream of a river), as in Karl's New York, there is no vantage from which to judge what is going on, which just goes on, in any case, indifferent to the terrible scene that has just been played out.

"June 7. Bad. Wrote nothing today. Tomorrow no time," Kafka writes in his journal. He is often seen as a writer with despair at the core of his work. And that's partly true; certainly he draws a good deal of dark humor about the hopelessness of it all. And then Kafka, like Kubin in his seedy way, speaks at a time when old forms seem exhausted (empire, marriage, the novel) while the present is endlessly consumed by work time, leisure time, family time, modern times, with all the endless demands that Charlie Chaplin captures in his comic epic *Modern Times*. Overall, however, the wonder of Kafka's work is how exhilarating it is to watch his strange stories and wild sentences go careening on. They are queasy and uneasy and horrifying and terrifying and, finally, euphoric. He writes in ecstasy, Brod says, and ecstasy and physicality are as much as anything what Kafka's work is about:

> If one were only an Indian, instantly alert, and on a racing
> horse, leaning against the wind, kept on quivering jerkily over
> the quivering ground, until one shed one's spurs, for there
> needed no spurs, threw away the rein, for there needed no reins,
> and hardly saw that the land before one was smoothly shorn
> heath when horse's neck and head would already be gone.

That's "The Wish to Be a Red Indian" (all of it), and let's not forget that "Red Indians" are a subjugated and nearly exterminated people: victims of the forward march of time that, with the turn of the century, as for so much of the previous century, was deemed to be full of so much promise—or was that promise only one of destruction? In Kafka, however, ecstasy is always kin to destruction, and destruction is always kin to creation, one reason why his three novels, however fragmentary their final state, all feel like wholes.

4. YOUTH AND AGE

COLETTE'S *CLAUDINE AT SCHOOL* AND
RUDYARD KIPLING'S *KIM*

The novel has always liked the young. The young, after all, have so
many places to go; only one end awaits the old. The transformation
from youth to maturity is the story of stories: something everyone
has to go through and everything else must too: young marriages,
young countries, maiden voyages, first impressions, new outfits, all
getting old.

The twentieth-century novel likes the young too—and adds a fascination with youth itself. Being, or staying, young is as important as
growing up. In the first decade of the century—which brings Sir Robert
Baden-Powell and the Boy Scouts; naturist colonies; the Wandervogel
movement, in which young Germans take to roaming the countryside
as a statement against industrialization; and Jugendstil—the embrace
of youth reflects an eager desire for the new and for renewal, for being
done with the stuffy old ways. At this liminal moment, too, a literature
of, let's call it "extreme youth," echoing Colette, comes into its own—
stories about unusual youngsters that have an appeal to youngsters (this
is a world in which ever more children are reading and need reading
matter) but appeal to adults too. These are stories about characters who
won't grow up, who want to stay on the near side of maturity, anti-
bildungsroman. *Alice's Adventures in Wonderland*, published in 1865,
already displays a rebellious impatience with grown-up demands and
a determination to see things differently. *The Adventures of Pinocchio* (1883) is nominally about the making of a proper little boy but
is in fact about the fury of a renegade puppet. Alice and Pinocchio are

figures that will enter modern mythology, and so too will Barrie's Peter Pan, a smash hit onstage and later in a pair of novels. Teddy Roosevelt, from the Oval Office, declares his admiration for *The Wind in the Willows* (1908), with its gloriously unrepentant and immature antihero Mr. Toad, another book ostensibly directed at children that becomes a bestseller. More hauntingly, the eponymous hero of Robert Walser's *Jakob von Gunten* (1909), a book not written for children and yet childish in spirit, is a kind of naïf who enrolls in a school for servants where he is to learn not so much a trade as sheer subservience. School is the manufactory of maturity, but Jakob's special school is one at which he will master the skill of never having a will of his own. We are left to wonder whether his service to others is a matter of selflessness or a way of avoiding the business of making something of himself.

What's going on behind the vivid exterior of these stories is complicated. Their protagonists are mostly male (though Alice is an important exception), and the fantasies spun around them reflect a desire to escape the stifling bourgeois household, where mother rules while father is away at work. Seeking escape from the bourgeois household, the stories may also be said to uphold it, and of course they will become staples of bourgeois storytelling, reminding their readers, old and young, that in the end everybody has to grow up! (Note, in particular, how firmly the girls in these stories are sent back home at the end: Peter Pan's Wendy must become a mother, just as Victorian-era Jo in *Little Women* had to.) Offering an escape from the bourgeois household even as they sustain it, the stories also turn a blind eye to the world that has grown up and around it, the industrial world in which women work alongside men, the world in which sex exists apart from marriage and women work the street, about which Zola, making notes for his novel *Nana*, a portrait of a prostitute, can write, "Imagine a whole society hurling itself into the cunt."

It would be tediously reductive, however, to dismiss the fantasy of extreme youth, and the books that bring it to life, as nothing but escapist, or, for that matter, to think of escapism as anything but a reasonable desire. These are genuinely wild and unexpected books about childhood and about what it says about the world at large. Could it be that childhood escapes the limits of adult knowingness and complacency, or of its own purported innocence? Childhood in these books is being seen not as a state of exemption from experience but of unclouded questioningness, and it has the power to tell us something unignorable, perhaps even transformative, about the world we live in.

What begins in escapism may end in liberation. Rudyard Kipling's *Kim* starts as a story of youthful escape and ends with a vision that is political, mystical, and deeply personal. Colette's *Claudine at School* begins as a story of high school high jinks with a titillating edge, and it grows into an exploration, neither sentimental nor moralizing, of the scope of human sexuality.

From the first pages of the book, we know that Claudine is a force to reckon with:

> My name's Claudine. I live in Montigny. I was born there in 1884. I won't die there I bet.

We've heard this staccato *I* before, from the Underground Man, from the immoralist, in their case an *I* that is more desperate and selfish than expansive and celebratory. Claudine's is very different. Confident, cocky, curious, Claudine is who she is, quite unafraid of taking issue with authority:

> My handbook of departmental geography puts it like this: "Montigny-en-Fresnois, a pretty little terraced town of 1950 inhabitants rising above the Thaize, notable for a well-preserved Saracen tower . . ." This makes no sense at all to me. For one thing, there is no Thaize . . .

And she goes on to describe things the way she sees them. Montigny is "not so pretty, but [still a place] that I adore." It is very much a country town, embedded in a landscape to which Claudine is delightedly attached, roaming fields and woods, loving the feel of soil underfoot, unafraid of scratches and bruises. She relishes the variety of vegetation and the hum of insect and animal life. She is a child of nature, as good as parentless. Her mother is dead. Her father is an eccentric old duffer, entirely absorbed by his study of mollusks. If Claudine seems precociously self-confident, that's just as well; really, she has only herself to depend on.

But the story she has to tell in her "diary, because this is definitely a diary, or almost, that I'm starting" is as social and political as it is personal. "When, two months ago, I turned 15, I let my skirts down to my ankles, the old school was demolished, and they changed the principal. The long skirts were necessary because of my calves: they were attracting glances . . ." Claudine, writing in 1899, is in her final year at a local public school where, among the daughters of farmers, laborers, and small shopkeepers, she is the lone middle-class girl. (Usually a girl of her class would be sent to a convent school, but Claudine's father is too preoccupied with his mollusks to care.) Her native smarts put her among a handful of girls who are preparing to take qualifying exams at the end of the year to attend a training college for teachers.

Claudine is about the social life of growing girls, their rivalries, gossip, crushes, and catfights; it is also about the growth of the new social state, which has ordained that the old school will come down to be replaced by a much bigger new one. The new principal, Mademoiselle Sergent, who has been brought in to oversee the transition, is accompanied by her old, silent peasant mother; the principal herself is a product of the changing world. Her patron is Dr. Dutertre, the district superintendent of schools as well as the physician for the local orphanage (another state institution). Dutertre harbors political ambitions—he hopes to rise to departmental deputy—and Mme Sergent is very aware that her fortunes are linked to his.

Behind all these bright, shiny new public opportunities for women lies a harsh reality of sexual subservience. Describing a world of near unlimited scandal defined by the free trade of sexual favors, *Claudine at School* distills the cynicism of the decade of the Dreyfus trials. Perhaps the chief duty of Mme Sergent's assistant teacher, Aimée, is to sleep with Mme Sergent, and Aimée accepts this as her lot. (Claudine, walking past the construction site of the new school, overhears the workers describing goings-on glimpsed through the principal's window.) Then again, Aimée, as Claudine enviously notes, turns heads wherever she goes, and soon enough a male colleague falls for her and proposes, opening an escape hatch from Mme Sergent's hold—one that, however, slams shut when he discovers that Aimée has also been ministering to the sexual needs of the perpetually leering Dutertre, at the obliging instance of Mme Sergent, no less.

Claudine has sex on her mind too. She sizes up the male teachers, as they do her ("My friend, I believe that child knows more about what she shouldn't know than she knows about geography"), and at the start of the book she too has a crush on the irresistible Aimée. The other girls are equally keyed up, and Aimée's younger sister Luce has eyes for Claudine, who both leads her on and fends her off. Claudine avidly chronicles these various flirtations—innocent enough, especially by comparison to what's going on in official circles—along with the life of the schoolyard and the classroom.

In May, Mme Sergent escorts the gifted students to the departmental seat where they will take their exams, a moment of truth, since "for most of the girls their entire future is at stake." Precociously perceptive as ever, Claudine muses, "To think that this is all to become teachers, to labor from seven in the morning to five in the evening, trembling before a principal . . . in order to earn 75 francs a month. Of these sixty young girls, forty-five are the daughters of peasants or workers, and so as not to turn the soil or tend the loom, they prefer to let their skin grow yellow, their chests hollow, their right shoulders hunched . . . But at least they will wear a hat and won't have to sew clothes for other people, or tend to animals, or draw water from a well, and they can view their parents with contempt."

Claudine and most of her companions pass, and the book comes to an end with the inauguration of the new school, right next to the town hall. It is a great day, and Montigny is all decked out for the occasion, much as Paris would be for the World Fair of 1900, which opened shortly after *Claudine at School* was published. Dutertre has persuaded the minister of agriculture to preside over the festivities. Claudine and two classmates are kitted out in the red, white, and blue of the French flag and delegated to meet the minister. The whole class

stands to sing a "Hymn to Nature" and then sits down to provide a female backdrop to the speechifying male dignitaries. A dance follows,
and all the girls are waltzing merrily when terrible cries interrupt the
fun. Mme Sergent's mother, the old peasant woman, has caught her
daughter in bed with Dutertre. Dutertre has fled the scene, while the
elder Mme Sergent—the voice of the old order indignantly denouncing the scandal of the new—descends the stairs and with shouts of
indignation hurls his boots down onto the dance floor.

A farcical end to an often flippant, sometimes conniving book whose
cynicism and little kinks no doubt recommended it to readers (not that
it would have seemed unusual or shocking in the Paris of 1900), but
that balances the jaded with the genuinely refreshing. Claudine, mocking, fond, a bundle of energy, whip-smart, impertinent, and sometimes
impudent, but above all alert and curious and endlessly resourceful, is
a new kind of character: a real-life teenage girl. A real-life girl, a reader
might question, when she is served up so obviously as an object of prurient attention? When at the end of the book we learn that Claudine
will not be going to training college, but will instead move to Paris with
her father to "enter the world," don't we just imagine what discoveries
await a real-life girl there? But Claudine withstands salaciousness and
skepticism. On the threshold of life and a new century, her precocious
self-regard and effortless confidence add up to a commanding innocence. She is herself, and she is equal to what will come, and she looks
back at whatever glances we, or Dr. Dutertre, might cast her way un-
ashamed and unappalled: "I won't die there I bet."

When *Claudine at School* was published in 1900—it proved the runaway French bestseller of the year—it didn't come out under the name
of Colette but of Willy, the pseudonym of Henry Gauthier-Villars, a
fixture of the Parisian literary scene, a bon vivant, a rake. Willy was
an operator. He came from a conservative, devoutly Catholic and
prosperous family (they owned a publishing house), and after establishing himself as a music critic, he set up as a writer of novels per-
fumed with sex and scandal and stylish turns of phrase. Willy was
so busy publishing books in his own name, he had no time to write

them. He employed a range of ghosts—or as the French called them, *nègres*—who roughed out stories to which he applied a final touch, giving them the je ne sais quoi that was Willy: a snap, crackle, and pop of puns, literary allusions, and bon mots, the casual brilliance and expert worldliness of the successful scenester of the day.

In 1893 Willy married a woman more than a decade his junior, a girl of twenty, Sidonie-Gabrielle Colette, who came from a bourgeois family in the country, although one fallen on hard times. Colette, as she called herself, was very much part of Willy's act. The couple made a name for themselves at the intersection of high life (a term coined in these years), low life, and the avant-garde. They were in the audience for the first performance of Jarry's obscene modern send-up of classical tragedy, *Ubu Roi*—the defining artistic outrage of the '90s—and Colette was very close to the play's dedicatee, Marcel Schwob, a writer of beautiful, unplaceable texts, later much admired by Borges. At the same time, Colette, having debuted on the social scene as an ingénue from the country, was becoming famous for showing up in public— Willy alongside—provocatively dressed as a man, which was still forbidden by law to women other than actresses. This was how she made her appearance at the salon of of Mme Arman de Caillavet, a fashionable society lady who supplied some of the features of Proust's Mme Verdurin.

Claudine's story was very close to Colette's story, and Colette had largely written the book, as Willy would eventually, grudgingly, acknowledge. After *Claudine at School* came out and sold, in a mere couple of months, some forty thousand copies, a sequel was quickly arranged, to be followed by three more. *Claudine in Paris*, the immediate successor to *Claudine at School*, recounts Claudine's introduction to society, the sexual marketplace (Luce also comes to town and is soon established as a kept woman), the varieties of sexual experience (Claudine's cousin Marcel is very clearly gay and a masochist), and her falling in love with a much older but supremely mondaine and seductive diplomatic journalist, Renaud, whom she marries.

If *Claudine at School* looks forward to books like *The Catcher in the Rye* and shows like *Girls*, its successors anticipate reality TV. It was an open secret that in these books Willy and Colette were now essentially performing their private life publicly—and at this point Willy could be taken not just to be presenting the unfiltered thoughts of a brash young girl but to be pimping his wife to the world. Not only on the page but, soon enough, onstage. Happily riding the wave of scandal and gossip, Willy turned *Claudine in Paris* into a theatrical success of an even greater order. With Claudine played by the cabaret singer and actress Polaire, the play ran for five months, while Willy saw that "Claudine collars, lotion, hats, ice cream, cigarettes, perfume, candies, photographic paper, and even Willy rice powder" were available for purchase. Willy also produced a set of twelve louche postcards depicting a scantily clad Colette dancing attendance on him and made a point of parading around town with Polaire and Colette on either arm. In her biography of Colette, Judith Thurman tells us that soon enough every bordello in Paris featured a Claudine, and in the account of her relationship with Willy that Colette wrote in 1935 she says, "I have this moment received a letter from a shirt- and blouse-maker offering me three new [sic] styles in collars, just recently named: Claudine à l'Ecole, for morning wear; Claudine à Paris (book-muslin and stitched pleats); and (we must not forget summer and the call of the wilds) Claudine s'en va."

Colette and Willy, now mainstays of the popular press, bought an expensive apartment and filled it with portraits of themselves, and the content of the *Claudine*s grew ever more titillating, becoming a kind of folie à deux. By the time *Claudine Married* (1902) reaches its end, Renaud has propelled Claudine into the arms of Rezi, a rich, stylish, very modern married woman ("a black velvet dress, its too sumptuous material very plainly cut, clung to her round, mobile hips and her slim but not squeezed-in waist") with whom he is also sleeping, as Claudine discovers. Celebrity brought strains to the real marriage, and by 1906 the couple had separated, though they continued to collaborate for a while. Colette began an exercise regimen, went onstage, published a book under her own name, and succeeded in forcing Willy to recognize her claim to the *Claudine*s, though in a moment of weakness that, she said, she would never forgive herself for, she had allowed Willy, who had run through all his money, to persuade her to sign away their copyright to the book. She became the lover of Sophie

Mathilde Adèle Denise de Morny, the Marquise de Belbeuf, known as Missy, a notorious lesbian. At the Moulin Rouge, Colette and Missy performed in a skit (Willy remained involved as producer) that ended with a lingering kiss—and caused a riot.

"You can't get away from it," Colette recalls the poet Catulle Mendès saying to her about Claudine, "You've created a type." In *Claudine at School* and *Claudine in Paris*, Colette invented a hero for a new age, the unattached, undaunted girl. The Claudine sequence as a whole sees Colette inventing another, more challenged and stranger figure: Colette herself. Publicly recognized as a writer in her own right, she had also found a style and voice of her own. Claudine's voice is colloquial and irreverent, though at times there is a tinge of arch insinuation that may still be Willy. Colette's own voice is sensuous and unfailingly intelligent, with a steely exactitude.

Consider:

> I would avidly watch his eyes glaze as he tensely watched mine glaze . . . For a long time I retained—and to tell the truth I still retain—a slight terror of . . . how can I put it? I think "marital duty" is the usual term. This potent Renaud made me think . . . of that great gawk Anaïs, who had a mania for cramming her large hands into gloves too tight for them . . . It is pleasant to begin in complete ignorance and then to learn so many reasons for giving nervous laughs and nervous cries, for uttering little muffled moans with your toes curled up with tension.

That is Claudine describing the early stages of her sex life with Renaud. Consider in turn:

> Her eyes are cold, rather severe. She gets up, takes three steps, and sits down again. Then, irrevocable decision, she jumps off the bed, runs to her tray, scratches . . . and there is nothing at all. The indifferent expression returns. But not for long. Her anxious eyebrows draw together: feverishly she scratches the sawdust again, tramples it down, looks for a good place, and, for three minutes seems lost in bitter thought, her eyes

fixed and starting out of their sockets. For she is, deliberately, slightly constipated. At last, she slowly gets up and, with minute precautions, covers the corpse, wearing the earnest expression suitable to this funereal operation. A little supererogatory scratching round the tray, then she goes straight into a loose limbed, diabolic caper, prelude to a goat-like skipping and leaping, the dance of liberation. At that, I laugh and call out: "Melie, quick! Come and change the cat's tray!"

Both passages are meticulously observed—both passages concern, among other things, observation—and display the almost clinical precision with which Colette would approach life, sex, love, and other emotions, as well as the animal and natural worlds that would always mean so much to her: the inhuman on the other side of the human, which offers relief from the human. In the *Claudines*, Fanchette the cat may be Claudine's one true familiar, and Colette, you could say, takes a cat's view of human life.

Colette had made her name, found her style, and found, importantly, a certain attitude toward her work, which she had to fight to take control of. As a novelist, she would treat writing as a particular kind of job, a profession as much as a vocation, in the practice of which she exercised, she boasts in her memoir, "hard work and almost finical punctuality that would have given points . . . to almost any storekeeper's staff." The job took her out into the world and back to her desk, and it did not preclude her taking other jobs: she would have an ongoing career as a comédienne, and in the 1930s, with great fanfare, she would open a beauty salon. Colette the writer found acclaim for her writing but also as the producer of a distinctive product. Willy had run a factory, and now she had one too, of which she was the proprietor and the brand manager. Her role as Colette, not unlike her cross-dressing and bisexuality and several subsequent marriages, gave her a certain latitude in relation to her identity, and her work may be seen as rejecting the very idea of people having a defining identity, apart from what they make up or succumb to in the course of living. In her memoir, Colette describes how Willy systematically and speedily crushed her girlish spirits as soon as they were married and in Paris. Slowly, however, she found the courage to "value a little more highly what there was in me that was unusual, attractive, desolate, secret," becoming at last "a sovereign ruling and moving in the shadows, followed by her long tresses." The long tresses would go, but the sovereignty of the writer would remain.

In Colette's mature work she explores the sensibilities and desires of mature women and examines the strange, impersonal, confounding power of sex and love. She was fascinated by the play of desire and domination that had shaped her relationship with Willy, and in the two Chéri novels and in the scenes from the erotic, largely lesbian demimonde that make up her 1932 collection *The Pure and the Impure*, she provides near clinical descriptions of human dependency and self-destructiveness. She shares with Freud a sense of the fluidity, obsessiveness, and drivenness of sexual desire, though she is always matter-of-fact in her portrayals. For her, sex—and perhaps even more, that unaccountable thing, love—constitutes an essential, and terrifying, strangeness within. Sex marks the limits of the self, takes us out of the self, summarily returns us to the self, which is why—this is the burden of *The Pure and the Impure*—for so many people, seeking to slake and quell this thing, this desire that has them in its grip, it takes the form of self-obliteration. Colette's work is clear-eyed, unsentimental, and full of sensual detail. It is also profoundly elegiac. "Among all the forms of courage," she writes in *My Apprenticeships*, "the courage of girls is outstanding," by which she means the courage that brings them to a man's bed and the challenge of sexual existence. To enter the sexual world is not to be ruined, as the Victorian moralizers would have it, but it is to live in a world in which gratification is always accompanied by loss. Her later work celebrates the courage to go there even in light of the mournful knowledge it must bring.

Claudine is endlessly active, all leaps and bounds. In old age, Colette grew corpulent. Crippled with arthritis, she could walk only with canes and then not at all. Still, she continued to present a carefully cultivated image of herself to the world: the powdered old woman with a crown of dyed curls living alone in the Palais Royal was the intimate and monarch of the bed, the boudoir, the body, whose innocent hungers hold everyone in thrall.

In her literature class, Claudine hides a book of her own behind the course textbook: the stories of Rudyard Kipling. Today Kipling's reputation as a writer is chiefly as an unbending apologist for British imperialism, a blustering little man parading behind steel spectacles and a bristling mustache, excoriated for writing such lines as "East is East and West is West/ And never the twain shall meet" and "Take up the White Man's Burden." This is a caricature of a complicated man and writer, a great storyteller, and a stylist whose taut sentences and alert descriptions set a standard for twentieth-century prose, a gritty realist with a visionary streak that Brecht appreciated. T. S. Eliot, another admirer, said that Kipling "knew something of the things which are underneath, and of the things which are beyond the frontier." Kipling was forty-one when he won the Nobel Prize in 1907, the first English-language writer and (to this day) the youngest writer ever to receive it. By that point he was renowned internationally not only as a prodigy but also as an explorer of the backwaters and dangerous spaces of the world. His poems had brought the language of the streets and barracks into the padded parlor of Victorian verse. He had brought back stories from places far and wide. Kipling was unvarnished and for real. He was news. In a young century, he represented the spirit of youth.

Kipling was a public figure and a model of confident know-how, a bluff exterior that he had assumed after an unusually difficult upbringing. His father was a sculptor and teacher of art and design; his mother, very beautiful, a charmer, the niece of the Pre-Raphaelite painter Sir Edward Burne-Jones. Members of the educated middle class but without inherited wealth, they went to India, which they saw as a field of opportunity and a place in need of enlightened uplift. In 1865 Kipling was born in Bombay. "My first impression," he recalled in his posthumously published memoir, *Something of Myself,* "is of daybreak, light and colour and golden and purple fruits at the level of my shoulder. This would be the memory of early morning walks to the Bombay fruit market with my ayah." His ayah, or nanny, was of course Indian. He passed his first years among Hindus (with their "dimly seen friendly Gods"), Muslims, and Parsees, watching dhows pass in the harbor and living not far from the Towers of Silence, where the Parsee dead were left to be consumed by vultures. He "did not understand [his] Mother's distress when she found 'a child's hand' in the garden." His first tongue was an Indian tongue.

At five, however, his parents dispatched him to England to learn English and Englishness. It was the done thing. The boy found himself in "a small house smelling of aridity and emptiness." This was Lorne Lodge, where Kipling was to board, consigned to the untender mercies of its owner, Mrs. Holloway, a fanatical evangelical Christian, and her bullying (also very Christian) son. At Lorne Lodge (dubbed the House of Desolation in the memoir), Kipling was subjected to every piously improving torment that Holloway and son could possibly devise, and they were ingenious at it. Deemed an irredeemable sinner, he endured an unending round of renewed scoldings, beatings, and other punishments. After one childish infraction, he was made to walk though the streets of the town wearing a placard inscribed LIAR. And so, Kipling allows, he became one. Condemned in advance, what else was he to do? The situation, he remarks in *Something of Myself*, "made me give attention to the lies I . . . found it necessary to tell . . . I presume [this] is the foundation of all literary effort."

Lies sustained him. So did the books sent to him by his family in faraway India—*The Arabian Nights* especially—though his love of reading inspired the Holloways to confiscate his books on any pretext. But books possessed magic. Locked up alone for hours in the "mildewy basement," Kipling was inspired by *Robinson Crusoe* to imagine himself a "trader with savages." Surrounded by "a coconut shell strung on a red cord, a tin trunk, and a piece of packing-case which kept off any other world" ("the magic lies in the ring or fence that you take refuge in," he explains), he was safe, at least for a while, in a world of his own.

It was not until he was eleven that Kipling's family realized something was amiss at Lorne Lodge and released the boy from captivity. He finished up his education in England at a modest, comparatively humane boarding school before returning at seventeen to live with his family in Lahore, where his father was now the director of the local museum and where he found Kipling a job providing "scraps" for the local paper, *The Civil and Military Gazette*. Lahore, after the years in England, was deeply disorienting. Kipling arrived to find himself "moving among sights and smells that made me deliver in the vernacular sentences whose meaning I knew not." The tiny Anglo-Indian community (some 1,200 people) was insular, claustrophobic, given over to gossip and backbiting, and as resentful of the folks living the easy life back home as they were homesick; all around them, "in the growling, flaring, creed-drunk city," was the alien population (150,000) that they presumed to rule, who not so long ago had risen in bloody rebellion. Life was never less than difficult, and summers, especially, were terrible. The heat made sleep impossible, and dysentery, typhoid, and cholera were rampant. "My world was filled with boys . . . who lived utterly alone, and died from typhoid mostly at the regulation age of 22," Kipling writes. Indeed "the dead of all times were about us . . . Skulls and bones tumbled out of our mud garden walls, and were turned up among the flowers by the rains."

Kipling's "chief" at the *Gazette* was a son of a bitch, and Kipling loathed him. He also learned from him. Kipling began as a subeditor, digesting the news that came in from other parts of the British Empire and all over the world. After a time, he was put on the local beat—reporting on receptions, accidents, disasters, divorces, brawls, murders—and soon he was covering the region at large. "All the queer outside world dropped in at [the] office," Kipling says, even as by day (and in summer by night) he roamed the city, growing familiar with its backstreets and hidden corners, opium and gambling dens, brothels, liquor shops, and street entertainment. He saw the parties and hanky-panky at the hill station of Simla, where the better sort retreated for the summer, and the grim lives led by British soldiers in their remoter and drabber stations, and he began to write poems and stories about what he saw. The poems were patched into the paper as filler. The stories ran as "turnover stories" that compelled the reader to turn past the front page to finish.

Before long, Kipling, a brilliant packager of his own work, brought out *Departmental Ditties*, his first book of verses, with a clever cover that looked just like a brown paper government envelope crisscrossed with red tape, while a collection of stories, *Plain Tales from the Hills*, was rapidly succeeded by the six small volumes called the Indian Railway Library, perfect diversions for long journeys by train across the vast subcontinent.

In 1889, Kipling, now twenty-three, decided it was time to take his act back home, if England was home. Traveling by way of China and Japan and America, he came to London, found a room close to the music halls whose entertainments he adored, and prepared for the English publication of the railway stories. They were an immediate and immense success. Kipling had made it. When he sought to join the prestigious Savile Club, he was sponsored by Henry James—James would call him "the most complete young man of genius"—and Thomas Hardy, among other well-known writers of the day.

But Kipling was restless. He left London to build himself a house in Vermont (he had married an American), where he was as productive as ever, though he came to dislike what he saw as the unabashed greediness of the American way of life. After an ugly legal dispute with his brother-in-law, he returned with his family to the rural south of England, whose deeply historical natural landscape he would evoke in the beautifully atmospheric stories of *Puck of Pook's Hill* and *Rewards and Fairies*. He loved that England, but every winter he regularly left it for Cape Town, and during the Second Boer War he reported from the front. One place he never really went back to was India—one brief visit, and that was it. He revisited it in writing, however—in *The Jungle Book*, which cemented his international reputation, and then in *Kim*, which emerged slowly over the course of almost a decade, coming out in book form in 1901. Kipling rightly considered it his best novel; it was also singled out for special mention when he was awarded the Nobel Prize.

Kim is a mongrel book with a mongrel hero. It opens on a bold note: "He sat, in defiance of municipal orders, astride the gun Zam-Zammah." Bold and disorienting. Who is this? Where are we? The early-orphaned child of an Irish soldier and a nursemaid, raised by a "half-caste" woman, Kim when we encounter him is a child of Lahore, streetwise, dirty, fluent in the local languages and their various dialects, adept at insult and invective, endlessly inquisitive about and observant of the ways and whims of the different people and peoples—Muslims, Hindus, Sikhs, Jains, Afghans, Pathans—who live in or pass through a city at once ancient and modern. Kim has grown up living "a life wild as that of the Arabian Nights," executing "commissions by night on the crowded housetops for sleek and shiny young men of fashion," and "knowing all evil since he could speak." Fondly, but not unironically, nicknamed "friend of all the world," he is a shapeshifter, trickster, sneak thief, pickpocket, letter bearer, guttersnipe—and pure potential. And yet, if he has any ambition above and beyond survival, it is not to be cultivated by the missionaries who might recognize the European behind the sunburn and native clothes and seek to collar him and make him a good boy.

Kim's perch on the cannon Zam-Zammah (imperial war booty) is precarious as well as defiant, and it is there that he has the first of two encounters that will determine his fate. When a Tibetan lama shambles past, a figure exotic even to Kim, he sets out to "investigate further, precisely as he would have investigated a new building or a strange festival." The lama, he learns, seeks enlightenment, "to free [himself] from the Wheel of Things" by bathing in the river that, it's said, sprang up at the place, a place beyond all places, to which the young Buddha, in a youthful trial of strength, once sent an arrow flying. Now, however, the lama is "old, forlorn, and very empty." He slips into sleep, while Kim takes his begging bowl and goes to beg for him. When he wakes, the lama is convinced that Kim has been providentially sent to be his *chela* (disciple). He proposes that the boy accompany him on his quest, and Kim readily agrees.

Benares is the lama's immediate destination, and Kim suggests that they take the train, allowing Kipling to depict—in the squabbling but good-humored passengers from various walks of life—an India very much in transition, the India that right at the beginning of the book was described as "the only democratic country in the world."

The clatter and noise of the train is not, however, to the lama's taste. He insists that they walk.

> [The road] was built on an embankment . . . so that one walked, as it were, a little above the country, along a stately corridor, seeing all India spread out to left and right. It was beautiful to behold the many-yoked grain and cotton wagons crawling over the country roads: one could hear their axles, complaining a mile away, coming nearer, till with shouts and yells and bad words they climbed up the steep incline and plunged on to the hard main road, carter reviling carter. It was equally beautiful to watch the people, little clumps of red and blue and pink and white and saffron, turning aside to go to their own villages, dispersing and growing small by twos and threes across the level plain.

This is is the Grand Trunk Road, sprung into life as if at a click of the lama's prayer beads, "which runs straight, bearing without crowding India's traffic for fifteen hundred miles—such a river of life as nowhere else exists in the world," and this is the first of several visions in a book full of remarkable sightings, extraordinary, sinister, or vivid, and as fleeting as "ragged Kim against the purple twilight." "This is a great and terrible world, I never knew there were so many men alive in it," says the lama, unconsciously echoing Miranda in Shakespeare's *Tempest* (*Kim* is a book of echoes as well as visions), and it leaves Kim himself "in the seventh heaven of joy." The distance, the detail: Kipling's stately prose dilates on and delights in India's immensity.

Here on the Grand Trunk Road the second encounter that will decide Kim's fate takes place. Back in Lahore, a Pashtun trader had given him a message to deliver to a certain Englishman. Mission accomplished, Kim hangs around to eavesdrop, picking up on a rumor of war. Encountering an encampment of British soldiers on the Grand Trunk Road, he thinks to investigate further—and falls prey to the thing he has always dreaded most. He is nabbed by two holy men, an Anglican and a Catholic, hell-bent on converting him into a working Englishman. (Here we discover that Kim, so fluent otherwise, has only "tinny saw-cut English," which means that much of the book we have been reading has, up to now, effectively been in translation.) Luckily, the boy's talents are recognized by Colonel Creighton, an ethnographer who is also the head of the secret service (again we see the spreading reach of the new social sciences in the new social state). In Creighton, the orphan Kim finds an English father figure to balance the lama, and Creighton prepares him to be a player in what Kipling calls the Great Game, the deadly serious competition to secure tribal allegiances along the tense border with the Russian Empire. Kim is finally forced to squeeze into a school desk, but the astute Creighton gives him a special dispensation to rejoin the lama on holidays. So Kim continues his wanderings in India, excellent training for a spy.

After some years, and after a Himalayan initiation into the so-called Jewel Game (*Kim* is a book full of games, masquerades, pranks, riddles, as well as visions, and this graduation-level game teaches the lesson that what you see is not what you get), Kim's education is complete. He is ready to go to work, and the last part of the book is taken up with an exciting description of his first mission. He is sent north on the trail of two spies, one Russian and one French, purported cartographers, who aim to forge an alliance with Afghan chieftains, and he invites the lama to come along with him—as the lama's *chela*, he will be well disguised. The lama, homesick for his native highlands, agrees, temporarily abandoning his spiritual quest down on the plains. Kim's partner in the operation is the enormously fat and voluble Bengali master spy, Hurree Babu, who eventually insinuates himself into the foreigners' entourage as their interpreter.

Hurree is a great creation, a learned man—like Creighton, he is a student of ethnography—self-taught, and even more than Kim a master of disguise, a vivid and poignant character. Hurree, seemingly never at a loss and everywhere at home, immense in girth, wonderfully fluent in speech, embodies a condition of essential otherness. His very language, a torrent of tongues and idioms, a continuous feat of inspired invention, reveals—or you could say betrays—as much: it is a universal language; it is also a private language, his alone. And

Hurree's situation, one realizes, is to a greater or lesser degree that of all the characters in the book, from the lama to Creighton, all far from or without a home. The agents caught up in the secrets of the Great Game, the empire's most loyal defenders, are as much outcasts as insiders, anonymous, going under code names, unrecognized, condemned to live and die under disguise. Agent E.23 tells Kim, "We of the Game are beyond protection. If we die, we die." And the game is greater than the Great Game. It is life. As Hurree Babu says, "When everyone is dead the Great Game is finished. Not before."

Kim's mission is a success: the spies are routed. Kim's mission is also a disaster: set upon by the Russian, the lama strikes back in self-defense, for him a crushing spiritual defeat, though it was only to be expected, he now reflects, mortified, since in coming north he has turned away from his pursuit of purification. And Kim is no less mortified. In using the old man as a cover, he has, he realizes, abused the trust of the person who has been, as much as anyone, his guide to life. The lama falls gravely ill—Kim carries him on his back down to the plains—where Kim also falls gravely ill.

Old man and young, each, in entering the Great Game, has played himself false. But then who are their true selves? *Kim* is a book haunted by the question of identity. Kim and Hurree and the whole corps of spies are outsiders, while the lama seeks to shed selfhood and attain selflessness. All of them, in a sense, serve what the lama at the beginning of the book calls "the Excellent Law" ("Kim," the book continues, "accepted this new God without emotion. He knew already a few score"), a law that is impersonal and demands selfless service. Kim will become its servant too, yet Kim is too much Kim, too alive and individual, not to go on being himself. But just what is that? Who is Kim? We see him early on the Grand Trunk Road, supremely unselfconscious, identified with his world: "India was awake, and Kim was in the middle of it, more awake and excited than anyone." Later, however, booted and suited and sent to school and made a sahib, he is assailed by self-awareness, and with that comes doubt: "'I am Kim. This is the great world, and I am only Kim. Who is Kim?' He considered his own identity, a thing he had never done before, till his head swam." Initiated into the Great Game, the doubts grow. "Now am I alone—all alone," Kim thinks. "In all India is no one so alone as I." Kipling continues:

> A very few white people, but many Asiatics, can throw themselves into amazement as it were by repeating their own names over and over to themselves, letting the mind go free upon speculation as to what is called personal identity. When one grows older, the power, usually, departs, but while it lasts it may descend upon a man at any moment.

"Who is Kim—Kim—Kim?" A question that comes back yet again at the very end of the book: "'I am Kim, I am Kim. And what is Kim?' His soul repeated it again and again . . . He did not want to cry . . ."

But he does. He weeps, only to have the world, "the wheels of his being," reassert itself. The book ends:

> Roads were meant to be walked upon, houses to be lived in, cattle to be driven, fields to be tilled, and men and women to be talked to. They were all real and true—solidly planted upon the feet—perfectly comprehensible—clay of his clay, neither more nor less. He shook himself like a dog with fleas in his ear, and rambled out the gate.

"Like a dog" (the same words come to the mind of Kafka's Josef K at the end of his own confrontation with the law): Kim is a mongrel, and so, as I said to begin with, is *Kim* the book. It is an adventure, a tale of nearing disaster and narrow escapes (as the lama says, "We be all souls seeking escape"), a spiritual quest, a book about growing up, and a book about not growing up, celebrating the eternal child who outwits all the grown-ups. It is about finding yourself, and it is a guidebook to getting lost. It is a game of make-believe and a story of real danger. It is a paean to India, a mix of grit and stink and perfume, as well as—for many contemporary readers this can only be disturbing—an apology for empire.

For only Empire, Kipling felt, could contain the manifoldness of India, rising above the self-interest and prejudices of family, caste, class, tribe, nation. Only Empire could provide an enduring center for a world that, without it, would be sure to collapse into endless factional fighting. Only Empire could allow England to transcend the ugly certainties of Lorne Lodge. Empire is a home away from home; Empire is the heart of exile. Empire seemed to Kipling, much as world government would for Wells, the only realistic bond for a riven world, an idea that, in retrospect, can only seem fantastical—not unlike the magic circle he drew around himself in the basement of Lorne Lodge. But then *Kim* is a fantasy, and one of the things that makes it not only a marvelous but a poignant book is that the reader senses that it is, among all the endless other things it is, an imaginary autobiography, Kipling's dream of the other Indian boy he might have been, or perhaps at heart is.

Kim, like the Buddhist wheel of life, circles back on itself: Kim, who straddled a cannon at the start, awakes from sickness in the shade of a cart at the end. It is a vision of the world and a visionary book, but perhaps even more than that, a book of different voices and different tongues. It is certainly a brilliant display of writing. The text shifts shape as deftly as its hero (who, we are told, stammers in English, dreams in Hindustani, and resorts to Urdu as needed). It can be sonorous and Virgilian, terse and scriptural (drawing on Eastern scripture as much as the Bible), or modern and technical. Shakespeare is ever present (Hurree Babu enjoys a private, slightly bitter joke when he borrows Othello's language to tell the Russian spy "he has done the state some service"), as is slang ("Wow," a soldier bursts out), and no bones are made about cursing and obscenity.

Kim is the story of an orphaned kid that looks like a kid's story but reveals itself to be a story full of wonder and fear that asks the reader to wonder, What is this world we live in and what does it mean to live there? Readers in India as much as in the West have been responsive to that wonder—the book has been recognized as a great Indian novel—notwithstanding Kipling's embrace of empire. That, I think, is because there is nothing naive about the wonder Kim awakens, and nothing exoticizing about the novel, apart, perhaps, from some of the machinations of the Great Game, which may be the most childish thing about the book. Kim, rambling off "like a dog" to who knows what new beginning at the end of his story, is much more real than the Kim who is supposed to grow up and take his place among the servants of empire, like Claudine's classmates training to be teachers. The book registers the reality of the divided consciousness that Kipling's fantasy of empire exists to deny. If it is an apologia, it subverts itself.

In *Kim*, as in *Claudine*, a child protagonist allows the author to unsettle our sense of the world, and Kipling accomplishes this thanks to his reporter's eye for detail and character and his love of a good story, but above all—and in this his achievement is comparable to Kafka's—by his extraordinary sense of language. The language of *Kim* is polyglot: foreign names and words—*shabash, madrassah, ticca-ghari, hoondis, Pahari, Bilaur, koss*, not to mention *ne varietur*—are ubiquitous on the book's pages. The question of how language shapes understanding and life—a question Kipling himself had confronted from his earliest years—is worked into and echoes throughout *Kim*, which derives much of its power by tapping the primal sources of speech, the babble of our beginnings. What are the terms by which to understand our various meanings? Politically, Kipling sought in Empire a refuge from a dangerous and fractured world. Imaginatively, his answer was the question, the action, the supremely individual feat of language-making we find in *Kim*, its language dense, plastic, encrypted, and alive, iridescent like a fish in water, a language for a new century that is as distinctive and original as Kafka's euphoric sentences and that anticipates the murmurous, echoic dream language of the anarchic empire of the night that is Joyce's *Finnegans Wake*.

5. THE AMERICAN SENTENCE

GERTRUDE STEIN'S *THREE LIVES*

Locked out for the night on Brunelda's balcony, poor Karl Rossmann despairs of ever being big enough for America. Perhaps he would have taken some comfort if he had known that writers in the United States of America did too. They were in a fix. Here they are in this great new nation, in a great new continent that is filling up with great numbers of new people from all over the world and advancing a great new political model supposed to represent not just a local way of doing business but a universal ideal, all of which was without doubt a great thing—but how to represent it? The handy cliché is that the United States is an experiment, its potential unlimited. Pure potential, however, defies description or degenerates into boosterism, while in light of it, the actual details of everyday life in America's widely scattered—and in many cases not just provincial but primitive—settlements or its crammed and underserved cities seem all too limited. Experiments can also go wrong, and from the start, the United States raises and faces the question of how it is that a nation dedicated to the proposition that all men are created equal is equally founded on slavery. Americans live with the consequences of that paradox to this day, and when it led the nation to collapse into a civil war of unprecedented murderousness some eighty years after its founding, the world wondered just what kind of example the idealistic new nation actually constituted. Dostoevsky's Underground Man makes a point of that.

Karl Rossmann saw America as too big for him; a young Henry James, writing about Hawthorne in 1879, notoriously remarked, "One might enumerate the items of high civilization, as it exists in other countries, which are absent from the texture of American life, until it should become a wonder to know what was left." For James, Hawthorne's country had been a void, as immensely small, you could say, as it was big (which presented a daunting prospect for the writer), but certainly different from the clearly marked boundaries of nation and class that European writers had been accustomed to patrolling and negotiating. The problem of America is in effect a problem of scale and measure, not just how to measure the immeasurable but how to measure up to it, and in that way, like the Russian novel, it anticipates the problems of accounting for the unaccountable that will confront the twentieth-century novelist. Gertrude Stein, twenty-six as the century begins, saw this as clearly as anyone. America, she wrote in 1932, is "the oldest country in the world because by the methods of the civil war and the commercial conceptions that followed it America created the twentieth century, and since all the other countries are now either living or commencing to be living a twentieth century life, America having begun the creation of the twentieth century in the sixties of the nineteenth century is now the oldest country in the world." In this nicely gnomic pronouncement there's the wit of Oscar Wilde as well as—looking at the Civil War as method—an almost Leninist realism and sangfroid, not to mention the familiar twang of American self-promotion. It is a characteristically insightful and provocative comment from a brilliant woman who grew up in America with an ineradicable sense of the foreignness of her German-Jewish immigrant family and went on to live all her adult life as an American in Europe. Stein, of course, was not in any sense alone in seeing America as a central presence in the new century—the American Century, as it would be called by many people with varying degrees of hope, resentment, and dread—but she was unusually sensitive and responsive to American formlessness. She found, not without a good deal of searching, a way of working with it that worked for her. In doing that, she also helped to transform not only the American novel but the twentieth-century novel.

Stein began in an unlikely, lonely place. The youngest of five children of Daniel and Amelia Stein, first-generation German-Jewish immigrants and members of a prosperous merchant family, she grew up between America—she was born outside of Pittsburgh in 1874—and Europe, to which her restless father removed the family for a spell of years almost immediately after her birth. She grew up between continents, and she grew up among languages, speaking German (the language of her home) and French before English, which she initially picked up from books, and once back in the States, she grew up between the coasts. The Stein family was largely settled in Baltimore, until Daniel decided he'd be better off in Oakland, of which Stein would famously quip "there is no there there." In a big house on the sparsely settled suburban outskirts of the expanding western port, Stein's mother fell ill and slowly died while her father grew ever more irascible and demanding, and Stein buried herself in books: Shakespeare, Trollope, *A Girl of the Limberlost*.

Daniel died suddenly in 1891 and was neither mourned nor missed. His son Leo, to whom Gertrude was close, went east to Harvard; Gertrude followed him to attend classes at Radcliffe, where she studied English literature and took an interest in psychology. Henry James was a favorite writer of hers, and his older brother, the psychologist and philosopher William James, now became her teacher. He made a strong impression, and she impressed him; he encouraged her scientific ambitions, urging her to go to medical school at Johns Hopkins at a time when few women had MDs and those who did were often unable to practice. Leo was already at Hopkins, pursuing a degree in biology, and Stein joined him at the university, but instead of studying, she fell in love with a fellow student named May Bookstaver and became entangled in a tormenting lesbian love triangle. Leo left for Europe, in order to learn "all about art" at the foot of the famous connoisseur and socialite Bernard Berenson; escaping Bookstaver, Gertrude once again set out after him. At Berenson's house in England, Leo and Gertrude met and argued about politics with Bertrand Russell, and Gertrude stayed on through a bone-chilling London winter. But then she went back to Baltimore and Bookstaver, only to flunk her qualifying exams. A medical career was not to be.

She wanted, in any case, to be a writer. Imitating Henry James, she wrote a novella called *Q.E.D.*, about her relationship with May Bookstaver, that she promptly packed up and forgot about. Then she started a novel about a German-Jewish American family like the Steins. It was to be called *The Making of Americans*, and it seems to have begun conventionally enough, until Stein, apparently dissatisfied with the results, had another idea. Recalling some of the research she had conducted under William James, she decided that her novel should constitute not just a family history but a comprehensive inventory of every type of human character. "I began to be sure," Stein later said, "that if I could only go on long enough and talk and hear and see and feel enough and long enough I could finally describe really describe every kind of human being that ever was or is or would be living." This was certainly an unusual project, but the more Stein pursued this encyclopedic butterfly, the farther out of reach it flew. She would come back to *The Making of Americans* later, completing it after almost a decade—an immense work—and she would always promote it as her greatest achievement. She did not hide what a struggle it had been. Years later, as a traveling celebrity in America, she delivered a lecture on "The Making of *The Making of Americans*," and the quotes she culls from the book's pages are telling: "I am altogether a discouraged one. I am just now altogether now a discouraged one . . . I do a great deal of suffering."

It was 1905, and Stein had picked up and followed Leo to Paris, but in a sense she was still where she had always been: betwixt and between continents and languages and caught in the thick of family. Leo, however, had at last found his calling: having discovered Cézanne, he set up as a "propagandist" for modern art. Leo and Gertrude and their oldest brother, Michael, who looked after the family business and had also come to Paris, were all busy collecting the work of young artists, and they were surrounded by them—Matisse and Picasso were their friends—and absorbed in questions about art and innovation and the somehow related question of their Americanness, which defined them in their own and others' eyes. ("They are neither men nor women," Picasso said of the Steins. "They are Americans.")

And for Stein of course there was the question of her own character and loneliness and work. Leo suggested that she translate Flaubert's *Three Tales*, a literary touchstone of the turn of the century. The task would improve her French and perhaps give her ideas. It did, but not in the way Leo intended. "A Simple Heart," the most famous of Flaubert's *Three Tales*, tells the simple story of the life of a French servant woman. No, Stein would not translate it. She would write three lives of her own: American lives—American lives and women's lives and lives that all bear a certain resemblance to the life of Gertrude Stein. The lives of the Gentle Lena and the Good Anna bookend Stein's collection. These are poor German immigrant women toiling away dutifully as servants all their life long, their gentleness and goodness as much bane as boon. In the middle is the story of Melanctha, a "complex and passionate" young woman, a "searcher." Melanctha is black and, by the conventional standards of Stein's day, not good at all. All three women live in a fictional American city called Bridgepoint (which is to say neither here nor there, but on the way to somewhere, the American situation par excellence), and all three are poor and, though very much American, in another sense, not: foreign-born, black, speaking nonstandard English, they are very much outsiders, just like their creator in Paris.

"Melanctha" is the longest story in *Three Lives*, and it was in telling the story of Melanctha that Stein discovered herself as a writer. Melanctha is the child of parents who resemble Stein's—the father angry and threatening until he simply disappears from his daughter's life, the mother present only in her being interminably ailing—and the story starts when she is a teenager, avid to find out what she can about life. Hanging out at the train station, she finds out something about sex and men. She finds out more about sex and men from an older woman, educated, experienced, hardened—her name in fact is Jane Harden—who takes her under her wing and perhaps into bed, and then she begins to find out about love from the young doctor attending her mother. Jefferson Campbell is very much the opposite of the

mercurial Melanctha—he is a "good negro" determined to be "a credit
to his race"—but then opposites attract. Melanctha and Jeff grow
close—he is infatuated—yet when Melanctha hints suggestively at her
sexual history, Jeff turns jealous. Melanctha resents what she encouraged, and the relationship turns into a torment. Melanctha and Jeff
break up, and she takes up with a gambler, who is of course "no good."
Depressed, Melanctha comes down with TB and dies. "Melanctha" is
done.

The story is quickly told and in a sense not much of a story at all.
Sometimes it seems like a nineteenth-century cautionary tale about
how bad girls come to a bad end, or perhaps a tongue-in-cheek send-up
of such a tale. At other times it might be taken as the story of a good
person whose life is blighted by racial prejudice and social intoler-
ance, a sad story, though told with a certain off-putting ruthlessness.
"Melanctha all her life never could tell her story wholly," Stein writes
toward the end and obligingly kills her off. In places, it appears to be
a kind of modern fairy tale, almost willfully naive, while elsewhere
and quite differently it comes off as a near clinical examination of the
psychological dynamics of love, not unlike the sorts of things Marcel
Proust and D. H. Lawrence were starting to write at around the same
time.

"Melanctha" is all those things and none of those things, and sometimes it seems like it is really nothing much at all. The main reason it's
so hard to pin down what "Melanctha" is getting at is that the story is
so very long in the telling, not to mention the ever more peculiar language in which it is told. "Melanctha" is 120 pages long, composed in a
manner that might be best described as conspicuously wordy:

> Life was just commencing for Melanctha. She had youth and
> had learned wisdom, and she was graceful and pale yellow
> and very pleasant, and always ready to do things for people.
> And she was mysterious in her ways and that only made belief
> in her more fervent.

What wisdom had she learned? What did she do for other people?
Whose belief is it that grew more fervent? Her own beliefs (in what?)

or others in her? (Both readings are possible.) "Melanctha" is full of
vague sentences like these—filled out with conventional descriptions
and polite nothings and sentimental or racist turns of phrase like "the
warm sunshine of negro laughter"—and as it goes on, those sentences
tend to grow longer and more and more and more repetitive:

> "Melanctha Herbert," began Jeff Campbell, "I certainly after
> all this time I know you, I certainly do know little real about
> you. You see, Melanctha, it's like this way with me . . . You
> see it's just this way, with me now, Melanctha. Sometimes you
> seem like one kind of a girl to me, and sometimes you are
> like a girl that is all different to me, and the two kinds of girl
> is certainly very different to each other . . . I certainly know
> now really, how I don't know anything sure at all about you,
> Melanctha."

"I certainly know now really, how I don't know anything sure": I am
not sure that Stein knew for sure what she was up to as she hit on this
style, which—with its limited vocabulary, ever-expanding paratactic
sentences, and repetition compulsion—might be dismissed as both
flat and flatulent, maddening and even perhaps a bit mad, but as "Melanctha" proceeds becomes ever more recognizable and unignorable.
Stein may have been up to a number of different and not, at first sight,
necessarily compatible things. Here she is finding words at last to tell
her own story, the Bookstaver story. Bookstaver would later remark
that Jeff and Melanctha's grinding exchanges were little more than
transcripts of hers with Stein. In that sense, the language of "Melanctha" might be considered symptomatic on the one hand and therapeutic on the other, a way for Stein to get something off her chest
and put it behind her. Then again, she is also finding words to tell the
story of a woman, Melanctha, deprived of the authority or capability
to tell her own story, someone whose sex and race and life place her
outside the space of "proper" storytelling. To that extent, her writing
of Melanctha is as public and political as it is private and therapeutic. Though Stein was never an overtly political writer—she didn't do
messages—and her actual politics involved an unsavory fascination

with such putative strong men as Napoleon and Marshal Pétain, she was alert to politics (that "method of Civil War") and to the political nature of language.

In the end, however, "Melanctha" is not so much about telling anyone's story as it is about putting story aside. Here, Stein, trained in scientific experiment and emboldened by the experimentation of the artists around her, turns from story to take a new look at what stories are made out of: language, sentences, words. "Melanctha" is written out of an intense, even desperate awareness of how language shapes experience—its imprecisions, its evasions, its formulae, its structure, its unavoidable limitations. She takes, for example, the clogging *ings* and jingly *lys* intrinsic to the English language, and instead of playing them down, as "good" writers have long been taught to do, she lets them loose. Is what results "bad" writing? It is writing that tends toward a drone, and a drone is perhaps the tone of boredom, depression (the melancholy inscribed in Melanctha's name). Certainly, to echo Stein, one of the things this sad tale of an unrealized life is designed to do is to make the reader feel language and also feel language fail.

And it does that, but then again (as I keep having to say) it does something else: it gives language, rather miraculously, a new life. Stein's drone begins to gather overtones, until Melanctha's story breaks the bonds of story and conventional usage to become an exploration of and a meditation on the possibilities of language, language that exists in and for, as she would come to define it in a later essay, "Composition as Explanation," a "continuous present."

Repetition renders Stein's simple words and chain-link sentences surprisingly complex in effect, opening them up to multiple and shifting registers. The language of "Melanctha" can be read as black American dialect (at least that is what a lot of Stein's early readers took it for), and Richard Wright later told a story of reading it aloud to an illiterate black audience who responded with immediate recognition. The language of "Melanctha" is dialect, and it is also language as it is spoken, in which we often return again and again to the same words to try to get a point across. Then again (again), the language of "Melanctha" is very much written language, an oddly unreal and quirky idiom of the printed page on which, by dint of its repetitions, it practically prints patterns (which is to say that the language of "Melanctha" is visual, too). It is also musical, echoing and chiming, and abstract and philosophical: all those *really*s and *certainly*s and *truly*s not only reflect how we speak but raise the question of what we speak in the hope of, what certainty, what truth, what reality? Finally, the language is erotic, shot through with sexual innuendo—"Jeff took it straight now, and he loved it . . . it swelled out full inside him, and he poured it all out back"—and the rhythms (and perversity) of sex:

> "But you do forgive me always, sure, Melanctha, always?" "Always and always, you be sure Jeff. And I certainly am afraid I can never stop with my forgiving, you always are going to be so bad to me, and I always going to have to be so good with my forgiving." "Oh, Oh!" cried Jeff Campbell, laughing, "I aint goin to be so bad for always, sure I aint, Melanctha, my own darling. And sure you do forgive me really, and sure you love me true and really, sure, Melanctha?" "Sure, sure, Jeff, boy, sure now and always, sure now you believe me, sure."

Much influenced by visual artists, Stein's work would in time prove an inspiration to such very different American composers as John Cage and Philip Glass, while "Melanctha," shot through as it is with the rhythms of black American speech, brings to writing something of the incantatory eroticism of the blues and soul music.

With "Melanctha," Stein had found a way of writing that was all her own, a no-language and a new language that sounded a little bit like lots of things and like no one else. Overcoming the sense of uncertainty and inadequacy and isolation that had marked her childhood and her intellectual and sexual coming-of-age, she had fashioned an instrument that allowed her to air and explore her most characteristic and intimate concerns—her sexuality, her feminity, her philosophical turn of mind, her love of words and wordplay at once childish and sophisticated—in entire freedom and in depth.

It was her way of writing, and it was her way of being an American writer. If, as a child in America, Stein had felt hardly American, and as an adult in Europe, at times helplessly American, on the page she was free to be her American self and, more than that—having arrived at this moment of revelation, she would have an unwavering sense of prophetic purpose—to free American literature to be itself.

She returned to *The Making of Americans*, and as she worked on this, her magnum opus, she also worked out a theory of the Americanness of American literature, in which the problem of scale (something Melville and James and Whitman had in various ways confronted without, however, formally defining it) became—this was Stein's discovery—central to its promise. She develops her ideas in a lecture on English literature that she delivered in 1934. England, she said, an island nation, had naturally produced a literature marked by a delimited sense of scale, which provided a background for stories of "daily living." English literature had been a glory in its day—Stein was steeped in it, and she paid homage to it—and it had gone through several phases, from the invention of English as a literary language in the work of Chaucer through the subsequent enlargement of its vocabulary to the muscular and mature syntax and sense of Dr. Johnson. By the nineteenth century, however, English literature had been reduced to mere phrasemaking, saying the expected thing and saying nothing much while having things both ways, a convenient accommodation of God and Mammon that you would expect from an island empire anchored in the harbor of its self-regard. Here Stein, like Gide or Wells, rebels against the balance of the nineteenth-century novel.

English fiction, the fiction of a closed circle, had lost its honesty and its power, just as England had lost the power to dominate a world that had begun to expand continuously and violently outward— a world that could be said to have begun with the discovery of America and that looked like America more than anything else. England had the defined shape of an island, but America had no defined shape: it was a frontier, moving, the eccentric center of a widening world, a world not of settled definitions, but of unending exploration, where everything was in question. James, in Stein's view, had been the first American writer to catch a glimpse of this new, decentered reality, for though he had worked with an inherited English sense of the shape of

the novel, he also had, in her words, "a disembodied way of connecting something from anything and anything from something [that]
was an American one." This accomplishment had paved the way for
Stein, who not only recognized it for what it was but formalized it,
isolated it, as a researcher might a strain of bacteria, and made it into
a matter of conscious procedure:

> I went on to what was the American thing the disconnection
> and I kept breaking the paragraph down, and everything
> down to commence again with not connecting with the daily
> anything and to really choose something.

So she characterizes her way of working in "The Making of *The
Making of Americans*," and she goes on from there to describe how
this new way of breaking things down became a way of building
things back up, and so on. The work was forever ongoing, a continuous revelation of the writer's power not to reflect given realities in
given forms, but, as Stein says, "to really choose something," and from
it emerged a vision of a new kind of wholeness born of words: "I made
a paragraph," she boasted, "so much a whole thing that it included in
itself as a whole thing a whole sentence."

And this is the key thing that Stein discovers and passes on: putting the sentence at the center of writing, a sentence that can go on
and on or be cut as short as can be, but that one way or another, as a
kind of exploratory probe, takes precedence over the idea of the work
as a whole. You start with the sentence and the sentence finds out
where it is going and you go from there. This American "disembodied
way of connecting something from anything" goes on finding its own
path across the page: "Then at the same time is the question of time.
The assembling of a thing to make a whole thing and each one of
those whole things one of a series."

She concludes: "I felt this thing, I am an American and I felt this
thing, and I made a continuous effort to create this thing . . . a space
of time that is filled always with moving."

With *Three Lives*, Stein knew she had pulled off something remarkable. She was eager to publish the book and show it to the world, and this is when a young fellow Californian, Alice B. Toklas, showed up at her door and volunteered to type it. The two women took to each other and would become a famous couple, but the typescript found no takers, and after three years Stein turned to a vanity press in the States. Receiving the manuscript from France, the director of the press, a bemused Stein later recorded, surmised that the writer must be a foreigner and obligingly offered to clean up her irregular sentences. The book came out with a blurb from "Miss Georgiana Goddard King, Reader of English at Bryn Mawr College." Astutely, Miss King praised Stein for pushing "the method of realism as far as it would go," for setting "down all the repetition and recurrence, the casting back, the weary round of those faint stirrings in the brain that we call human thought." Perhaps no less astutely, she also compared Stein's "odd style" to listening to a broken record.

Something broken and yet—this was King's adjective—"astonishing," something that didn't work and yet, weirdly, did, *Three Lives* attracted more attention than might have been expected. It was reviewed in a number of prominent places—*The Nation*, which found in the book an "urgent life" that made it kin to the Russians; a Chicago paper that saw a resemblance between Stein's "murmuring people" and the continually "moving [human] 'situations'" in the work of Henry James. Stein sent it to H. G. Wells, who was struck by it, and it caught the attention of Sherwood Anderson, a self-made businessman who had recently walked out of his office and marriage to make a go of it as a writer. Stein's work had a profound effect on Anderson, a child of the empty spaces—actual, social—of the American Midwest. He listened carefully to her sentences, and they helped him fashion a style that can sound as flat as sheetrock (a product first brought to market at just this time). Anderson wrote novels and short stories about the deprivations of American life, especially small-town life, and his heroes and heroines were sensitive souls pining for sensual and spiritual fulfillment that was hardly to be had. "Out of Nowhere into Nothing" is the characteristic title of a short story, and at his best Anderson was able to capture a genuine sense of American dread that Stein herself fought shy of.

Anderson's novels, and especially Anderson's style, made a mark on younger writers—Hemingway and Fitzgerald and Faulkner all went through a period of infatuation, and *The Great Gatsby* in particular is inconceivable without Anderson's example—and he helped the new generation discover Stein's work. In 1922 he wrote the introduction to her first commercial publication, a collection of shorter pieces called *Geography and Plays*, praising her in terms she would certainly approve:

> For me the work of Gertrude Stein consists in a rebuilding, an entire new recasting of life, in the city of words. Here is one artist who has been able to accept ridicule, who has even forgone the privilege of writing the great American novel, uplifting our English speaking stage, and wearing the bays of the great poets, to go live among the little housekeeping words, the swaggering bullying street-corner words, the honest working, money saving words, and all the other forgotten and neglected citizens of the sacred and half forgotten city.

Anderson also wrote a letter introducing Hemingway to Stein when Hemingway, shell-shocked from his military service in World War I and bored by the newspaper job he was holding down in Kansas City, abruptly decamped—almost like Anderson, altogether like an Anderson character—for Paris. Stein liked the handsome young American, and Hemingway listened very carefully to her work and to what she had to say about his work. Stein, Hemingway would say, taught me to write. Famously, she also provided the epigraph to his first novel, *The Sun Also Rises*: "You are all a lost generation."

Stein had become a presence. In 1926 she delivered her crucial critical essay, "Composition as Explanation," in England at the invitation of Leonard and Virginia Woolf; and then came the success of the publication of *The Autobiography of Alice B. Toklas*, which is not that, but Stein's autobiography, replete with catty anecdotes about Matisse and Picasso and Hemingway. Stein was now a public figure, with a carefully cultivated image—impassive as an idol, with her androgynous cropped hair and waistcoat—that reflects Picasso's famous 1906 portrait of her.

(She was working on "Melanctha" at the same time she was sitting for him.) She bore more than a passing resemblance to Henry James, too. By the time she died, in 1946, New Directions, the most important American publisher of new writing, had reissued *Three Lives* as—the term would have still seemed something of an oxymoron—a modern classic, "the revolutionary explosion . . . which produced the lean, hard, accurate styles" of Anderson and Hemingway.

This was true enough, yet it also somewhat misrepresents the character of Stein's influence or, more to the point, the special brilliance of her work. I've spoken of Kafka's sentences, how they catch the continuous disappearance of things in time, and of Kipling's great liberation of language. Stein's discovery is not unrelated to theirs, but it is also related to a larger emphasis on the material and formal properties of art in the paintings of Cézanne, Matisse, and Picasso that she collected and compared her own work to. Kafka's and Kipling's ways of handling words are brilliantly individual, and we still feel their distinctive effect and the authority of that effect, how it makes us feel things in general differently. Stein's influence as a writer, however, comes not from her specific style, her own highly mannered effects, so much as it does from her singling out the question of the sentence and its scale as the generative core of writing. How to describe her discovery? We know—it's a commonplace of art criticism—that behind Jackson Pollock's swirls and skeins and Barnett Newman's color fields, those vast compositions of the mid-twentieth century, lie the fractured panes of Braque's and Picasso's first cubism of the teens, as different as the idioms and interests of these artists otherwise are. Braque and Picasso opened up the full space of the canvas, presenting the picture to the viewer as an object, and Stein, partly in response to their example but most of all out of the exigencies of her own American experience, opens up the sentence in similar fashion. She had come from a place where "there was no there there," and she had turned it into a written space where that very absence of definition, of given form, became an invitation to continual reinvention. Stein is as much inventor as author—a very American thing to be.

In time, the rumor of Stein's American sentence came to fill the world, spreading first through the work of her American admirers and then, as their work came to be translated and imitated, more widely. In Anderson's hands and in Hemingway's, this new central- ity of the sentence answers to a point of American pride about doing things "my way," even as it touches on American anxiety about per- haps not knowing the right way or not having—in a nation of peo- ple displaced from the old ways—the right materials at hand to do things as they used to be done. Stein's liberation of the sentence left writers free to do things their own way, and American writers would leap in to enjoy this new amplitude and latitude, this new very Amer- ican space that Stein had pioneered. It was an invitation, a challenge, a provocation, and you can feel it at work both in the edgy discipline of Hemingway's self-conscious simplicity and in Faulkner's immense baroque exercises in rolling counterpoint, as well as in the overplus of graphomaniacs like Thomas Wolfe and Jack Kerouac. The work of these writers works from the sentence up, and the influence of these writers—Hemingway is still read all over the world; Faulkner would shake up European writing in the 1930s, well before he had an Amer- ican audience—reshaped the twentieth-century novel at least as much as the metafictional conceits of Gide and the speculative fiction of Wells. Jean Giono, Cesare Pavese, Thomas Bernhard, Bohumil Hra- bal, José Saramago: most of these writers never read Stein, I suspect, and as for Pavese, who translated *Three Lives* into Italian, he dismissed the book as unreadable. And yet their work is marked through and through with the generative power of the American sentence that she revealed.

6. A WORLD OF LITERATURE
MACHADO DE ASSIS'S *THE POSTHUMOUS MEMOIRS OF BRÁS CUBAS* AND NATSUME SŌSEKI'S *KOKORO*

In March 1880, not long after Gertrude Stein and her family moved back from Europe to the United States, the first installment of *The Posthumous Memoirs of Brás Cubas* appeared in *Revista Brasileira*, a monthly journal of arts and sciences published in Rio de Janeiro. Brás Cubas was an important sixteenth-century Portuguese conquistador and a common Brazilian name, but as to posthumous memoirs, well, that must have presented a puzzle. Could these be newly discovered memoirs from what would have been thought of as Brazil's heroic age of discovery? Or was this an allusion to the voluminous and popular *Memoirs from Beyond the Tomb* of the French aristocrat Chateaubriand, published after his death, in 1848? Chateaubriand, a man of the world, a man of letters, and one of the great figures of French Romanticism, had spent some years in American exile after the French Revolution, and he had become famous as a writer with the novella *Atala*, a tale about the Indians of Florida. A European touchstone for depictions of the New World, *Atala* had made an impression in Brazil, where ambitious writers, like their North American counterparts Fenimore Cooper and Longfellow, saw the lives and legends of the country's indigenous peoples as a resource from which to construct a new, local literature. Mid-nineteenth-century Brazilian writers were eager to transcend European literary prototypes—all the more so because they were painfully aware of their continued dependence on them—and the odd harnessing of a Portuguese explorer and a French writer, two very different kinds of "great men," that takes place in the title *The Posthumous Memoirs of Brás Cubas* might well have teased at readers' awareness of that predicament—unless, that is, the reader picked up on another echo: *The Posthumous Papers of the Pickwick Club*, the book with which Dickens had made himself known throughout the world.

Chateaubriand was a grand figure, and his memoirs are a work in the high style: a voice sounding out of the grave as if for all eternity, florid and magisterial, uncanny but also canny enough, since, after all, the whole point of posthumous publication was to avoid making enemies until you were well beyond their reach. It is the voice of authority and adventure. Pickwick, genially bumbling circus master of a comic romp, has something else entirely, the energy of anarchy. And these *Posthumous Memoirs*?

> I hesitated some time, not knowing whether to open these memoirs at the beginning or at the end, i.e. whether to start with my birth or with my death. Granted, the usual practice is to begin with one's birth, but two considerations led me to adopt a different method: the first is that, properly speaking, I am a deceased writer not in the sense of one who has written and is now deceased, but in the sense of one who has died and is now writing, a writer for whom the grave was really a new cradle.

These *Posthumous Memoirs* begin in uncertainty and immediately proceed to absurdity, awakening readers' incredulity rather than suspending their disbelief. This book is neither imposing, like Chateaubriand, nor unbridled, like Dickens, but rather hedged, ironic, and not a little self-mocking. Brás Cubas seems not only to anticipate but to invite a skeptical response from his readers: when it comes to comparisons with the canonical books of the Old World, he immediately ups the ante. This novel form of composition of his, he tells us, is in fact not entirely original to him, though he could be said to bring to it a new "merriment and novelty. Moses, who also related his own death, placed it not at the beginning but at the end: a radical difference between this book and the Pentateuch."

The author of *The Posthumous Memoirs of Brás Cubas* was Joaquim Maria Machado de Assis, and by 1880 this was a name that
would have been familiar enough in Rio, where Machado had been
active on the local literary scene for a good two decades. He had come
from nowhere and had made a name for himself. Machado, born in
1839, was mixed-race. His father was black; his paternal grandparents
had been slaves. And since slavery was not abolished in Brazil until
1888, he was someone who had spent much of his life surrounded
by slaves and the slave business, aware of its horror and injustice (he
denounced it), but presumably also conscious of it as a background he
had succeeded in leaving behind. The Brazil of Machado's day was in
many ways an anomalous place. A vast, largely unsettled and unex-
plored territory parceled out among big landowners, it was an empire
overseen by a constitutional monarch of distinctly liberal sympathies,
Dom Pedro II, who sought to build and strengthen national institutions, political, cultural, and economic, and who worked toward
the gradual end of slavery, to which he was actively opposed. Under
Dom Pedro's long reign, Brazil was prosperous and, especially compared with neighboring Argentina, stable, and the country attracted
a growing influx of immigrants from Europe. But Dom Pedro's reign
ended in 1889 with a military coup—military influence in Brazil's political affairs would be a constant for much of the twentieth century—
one in which he himself has been judged to be essentially complicit:
his only legitimate successor was a woman, an impossible thing, all
concurred at the time, and weary of so many years of ruling, the
emperor made it clear that he was perfectly content to depart into
comfortable exile in Europe.

Machado's Brazil was at once old-fashioned and newfangled, quasi-
feudal and forward-looking—all of which was reflected in Machado's
own family circumstances. His father was a housepainter who married a white girl from the Azores, and together they went on to spend
their life working on the estate of a rich, politically connected woman.
Machado's parents seem to have enjoyed a secure position as depen-
dents, and their son found favor with their patron, who took an active
interest in his education and eventually adopted him as her godson.

Machado's education was on the random side—he is said to have learned French from a baker—but he had formidable drive, and he became a man of extensive learning and remarkable productivity. At sixteen, he published his first poem, and he found a job as a typesetter and proofreader at the national printing house, an important cultural institution that offered an entry into Rio's literary circles. Machado, born five years before the first Brazilian novel was published, was soon producing work in a range of genres: poems were followed by plays and stories and critical and political essays; he translated Dickens and Hugo; and he was a master of the glancing, witty accounts of current affairs and fleeting events that Brazilians call *crônicas*. Machado published in periodicals and he published books and he published under his own name and under curious pseudonyms such as BB, OO, and ZZZ. He competed in chess tournaments, belonged to the Beethoven club, and ran for political office. He advanced through a series of posts as a government official, and in 1869 he married Carolina Novaes, a woman of Portuguese birth and the sister of a fellow writer, to whom he was devoted. He did all this even as he suffered from epilepsy as well as rickets. (Apparently, patronage hadn't spared him from childhood malnutrition.) In 1908 he died at the respectable age of sixty-nine, having been elected the first president of the Brazilian Academy of Letters in 1897.

Machado turned to the novel rather late in his early-blooming career—his first, *Resurrection*, appeared in 1872, though with characteristic energy he wrote three more before the decade was out—and when he did, it was with a particular critical agenda in mind. (The Latin American novelist, like American and Russian novelists, was condemned always to be proving something, not least about the Latin American novel.) Machado was, on the one hand, a critic of the Brazilian writers who set out to construct a new national literature from its indigenous past. He believed that the novel should function not as an instrument of romantic fabulation or national mythmaking, but as a faithful engagement with the problems of modern life. On the other hand, he was no less critical of the social realism that took its bearings from Flaubert and Zola and whose preeminent practitioner in Portuguese was his slightly younger contemporary Eça de Queirós, a wonderful novelist, though not to Machado's way of thinking. Machado dismissed the shocking revelations of Eça's novels as lurid and superficial. The Brazilian novelist, he argued, should seek to attain the universality of a Shakespeare, and universality was not to be gleaned from documenting the world's nasty corners and ugly accidents. The novel could only be true to life and more than provincial if it put life into a meaningful perspective.

Machado's aspiration, in other words, was essentially to write a conventional nineteenth-century European novel, but the problem was that the Brazilian realities he also wished to attest to didn't permit it. His early novels depict a country in which rigid hierarchy and pure contingency dispute each other's claims as they reel from one improbable situation or event to another in pursuit of a reasonable conclusion that surely exists, except it doesn't. Thus his *Helena*, published in 1876, is the convoluted story of the illegitimate daughter of a rich and powerful man who dies on the first page, leaving a will that, to the dismay of his family, recognizes her. But it turns out that Helena isn't the dead man's illegitimate daughter and isn't illegitimate at all (apart from being illegitimately illegitimate), and meanwhile, to complicate things, the legitimate heir falls in love with her—his half sister, as he believes. At last, unable to make her way out of this thicket of illegitimate representations, Helena dies of a broken heart. In this mediocre book, Machado confuses plottiness for coherence, and in this it is not all that different from the lesser novels of such contemporaries as Wilkie Collins and Thomas Hardy. It is a novel that is all grinding gears.

An impossible novel, a parody novel: with *The Posthumous Memoirs of Brás Cubas*, however, Machado managed something altogether other and original. He wrote an impossible novel for real.

Machado starts with the dead author describing his death: "At two o'clock of a Friday afternoon, in the month of August 1869, at my lovely suburban home in Catumby . . . sixty-four, prosperous, single, worth about 300 contos." With this, Brás Cubas reveals himself to have been a man of means—those three hundred contos are serious money—but he makes no bones about not being a man of note. His death does not recommend him to our interest (what is more ordinary than death?), though he drops in passing that a "mysterious lady" figured among the bare eleven people who accompanied his coffin to the cemetery. Perhaps that will excite our curiosity. So he insinuates, and with this hint the book not only introduces author to reader but puts the reader on the spot. Are you that kind of reader who needs that kind of love interest to take an interest in a book? Or are you the kind of reader who recognizes just how hackneyed, how uninteresting that kind of authorial bid for the reader's attention is? In either case, this book is for you—or not.

The Posthumous Memoirs of Brás Cubas is a book of two hundred plus pages comprising 160 chapters; it was initially serialized over a period of months. The chapters are short and, one after another, brought up short: teasing, sarcastic, aphoristic, episodic, arresting, they leave the reader wanting—more, perhaps less. A chapter will arrive at one conclusion only to have the next reverse it. From early on, the book announces itself as an exercise less in provocation than in equivocation, a parade of appearances that exist to be continuously dismantled and reassembled. Brás Cubas, for example, wastes no time in exposing himself, or at least his family, not only as being of no great interest, but as phony: rich, yes (the clink of money resounds throughout the book), but its famous name is actually an utterly ordinary name— *Cubas* means "cooper," and that was the family trade. His father, having made some money, decked it out in pretended historical finery in hopes of helping his heir to a political career. It's all a sham, a production, as even Brás Cubas's death will prove to be. What happens when you die, or rather is said to happen? Your whole life goes by before your eyes. What happens at the decisive moment to Brás Cubas, that world-historical nonentity? All of human history is revealed to him. He zooms back to the beginning, and he zips forward to the end— almost—but then the vision ends. He comes to once again in the same old Rio suburb of Catumby, where his cat, Sultan, is batting a ball of string while Brás Cubas dies "calmly, methodically, hearing the sobs of the ladies, the soft words of the men, the rain drumming on the taro leaves, and the piercing noise of a razor being sharpened by a knife grinder outside."

Sultan the cat, the shrill rasp of the sharpened razor: everything in Brás Cubas's world is prone to being converted into a symbol of how narrowly conventional and symbol-ridden and killing that world is. Then again the sobs, the soft words, the drumming rain: these are observed details from everyday life, and even if the sobs are purely pro forma and all the talk is of the next order of business, they alert the reader that Machado has somehow found, on the far side of futility, bitterness, and arch humor, a way to describe his Brazil.

In the topsy-turvy world of *The Posthumous Memoirs*, death must of course be followed by birth, and before long Brás Cubas provides us with a more or less conventional account of his life and his times. Born on October 20, 1805, "washed and diapered, I immediately became the hero of the house," a spoiled brat, doted on by his mother and groomed by his father for the political career that would cement the family's social position. His youth? He had a torrid affair with a beauty of Spanish descent who fleeced him until his father sent him away to study in Portugal. His education? He studied everything and nothing before returning to Rio and the prospect of an advantageous marriage to a certain Virgilia—her classical name is as much a marker of provincial social jockeying as Brás Cubas's own ersatz moniker—which, however, came to nothing when Virgilia encountered a suitor with better credentials. Brás Cubas's father died of the disappointment, and the son was left to live off his fortune, "to write on politics and dabble in literature," and to nurse a sense of grievance at his bad luck.

Which is pretty much all he will do till the day of his death, except that there is that promised love interest to provide a twist—or knot—in the otherwise foreordained plot: the love interest is the very same Virgilia who, after marrying and moving to São Paulo, returns to Rio and Brás Cubas. They set up a love nest outside of town, and Virgilia's politically prominent husband, Lobo Neves, either remains or chooses to remain in the dark: he and Brás Cubas are for a while bosom buddies. Brás Cubas and Virgilia are really in love, but their love can hardly come out of the shadows without provoking complete social ostracism, especially for Virgilia, and perhaps both of them are happy enough with things as they are, happy to be able to escape from society at large to their little world apart and from there back to society at large. There is a moment when love threatens to turn into something lasting: Virgilia is pregnant, and Brás is elated at the prospect of having a child of his own. When, however, Virgilia miscarries, he is left to commiserate with Lobo Neves over the loss of Lobo Neves's child—and who is to say it wasn't? The web of deceit is tightly woven, and one day—when Virgilia departs to a distant province of which Lobo Neves has been appointed governor—it's gone.

Brás Cubas himself now goes into politics. Among the many chapters of *Posthumous Memoirs*, the one devoted to "How I Did Not Become a Minister of State" is one of the most memorable:

. . . .

. . . .

. . . .

. . . .

. . . .

And what is there to say after that? Brás Cubas has spent his life going through the motions. He has been litterateur, lover, lawmaker, to which he can add newspaper owner and entrepreneur (he invents the Brás Cubas anti-melancholy sticking plaster, the Prozac of an earlier day)—so many ways of leading a productive or meaningful modern life, and he has found them, or has been found, wanting. There is really nothing left for him to do except what he has already done: die.

So the book comes full circle, a perfect whole or a wholly pointless one, ending where it began as if it had been all over before it began. But has Brás Cubas's life been a total waste? The novel wraps up:

> This last chapter consists wholly of negatives. I did not achieve celebrity, I did not become a minister of state, I did not really become a caliph, I did not marry. At the same time, however,

I had the good fortune of not having to earn my bread by the sweat of my brow. Moreoever, I did not suffer . . . nor did I lose my mind . . . Adding up and balancing all these items, a person will conclude that my accounts showed neither a surplus nor a deficit and consequently that I died quits with life. And he will conclude falsely; for upon arriving on this other side of the mystery, I found that I had a small surplus, which provides the final negative of this chapter of negatives: I had no progeny, I transmitted to no one the legacy of our misery.

It is a note of conclusive, almost sumptuous irony—if, that is, irony can really be conclusive.

The Posthumous Memoirs of Brás Cubas is a doleful book but often a delightful one, surprising and confounding, and I think it may well have been as much of a surprise to its maker as it remains to readers today. We don't really know anything about how Machado came to write the book or how he went about it—his busy professional life, like his parental background and impoverished childhood, remains essentially opaque—but it seems likely to me that the book began as a sketch, even caricature, of a certain type of second-generation Carioca arriviste, privileged and pampered but still promising, who, instead of realizing that promise, lapses into a life of sterile leisure. A conventional enough sort of literary production, such a book would have been partly topical and satirical, shining a light on the criminal frivolity of the Brazilian elite, and partly rueful, as we witness an appealing man undermined by that frivolity. Both Brazil and Brás Cubas would have emerged from the pages of Machado's book as perpetrators and victims of a shared failure of national moral imagination and will, while Machado the writer would be credited with having concentrated the nation's predicament in a specific type— a local variant, you could say, of a charming, sponging ne'er-do-well like Harold Skimpole in *Bleak House* or an ineffectual upper-class superfluous man of the sort that Turgenev—whom Machado could very well have read in French translation—had made a mainstay of Russian literature. Readers would have put the book down with a sense of amused recognition, gratified by the whimsy, precautioned by the waste.

And in many ways *Posthumous Memoirs* is a fairly conventional nineteenth-century novel of social critique. Certainly, behind Brás Cubas's off-the-cuff witticisms and sardonic asides, we are given a picture of a society driven by greed, awash in hypocrisy, and cruel to the core. There is, for example, the sad story of Dona Plácida, the poor woman who keeps the little house to which Brás Cubas and Virgilia retreat. One day, to while away the time—Brás Cubas is waiting impatiently for his lover—Dona Plácida tells him all she has gone through. He is so impressed by her tale of unremitting deprivation that he entertains a fantasy of her, in the life to come, confronting her progenitors: her mother, a prostitute who pushed her daughter toward prostitution, too; her father, a straying priest who never recognized his offspring. "Here I am," Brás Cubas imagines her saying to the two of them. "Why did you summon me?"

They answer:

> We summoned you so that you would burn your fingers on pans and your eyes in sewing; so that you would eat little or nothing, rush around, become sick and then get well so that you might become sick again; sad today, desperate tomorrow, finally resigned, but always with your hand on the pot and your eyes on the sewing until you wind up in the gutter or in the hospital. That is why we summoned you, in a moment of love.

It is a powerful passage, but having conjured it up so vividly, as far as Brás Cubas is concerned it is something to knock off like the ash of a cigar—an aside like everything in the book (the shortness of the chapters of *Posthumous Memoirs* serves partly to chart a serious case of moral attention deficit disorder)—or to pack carefully away in the excelsior of the Schopenhauerian pessimism he acquired in the course of his European education. In any case, he now reflects (like an upper-crust version of the Underground Man), why would Dona Plácida bother to tell him about her sad life unless she wanted to get something from him? Her story is told, and the matter is settled. He gives her a tip.

"There is nothing in the world," Brás Cubas says at one point, "so monstrously vast" as the indifference of the dead. The novel, however, makes it clear that it cannot conceivably be as vast as that of the living. There is the plight of poor women like Dona Plácida, too worn-out to do anything more than to be an accessory to their own degradation. Beyond that, there is slavery. Throughout *The Posthumous Memoirs of Brás Cubas*, slaves come and go in the background and, for the most part, only in the background. They are, after all, taken for granted, and Brás Cubas records that he used to ride around on the back of the family slave Prudêncio (Plácida, Prudêncio: note how virtuous are the names of the oppressed!), kicking him all the while to giddyap, a story he tells to illustrate just how spoiled a child he was, as indifferent to Prudêncio's humiliation now as he was then. Grief-stricken at his mother's death, Brás Cubas retreats to the country, remarking, "I put together a rifle, a few books, clothes, cigars, a young slave." Brás Cubas, whose life spans the years in which the slave trade was outlawed in Brazil, disapproves of slavery, it should be said, viewing it as outmoded, and looks with distaste on the activities of his brother-in-law, a slave smuggler, which means he does his best to turn a blind eye to them. One day, Brás Cubas tells us, he encountered Prudêncio again, now a freed man, beating a slave of his own. Brás Cubas intervenes and chides his former chattel, and he reflects:

> On the outside the episode I had witnessed was grim, but only on the outside. When I opened it up with the knife of rational analysis I found a curious and profound kernel . . . I, as a child, had sat on his back, had put a rein in his mouth, and had beaten him mercilessly; he had groaned and suffered. Now, however, he was free and could move his arms and legs when and as he pleased . . . Now he rose and became top man: he

bought a slave and paid to him, in full and with interest, the amount he had received from me. See how clever the rascal was!

Yes, slavery makes you think.

You could look at slavery as the master metaphor of the *Posthumous Memoirs*, which describes a world that is, from top to bottom, in thrall to corruption and enslaved to illusion. A world that is dead at heart. A world of dead people. And you could add that to denounce the world in this way only compounds, or echoes, its particular horror: to say that slavery provides a master metaphor for the world is to forget that it is full of slaves who are not metaphorical at all. There is nothing to say for this world, which is so far gone as to make it impossible to say anything about it.

You can read the book this way, which would be to read the book as being all in character. The wit and charm and insouciance of its pages are nothing but evidence of its protagonist's monstrous heedlessness, which Machado's book exists first and foremost to expose to our appalled recognition. You can read the book this way, and I think Machado may even have meant it to be read that way—but in the end that is not how the book reads. The book we have is a much stranger and slipperier sort of thing, both more entertaining and more unsettling than the moral outing of the seedy but seductive operator I just described. The protagonist, and putative author, has many limitations and is indeed a kind of monster, but there is something winning about him, too: after all, he knows his limitations. (What greater limitation can there be than being dead?) He holds our attention and does so from the moment he introduces himself as already having graduated to eternity. And what's the relationship of Brás Cubas, Machado's creation, so questionable, so engaging, to his well-known creator, the reader has to wonder? Because Brás Cubas demonstrates, as nothing had before, Machado's powers of invention. Brás Cubas is the making of Machado as an author. You, the reader—and as I have said, quite possibly Machado the author—may wish to distance yourself from Brás Cubas, to hold on to the disapproval he so amply merits, yet he insinuates himself; he insists on coming close. You may want to know what Machado is up to here, but the more you try to define it, the more you doubt you know: instead the book has developed a life of its own, succeeding in gaining our recognition, and affection, while the character presented for our judgment has come to question, or implicate it, in turn.

The challenge for Machado, as the realistic and also universal and edifying novelist he hoped to be, was to be true to life in Brazil and also truly Brazilian. In *Posthumous Memoirs* he succeeds in being both, and in the most unforeseen of ways. Being true to life in Brazil meant reflecting its structures of domination and gross inequalities but also its unexpected opportunities, as well as the uncertain and unsettled foundations of a vast empire in which, among many unlikely things, the emperor could play along with his own overthrow. Reflecting that truth would seem to call for unflagging critical vigilance and unwavering moral clarity, yet here in the *Memoirs*, Machado divests himself of both. His elusive protagonist is a monster, yes, but also a pleasure, a cautionary example but also, as used to be said, a caution, a cutup, outrageously seizing and gratifying our attention. We are happy to be in his company because we do not know what to make of him or expect from him—but then again, we know that all too well. And there we are as readers, at once engaged and put on the spot.

As to being truly Brazilian as a novelist, well of course that began with describing some of the country's weird and disturbing doings recognizably and memorably, but it also called for doing it with an originality that bore the trace of its origins. The *Posthumous Memoirs* is certainly original, and yet—here's the trick—the way it arrives at that originality is, from start to stop, by making a point of how very unoriginal it is. The title, as I began by saying, already suggests an essentially derivative production, and when the novel came out in book form, Machado added a note, in Brás Cubas's voice of course, to underscore the point. The book, the note says, is obviously composed in the tradition of Laurence Sterne and Xavier de Maistre, though Brás Cubas does allow that he may have added "a certain peevish pessimism of his own." What Machado is doing here may sound like classic rhetorical authorial self-deprecation, but it's quite different in effect. Tacitly, he is making a wider point about the dependency of Brazilian literature on European models, a dependency that Brazilian authors were always trying to get out from under; he, however, instead of trying to do that, as all those Brazilian authors so predictably and ineffectually labor to do, will embrace and announce that dependency. He goes further, really, since he as good as says his book is dead from the start—a forthright claim of unoriginality that is startlingly and entirely new because it's just the sort of thing that is never done, not in Brazil and not in Europe, either. Many twentieth-century novelists will look at times to the eighteenth century, as we have seen Wells look to Swift, for an approach to the novel that is both more concrete and more intellectual—less mealymouthed—than the elaboration and popularization of the form had made it in the nineteenth century. Machado is doing that, but he is doing something more: not just following a model but boldly seizing the opportunity to proclaim himself a mere imitator—and by that setting himself apart. The Brazilian critic João Cezar de Castro Rocha brings out the daringly paradoxical nature of Machado's way of positioning himself in the world of literature when he speaks of Machado's poetics of plagiarism.

   In logic, anything follows from a contradiction, and the self-negation of the author in *Posthumous Memoirs*—the snap of the fingers and shrug with which the book begins—proves a powerfully effective way to reveal the rigidity and contingency of Brazilian social reality while eluding its limits. The book represents Brazil's complexities without getting caught up in them or trying to answer for them in ways that would be all too likely to strike readers, as his earlier books do, as trying too hard. Undercutting his authority, he undercuts all sorts of authority, astonishing us in the act. In a world where everyone has his place or is seeking to assert himself, he finds something unsuspected: a way to call everything into question, a way not to be pinned down, a way, in a country of slaves, to slip free.

What was your original face, the one you had before your mother and father were born? Sosuke, the protagonist of Natsume Sōseki's novel

The Gate, retreats to a Zen monastery, where the roshi assigns him
this koan. Sosuke is a lowly salaryman, underpaid and overworked,
who has been ostracized by his family after marrying, against their
wishes, for love. Cut off from his larger family, he is cut off from the
customary life of old Japan; returning day after day to the office, he
is helplessly caught up in the degrading modern business of making
a living. The subject of Zen (which in 1910, when Sōseki's novel was
published, would have been unknown outside of Japan and considered hopelessly old-fashioned within) comes up in a conversation
with a coworker. It intrigues Sosuke, not least because it is so much
a thing of the past. But when he eventually visits the monastery, he
finds no answers to his problems, only this maddening riddle, and
though he sits and meditates and aches and watches his thoughts
wander so widely that they no longer seem his thoughts, he can make
nothing of it. Well, he does ultimately come up with something—not
that we're told what it is—but it is summarily dismissed by the master,
and Sosuke is not surprised. After a few weeks at the monastery he returns home, looking, his wife observes, more haggard than ever. The
gate is an ancient Buddhist symbol of enlightenment, but *The Gate* is
a novel about not passing through the gate, of vision denied.

   In the early 1890s Sōseki himself had gone to a Zen monastery to
escape from his troubles. There he was assigned the same koan that
bedeviled Sosuke, and he found himself no less unable to respond to
it. It continued to haunt him. Donald Keene, the American scholar
and critic who devoted his career to the understanding and translation of Japanese literature, has suggested that the koan represents "the
fundamental question of Sōseki's existence, of his original sin."

   Not only of Sōseki's existence, you could say, but also that of Sōseki's Japan, the Japan of the turn of the century and the Meiji dynasty
which, lasting from 1868 to 1912, almost entirely encompassed Sōseki's own life (1867–1916). During the long Edo period (also known
as the Tokugawa shogunate) that preceded the Meiji, Japan had been
governed by a series of feudal warlords who sought, for many years
successfully, to cut the country off from Western influence. In 1853,
Admiral Perry's gunboats showed up to "open the country" to international trade (naturally on terms favorable to the Western powers),

leading, after more than a decade of internal confusion and conflict, to what has been called "a revolution from above." During the Edo, Japan had been without an emperor; now the position was revived, a symbol of the country's ancient integrity. But as a gesture toward the future, the new young emperor took the name of Meiji, "enlightenment," promulgating a new program explicitly dedicated to national reform and international outreach: "Evil customs of the past shall be broken off," reads the fifth of the five oaths that were published in his name on his coming to power; "Knowledge shall be sought throughout the world." The new government of the newly restored emperor gave a new name, Tokyo, to a new capital from which, in short order, it oversaw the creation of a new military, a new legal code, a new constitution, a new parliament, new industries, and new institutions—schools, universities, banks, and newspapers—all of which, some twenty-five years earlier, not only did not exist but would have been inconceivable to the vast majority of the Japanese.

Basil Hall Chamberlain, an Englishman who was professor of Japanese at Tokyo Imperial University at the time, described the bewildering character of the experience:

> To have lived through the transition stage of modern Japan makes a man feel preternaturally old; for here he is in modern times, with the air full of talk about bicycles and bacilli and "spheres of influence," and yet he can himself distinctly remember the Middle Ages. The dear old Samurai who first initiated the present writer into the mysteries of the Japanese language wore a queue and two swords . . . His modern successor, fairly fluent in English and dressed in a serviceable suit . . . might almost be European . . . Old things pass away between a night and a morning.

Where was this transition leading? What was this new Japan? The Englishman was uncertain and distrustful: there is no missing the note of disdain in the "serviceable suit" of the "almost European." So were the Japanese. The power and prosperity that industrialization and political reorganization had brought to the country were a matter of pride—no country, Western or Eastern, had ever accomplished anything like it—but it was also the source of a corrosive anxiety and self-doubt. Japan might be coming into its own; it might even be on the verge of becoming a new international model, as the popular slogan about combining the best of the East and the West suggested, the sun of its flag rising to illuminate the world. Then again, Japan might be losing touch with everything that made it Japan, succeeding merely in being "almost European."

It's in this context that we must hear Sōseki's invocation of the Zen koan. This legacy of old Japan seems to respond directly to the problem of identity afflicting a modernizing Japan, to identify it and to offer a solution: identity is an illusion; the problem is no problem; that is the old wisdom. To Sōseki, or Sosuke, the koan has a haunting appeal, yet it resolves nothing. It comes to them from an irretrievable past, even as they are irreversibly fated to be modern.

The novel had been imported from the West to Japan as part of the Meiji's forced march to modernity. (The celebrated medieval *Tale of Genji* figured as something else altogether.) No Western books had been known in Japan before the Meiji, and translation first served largely as an aid to language acquisition and to introduce Western ways and ideas. Samuel Smiles's *Self-Help* and John Stuart Mill's *On Liberty* both made a big impression in the early years of the Meiji. The first novel to find an appreciative audience was *Ernest Maltravers*, by the popular Victorian writer Sir Edward Bulwer-Lytton, translated as *A Spring Tale of Blossoms and Willows* in 1879. This was a novel about political life—what's come to be known as a Condition of England novel—but what astonished and fascinated Japanese readers was that Bulwer-Lytton added an unexpected dollop of romance to the story. Translations of other political novels, like Disraeli's *Coningsby*, soon followed, gaining increasing recognition for the novel as a genre. If the British prime minister could devote time to writing such a thing, Donald Keene says the calculation went, well, then it must certainly be a worthy endeavor.

One of the first modern Japanese novels, *Chance Meetings with*

Beautiful Women, published in one of the new newspapers in 1885, opens with the main character, the so-called Wanderer of the Eastern Sea, walking into Independence Hall in Philadelphia: he observes "above him . . . the cracked Liberty Bell, below him the Declaration of Independence," and soon he encounters the promised beautiful women with whom he discusses the significance of what he observes. The formula was so successful that new installments of the novel continued to come out until 1897, even as translations of novels from around the world picked up. English novels had come first, England being the dominant economic power but soon French and Russian novels were added to the mix (by 1892 *Crime and Punishment* had come out in a translation from the English), giving rise to more and more Japanese novels. Some were written in colloquial Japanese rather than the formal language traditionally reserved for literature. Some sought to analyze character in depth or to depict social problems in the manner of Western novels. Some returned to older Japanese traditions of narrative fiction for inspiration, and along with them there was more and more discussion of what the novel was—and what it was, or could be, for a novel to be Japanese.

The novel came from afar and came as news, but Sōseki came from the old Japan, where the only kinds of Japanese narrative fiction that were known were either ancient, like *The Tale of Genji*, or little regarded, like the prurient gesaku stories that emerged from the pleasure quarters, the so-called floating world, of the vast city of Edo. Natsume Kin'nosuke, Sōseki's name at birth, descended from a family of Tokugawa government functionaries whose fortunes had fallen in the Meiji. He was an eighth, unaffordable child, fobbed off on a local grocer by his parents. The grocer's family was too busy to look after the baby boy, and the story is that his older sister, finding him lying outside in a basket, picked him up and took him back home. Put up for adoption again, he was taken in by a farmer, and there he remained for some years, until the farmer and his wife divorced and he was taken back by the Natsumes, exchanging the farmer's family name for his original name. Named and renamed, it is perhaps not surprising that he eventually gave himself a name of his own choosing in emulation of an old practice of the Chinese literati: Sōseki, which

Kin'nosuke adopted in 1889, comes from a Chinese word meaning "gargler of stones."

Notwithstanding his difficult family circumstances, the gargler of stones was a brilliant student from early on, and by high school he was determined to make his mark. At first he wanted to be an architect—intending literally to structure a new Japanese order—but a friend persuaded him that he would do better as a writer, and so he set out to "startle westerners by producing terrific works written in a foreign language." Having already mastered classical Chinese—the traditional foundation of a Japanese education—he majored in English at Tokyo Imperial University while also studying French and German. On graduation, he left the city to teach English in a country school, where he wrote essays about Walt Whitman and Machado's beloved *Tristram Shandy*. He then received a government scholarship to study English in England, and in 1900 he traveled from Japan to England, only to discover that his funding could not support him at his intended destination of Cambridge. For the next two years, he lived in London, rooming in cheap boardinghouses, sitting in on lectures at University College before deciding that they were hardly worth his while, reading deeply in English literature, and walking the streets, always lonely, with a growing loathing of the commercialism of English life, but also of his own, as he saw it, meager dark reflection in the unending shopwindows.

Living in London was a transformative experience—one Sōseki never recovered from. After London, no matter where he went or what he did, he would always feel displaced, and back in Japan, he immediately suffered a nervous breakdown. On recovery, however, he was appointed professor of English at the University of Tokyo, the first Japanese person to hold that post. Sōseki's lectures were criticized for being overly theoretical—he was determined not to teach as he had been taught, when all that was asked of him was to know such things as "the dates of the birth and death of Wordsworth [and] the number of pages in Shakespeare's manuscripts"—but they were a success, though he did not enjoy his success. His mental health continued to suffer, and it was supposedly as a lark, in order to distract himself from his day job, that he began a comic novel, *I Am a Cat*, in the outlandish spirit of Sterne. Here he depicted himself and his intellectual circle and the foibles of modern Japan through an exacting feline eye.

I Am a Cat, serialized in a popular newspaper, was a hit, and Sō-seki embarked on his prolific, restlessly exploratory career as a writer. He followed his first book with *Botchan*, which means "the young master," relating the adventures of a charming young rebel in a country school, a book that is sometimes compared to *Huckleberry Finn*. Then, within the same year, 1906, he published something quite different: *The Grass Pillow*, a novel he described as a haiku, which, he boasted, had "no counterparts in the west."

Sōseki kept on writing new novels, and they kept on making a splash—Tokyo department stores sold clothes in poppy prints to mark the publication of his *The Poppy*—and in 1907 he resigned from the university after being commissioned by the newspaper *The Asahi Shimbun* to write a novel a year for serialization. He continued to experiment with the novelistic form and subject matter while working in a wide range of genres—travel books, criticism, memoirs, and poetry in Chinese—in spite of mental turmoil, physical ailments, and that not unusual accompaniment of the writing life, a bad marriage. A circle of young admirers gathered around Sōseki—some of them would go on to become major writers themselves—but he repeatedly declined public honors from the press and the government. He died in 1916, from overwork as much as from the bitingly painful stomach ulcers he had suffered from for years.

The Japanese novel had begun as an imitation of the Victorian Condition of England novel, and for all the variety of Sōseki's novels, they continued to consider the condition of Japan, and especially the private damage wrought by its ongoing public transformation. *Kokoro*, published in 1914, is the most famous work of the novelist whose face would, after World War II, figure on the thousand-yen note. In it, Sōseki directly engages with the question of the legacy of the Meiji dynasty and the unresolved character of modern Japan.

Kokoro is a Japanese word that doesn't translate easily. It means "heart," as the seat of feelings and the physical motor of life; it also means "mind," and depending on how it is used, it can mark a state of unusual unity or one of division. The American writer Lafcadio Hearn, Sōseki's predecessor as professor of English at the University of Tokyo, had used the word as the title of a book celebrating the virtues of old Japan. Sōseki had something else at heart and in mind.

"Loneliness is the fate of modern man," says one of the two central characters in *Kokoro*, a story of disastrously riven lives in a book that is itself split between past and present, with a climax that is carefully dated just after the Meiji emperor's death, in 1912. The first two parts of the book are in the voice of a young man, the younger son of a prosperous farmer who has sent him off to the University of Tokyo. The story begins while he is on summer vacation, just before his final year of studies. At a swimming resort, he runs into an older man who seems to possess a mysterious authority. Back in Tokyo, he calls on him, hoping he will prove to be a teacher of the sort that he has failed to find at the university. Sensei, he calls him, very much against the older man's wishes. Sensei insists that he has nothing to teach.

He has nothing to teach and much to regret, he lets on. Regret and remorse have kept him from the success that might have awaited such a cultivated man. This makes Sensei that much more fascinating to his young admirer, who is also intrigued and puzzled by the man's unusually close yet somehow strained relationship with his beautiful wife.

What is Sensei's dark secret, the young man wonders. His visits verge on being a nuisance, yet Sensei does not turn him away. Fascinated with Sensei, he is also worried about himself. What is he going to do when his studies are done? Soon enough, they are, and there is very little for him to do except head back home for the summer. His father is old and ailing, his brother is in business, and it is a younger son's duty to look after his parents and the farm, something he has no wish to do. How to resolve this predicament? He writes to Sensei for advice, and his parents are also hopeful that this eminent man will tell their son what is the right thing to do. Sensei doesn't write back.

"Sensei and I" and "My Parents and I," are the first two parts of *Kokoro*. They are cast as a confession, though it is unclear to whom the student is confessing and to what end. As for the story itself, it takes place over successive seasons and develops through a series of short, often seemingly inconsequential or inconclusive encounters—visits, walks, talks, the occasional tea or meal, Sensei's hat blowing off, Sensei terminating a conversation to urinate—in which what is said is more often than not said in order to avoid saying something else. Sōseki displays phenomenal authorial poise in depicting this pattern of avoidance, and the reader is more and more caught up by the spreading silence of the many things that appear to be unsaid. The student's story holds the reader spellbound much as Sensei does the student, and like the gauche and green student, the reader is both eager for enlightenment and filled with a sense of dread.

Summer is ending. The father is dying. At last Sensei's letter comes, surprisingly long, given that he "hates to write at all." The student puts the letter aside to tend to his father; then, back in his room, a sentence from it catches his eye: "By the time this letter reaches you . . . I shall in all likelihood be dead."

Leaving his dying father, the student rushes to catch the train to Tokyo: "All I wanted to know at that moment was that Sensei was still alive."

The last part of the book is Sensei's letter, his long-awaited teaching, you might suppose. He writes, he says, to the student "alone, among the millions of Japanese." "I . . . am about to cut open my own heart and drench your face with my blood." And so his story unfolds.

Once upon a time Sensei was also a student in Tokyo. An orphan, he had been raised by his uncle, who robbed him of his inheritance, leaving him poor, embittered, and full of distrust. Lonely, he befriends a fellow student, K, who is even more of an outsider than he is: K has been ostracized by his distinguished family after secretly giving up his medical studies to study religion instead.

K is harshly judgmental of others and himself. He scolds Sensei for his worldliness: "Anyone who has no spiritual aspirations is an idiot," he declares. Impressed, Sensei asks K to room with him. Sensei and K are both secretly attracted to their landlady's pretty daughter, Ojosan, and Sensei even wants to marry her, but "I stood still, not daring to take a step in any direction." Only when the tormented K confesses his own love to his friend—"I have found I am a weak man and am ashamed . . . You see I am lost and have become a puzzle to myself . . . I cannot bear this pain"—does Sensei ask Ojosan's mother for her daughter's hand, and his offer is accepted. He is afraid to tell K the news, though K is sure to learn it. One night, coming into their shared quarters late, Sensei finds K's door open; through it, he sees K sitting and facing the wall; then he sees "the blood on the wall." K has killed himself, after writing Sensei a letter in which he asks him to inform his family and tend to the funeral rites. "Why did I wait so long to die?" it ends.

"Too late, too late," Sensei claims to have thought at the moment. And ever since, Sensei has lived as if it were too late.

But in fact it is not, he now exultantly writes to his would-be student. It is never too late, he has realized. The Meiji emperor has died, and after his death Admiral Nogi, the head of the navy, committed suicide, making good on the debt of honor he had carried since losing a sea battle to the Russians early in his long career. It is never too late to make things right through suicide.

"I was born an ethical creature, and brought up to be an ethical man," Sensei writes. "My ethics may be different from those of the young men today, but at least they are my own." Sensei is careful to set himself apart from the new era—he grew up when "such phrases as 'the age of awakening' and 'the new life' had not yet come into fashion"— but "at least they are my own" sets him apart from the old one, too. Being an ethical man, however, begins with recognizing obligations to other people, and Sensei is effectively saying that he recognizes no such thing: he is a law unto himself. To the young man he now writes that in handing over his past, "this thing which is mine," to him, his hope is that "when my heart stops beating, a new life [will lodge itself] in your breast." By the time the letter—and the book—has come to an end, Sensei resembles a vampire more than a troubled man.

And what, at the end of this story of student and teacher, has been learned? It is too late, we know, for the student to save Sensei or his father. It is too late, and it is time. As we read the last section of *Kokoro*, fictional time and real time become one. The student is reading the letter; we do not know what he will make of it. And we are reading the letter at the same time—time that, like the train, is rushing forward while we read, and what are we to make of it?

Kokoro is a book of urgent irresolution. It combines the breadth and detail of a novel with the knotty concision of a koan, and I read it as Sōseki's novelistic response to the koan he had been unable to find an answer for in its own terms. Its characters are types tormented by their individuality and individuals desperate to know their roles, characters without faces, and as to the book's mix of unimportant detail and growing portent before the explosion of deaths with which it concludes—there is no antecedent in the Western novel for this way of telling a story. Sōseki has written a novel about the new Japan that is also a new kind of—thoroughly Japanese—novel. The suicides at the end encompass and question a whole society, from its top brass to middle-class Sensei to K, scion of an old priestly family, and when we have come to the end of the book, it also makes us look back and question everything we have read so far, for the student's narratives, we now see, could only have been written with the knowledge of the book's end, that disaster from which, however, it draws no conclusion, but only returns to repeat at the end.

Looking back, we also see that from its beginning the book has been haunted by the question not only of what is wrong with Japan, but with West and East. Its opening scene, in which the student first catches sight of Sensei, is set in Kamakura, which Japanese readers would have known as a popular beach resort in a town famous for its venerable Zen monastery, where workers from the city blanket the sand while the McMansions (an apt enough anachronism here) of the Meiji nouveau riche encroach upon peasant rice fields. The reason the student notices Sensei is that Sensei is there in the company of a Westerner, an unusual pairing made all the more unusual by the Westerner's wearing a Japanese swimsuit, revealing compared with the Western bathing clothes of the time. The two men swim out to sea together and they swim back, and the student watches them, and this is the last we ever see or hear of this mysterious Westerner, the only friend, apart from K, that Sensei is given in the book. The scene seems almost meaningless, but on reflection it is charged. This scene—in which Sōseki captures the vague wandering and sudden fixation of attention so characteristic of the way we experience the beach, the street, or cafés and restaurants, those modern spaces whose defining feature is that they are full of strangers—signals quietly but distinctly that this is not only a book about Japan, but about a whole world that has been set afloat, personally and politically as well.

"I have done my best to make you understand the strange person who is myself," says Sensei. The very sentence is strange! Hopelessly earnest and yet detached, baffled and baffling. At the time Sōseki was writing *Kokoro*, he delivered a lecture to students at an elite Japanese academy (students he knew were going to go on to be "important people") that was published under the title "My Individualism." Sōseki didn't boast about his achievements as a writer. He talked about his time in London, how alone and diminished he had felt there and how long it took him to give himself permission to admit his discomfort or disagreement with English ways. Eventually, however, he could not help it. He simply was not their kind of person, and his burden was not to pretend to be, but to be true to the different person he was. And who was that? This question would not go away. Speaking to the students in this way, Sōseki is—as is almost always the case in his work—seeking to fill them with the powerful and generative sense of difference that drove him to shift his approach to the novel throughout his career and that sees him, in *Kokoro*, reworking a theme of a suspect legacy that is common in European novels—the story of Sensei and the student has a certain resemblance to the story of Pip and Miss Havisham in *Great Expectations*—in a distinctly Japanese way, marked by a particular, staggered rhythm of hesitation and revelation that is all his own. To the group of Japanese students, he says, We are different from the English, yes, and once we see that, we can also see that we are different from each other. Cultivate your individuality— not English individualism or commercialism, not Japanese nationalism and corporatism either; Sōseki specifically warns against the latter, and he would become a target of nationalist opprobrium as a result—because we are, one and all, different through and through. It is out of the awareness of differentness, Sōseki argues in "My Individualism," that the "world of literature" is brought to light, the world of literature that suddenly opened before a shy young Japanese student of English literature in London when he realized he was free to disagree with "the ideas of a native English critic." "World of literature" is a striking formulation. This is not Goethe's *Weltliteratur*, which speaks across boundaries of time and space to some ideal human form of elevated feeling and expression. Nor is it a prototype of the sort of international novel, aspiring to be the literature of a global world, that will come into existence much later in the century. Distinct from either of those endeavors, it admits and preserves boundaries—they are always there, they need to be there, we would not know where or who we are if they were not there—but admits, even insists, that they are also and always there to be breached. Literature is the power to breach, and one thing the new century asks of the novelist is to imagine and give form to this breach, however tiny or immense. How? Sōseki comes back to that London from which he could never get away and where he was, he says, utterly paralyzed, "like an isolated being surrounded with mist . . ." A commonplace simile, you could say, and yet then it opens up. That mist is London's notorious noxious fogs, isolating and smothering the individual, but it is also, in Sōseki's hands, something else—the misty distances of Chinese and Japanese painting, those spaces in which being and not-being are at play, the primal void out of which everything arises and to which it returns. Then again, in that mist we might equally see the blinding smoke of the train in which the young narrator of *Kokoro*, who does not even have a name that we are told, hurtles off into the world of literature.

1. HIPPE'S PENCIL

THOMAS MANN'S *THE MAGIC MOUNTAIN*

Nineteen thirteen: Thomas Mann, not just successful but celebrated as a writer, is a restless man. What does he have to complain about? He is not yet forty, and his publisher is already contemplating commissioning a biography. He has been famous since the publication of his first novel, *Buddenbrooks*, the story of the decline of a prosperous merchant family from the north German harbor town of Lübeck— a family very much modeled on Mann's own.

Buddenbrooks, a big book completed when Mann was a mere twenty-five, spans much of the nineteenth century and came out in 1901. Mann's remark, much later in life, that the book "was the German novel's breakthrough to World Literature" may, as his biographer Anthony Heilbut observes, appear "inordinately vain" (Mann was inordinately vain) but is "correct." *Buddenbrooks* unfolds with the leisure and certainty and attention to detail cultivated by a haut bourgeois family like the Buddenbrooks, and it makes their table settings, business deals, seaside vacations, medical problems, dreams, and deaths as solidly present to the imagination as either Miss Havisham's or Madame Bovary's wedding cakes. It is a nineteenth-century novel of the sort Germany had not really seen before, but an entirely German one, which is also shot through with fin de siècle anxiety. The Buddenbrooks suffer from a certain nervous sensitivity, a proclivity to excessive introspection and daydreaming, a taste for sensual pleasures, and a susceptibility to music that can only undermine the austere Protestant resolve that had built their fortune. Similarly, part of the effect of

Buddenbrooks as a novel is to call its own too, too solid existence into question, implicitly asking what lay in store, not only for the bourgeoisie but for the novelist of bourgeois life, in the century to come.

Mann had married in 1905—his wife Katia came from a rich Jewish family, much richer than Mann's own—and it was a long, happy marriage that would produce six children within a little more than a decade. At the same time, there was a homosexual side to Mann's imagination that figured increasingly in his work and was all-important to his conception of it. (Whether Mann's desires ever found physical expression, no one knows.) *Death in Venice*, which came out in 1912, develops the theme in a dark key. Gustav von Aschenbach, the protagonist of the story, is a writer, not an artist (his features are those of the composer Gustav Mahler). He is fifty and not just established but, like Mann, celebrated, the article of nobility that he sports having been awarded to him in recognition of his achievement by the kaiser himself (a kaiser renowned for his philistinism). But Aschenbach has grown weary of the world and of his own words. Perhaps travel will restore his spirits and renew his inspiration. He is drawn to Venice, a city like no other, a city of great beauty, ancient memories, and decayed glory, but also distinctly modern, a tourist resort, a stopping place for a transient population from all over the world. In Venice, staying at the Lido, Aschenbach glimpses a beautiful Polish teenage boy, Tadzio, a name that, to the writer, echoes *adieu*. He gazes at him on the beach and, comically but also creepily, takes to trailing around after him and his older sisters in town; to spruce himself up, he lets the barber black his lashes and rouge his withered cheeks. At the end of the story, Aschenbach, perhaps a victim of cholera, perhaps worn out by a writing life dedicated not to the expression but the suppression of desire, perhaps simply from love, dies, as we have known from the start he must, stretched out in a beach chair, gazing at the beautiful Tadzio and the sea.

Buddenbrooks, after attracting scant attention, had gone on to enjoy an ever-growing success. Mann's publisher decided to reissue the book in paperback, a new format, and Katia Mann would later recall seeing trucks loaded with her husband's book pulled up outside his publisher's offices. (By the early 1920s, Mann's family home would be converted into a tourist destination for fans of the novel.) *Death in Venice* was also a success. It was a story about desire, whatever form that strange, demonic force may take, while homosexuality—already, as we have seen in Gide and Colette, a major concern for the twentieth-century novel—was topical in Germany when the novella came out: a few years earlier, the homosexuality of two of the kaiser's confidants had caused the sort of scandal the Wilde trial had created in England. And politics and history, along with questions of sexuality and desire, also shadow the pages of *Death in Venice*. It opens "On a spring afternoon in 19—, a year that had been glowering so ominously at our continent for months," and though the conflict referred to is probably one of the Moroccan crises that early in the century aggravated Franco-German hostility, that "19—" points to the prospect of a whole century at risk, just as the setting of Venice suggests a deep historical background in which empires and republics have come and gone.

Though pleased by his successes, Mann remained dissatisfied. *Buddenbrooks*, he wrote to his older brother, Heinrich—a successful novelist himself, who was both a rival and his closest confidant apart from his wife—"was a bourgeois book and has no more meaning for the twentieth century." As for *Death in Venice*, well, one of its themes is, as Mann wrote to another correspondent, "that the fame of the artist is a farce." In yet another letter to a fellow writer, Mann wondered whether the very elegance of his own story didn't indicate that "perhaps a war is needed."

And then the war came. Mann, like so many people throughout the countries involved, rich or poor, educated or uneducated, on the right or on the left, was thrilled. The war was "great, fundamentally decent, and in fact stirring." A "stronger, freer, happier German soul" was sure to emerge from it. Mann shared the widespread German view that the attack on France via neutral Belgium was perfectly justified in light of the obvious determination of Germany's enemies to encircle and neutralize Germany itself, whose growing industrial and military power filled them with envy. In September 1914 he published some enthusiastic "Thoughts in Wartime," which he followed with

a historical study comparing the present campaign to Frederick the
Great's heroic and wily struggle to assert Prussian might and right in
the eighteenth century. By the end of the year, Mann's contributions
had been gathered into a little book that, he was proud to hear, had
been added to the gear of soldiers on the front. Mann himself didn't
volunteer to fight, and when, as the war ground on, conscription was
instituted, he was exempted as unfit.

Heinrich Mann opposed the war. The brothers were at odds from
the start: when Heinrich told Thomas that the war was not only un-
justified but certain to end in German defeat, his younger brother responded with patriotic outrage. Then, at the end of 1915, Heinrich
published a long essay about Zola and the Dreyfus affair that was
clearly intended as a reflection on the conduct of German intellectuals in the face of the war. Heinrich describes the ostensibly principled
persecutors of Captain Dreyfus:

> Traitors to the intellect and to the human being . . . they run
> together [with the people] and their most disgusting corrupt-
> ers, encouraging them in the injustice they are being enticed
> to commit. They, the intellectual fellow-travellers are more
> guilty than those in power . . . One has chosen between the
> moment and history, and one has admitted that with all one's
> talents one has still only been an entertaining parasite.

Thomas was disgusted to see Heinrich setting up a French novelist as a model for Germans. But what really infuriated him was the
phrase "entertaining parasite." Because that, Thomas Mann knew,
could only mean Thomas Mann himself.

For Mann, a new war now broke out, a war with his brother, which
soon overshadowed the real war, whose trenches kept on spitting out
dead men. Setting aside the book he had begun to work on before
war started—a satiric pendant to *Death in Venice* that would be set
in a TB sanatorium high in the Swiss Alps, which he was thinking of
calling *The Magic Mountain*—he began a literary campaign against

his brother and everything his brother represented. Over the next two years he poured out a wild torrent of words that he finally published as *Reflections of a Nonpolitical Man*, a book of more than six hundred pages, in March 1918—six months before the unconditional surrender of the German military would lead to the complete collapse of imperial Germany.

Reflections of a Nonpolitical Man is a fascinating, uncategorizable book, the most directly personal book Mann ever wrote, a kind of tantrum of the spirit. In it, he argues that Germany is the most moderate and conservative—*bürgerlich*, as he puts it—and exemplary of European nations, the indispensable fulcrum, balancing on the one hand barbarous and mystical Russia and on the other revolutionary and secular France, whose corrupting influence is concentrated in the character of Civilization's Literary Man (read, brother Heinrich). Civilization's Literary Man pretends to speak in defense of universal truths, but he in fact aims to destroy everything local and individual that enriches human life and constitutes culture itself, replacing them instead with political calculation and legal proceduralism that make for a shallow public show glorified as democracy. Sentimental, platitudinous, cynically manipulative, unnatural, arty (he ogles "anthropophagous sculptures" at art galleries), superficial (he dances the foxtrot at the St. Moritz), Civilization's Literary Man is above all a dyed-in-the-wool hypocrite. What is at stake in this war? Mann demands in conclusion. German defeat would mean nothing less than the end of music; *finis musicae*, Mann says, flourishing his Latin.

And yet, notwithstanding such passionate, even hysterical protestations, when the end of the war at last came, Mann accepted German defeat with remarkable equanimity. His diaries excoriate vengeful Clemenceau and priggish Wilson, and the postwar success of Heinrich's novel *The Underling*—a scathing depiction, usually translated as *Man of Straw*, of a German businessman of the prewar era as a boorish, gutless, treacherous timeserver—infuriated him, as did Heinrich's speeches in support of the new democratic political order. And yet, slowly but surely, Mann's own political views began to shift until, by 1922, he himself was singing the praises of democracy. In "The German Republic," presented as an address to German youth, he stage-manages a spiritual marriage between the aristocratic German Romantic poet Novalis and Walt Whitman, the democratic, and very homoerotic, man of the people par excellence, presenting it as a timely and necessary commitment to a generous new common manliness. Criticized for changing his colors since *Reflections*, Mann replied that, no, he was delivering the same old message but in a form that was appropriate for a new world. Hadn't the message of *Reflections* been "Conservatism equals irony with eroticism"? Still, his support for the fledgling and struggling Weimar Republic was a real change, and it required courage to announce it in public.

The new shape in which Mann had come to see the world comes out most clearly in the new novel—*The Magic Mountain*—which he had resumed work on almost immediately after the war. Originally conceived of as a short work, it now began to swell and swell, and while inflation ravaged the German economy, Mann supported his family by giving well-attended and well-remunerated public readings from the book. He had fiercely denounced America in *Reflections*; now he was eagerly composing short pieces about life and culture in postwar Germany for the American journal *The Dial*, which brought him the hard currency of dollars along with a new international audience. By the beginning of 1922, as his fortunes prospered and he worked hard on his new book, he even made up with Heinrich.

The Magic Mountain is a story about a very ordinary young man—it even begins with the words "an ordinary young man"—Hans Castorp, who, like Thomas Mann, comes from a prosperous family of merchants. Hans is a hearty fellow of healthy appetites; he likes his cigars and has trained to be an engineer. The book begins as he is about to start his professional career. Before he does, however, he wants to pay a visit to his soldier cousin Joachim, who is in a sanatorium in the Swiss Alps because of a spot on his lung. Hans hopes to raise his ailing cousin's spirits and to have a good time.

The sanatorium is luxurious, the clientele international. The therapeutic daily regime of "airbathing" in the crisp mountain atmosphere is strictly enforced, though at the end of the day it is followed by an elegant and ample meal, washed down with copious amounts of excellent wine. Visitors must also observe the house rules, and Hans does, with the surprising result that he begins to feel increasingly ill. Feverish. Even his cigar tastes bad. Hans goes to the doctor for a checkup, and it turns out that he, like Joachim, has a spot on his lung. Hans must stay with his cousin on the mountain to be cured.

These first three weeks have taken the first four parts of the novel and some two hundred pages to recount, and by the end of the book, Hans will have stayed at the sanatorium for seven years. The symbolic number seven underscores that the sanatorium is a symbolic place, both the world in a nutshell—it contains the proverbial all sorts that it takes to make a world—and a world apart, where the usual expectations are suspended and there appears to be all the time in the world, even though for its residents, time is always threatening to run out. They gossip and bicker, fall into bed and fall out with each other, follow fads, and do what they can to pass the time. From time to time someone takes a turn for the worse and disappears to die. From time to time, someone, cured at last or simply sick of being sick, departs, though some in time come back. Meanwhile, poised between the passing instant and the unimaginable immensity of eternity, the book unfurls at enormous leisure, as slowly, experimentally almost, Hans Castorp is introduced to the defining contraries of the human condition: love and hatred, mind and body, art and science, sickness and health, life and death. The simple sense of who he is that Hans brought up to the mountain like a monogrammed piece of luggage will be increasingly challenged, and the reader, drawn into this very long book and left for long spells at a loss, will share in his experience.

The Magic Mountain is a book of studiously juxtaposed contraries. It is symbolic, but it is also thoroughly realistic. It is an allegory, and as such supra-historical, but it is also set at a specific historical moment, as Mann makes clear from the start:

The extraordinary pastness of our story results from its having taken place *before* a certain turning point, on the far side
of a rift that has cut deeply through our lives and consciousness. It takes place, or, to avoid any present tense whatever, it
took place back then, long ago, in the old days of the world
before the Great War, with whose beginning so many things
began whose beginnings, it seems, have not yet ceased. It took
place before the war, then, but not long before. But is not the
pastness of a story that much more profound, more complete,
more like a fairy tale, the tighter it fits up against the "before"?
And it may well be that our story, by its very nature, has a few
other things in common with fairy tales.

The function of this is, of course, to remind the reader that he encounters the book at a no less specific time: after the war. The book, in
other words, is as much about after as before, bracketing the immensity of the war like a parenthesis.

"Only thoroughness can be truly entertaining," the narrator announces, and *The Magic Mountain* is nothing if not thorough. The
story emerges as a sequence of digressions (a kind of considered and
corrective reprise of the wild gesticulations of *Reflections*), of accidents
and encounters, as Hans, as curious as he is bored by his monotonous
invalid's life, struggles to pass the time. One of his first encounters
is with the Italian journalist Settembrini, a Freemason and free-
thinker who takes the young man in hand, dubbing him Life's Problem Child, and sets out to explain the world to him. Settembrini is
the liberal progressive par excellence—a more sympathetically drawn
version of Civilization's Literary Man—genial and decent, though
given to moments of acid condescension, and the freethinking in
which he schools Hans will eventually lead Hans to question him in
turn. Settembrini's great cause is to eliminate pain from human life,
and Hans comes to wonder how realistic such a goal is, and what pain
may lie behind it.

The balanced design of *The Magic Mountain* means that Settembrini must have an opposite number, and so he does: Naphta, a tortured spirit whose essential incoherence inspires him to flights of dazzlingly perverse argumentation. Naphta is a Jesuit novice, a classical scholar, and a Jew, who as a child witnessed the death of his father, a ritual butcher, crucified in a pogrom. Small and ugly to the point of deformity, an aesthete and a lover of fine things, Naphta preaches the violent revolution and dictatorship to come not as liberation, but as the necessary recognition that only terror—the threat of pain that his opposite number seeks to eliminate—can root human community. Settembrini, the scourge of religion and superstition and the lover of democracy, is appalled but also fascinated by this man, who does not seek to deny or overcome his pain, but embraces it, maintaining the reality of hell over any image of heaven. The two men enjoy sparring with each other, at least to begin with. Their argument—representative of political arguments that went on both before and after the war, and Naphta, it should be said, is as nearly a fascist as a communist—goes on and on, becoming increasingly exhausted and exhausting as it does. It is not after all a question of reasons, but of life and death, and one of the triumphs of Mann's book is to make the reader see the suffering that lies behind the sophistry of these two men.

Life's Problem Child is designed for life, though. He moves on. Politics may be helpless to explain or assuage the human condition, but perhaps science can illuminate it. Dr. Behrens, the sanatorium's medical director, is an amateur painter, and one day he invites Hans and Joachim to his apartment to see his work. Mostly it consists of alpine landscapes, painted with "brash clumps of color that often looked squeezed onto the canvas directly from the tube . . . a technique occasionally . . . effective at covering bad mistakes," but what captures Hans's attention is a portrait of a fellow patient, Clavdia Chauchat ("hot cat," the name translates), an exotic Slavic beauty, very likely the doctor's mistress. Hans has a crush on her. It's as crude as all the other paintings, but Hans's admiration leads the doctor to hold forth about the wonders of the skin, that border between inner and outer worlds, and, inspired by Clavdia's throat and breasts, to lay

out the mysterious working of the lymphatic system in a passage that
is clinical and comical and laced with sexual innuendo. Hans's interest is thoroughly aroused. "I could easily have become a doctor," he
cries. "The body?! the flesh! The human body! What is it? . . . Tell us
now!" "Water," the doctor says, "to which a little fat and salt is then
added"—reserves that slowly but surely are exhausted. "So," Hans
asks, "if someone is interested in life . . . it's death he's particularly
interested in?" Right, the doctor affirms, and goes to take a nap.

Behrens's lecture prompts Hans to strike out on a course of scientific study: he immerses himself in textbooks on chemistry, biology,
anatomy, physics. From larger physiological structures he is led to
ponder smaller and ever smaller ones: the cell and its interior, the gene,
the protein, the molecule, and the atom, that "tiny, initial, ephemeral
concentration of something immaterial . . . not yet matter, but related
to matter—of energy, that one could not yet, or perhaps no longer,
think of it as matter, but rather as both the medium and boundary
between the material and the immaterial. But that posed the question of another kind of spontaneous generation . . . the generation of
matter from nonmatter." At which point microcosm yields to macrocosm: Hans turns his gaze outward—toward the world at large
and the cosmos—arriving at last at what is in no sense a conclusion:
"Concepts like inner and outer had now lost their foundation . . . The
very moment when one thought one had reached the outermost edge,
everything began all over again."

It all leads nowhere, in other words, though for a while it leaves
Hans elated, his exploration of the natural world and human knowledge deepening his own understanding and wonder and giving him
a great deal of pleasure. This whole section of the book is a brilliant
display of Mann's astonishing gift for using apparently contradictory
terms to illuminate each other, of his supremely confident, high-
spirited unleashing of paradox and irony. Here he captures a whole
prewar climate of opinion—here for example is the nagging question
of the relation between exterior and interior perspectives that we
saw in Wells and Gide—seeing it in the round, and so in some sense
moving beyond it, without forgetting how meaningful it continues
to be. Here too, even more dazzlingly, starting with Behrens's not

very remarkable painting of Clavdia (it makes plain how limited art's means are to depict the fullness of a person or a body), Mann passes from the limits of art to the allurements of science to an exposition of science's own limits in what, finally, can only be taken as a spectacular demonstration of the reach of Mann's own art.

And yet for Hans, disappointment follows hard on the heels of his earlier elation. Soon he gives up his scientific studies and devotes himself instead to what passes for a life of action, of moral engagement. In the sanatorium, the dying are shunned, and they themselves shun the merely sick. They disappear into their rooms, and no more is said. Now Hans and Joachim resolve to visit and tend to the terminally ill. Death must be faced in fact, not just in theory.

Throughout all this, Hans is haunted by a peculiar memory, something he'd entirely forgotten, which comes back to him with hallucinatory force when, early in his stay on the mountain, feverish, he dozes off on a bench. At thirteen, Hans had fallen in love with a schoolmate, Pribislav Hippe, a grade ahead of him, a model student whose blond splendor was accentuated by the Slavic tilt of his startling blue eyes. For almost a year, Hans had gazed at Hippe in secret, never saying a word, until one day, in the interval between history and drawing class, Hans realized that he lacked a pencil, and screwing up all his courage, he approached his beloved to ask to borrow one. Gladly, Hippe responded, handing him a pencil—saying just make sure to return it. Hans took the pencil, sharpened it—"he kept three or four of the red-lacquered shavings in the drawer of his desk for a year or two"— drew with it, and finally, blissfully, gave it back. "Hans Castorp had never been happier all his life than during that drawing class," though he never spoke to Hippe again. It is after recalling this episode that for the first time Hans coughs blood.

Clavdia Chauchat shares Hippe's slanting Slavic eyes—Hans quickly recognizes the resemblance—though she is otherwise quite unlike him. Hippe was upright and attentive. Clavdia is careless and louche, slamming doors, with a slinky walk and bitten fingernails that are, Hans notices again and again, never quite clean. Still, she fascinates him as much as the boy did—she notices her effect, too—and things come to a head at the midpoint of the novel, on Mardi Gras. Masks are donned, honorifics cast off, the intimate rather than the polite form of speech is embraced as the residents of the hotel engage in an orgy of trivial pursuits, one of them a game of drawing blind, and Hans, wanting to play, lacks a pencil. He turns to see Clavdia and tremblingly approaches her—this is the first time he's spoken to her—to ask if she'll lend him hers. The conversation that ensues ranges ever more widely. Though not cured, Clavdia is, as Hans has heard, leaving the sanatorium to rejoin her husband in Daghestan, and as to that husband, well, she is married only so far as marriage allows her her freedom. A riddler, Clavdia tells Hans that morality is not to be found in "virtue . . . [but] in sin, in abandoning oneself to danger." Hans finally unburdens himself—"I love you . . . I have always loved you . . . You are the 'intimate you' of my life, my dream, my destiny, my need, my eternal desire . . ."—to which Clavdia responds, "My little bourgeois . . . with the little moist spot . . . Is it true that you love me so much?"

Hans falls to his knees:

> The body, love, death, are simply one and the same. Because the body is sickness and depravity, it is what produces death, yes, both of them, love and death, are carnal. That is the source of their terror and great magic . . . Death is much more lofty than a life spent laughing, earning money . . . much more venerable than progress . . . It is history, nobility, and piety . . . In the same way, the body, and the love of the body, too, are indecent and disagreeable . . .

And yet:

> Consider the marvelous symmetry of the human frame, the shoulders and the hips and the breasts as they blossom on each side of the chest, and the ribs arranged in pairs and the navel set in the supple belly, and the dark sexual organs between the thighs . . . What an immense festival of caresses

lies in those delicious zones . . . ! A festival of death with no
weeping afterwards . . . Let me touch in devotion your pulsing
femoral artery where it emerges at the top of your thigh . . . !
Let me perish, my lips against yours!

At which point Clavdia, smiling, gets up to leave, though not without
admonishing him to return her pencil.

This time he doesn't.

Is the relationship consummated? Mann is supremely coy about
the question. Does it really matter? Like sex, Hans's speech is effortful
and absurd and finally orgasmic. Before Clavdia leaves, she does make
Hans a promise—she will come back (she does)—and she gives him a
memento: her X-ray—"a little plate of glass in a narrow frame . . . the
portrait of Clavdia's interior without a face, but revealing the organs
of her chest cavity and the tender framework of her upper body, del-
icately surrounded by the soft, ghostlike forms of her flesh." He will
cherish it. Hans's declaration, "their riotously sweet hour together,"
and Clavdia's departure occur nine months after Hans's first arrival.

After this delirious outburst *The Magic Mountain* takes a darker
turn. Hans will remain on the mountain for another six years and
more, but in the second half of the novel they go briskly by. Love
has been declared, but now it is the necessary alliance with death
that Hans also declared that comes to the fore. The book becomes
a chronicle of exhaustion. The subjects that seemed of such feverish
and consuming interest early on now reveal their diseased essence.
Seemingly comic, Settembrini and Naphta's endless arguments—and
the perverse marriage of opposites that binds them together—come
to a tragic end. Meanwhile, the residents of the sanatorium take up
one fashionable craze after another. Honest Joachim, fed up with the
whole situation, departs the sanatorium for the army, determined to
be of service. He is soon back, however, and once back, soon dies. Now
conducting séances becomes all the rage (as it had been before the war
and was again after, as bereaved parents sought to make contact with
their dead), and Hans, though entirely skeptical, has nothing better

to do than take part. The medium summons Joachim, who appears for an endless instant, immensely sad, speechless. Forgive me, Hans stammers out. Forgive me.

Joachim is dressed in a strange uniform, unfamiliar to Hans and the other participants in the séance. He wears a heavy, almost funny steel helmet. It is a helmet from the war to come. At the end of the book, that war will break the spell Hans has been under for so many years, returning him to the lowlands and consigning him to the trenches. We are left with a bird's-eye view of him, marching into battle while singing Schubert's "Lindenbaum" (the tree grows over a grave where, the lyrics go, "I too will find rest"), before he is hurled to the ground by an exploding shell. Does he survive? Mann doubts it. We can't know.

I have described how, early in *The Magic Mountain*, Hans goes out for a walk and, exhausted, falls asleep and dreams of his beloved Hippe. Late in this book of endless echoes and reflections, he goes on another excursion and again falls asleep. He is skiing in the mountains, feeling vigorous, not sickly, this time, when he is overtaken by a blizzard. In its blinding whiteness, he soon loses his way, and he stops, as he knows he shouldn't, to rest. Now he has a vision of:

> [A] whole sunny region . . . [that] was populated in all directions: people, children of the sea and sun, were stirring and resting everywhere, intelligent, cheerful, beautiful, young humanity, so fair to gaze on . . . Lads exercised trotting whinnying, head-tossing horses . . . The muscles of the boys' golden tan backs played in the sunlight and the cries that they exchanged or shouted to the horses seemed inexplicably enchanting.

And so on—it is an almost clichéd vision of classical sensuality and order, and Hans, "opening his heart" to it, risks sinking into a final and fatal repose. Then, however, his vision turns dark. He finds himself at the base of a flight of monumental stairs. He mounts them. The doors to the temple are open:

> Two half-naked old women . . . among flickering bra-
> ziers . . . [with] tits long as fingers . . . were dismembering
> a child . . . the brittle little bones cracking in their mouths,
> blood dripping from their vile lips.

A vision of horror that makes Hans start awake, saving his life. And now, after these successive visions, he thinks:

> Man is the master of contradictions, they occur through him,
> and so he is more noble than they. More noble than death,
> too noble for it—that is the freedom of his mind. More noble
> than life, too noble for it—that is the devotion of his heart . . .
> Death and love—there is no rhyming them, that is a prepos-
> terous rhyme, a false rhyme. Love stands opposed to death—it
> alone, and not reason, is stronger than death. Only love, and
> not reason, yields kind thoughts. And form, too, comes only
> from love and goodness: form and the cultivated manners of
> man's fair state, of a reasonable genial community—out of si-
> lent regard for the bloody banquet. Oh, what a clear dream I've
> dreamed!

In the meantime, the sun has come out, and Hans makes his way safely back home. It is a dream that builds on and goes beyond the merely personal love that Hans felt for Hippe and Clavdia. But is the dream so clear, and if it is so clear, isn't it a little pat? "Love triumphs over everything." Aren't Hans's reflections so many pretty platitudes? But maybe he has lived through enough on the mountain to make this realization genuinely meaningful. And yet, he still has to go to war.

In 1918, just after *Reflections* came out, Mann described his book as "more than 600 pp about the 'whole thing.'" Wholeness lies at the heart of *The Magic Mountain*, too, a whole new effort not only to grapple with the whole disaster that the war had been, but also to preserve a vision of beneficent wholeness that that disaster might well seem to have called into question once and for all.

Certainly many people thought that it had, and the irruption of revolution, the collapse of empires and economies, and the struggles of new nations and well-meaning new organizations like the League of Nations that followed the war only confirmed that despair. The war had changed everything—that was a cliché after, during, and even before it broke out, when its advocates had eagerly imagined that it would do precisely that. Mann's response to this world in which everything had changed was, simply and boldly, as we have seen, to put everything in his book: art, science, politics, sex, gramophones, love, and death— and finally and unavoidably, the war. It was a kind of encyclopedic museum of what, after everything had been destroyed, was left.

Here in *The Magic Mountain* was all the superficiality of prewar life, now depicted with the paradoxical awareness that as much as that shallowness and blindness could be said to have brought on the war, the years in which they had thrived had at least been years of peace, undervalued peace, and perhaps what had been shallowest of all had been to yearn, as Mann had, for a purifying war. Here too was the question of national character, of the Germanness that had seemed to Mann both underappreciated and actively threatened during the war, brought out through the musical character of Mann's book, with its slow variation and development of interconnected themes over time and with, at the same time, its peculiar fusion of the bildungsroman and the fairy tale, those defining and contrasting German literary genres, one of which speaks of the processes of cultivation and maturation, the other of eternal childhood.

The German imagination, Mann was as much as saying, had survived the war even if the distortion of it that was imperial Germany— and this was just as well—had not. Here too is Hans, that German everyman, earnest and blundering, and here too is the knowing drone of the narrator of Mann's novel, a never-identified, presumptive "we," as arch as Hans is unremarkable. Here then was Germany, but here also was the world at large, the human spirit at large, which Germany enlarged and by which in turn it was enlarged. While at work on the book, Mann wrote his fellow novelist Arthur Schnitzler that it was connected with his "infatuation with the idea of humanism." In another letter, written after the book had come out, he described Hans as "sens[ing] . . . some glimmering of the 'truth,' of future humanitas," at least "before he is wrenched into the war."

It was all there, and then again it was hardly there at all. Certainly, as anyone reading it would have noted, there is nothing about the squalor of the trenches, the needless slaughter of millions upon millions, or the deprivation and starvation on the German home front that had people wearing paper clothes before at last they and the troops openly rebelled against the kaiser and his military advisers' war—though of course you could say that all that went without saying, especially by Thomas Mann, who could hardly claim to have experienced it. (In *Reflections*, he does complain about how cold his study could get during the war.) All of which is to say that *The Magic Mountain* is less an imposing whole than the strangest, most unnatural of hybrids, at once a monument and a caprice. It is certainly an extraordinarily self-conscious book, perpetually looking over its shoulder, checking itself out in the mirror, fussy and vain of its looks. It's an act that not infrequently seems as if it can't and shouldn't work, though Mann, the great connoisseur of irony, might have been at peace with the thought that a book that sets out to do everything must of course also fail.

It succeeds however as a twentieth-century novel—what before the war Mann had felt he must and yet could not write—and above and beyond that, as a new form of the twentieth-century novel, a form born of the war whose new significance could only be fully appreciated after the war. Devoted as it is to preserving a vision of wholeness in light of the whole disaster that was the war, *The Magic Mountain* inevitably begs comparison to the kind of wholeness—the studied balance of the competing claims of self and society—that characterized the novel in the nineteenth century. It seems, in fact, to look for and to possess something of that balance, very much by contrast with such novelists as Gide or Wells or Kafka, who, as we have seen, deny, resist, and challenge it; who suffer from a divided sensibility and embrace it, affirming that it is only intransigence that makes the novel suitable to a new age. Mann's book does something different. It preserves an image of unity by telling the story, down to the last detail, of a world whose pieces no longer come together. A world that was, the reader knows, in fact doomed to explode.

It exists as a book about a questing and questioning young man that, as a book, makes a point of raising a host of questions about the kind of book it is—and even that pose can only be viewed with suspicion. How can a book about the war ignore, or pass over in silence, the war itself, taking it as an occasion for allegories of human flourishing and sacrifice, for a vast exhibition of quasi-musical sleight of hand? Isn't this, after all, only a kind of evasion of the sort Mann specialized in, having his cake and eating it too, in true bourgeois fashion? Mann, the bourgeois paterfamilias, immaculately decked out in the correct and seasonable outfit of his class, harboring his fantasies about young men; Mann, whose big, happy family hid a wealth of unhappiness (his sister committed suicide, as did his openly gay son, Klaus, also a novelist, and as his youngest son, Michael, may well have done too); Mann, who when he was forced into exile by the Nazis would say, "Where I am is Germany," a great spirit but also an inexhaustible source of vanity and pettiness. So we wonder, but it is the book that makes us wonder. We wonder how to reconcile the contradictions that Mann so assiduously cultivates, like hothouse flowers. But then the peculiar courage and beauty of his book is to expose itself to that question, thanks above all, it has to be said, to Mann's unnerving eye for detail, the eye that sees in the broad brushstrokes of Behrens's amateurish painting of Clavdia "perspiration, the invisible vapors of life, rising from the flesh . . . If you were to press your lips against the surface, you would smell a human body, not paint and varnish."

And there it is: an immense book that is also in a sense an empty book, a book full of clues and down and across columns, like a vast crossword puzzle the reader is left to fill in, as much minor entertainment as masterpiece and no less a masterpiece for that; something to while away the time; a heavy book and a light one, like an iridescent bubble; a great performance that may perhaps be best seen as something small and dear and useful in the face of the terrifying new world at hand—like, say, a pencil.

8. WHAT DID YOU DO IN THE WAR?

MARCEL PROUST'S *IN SEARCH OF LOST TIME*
AND JAMES JOYCE'S *ULYSSES*

Conceived before the war in a world that the war would destroy, but largely written after the war was over, *The Magic Mountain* is centrally a book about the war, even if it's about many other things (everything) as well, and even if the war itself enters the book only in its last pages. Marcel Proust's *In Search of Lost Time* and James Joyce's *Ulysses*—no less monumental books that, like Mann's novel, would take final form in the early 1920s and find, almost immediately, an international audience—were also conceived before the war but written, and rewritten, as it was going on. They are not war books—*Ulysses* is set in 1904—yet they were shaped by the war in ways their authors had not—could not have—foreseen, and it was, I think, very much in light of the disaster of the war that, as works of literature, they would take on the eminence and urgency that postwar readers would find in them. They are not war books, yet they might be described, together with Mann's, as having been written by the war.

Marcel Proust was born a few years before Thomas Mann, in 1871, the son of a Jewish heiress and a physician with a distinguished career in public health. Well-educated, well-connected, well-read (he had a special passion for English literature), at an early age he set out to write a great book, without much success. An attempt to write an autobiographical novel came to nothing, and instead he produced self-consciously little things—a translation of and commentary on Ruskin's book about the cathedral of Amiens, a set of clever pastiches of famous French writers—and was known chiefly as a social butterfly. In Colette's *Claudine Married*, Proust makes a brief appearance as "a young attractive literary man (beautiful eyes . . . a faint touch of blepharitis)" who, meeting the short-haired, boyish Claudine at a dinner party, enthusiastically compares her "to Myrtocleia, to a young Hermes, to an Eros by Prud'hon," flattering her so continually and shamelessly that he almost spoils her appetite for the sumptuous dinner their rich hostess has set before them.

Sycophantic, a social climber, sickly, as sexually repressed as self-evidently gay, though given to hopeless crushes on both men and women, Proust had earned a solid reputation as a thorough lightweight, when, after the deaths of his intimidating father and too-loved mother, he curtailed his worldly ways and began to write in earnest. It was not a novel, however, that he set out to write, but an essay about Charles Augustin Sainte-Beuve, the major French literary critic of the nineteenth century who had argued that it was an author's life that provided the key to understanding his work, a view Proust vehemently rejected. *Against Sainte-Beuve*, as Proust called this work, swelled and drifted—Proust turned from Sainte-Beuve to his contemporary Baudelaire, the great poet of the corrupted heart and its destructive desires, misunderstood and even betrayed by the critic—and then, in a series of passages addressed to his mother, took an autobiographical turn. Eventually these passages gave birth to a novel that, by 1910 at the latest, he was working on with confidence and enthusiasm.

It would be a big book about a young man, a sensitive soul and a great reader and an aspiring novelist who wasted his time in pursuit of social standing and love and through plain old procrastination—all of which would be exhaustively chronicled—before, in the end, against all odds, the waste would be made good, shown to be the necessary precondition for the narrator's final and complete and triumphant commitment to the work of art that would both contain all the waste and then convert it, by a kind of literary alchemy, into gold. It would be a novel in the form of a Möbius strip, a single twisted band that would accommodate, along with the story of a sensibility unfolding into the larger logic of the work, a comprehensive picture of French society, its private and public passions, at the end of the nineteenth

century and the beginning of the twentieth. It would be a book about
the workings of memory. It would be a book, in short, about everything Proust had ever known or felt or read or thought about or done.

As a project, it has to be said, this seems not so much supremely
ambitious as hopelessly naive: this is the book every young person
dreams of writing, which is essentially unwritable, as it had proven
for Proust up to that point. Starting with the reflections and sketches
of *Against Sainte-Beuve*, he had, however, found his way to a method
of composition—dispensing with plot, he worked with bits and pieces
that he moved around at will and reworked in the process, waiting
for them to find their proper place in the expanding mass—and, even
more important, he had found a voice, a tone. That tone is pitched between the intimate and the impersonal, and the novel, with its flights
of description, its unexpected epigrams, its critical digressions on
music and art and style, its forensic analyses of sensations and emotions, its gossipiness, always retains a hint of the essay it grew out of. It
is this tone, as much as anything, that made the work possible—tone
and method are one and the same—and it is this tone that the work is,
among other things, about. Proust would continue to rework his book
until the end of his life, and if it is notorious not only for its length as
a whole but also for the length of its individual sentences, that is because in it the individual sentence often functions as a kind of sample
of the whole (the book is fractal, the poet Richard Howard once said
to me), going on until it seems at risk of losing its raison d'être, going
on until the reader may despair of its going anywhere—as Proust's
narrator repeatedly despairs that his life is not going anywhere—until
at last it does fall into place, does come to a point. Fairly early in the
book, Proust describes the phrases of a Chopin prelude "which with
the inordinate sinuous length of their graceful necks are so fluent,
flexible and tactile, which seem to be meandering off-course, far away
from their original direction, in an aimless tentative search for their
proper place, straying anywhere but towards the destination where
one might have expected to feel their final touch, but which are only
feigning these fanciful detours so as to return more purposefully,
more accurately, more knowingly, and as though ringing cut-glass
echoes that make one want to cry aloud, strike home to one's unsus-

pecting heart." The reader knows that this sentence is meant as a description of Proust's own sentences.

By 1912, Proust had written a thousand pages, and though he envisioned his whole book as containing at least as many more, he was eager to publish what he already had and to reveal his ambitious project to the public. The title of the whole work, *In Search of Lost Time*, combines the dryly scientific—the French *recherche* means "research" as well as "search"—with the impossibly quixotic. It is both abstract and vaulting. (And sardonic: it can also be read as "in search of wasted time.") By contrast, the title of the first volume, *Swann's Way*, was modest and casual, so much so that some of Proust's friends warned him it was effectively meaningless. ("By Way of Swann's" would be a more accurate rendering of the French, capturing the casual gesture at the commonplace question, Which way shall we go? that begins this great big book.) Proust's hope was that the book would be taken on by the NRF, Gide's new house, which had quickly established itself as the most venturesome and prestigious in France, and Gaston Gallimard, the publisher, expressed interest, but the editorial committee, led by Gide, turned the book down without much thought. Proust's book was eventually picked up by Bernard Grasset, another comparatively new publisher who was pioneering new forms of literary publicity and promotion. That appealed to Proust, who had no doubt that his book should and could attract a wide audience.

Swann's Way came out in 1913, and it included a prospectus on the volumes to come. It was about half the length of the thousand pages Proust had originally submitted—Grasset pointed out that printing presses simply couldn't handle such a bulk—but it set the terms of the work as a whole. The insomniac writer with which it begins, remembering himself as a sleepless little boy craving a good-night kiss from his mother that he knows his father will forbid, is everyone who has lain awake at night missing a lover or tormented by having missed out in general; the bed he lies in is the bed of birth and the bed of love, a sickbed, a deathbed, the bed of a dreamer. His memory involuntarily stimulated by tea and the famous madeleine, the narrator recalls the two walks his family took on summer vacations in the country, one by way of their neighbor Swann, another associated with the aristocratic Guermantes family, two walks that will come to figure in the larger book as the two paths through life that he will pursue as an adult, the path of art and the path of worldly ambition. The story of the fashionable and deeply intelligent and perceptive Charles Swann and his infatuation with a small-time courtesan, to whom he comes to sacrifice his individual sensibility even as she climbs on his back to the highest levels of society, stands as a premonitory and cautionary tale about jealous love and the social world. *Longtemps*, "for a long time," is the first word of the book; already Proust would have known that it must end as it began, as in time it would, with the word *temps*.

The book was immediately recognized as a major work. Excerpts appeared in the daily papers. There were many reviews, for the most part appreciative. Sales were good too. The book was reprinted, and Grasset had the second volume in the works.

Then the war intervened.

But no, before the war intervened, something else happened that would profoundly transform the character of the novel. Proust fell in love.

The spring prior to the publication of *Swann's Way*, a young man whom Proust had previously employed as a chauffeur, Alfred Agostinelli, showed up at Proust's door along with his girlfriend. (He said she was his wife.) Proust, whose sexual life seems to have been largely a matter of flirtation, masturbation, and voyeurism, and who always insisted that he did not have sex with men, was nonetheless quite open about being attracted to them, attractions that typically took the form of compulsive gift giving and ever more ferocious jealousy. In 1908 he had met and soon been drawn to Albert Nahmias, the young son of a banker, and though his feelings had since cooled, Nahmias had served as his secretary from 1910 on. Now, suddenly smitten by Agostinelli, Proust made him his secretary, too, unlikely candidate though he was, and Agostinelli and his girlfriend must have been happy to find a place to live. Proust, instantly jealous, wanted Agostinelli around all the time, and to guarantee that he would be, he began to shower him with money. The couple stuck around through the summer and fall, during which time Agostinelli developed an ambition to train as a pilot, and this trendy modern enterprise appealed to Proust, who encouraged him and paid for his lessons.

In December, however, just as Proust's novel was making its way into the world, the couple abruptly decamped. Proust, distraught and desperate, sent money to Agostinelli's family, begging them to make him return. Learning that he was in the South of France and continuing to train as a pilot (under the name Marcel Swann), Proust hoped to lure him back by buying him a plane and perhaps a Rolls-Royce. Agostinelli refused the gifts. The plane remained in the hangar, where Proust thought of having it inscribed with a famous line of poetry by Mallarmé, "*Le vierge, le vivace et le bel aujourd'hui*"—"the virgin, vital, beautiful today"—the opening of a sonnet about a swan frozen in place and haunted by the memory of all "the flights that he has never flown."

In April 1914, in the course of taking his second solo flight, Agostinelli crashed into the sea. His family wrote to Proust with the news, requesting that he pay to search for the body. It was found a few days later. Proust, heartbroken, was consumed by guilt. One of the high points of his relationship with Agostinelli had been a visit to the airfields outside of Paris. Wasn't it his fault that Agostinelli had taken to the air and fallen to his death?

Proust had always meant his narrator to suffer the same torments of jealous love that afflicted Charles Swann; he would have to undergo what Swann had undergone, to suffer even more in order to know better, in the end, than to do as his deceived role model had done, since the serial perdition of love is as central to Proust's view of the world as the insurmountable depredations of time. (One of the things that Proust's obsessive book could be said to be about is learning to be alone, to need neither mother nor lover to ease your solitude, to own it, which is to say to own your own death.) But, though Proust knew where he was going by the time he published *Swann's Way*, and he pretty much knew how he was going to get there, the Agostinelli affair gave his conception a new intensity and focus. Agostinelli was interred and commemorated and exorcised in Proust's pages as a new character—Albertine, met at the beach in volume two but coming eventually to occupy two whole volumes of her own, her name tolling through the pages of *In Search of Lost Time*. It is repeated, his biographer Jean-Yves Tadié says, 2,360 times.

There would have been no Albertine without Agostinelli; there would have been no Albertine without the war, either. It was the war that gave Proust time to develop her image. Grasset had readied the proofs of *In the Shadow of Young Girls in Flower*, the successor volume to *Swann's Way*, when conflict erupted. The lead for type was needed for bullets, and Grasset's house shut down.

Albertine is a strange character. She makes her first appearance as, effectively, an apparition, just one among a troupe of almost interchangeable girls traipsing by, but the narrator is smitten. Defined by her unreliability and unavailability to him, by contrast to her complete pliability with others, and by a certain superficiality, by her deceptiveness, Albertine is hardly a character at all; her story goes on and on, yet she herself is somehow never anything more, never any more present than she was in the narrator's initial glimpse of her, a kind of wraith. What in fact she actually looks like we never learn (just as, it should be said, we never know what the narrator looks like either).

In *The Prisoner*, the fifth volume of Proust's opus, we come as close to Albertine as we ever will. She is living with the narrator, "hidden by me from all the world," "her room some twenty steps away from mine, at the end of the hall" in a room that was once his father's, where "every evening, very late, before leaving me, she slid her tongue into my mouth, like daily bread, like nourishing food and with the almost sacred character of any flesh on which the suffering we have endured on its behalf in the end confers a kind of moral sweetness." Captive to holding Albertine captive in his Paris apartment, the two of them tended to by Françoise, the family servant the narrator has known since childhood, herself as wary and watchful as a jailer, the narrator becomes more and more persuaded that Albertine, who wants to go out, who wants out, is going out to cheat on him with other women. (She is.) Meanwhile he goes on not writing his book, the book that has led him to cut himself off from society. (Meanwhile, Albertine keeps asking him if he's making progress on his book.) The main action of *The Prisoner* takes place over three successive days—the numbering of them establishes that the days, each filling countless pages, are both interminable, all one and the same, really, and numbered—during which the narrator's jealousy swells to the hypertrophic dimensions of an immense, sickly-sweet tropical flower.

The Prisoner is the hellish center of Proust's research—and, like so much of *In Search of Lost Time*, it is organized as series of set pieces, scenes at once sharp and nebulous. The beginning of *The Prisoner* finds the narrator in bed—we are in a sense back at the beginning of the book as a whole, and he explicitly compares Albertine's kisses to the kiss his mother gave him that lonely, long-ago night when he could not get to sleep as a child—and again he is wide-awake, his head turned to the wall. He has been lying like that ever since the first hint of dawn, alert, listening, gauging the day's weather from the sounds that reach him from the street. "It was from my room above all that I perceived life on the outside at this period of my life"—and that remains no less true even though he goes out a good deal in the pages that ensue. That room, that place of terminal confinement, looks back to the Underground Man's mousehole and forward to the ever more constricting rooms and beds and jars and holes inhabited by Samuel Beckett's destitute narrators. Incapable of giving birth to anything except fear and hatred, that room is the exterior form of *The Prisoner*'s true subject, which is not love or even jealousy so much as subjectivity itself, the hell of consciousness, the unlimited interior disaster that it is to be a person, which desiring another person is supposed to relieve but only deepens. The book of Albertine is the book of the intolerable, inconsolable monstrous self.

From the beginning, the narrator knows it will end badly: "I sensed the nothing she was for me, and that I would be for her." He describes himself as "a man of habitual and infinite doubt," and so disqualified from committing himself to or feeling much for another, a doubt that makes him quite certain that Albertine's commitment must prove equally unreal. And yet the book begins in a comparatively celebratory vein, describing the couple's many kisses and intimate and interesting conversations and his opening Albertine's dressing gown to contemplate her small breasts, her belly, the declivity of her thighs. Other stranger things ensue. The narrator comes into Albertine's room and, like a dragon squatting and gloating over a hoard of treasure, contemplates her in her sleep. All "races, vices, atavisms, reposed upon her features." It seems to him that he possesses "not one, but innumerable young girls." A kind of Magellan, he then "embarks on Albertine's sleep," climbs into her bed, presses against her, and knowing "that he will not run up against the uncovered reefs of consciousness," wraps an arm around her, pressing lips to her "cheek and heart" while "his free hand" explores "all the parts of her body" and he savors the feeling of their two conjoined, breathing bodies. He does this, we are to understand, not once but many times, though sometimes, he allows, he also enjoyed "a less pure" pleasure with Albertine, still asleep, which he arrived at by placing his leg, "stiff as an oar dragged through the water," against her leg. (Through all this, what we would now see—and Proust might well agree with us—as the narrator's criminal intimacies are met and further awakened by the complete unconsciousness and unresponsiveness of Albertine.) The pleasures of watching her sleep, however, are as nothing compared with the pleasure of seeing her wake, her body stirring and stretching and, with consciousness restored, her turning to call him "*mon cheri*" and to say—Albertine now naming, like a mother, the narrator, one of only a handful of times that he is named in the book—a name that "were it the same first name as that of the author of this book, would be 'My Marcel.'"

Day two: he is wakened by the procession of street vendors outside his bedroom window. Proust offers us a little collection of their cries, cheery and brusque, though to the narrator they also sound plaintive, arriving "at little intervals like the [cries] of a dying animal." Albertine, we are told, loves these cries, as does the narrator, clearly, except they also stand "as the symbol of the atmosphere of the outside"—the outside where Albertine is forever proposing to go and where he cannot bear for her to go, the outside that is nothing but a continual clamor of solicitation, where everything, most of all love, is for sale. Now the street cries change their tenor, until the narrator imagines spending "all his time, all his money" on a woman.

And so on. The growth of the narrator's jealousy is charted on an axis of waking and sleeping, pleasure and pain, with these last two words, the echoing *douceur* and *douleur*, recurring with obsessive frequency. Pleasure in Proust's dark calculus can only be experienced as relief from pain, a pain whose return it only assures, since pleasure, of course, cannot last. Pleasure comes from and leads to pain, and love, similarly, which "in sorrowful anxiety as in happy desire, is the demand of the whole," will and must end with the renewed realization that to be a person is to be a person apart, alone, unloved. Pleasure, pain, desire, dread are, in other words, only different forms of the same hopeless craving for relief—*apaisement*, literally "to find peace," is the word Proust resorts to again and again—a relief that can only come from death. Indeed, though the outlines of the Albertine story derive from the Agostinelli affair—at the end of *The Prisoner* she too flees; at the beginning of the subsequent volume, *Albertine Gone*, she too dies in a freak accident, thrown from a horse—the deadlocked and destructive nature of the relationship between the two lovers resembles nothing so much as the war in the trenches that had yet to take place at the time the story is set, but that was going on and going nowhere as Proust wrote it. The narrator and Albertine are engaged, he writes, in a battle "on which everything depends," a battle, however,

> which resembles less those of the past, which lasted a few hours, than a contemporary battle which does not end the next day or the day after next, nor even the following week . . . One throws in all one's forces, because one continues to suppose that these will be the last of which one has any need. And more than a year will pass without any result.

Albertine's and the narrator's misery is mechanical and industrial and total, devoted, like modern war, to "the infinite production of pain."

Albertine is deeply attracted to women—that is one of the things that tends to make her relationship to the narrator a little problematic— and in the larger order of *In Search of Lost Time*, the story of the narrator's relationship to Albertine is part of the meditation on homosexuality that he had always intended to be an important part of the book, which he called *Sodom and Gomorrah*. In the book as a whole, the character who most clearly represents Proust's thinking about homosexuality is the Baron de Charlus. It is as a child that the narrator first catches sight of this imposing and intimidating figure, an aristocrat and an inflexible snob who strikes the boy as the most manly of men. Later, he comes to distrust this impression, and it is conclusively disproved when one afternoon he glimpses the baron, imagining himself unobserved, wooing a mere tradesman. This prompts a prolonged reflection:

> M. de Charlus belonged to that race of beings, less paradoxical than they appear, whose ideal is manly precisely because their temperament is feminine . . . a race upon whom a curse is laid and which must live in falsehood and perjury because it knows that its desire, which constitutes life's deepest pleasure, is held to be punishable, shameful, an inadmissable thing . . . sons without a mother, to whom they are obliged to lie all her life long and even in the hours when they close her dying eyes; friends without friendships; . . . lovers who are almost precluded from the possibility of that love the hope of which gives them the strength to endure so many risks and so much loneliness, since they are enamoured of precisely the type of man who has nothing feminine about him, who is not an invert and cannot possibly love them in return, with the result that their desire would be forever unappeased did not their

money procure for them real men, and their imagination end
by making them take for real men the inverts to whom they
have prostituted themselves.

This reduction of homosexuality to inversion—homosexual men
are really women inside, and vice versa—deeply distressed Gide, who
saw its self-hating character; he also found it distasteful, since it had
nothing to do with his own more straightforward desire for adolescent males. It is self-hating, and it is limited, but quite apart from that,
Proust's theory of homosexuality's "falsehood and perjury" is not really any different from his theory of love in general (and in fact there
is hardly a significant male character in the book, the narrator aside,
who is not eventually revealed to be homosexual). All love is a lie. All
love is doomed. Homosexuality is only the acutest manifestation of
this common human predicament, the purest because it is the most
purely hopeless. If Proust's novel is shot through with self-hatred,
if it is a kind of giant lie, the narrator pretending to heterosexual-
ity and observing the world of homosexuality from this ostensibly
more secure perch (even as the writer gives the women the narrator
falls hopelessly in love with names, Albertine, Gilberte, that mask the
names of men, dressing them in drag), that only makes the book as a
whole that much truer to the self-deception and destruction that are
at the heart of love. The heterosexual narrator in love with the homosexual Albertine is in precisely the same predicament as the baron,
loving someone whose appetites are not his own.

In *Time Regained*, the final volume of *In Search of Lost Time*, the actual war breaks out. In poor health after all his emotional ordeals, the
narrator has retreated to a sanitarium. In 1916, however, he returns
to Paris, where the war is on the tip of everyone's tongue. Come at
five to talk about the war, says Mme Verdurin, the ruthlessly ambitious bourgeois hostess who functions throughout the book as the
barometer of the changing weather of taste, opinion, and social standing. The war has changed everything, is what everyone says, and the

narrator observes that in the papers and salons, patriotic, chauvin-
istic, jingoistic, and jargon-ridden platitudes are the order of the day.
As the slaughter continues, some people are even looking ahead: "the
torment and ambition" of fashion designers "is [to] seek the new, distance themselves from banality, demonstrate individuality, prepare for
victory, and develop for the new post-war generation a new formula
for the beautiful."

M. de Charlus, it is true, takes a different view of things. He decries
the propaganda in the papers and denounces the militarism of the
moment. The war, as he sees it, is essentially vulgar: "The public that
resisted the modern in art and literature follows the modern wars," he
says, "because it is the done thing to think that way and because small
minds are overwhelmed, not by beauty, but by the enormity of the
action." The baron is also related to German nobility, a connection
that matters more to him than French citizenship. Unafraid of being
charged with "defeatism," he praises German military prowess and
admires the German successes on the battlefront, even as he insists
that their sole goal is "peace and reconciliation," which English and
French politicians are responsible for subverting. At the same time, he
has turned his house into a military infirmary, largely, one suspects,
to surround himself with young men.

All this the baron delivers to the narrator on a summer evening
in the streets, with rough trade hovering in the background hoping
to catch his eye, after which the two men go their ways. It is hot, and
after walking for a while, the narrator is thirsty, but the war has pretty
much shut the city down. Thinking he sees a friend slipping out of
the rare lighted door, he slips in after him—only to find himself in
a homosexual brothel run by the baron's sometime concierge and
procurer, Jupien. The "disagreeable atmosphere" of the place, which
is frequented by politicians and other important sorts, inspires "immense curiosity."

The narrator asks Jupien for a drink and a room to rest in, but
finds he is disturbed by cries from the room next door. "I implore
you, have mercy, have mercy, have pity, let me go, don't hit me so
hard . . . I'm kissing your feet. Look, I'm grovelling. I won't do it again.
Have pity on me."—"No, scumbag. Go on blubbering and crawling

around on your knees. That's why we're going to chain you to this bed. No mercy for you." Stepping out of his room, the narrator encounters a small window, conveniently uncurtained, and sees that the man chained to the bed, like Prometheus to his rock, is the baron, covered with blood and bruises. The young man is lashing him with a cat-o'-nine-tails.

It is the summer of 1916, the summer of the Battle of the Somme, in which casualties exceeded one million, and after close to five months of fighting, the British and French forces advanced their position against the Germans by about six miles. There is no separating that knowledge from the grotesque image of the bloody old man. Charlus, imploring his young attendant not to beat him, the better only to be beaten harder, grotesquely reverses the position of those other old men dispatching young men to their fates at the front. And yet even subordinate, he remains like them in power, his pitiable, appalling, childlike figure bringing into focus the much greater bloodshed occurring elsewhere. The war changes everything? This Mme Verdurin and Charlus agree on, Charlus regretting that the strapping footmen who used to flank the splendid staircases of the great mansions of the Belle Epoque have all been sent to the war. Superficially yes, the narrator acknowledges, though, as he notes dryly, "Life continued more or less as always for many of the characters who have figured in this account," which is to say its essential superficiality is unchanged. "Everything was really the same."

In the last, revelatory, scene of *Time Regained* the war has been over for several years. The narrator is on his way to a party given by the Prince de Guermantes (bankrupted by the war, the prince, the acme of aristocratic society, has now taken bourgeois Mme Verdurin as his wife), and as always, he is in despair over his wasted life. "But it is sometimes at the moment where all seems lost that a message arrives that might save us," he notes, resorting to a cliché, one often deployed in battle stories, to account for the accident that accounts for the book in our hands: the narrator stumbles over a cobblestone, and suddenly, unexpectedly, as with the madeleine, memory returns, this time, however, accompanied by the knowledge that he has the power to set it down. "As if by enchantment," his doubts are lifted at last.

He delays entering the party and stops in the prince's library to further absorb what has happened, what is still happening. The library is no mere background to what follows: it is the place where reading—and the narrator has been identified from the first as a reader—and writing meet, the place where his own book will in time take its place. "In reading," he reflects, "one seeks to come back to one's native country" and the writer is someone who "read the unknown signs of the book within, a reading that consists of an act of creation." Books of all sorts from all sorts of places are shelved in the prince's library, and the narrator is led to describe writing as fundamentally an act of translation, which may be the first time this idea, which takes distinct form in Walter Benjamin's essay "The Task of the Translator," finds expression in a novel. It must be the first time that a novel comes to the idea as one of its culminating realizations, and it is a curious note to strike. All through the nineteenth century, as more and more literature was published, more and more of it was literature in translation. The library in which Proust's narrator stands waiting is, among other things, an image of the book now taking form in his imagination, the book in hand, a book that is full of books, some imagined, others—Dostoevsky figures importantly—from the world of literature. It is a matter of fact, in other words, that more and more books exist in the library, and in the world, thanks to translation. To say, however, that the novel is essentially an act of translation is to stake a stranger claim: on the one hand that the novel is always derivative, unoriginal, that it has no proper language of its own; on the other that, triumphant in all languages everywhere, it has transcended language to assume a universal significance. We have a figure expressive of inadequacy and defeat that is also a figure of triumphant reconciliation. Which is it? Between these alternatives Lukács's line about the novel as the form of "transcendental homelessness" comes to mind.

We have already seen Proust echo Plato (Aristophanes in *The Symposium*) in describing love as the pursuit of the whole, even if love in Proust is no less an unending disaster. In the novel, however, despair

WHAT DID YOU DO IN THE WAR?

and salvation may meet. Jupien refers sarcastically to M. de Charlus's brothel, with its visitors from all over, as a house of all nations, a house of pain (taking us back to Dr. Moreau's island) that serves temporarily and perversely as a refuge from a world at war. And yet in the aftermath of war, the narrator, coming to his wits, recognizing his calling at last in the library, is freed to see in the novel a promise of peace.

The great final party he attends—his last party in a work that is full of parties and the last party he will go to before turning to that work—was part of his earliest plan for *In Search of Lost Time*. He always described the scene as a *bal des têtes*, a masked ball, but the only masks people wear are their own features, grown haggard and almost unrecognizable with age. Those features are revealed as the true face that lay hidden under the mask of youth, which it is the vengeance of time to uncover. This final party is explicitly compared with the first great party in the book, at Mme de Saint-Euverte's, attended by the narrator's alter ego, Swann. Mme de Saint-Euverte was the presiding social goddess of the Second Empire; the empire is long gone (with the war, the whole world of Continental empires is largely gone), and she is now forgotten. To go back to that early scene, as Proust invites us to, is to find those great, strapping footmen that M. de Charlus misses so, but also to find this description, through Swann's eyes, of the ugliness and unfamiliarity of the people at that party:

> The general's monocle, stuck between his eyelids like a shell-splinter in his vulgar, scarred and overbearing face in the middle of his forehead which it dominated like the single eye of the Cyclops, appeared to Swann as a monstrous wound which it might have been glorious to receive but which was indecent to expose.

Swann in other words sees a disfigured social world full of disfigured individuals (and the monocle is a straightforward enough symbol of seeing only one thing). The monocle, "indecent to expose," also represents the wound of sex and love, and here Swann also could be said to have an advance premonition of the Great War to come, though Swann dies long before it does come, and it was still in the future when Proust wrote this scene.

But then war was always central to Proust's vision of the world, born as it is of two warring elements. On the one hand, he has an unforgivingly deterministic vision of human nature in relation to the passage of time, by which our bad desires and bad habits—and since in Proust desire is always desire for the wrong thing and habit nothing but a misguided persistence—drag each and all of us to perdition and destruction. The bloody baron and the young narrator lying in bed craving a good-night kiss from his mother are finally one and the same. Then again, on the other hand, by contrast to this predestined doom, there is the saving contingency of the madeleine, of the cobblestone, of the piece of music or work of art that absorbs our attention and sets free our desire (or sets us free from it), moments of redeeming grace—everything that sets the narrator, the writer, apart from Charlus and everyone else. There is nothing we can do to make this happen, though when it happens, there is no denying it. Proust's novel is full of chance events, underwritten by the impossible conceit that the whole of it is one immense transport, a transcendental glimpse.

This uncompromising tension between dire necessity and utter contingency—a tension between two fundamental ways of explaining what happens—gave birth to what remains the most beautiful book of the twentieth century, the one that displays the amplest curiosity and deepest sympathy, and the one that, perhaps surprisingly, given its social and personal insularity, contains the most lived experience. It is hard to believe, however, that the book would affect us so if it had not been for the war. If the actual war had not occurred, the war metaphors of the sort one encounters in Swann's description of the party at Mme de Sainte-Euverte's would remain metaphors, images, part of the apparatus of a book laden with images. The book itself, I am saying, would never have outgrown its armor of prewar decor. The war freed Proust from his period; the Great War brought out his greatness by a contingency that is finally no different from the madeleine. It is an accident that Proust might have accepted sufficiently sorrowfully as the cost and limit of art; after all, he as much as Marx was conscious that "men make their own history, but they do not make it as they please." "A book," Proust writes in *Time Regained*, "is a great cemetery where the names on most of the tombs are too worn to read."

What did the war do? It put an end to the Russian, the Austro-Hungarian, the German, and the Ottoman empires and left the British Empire impoverished and weakened. It helped bring about the Russian Revolution. It led to the establishment of a whole series of new republics and nations: Poland, Czechoslovakia, Romania, and previously unheard of protectorates around the world that would become nations like Iraq. It led to women being given the vote in the United Kingdom and the United States. While it went on, many people thought it might never end. Many people thought that as soon as it ended, a new war would begin. H. G. Wells, as we know, called it the war to end all wars. It lasted four years. It killed and wounded some forty million people. The truism is true: it changed everything.

Mann, writing in a defeated nation, had no trouble granting that. Proust rejects the truism, but then his own conviction that the war simply revealed the unchanging destructive essence of everything isn't at heart different: it remains a transformative experience of an unprecedented order. The two novelists had a lot in common—both were fascinated with sickness, sex, social status, time—and among the things that their two great novels have in common is a critical tone, mixing the descriptive and the discursive, born of a larger sense that the novel is in crisis, a crisis that the war has invested with new urgency but also put into perspective. Both writers are impatient with the one-sidedness of the turn-of-the-century novel—the one-sidedness that Gide and Wells made a virtue of—and both of them are also nostalgic for the big comprehensiveness, the enfolding impersonality, of the nineteenth-century novel. In Proust, the narrator, as a young reader, is in awe of the style of the fictional novelist Bergotte; by the end of the book, however, its studied individuality has come to seem precious. Bergotte is shown dying after leaving his sickbed to see a show of works by Vermeer, dying as he admires the little dab of yellow paint that, he feels, makes all the difference in the painter's *View of Delft*, an insight that displays Bergotte's characteristic sensitivity and genius but also its limitations. It is a fatal madeleine. Mann, for his part, wrote in alarmed reaction to his brother Heinrich's outward-facing, satirical, activist conception of the novel. Proust is continually glancing over his shoulder at the great overflowing junk shop of Balzac's *Comédie humaine*, while Mann looks to Goethe, admiring not only his renowned intelligence and judgment but his erotic appetite and energy. They don't want to copy these writers, but they do hope to match them. Both reserve a special loathing for Romain Rolland, the pacifist Vedantist who won the Nobel Prize in 1915 for his "idealism" and would go on to further distinguish himself as a Stalinist stooge. Rolland's multivolume novel *Jean-Christophe* tracks the life of his eponymous character, singled out from birth to be a great composer, dramatizing and expanding on all the important and edifying things he finds out along the way. Both writers saw this highly improving work as wholly phony.

And then there is *Ulysses*, another book with time and sex on the brain, along with a musical scheme and a vision of life as a dream; another book that makes a point of making room for everything (and more than that, anything); another book that looks back, in Joyce's case not just to the last century, but to the origins of Western civilization in ancient Greece, in order to take the measure of contemporary life and show itself to be a novel unlike any novel anyone has ever seen. Another book featuring a young man yearning to be a writer but succumbing to intellectual and physical dissolution (Stephen Dedalus, as obviously the image of its maker as Proust's Marcel); another book that offers us, in the character of Leopold Bloom, adman, Irishman, cuckold, and Jew, an everyman whose experiences and reflections, like Hans Castorp's, help us appreciate the true meaning of the human.

And another book born of the war. The first inkling of the work—the idea of a story that would present a contemporary Dubliner as a counterpart to Homer's Odysseus, to whose adventures the book would present a parallel—dates to 1906, when Joyce was still focused on the stories in his first book, *Dubliners*. It was not until 1914 that he would begin to work on the book in earnest, however, and not until 1921 that it would be done. *Ulysses* took shape with the war in the

WHAT DID YOU DO IN THE WAR?

background, though Joyce's attitude to the war was altogether differ-ent from that of Mann and Proust. As an Irish Catholic, Joyce did not support the British; as an anti-imperialist (and, as a young man, a sympathetic reader of Marx and Bakunin), he could no more support the empires on the other side, though he was grateful to the Austro-Hungarian authorities for the easygoing style with which, when war broke out, they drove him out of Trieste, where he and his family were living at the time. ("They called it a ramshackle empire. I wish to God there were more such empires!") Resettled in neutral Zurich, Joyce was, in the words of Richard Ellmann, his great biographer, "supremely indifferent to the result, so long as gunfire could not be heard."

For years, Joyce's life had been a struggle. He had fought with his family and broken with the church, left Ireland (he had no more lik-ing for Irish nationalists than for the British Empire) for a life of self-imposed exile, struggled to make a living while also finding time to write, struggled to publish his books, which publishers and printers (tasked with vetting the decency of the books that came to press) had deemed risqué or a political risk. In 1914, however, his book of sto-ries, *Dubliners*, had come out (ten years after he had put it together), and though publication of his autobiographical novel *A Portrait of the Artist as a Young Man* was blocked in England, in 1915 an American house agreed to take it on. Wells admired the book, and soon Joyce was being championed by the indefatigable Ezra Pound. The war years were working to Joyce's advantage, and when he began to receive a substantial allowance from a secret benefactor, Harriet Weaver, the editor of *The Egoist*, in which *Portrait* had been serialized, he was free for the first time in his life to work on a novel in peace. And he was hardly unaware of the background of horror. "As an artist," he said, "I am against every state . . . The state is concentric, man eccentric. Thus arises an eternal struggle . . . Naturally I can't approve of the act of a revolutionary who tosses a bomb in a theatre . . . On the other hand, have those states behaved any better which have drowned the world in a blood-bath?"

Ulysses, of course, is set before the war, on June 16, 1904, a date chosen by Joyce because it was the date of his first meeting with Nora

Barnacle, the working-class woman he settled down with and eventually married. *The Odyssey* is the story of a man coming back from war and trying to reunite with his wife. Joyce took an unusual view of Odysseus. The Greek, Joyce said to Frank Budgen, a Zurich friend, may have been a warrior, but before that he was "a war dodger who tried to evade military service by simulating madness." . . . "He was the first gentleman in Europe . . . a complete man . . . a good man. At any rate, that is what I intend that he shall be." To his hero's accomplishments, Joyce also added the invention of the tank, seeing no essential difference between a metal box and a wooden horse full of soldiers, which is a thought that Leopold Bloom could well have had.

Bloom is a perfectly unheroic *homme moyen sensuel* with an inquiring mind ("do fish ever get seasick?" he wonders at one point) and a reflective streak and a deep love of his wife, even if she is cheating on him. Unheroic, but not uncourageous, Bloom takes action on two significant occasions in *Ulysses*—insofar as anything happens in the book (otherwise, he makes breakfast, buys a bar of soap, attends a funeral, masturbates, and finally comes home and goes to bed)—in both cases with the purpose of preventing conflict. The major, defining, action of the book is Bloom's meeting with Stephen, which counts, in the book's larger symbolic structure, as the meeting of father and son, the father that Stephen desperately needs (his own being lost to drink), and the son that Bloom, whose own son died as a child, wishes he had. The meeting takes place late at night in the red-light district, and it happens when Stephen, having drunkenly picked a quarrel with two English soldiers, is about to get beaten up and/or arrested. (Everyone in this, the book's Circe chapter, is turning into a beast.) Stephen gets knocked out by a punch in the face, but Bloom remains to pick him up and lead him off, after which they talk about this and that and take a convivial piss together before heading their separate ways. When it counts, Bloom acts, and acts in his modest way like a man.

Nationalism fuels the fight Bloom fails to avert between Stephen and the soldiers —Stephen slights the king. "I'll wring the neck of any fucking bastard says a word against my bleeding fucking king," says Private Carr—and nationalism also stokes the flames of the fight that Bloom avoids, though only just, earlier in the day. Seeking a friend,

Bloom steps into the pub, where he encounters the so-called Citizen, a "broadshouldered deepchested stronglimbed frankeyed redhaired freelyfreckled shaggybearded widemouthed largenosed longheaded deepvoiced broadkneed brawnyhanded hairylegged ruddyfaced sinewyarmed" champion of all things Irish. Talk turns to politics, and Bloom, with his moderation (he won't even have a drink) and his perpetual—as the section's cynical barfly narrator dismissively puts it—"but don't you see and but on the other hand," becomes the target of the Citizen's anti-Semitic mockery. Bloom keeps his head:

> It's no use, says he. Force, hatred, history, all that. That's not life for men and women, insult and hatred. And everybody knows that it's the very opposite of that that is really life.
> What? says Alf.
> Love, says Bloom. I mean the opposite of hatred.

Eventually Bloom provokes the oafish Citizen to fury—"Your God was a jew," Bloom says, "like me"—blind fury that allows him (this is the Cyclops episode of the book) to escape. He has saved his skin. He has also shown himself to be courageous and resourceful in the cause of peace.

Ellmann calls *Ulysses* a pacifist epic, which is to say an oxymoron, since epic heroes are fighters. Joyce's novel sets out to refashion the novel and with it our whole perception of literary tradition as willfully as Mann's and Proust's big books, and like them, it has to be seen as a kind of antidote to the toxins of the war, a love philter. (How strange and striking that these immensely long, complex books could all be said to enfold, like fortune cookies, a single platitude: love is all there is!) But *Ulysses* differs profoundly from *The Magic Mountain* and *In Search of Lost Time* in its relation to language. Proust and Mann are of course great artists in language, but the greatness of their art arises in relation to and serves to highlight language's capacity, sometimes treacherous, for transparency. *Ulysses* is not like that. *Ulysses* puts language up front and center. And *Ulysses* is completely without a

discursive or even reflective, much less edifying, dimension, a whole
dimension of literature that Joyce as good as rips up and throws away.
Charting the passage of a day, the book's effects are all present effects.
Joyce's distinctive take on stream of consciousness—"as if," as Ellmann beautifully describes it, "a multitude of small bells were ringing in the mind"—contributes to this sense of presentness, but more
than anything it is born of Joyce's endlessly inventive relationship to
words: nonce words, neologisms, foreign words, archaic words, ten-
dollar words, technical words, dirty words, unknown words, puns,
and countless plays on words are unrelenting and unending in *Ulysses*,
and there are times when the book resembles nothing so much as a
wall covered with graffiti.

The reader of *Ulysses* is always being made aware of the words on
the page and of Joyce's way with words, Joyce's ear for spoken speech
and gift for mimicry, his appetite for parody and pastiche. This can
try the reader's patience—it can seem a product of obsession as much
as artistry, especially since one thing Joyce did not always possess was
a sense of proportion—but then he will win back our attention with
the exactness of his observations of the world and the word. Pound
perceptively described him as a "composer of sentences"—in this his
achievement will prove complementary to Stein's, though Joyce is
quite free of Stein's taste for theory and wish to set herself and her
writing up as an example for others—and *Ulysses*, massive with minutiae, is a book in which the part dwarfs the whole. Bloom notices a
teapot: "It sat there, dull and squat, its spout stuck out." This is not just
a description; this is a still life in monosyllables, a sentence as definite
in shape as the thing it describes. He visits a busy newsroom, and
Joyce makes up a word—a word apt for a newsroom because it could
be taken for a typo—to describe what he hears: "That door too sllt
creaking, asking to be shut. Everything speaks in its own way. Sllt."

Everything speaks in its own way. In the "Circe" section, set in
a whorehouse and written as a theatrical extravaganza, a set of personified Waterfalls enter: "Phaucaphaucaphauca," they say, just like
Private Carr. The now familiar term *stream of consciousness* had been
taken from William James's *Principles of Psychology* by the novelist
May Sinclair to describe what Joyce was doing in *Portrait of the Artist*,

where his seeming transcription of raw thought served him by re-
leasing the self and the self's words for itself from their subservience
to conscience, the invigilator of church and family and nation. Describing the free flow of the stream of consciousness was a question
of honesty and veracity but also quite simply of freedom: that is how
it is, and there is no reason to pretend otherwise (or rather every reason not to). In *Ulysses*, however, Joyce goes beyond that to stream the
consciousness of language itself, saying to his expositor Stuart Gilbert, "From my point of view it hardly matters whether a technique
is 'veracious' or not; it has served me as a bridge over which to march
my 18 episodes; and once I have got my troops across, the opposing
forces can, for all I care, blow the bridge sky-high."

Stream of consciousness had been welcomed by advanced readers, but this new turn confounded even Joyce's staunchest advocates,
including Harriet Weaver, who was publishing chapters of *Ulysses*
in her magazine *The Egoist*. Pound suggested that Joyce keep his focus on Stephen, only to have Joyce respond, "Stephen no longer interests me. He has a shape that can't change." Stephen is a troubled,
self-thwarting character—he is in a rut, it is true—but here Joyce is
making a point not only about his particular character but about the
place of character in fiction, which was coming to matter less and less
to him. The "Oxen of the Sun" episode gave (and continues to give)
readers particular trouble, and it is certainly representative of where
he was going. Set in a maternity hospital, set at the physical center of
the book as a whole, it describes Stephen and his friends carousing
while a child is being delivered in the room next door—it is a scene
of impiety and excess that Joyce presents in the form of a wildly luxuriant, often inscrutable pastiche of the development of the English
language. "In woman's womb word is made flesh but in the spirit of
the maker all flesh that passes becomes the word that shall not pass
away. This is the postcreation," Joyce writes, echoing the Gospel of
John, and the postcreation—the reincarnations of the world in the infinite forms of the word—seems at times to matter more to Joyce than
creation itself, unless, that is, he is consumed by a hopeless desire
to return to the womb of the creative word itself. The stream of language will take him finally from stream of consciousness to the great

opaque and glittering swell of language that is *Finnegans Wake*: "river-run, past Eve and Adam's, from swerve of shore to bend of bay . . ."

"I can't express myself in English without enclosing myself in a tradition," Joyce wrote to a friend. "I'd like a language that is above all languages to which all do service." Joyce's dream of a metalanguage is comparable to Proust's describing all novels as translations, and the metaphor of domination here makes it that much clearer that his prolific, unfettered, spendthrift, debauched, often excremental language exists to resist domination by others. The late-Victorian critic Edmund Gosse, a sometime supporter of Joyce's work, was appalled and disgusted by *Ulysses*, but he saw things clearly enough when he said that "the character of Mr. Joyce's notoriety . . . is partly political," his book an "anarchical production, infamous in taste, in style, in everything." Every kind of language is admitted into *Ulysses*, and so language is set free and rendered innocent, like the newborn child whose babble all language is in the end as in the beginning, and the reader is set free too—though this is something Joyce's readers have often been curiously slow to grasp. The reader is under no obligation to figure the book out, much less decode it (though Joyce enjoyed the rumors that he had been a spy for the Germans during the war and the whole book was a cypher); readers are free simply to make their way through it, the way Bloom makes his way around Dublin, taking note of whatever strikes him along the way. *Ulysses*, like a day or a city or a language or a person, is in a profound sense meaningless. Then again, the book of a single day exists finally to celebrate the everyday while also observing the classical unities, but above all to preserve the vision of an eternal day that Joyce retained from his religious upbringing.

So what about the elaborate scaffolding, the carefully worked out correspondences to *The Odyssey*, the scene, hour, organ, color, symbol, art, and technic that Joyce told Stuart Gilbert he had assigned to each chapter, which Gilbert relayed to the world—all the arcana that scholars have devoted so much time to elaborating on and that readers have often felt they must, as best they can, master if they are to "get" *Ulysses*? Joyce described all this as "his way of working," and that pretty much seems the limit of the importance he assigned to it. He worked that way because his mind worked that way. In the 1930s, Nabokov dined with the master and was taken aback to hear him pooh-pooh the book's mythological underpinning—Joyce described Gilbert's book as a too-successful ad campaign—and the critic Hugh Kenner has even suggested that had Joyce not called the book *Ulysses*, no one would have even noticed the connection. The armature, in other words, is a kind of filing system that enabled Joyce to put stuff in and find a place for it, and of course it accommodates all kinds of things, including a host of explanatory systems, just as Bloom and Stephen spend their day trying to explain a variety of things. It's human to try to explain things, just as it's human to lust or take a dump. In any case, it's the stuff rather than the filing that matters, even if, in finding a classical precedent for his work, Joyce was doing what docile students had been immemorially urged to do by their professors. This good student, however, was bent on blowing the school up—or, as he famously joked, leaving the professors to go on studying what he was up to.

In the world of "leaflets, brochures, articles and posters" that the war had brought on, there was, Walter Benjamin remarked, no place left for the "universal gesture of the book." Mann, Proust, and Joyce could be said to have feared that that might be the case—they all had been educated in the nineteenth-century cult of artistic greatness—which is why they each tried to make just such a universal gesture. The war made such a gesture that much more necessary, and it was the willingness of these writers to risk it that immediately made them public figures. Some kind of writing that reflected the way things had fallen apart but also stuck them back together, that suggested it would be possible to put things together again, was called for. Mann, Proust, and Joyce worked from an old-fashioned conviction to which the war had given new urgency, and readers responded. Their work is ambitious and difficult and was met, in the case of Joyce, by legal prohibition, but not only was it not ignored, its centrality was almost immediately accepted, and on an international scale, and this as much because of the challenge to translation it presented as in spite of it. The towering uniqueness of the books was taken as a bid for universality. Interestingly, what people were not looking for right after the war was more war literature. Henri Barbusse's *Under Fire* came out during the war, an early version of Jünger's *Storm of Steel* just after the war, but most of the famous World War I novels—Erich Maria Remarque's *All Quiet on the Western Front*, for example—would wait until the late 1920s and the 1930s to appear. In the immediate aftermath of the war, the urgent business was not so much description as destruction of whatever had been complicit in the disaster and, beyond that, a vision of reconstruction. Perhaps even more to the point, *Ulysses, In Search of Lost Time,* and *The Magic Mountain* were books that remained, in the face of the innumerable trials and disasters of the heart and body and soul that they recorded as clearly as anyone ever had, massively imperturbable.

So yes, Mann, Proust, and Joyce showed that the universal gesture was possible, though the nature of the gesture in their work remains deeply ambiguous. The books are crammed with real life, but they are also dream books, fantasies. They explore a range of ways of explaining the world and then retract them. They offer paths to freedom but are almost hermetically sealed; they speak for everyone, yet they are self-absorbed; they are new but also oddly archaic; they contain the whole of reality but are wholly devoted to art. I have presented Joyce's *Ulysses* as a blow struck for freedom, and it was received that way. George Bernard Shaw called it "a revolting record of a disgusting phase of civilisation; but it is a truthful one." T. S. Eliot, who admired it deeply, wondered aloud to Virginia Woolf if it would not put an end to writing. *Ulysses* is a kind of time capsule of life before the war, as are *The Magic Mountain* and *In Search of Lost Time*, and like them, it is encyclopedic in scale and ambition, a monument to human civilization that looms all the more imposingly when the very existence of such a thing has been comprehensively called into question.

Ulysses, however, has a radicality that set it apart, and that still does: an extraordinary demonstration of linguistic absorption and invention whose power comes from its continuing willingness to court

failure, or its single-minded, even solipsistic, obliviousness to the possibility of failure, a solipsism that would be the end of language altogether.
"Ideas, classifications, political terminologies leave me indifferent; they
are things one has passed beyond," Joyce told a friend when he returned
to Trieste after the war. And when another old acquaintance inquired,
"And how have you spent the war years, professor?" Joyce answered,
"Oh yes, I was told there was a war going on."

PART II

A SCATTERING
OF SPARKS

9. FOR THERE SHE WAS

VIRGINIA WOOLF'S *MRS. DALLOWAY*

It had been, she realized, a very busy few days. First, the Americans had dropped by, "impressive to me . . . for their vivacity which combined with their large well-nourished bodies made them appear powerful . . . & then because they were simple and intensely in love with the League of Nations . . ." "Almost instantly," they had been followed by a less welcome visitor, Harriet Weaver, "the Editress of the Egoist . . . [in] her neat mauve suit fit[ting] both soul and body . . . her table manners . . . those of a well-bred hen." The next day, it was down to the country to visit an old friend, who held forth "about all manner of things; on growing old, on loneliness; on religion; on morality . . . on French literature; on education; on Jews; on marriage; & on the Lysistrata. Occasionally he read a quotation from a book by Proust . . ." Come morning, she returned to London to view two paintings another friend had just acquired at auction in Paris:

> There are 6 apples in the Cezanne picture. What can 6 apples not be? I began to wonder . . . We carried [the painting] into the next room, & Lord! how it showed up the pictures there, as if you put a real stone among sham ones; the canvas of the others seemed scraped with a thin layer of rather cheap paint. The apples positively got redder & rounder & greener.

The day ended with a meeting of a local branch of the Women's Co-operative Guild, a socialist-leaning group devoted to advancing working women's suffrage, health, and economic well-being. "In spite of their solemn passivity," she observes, "they have a deeply hidden and inarticulate desire for something beyond daily life . . . They wish me to get them a speaker on Sex Education."

This is Virginia Woolf's diary entry for April 18, 1918, her excitement and curiosity and wit and concern and ambition and not inconsiderable malice, her whole personality, marking the page, as they do throughout the wonderful journal she kept until the end of her life. Woolf's journal was a place not just to record whom she had seen and what she had done, but to practice writing: a sketchbook of sorts, but also a document that, she imagined, "old Virginia" might in future years go back to, to get a glimpse of who she had been, for better or for worse. This entry captures the tone of the diary, which is the core of Woolf's work as much as Gide's *Journals* are of his. It is also a glimpse of a whole new world that, with the end of the war, was coming into view—the actual world of the twentieth century—a world in which Woolf and her friends would play a decisive part.

Not that in April 1918 the war was over. It was raging, and the English and French had just suffered a defeat in the German spring offensive of 1918. Troops were still being shipped off to the front, and when in this same entry Woolf mentions her husband, Leonard, being out "visiting prisoners," she is referring to people—the philosopher Bertrand Russell was one of them—who had gone to jail as conscientious objectors. But though the war had not ended, it was clear that it had put an end, one way or another, to the world that existed before the war and that it was time now to give shape to the years ahead. Leonard Woolf, a political crusader throughout his life, had published an influential sketch of a plan for world government as early as 1915—hence the visit of those admirably "simple" Americans—while the friend bursting with the news of the French literary sensation, Proust, is Roger Fry, the art critic who had introduced postimpressionism to a scandalized London in 1910 and in 1918 was busy overseeing the Omega Workshops, where the decorative principles of the new art were applied to houseware and furniture and other practical objects, the better to liberate domestic life from Victorian stuff and upholstery. The friend with the Cézanne is John Maynard Keynes ("like quicksilver on a sloping board—a little inhuman but very kindly, as inhuman people are"), who in 1919 would participate in the Paris Peace Conference and who, in his *The Economic Consequences of the Peace*, would denounce the ensuing Versailles Treaty as a terrible threat to the stable and peaceful postwar international order that Leonard Woolf and his Americans were hoping for.

And here we see Woolf herself grappling with "the woman question" and the question of class that would loom large in the decades to come. In the UK, women gained the vote in November 1918, just as soon as the war ended, and it had become commonplace to say that the war would never have happened at all if women had been able to vote. Woolf had always supported female suffrage. She was conscious too of the toll economic inequality took on women's lives, and she went on to write *A Room of One's Own*, about the plight of women who lacked autonomy and independent livelihoods. At the same time, as a pure product of the educated upper middle class, she was acutely conscious of the difference between her, a "lady," and the other women at the local Women's Co-operative Guild. In 1919 she and Leonard brought out her story "Kew Gardens" from their new Hogarth Press (begun in 1917, almost as a hobby, it became an important institution of the postwar years, publishing translations of Dostoevsky and Gertrude's Stein's essay "Composition as Explanation," not to mention Woolf's own novels), and she was leery of showing it to the women in the guild, since it made fun of them.

As to Miss Weaver—the most prominent target of Woolf's snobbery—in the entry above she has come to see if the Woolfs would publish *Ulysses*, and the answer she received was that they would not. It was, they said, too long (even if at this point it was not finished), and though Leonard would have second thoughts, he soon decided that whatever the merits of the book as a novel, there was no chance of it not being prosecuted for indecency, as Joyce's *Portrait of the Artist as a Young Man* already had been. Virginia, for her part, thoroughly disliked Joyce's work—of *Portrait*, she had written to her brother-in-law, Clive Bell, "I can't see what he's after, though having spent 5/- on him, I did my level best, and was only beaten by the unutterable boredom." In her April 18 journal entry, the memory of Miss Weaver's prim presence leads her to wonder, "How did she ever come in contact with Joyce and the rest? Why does their filth seek exit from her mouth?" And yet Woolf came back to *Ulysses*, or it came back to her, because even before its publication in Paris in 1922, it had become the defining novel of the new moment. For Woolf, like many other writers of the next two decades, from William Faulkner to Louis Guilloux to Carlo Emilio Gadda to Ernest Hemingway, the book was an inescapable reference point, even if her relation to the book was one of antagonism. She disliked it intensely, but she could not dismiss it from mind. *Ulysses* was provocation; *Ulysses* was a challenge. Why did it matter so much to others when, to her mind, it so clearly fell short? The postwar era would be a new era, and that called for a new kind of novel, as distinctive as those apples of Cézanne's. *Ulysses* wasn't it, she believed, though many seemed to feel it was. What was?

And what kind of novelist was Virginia Woolf? That was another question. Because in 1918, for all her ambition and confidence and connections, she still felt herself very much on the uncertain threshold of her writing life. She was thirty-six, and though she had published a novel, *The Voyage Out*, in 1915, she was better known as the scion of a famous family than for her own accomplishments. Her father, Leslie Stephen, had been an eminent late Victorian, an influential editor and widely read essayist, bearded and beetle-browed, a courageous agnostic at a time when the educated still clung to God, a friend to everyone from James Russell Lowell—the poet who was the American ambassador to the Court of St. James's and Virginia's godfather—to Thomas Hardy and Henry James, all of whom would regularly visit the Stephens when Virginia was growing up. Her mother, Julia, also from a distinguished upper-middle-class family, was a celebrated beauty who dedicated herself to the care of the sick and dying. The Stephens epitomized the liberal intelligentsia of their day: sociable, cultured, high-minded, practical, and indefatigable in their devotion to clear thinking and worthy causes.

Julia Stephen died suddenly when Virginia, the youngest of her children, was thirteen. The event devastated Leslie, whose subsequent

self-pitying and self-flagellating gloom and misery not only trauma-
tized the adolescent Virginia and her older sister Vanessa but also
convinced them that there had been something rotten about their
upbringing. Losing their mother, they had also in a sense lost their
father, or rather found another who was cruel, childish, and false to
all the fine ideals he, as much as their mother, had espoused. When,
in 1904, to everyone's relief, Leslie died, Virginia, Vanessa, and their
brothers Adrian and Thoby all moved from the parental home to
the elegant but slightly raffish neighborhood of Bloomsbury, where
their house on Fitzroy Square served as a meeting place for a circle of
friends, many gay, that Adrian and Thoby had made at Cambridge.
(The sisters, it's worth noting, never attended any school of any kind,
though Leslie Stephen encouraged and admired Virginia's intellect
and imagination and daydreamed of her being a writer like him.) The
Bloomsbury circle, and they soon came to think of themselves as a
circle of the like-minded and enlightened, was determined to break
with the Victorian past: at Fitzroy Square they took down the curtains and let in the light, and they never ceased to marvel at how different everything looked. There were colors.

Virginia Stephen had married Leonard Woolf, another Cambridge
graduate, in 1912, and finished her first novel, *The Voyage Out*, soon
after. She then suffered a terrible mental breakdown, and, after the
publication of the novel in 1915, filled with dread that she would be
"jeered at," she suffered another. It took her almost a year to recover,
and Leonard worried that writing would cause her to fall apart again.
Yet in 1916 she was working on a new novel, *Night and Day*, which she
continued to labor at in April 1918, on her back in bed with, she later
told a friend, a strict limitation of her time to write.

The novel had required self-control and was itself an exercise in
control. Like her first book, it was about unconventional young people
trying to make sense of their lives, but it was even more conventionally novelistic in form: after finishing it in the fall of 1918, she compared it to an art student's careful study of a piece of classical statuary.
It was better than her first book, more grown-up, she felt, but she also
suspected that all the work that had gone into it had hurt it. To her
brother-in-law Clive Bell, whose criticism she feared, she described

it as "that crude laborious novel of mine." Her problem, however, was not so much the novel as it was that her critical standards had changed, largely in response to two influences: the Russians and modern painting. The Russians, especially Dostoevsky and Chekhov, seemed to her attentive to the shifting and treacherous currents of inner life in a way that no English writer was or had been. The painters joined formal rigor and personal vision with a flair that was entirely missing from the novel. They painted paintings that looked like no other paintings and nothing else—and they made you see the world anew. There was color.

So at the same time she was working away at getting *Night and Day* out of the way, she was trying her hand at something quite different, conducting a kind of experiment, making small, intimate sketches where she set out to track the movements of the mind and eye as closely as possible in a newly free and suggestive language, favoring texture, in terms Roger Fry had suggested to her, over structure or plot. She was seeking to be true to experiences and sensation rather than to the given forms of narrative; she was seeking a style of her own. (What she was doing may be compared with Proust's exercises in *Against Sainte-Beuve*, where he hit on the composition by tone that made *In Search of Lost Time* possible.) Meanwhile, she and Leonard were learning to work the printing press they had just acquired, partly as a therapeutic activity for her but partly because they wanted a press of their own. In 1917 they set up and printed 134 copies of a slim book, *Two Stories*, one by each of them. This was "Publication No. 1" of the Hogarth Press.

Hers was called "The Mark on the Wall," and in it the narrator of this story without a narrative perceives something, a mark, on the opposite wall and can't quite figure out what it is. Puzzling over it, she finds herself thinking about thinking—thinking about the ways we explain ourselves to ourselves and come to affirm who we are:

> All the time I'm dressing up the figure of myself in my own mind, lovingly, stealthily, not openly adoring it, for if I did that, I should catch myself out, and stretch my hand at once for a book for self-protection. Indeed it is curious how instinc-

tively one protects the image of oneself from idolatry or any other kind of handling that could make it ridiculous, or too unlike the original to be believed any longer. Or is it so so very curious after all? It is a matter of great importance. Supposing the looking-glass smashes, the image disappears, and the romantic figure with the green of forest details all around it is there no longer, but only that shell of a person which is seen by other people—what an airless, shallow, bald, prominent world it becomes! A world not to be lived in. As we gaze at each other in omnibuses and underground railways, we are looking into the mirror; that accounts for the vagueness, the gleam of glassiness, in our eyes. And the novelist in the future will realize more and more the importance of these reflections, for of course there is not one reflection but an almost infinite number; those are the depths they will explore, those the phantoms they will pursue, leaving the description of reality out of their stories, taking a knowledge of it for granted, as the Greeks did and Shakespeare perhaps—but these generalizations are very worthless. The military sound of the word is enough. It recalls leading articles, cabinet ministries . . .

"The Mark on the Wall" is as much manifesto as meditation, mixing up and mulling over the personal, the political, the sexual, and the aesthetic. One of the things that's striking about this particular passage is its studied irresolution. First it announces a problem of identity, its vulnerability, suggestibility, and susceptibility to misrepresentation, if not self-betrayal, its essential uncertainty and unreliability—all familiar enough. Then, in the figure of the "novelist of the future" (the novelist who in the future Woolf will be), it proposes a kind of answer to that problem, since the novelist of the future, like the greatest geniuses of the past, can be counted on to see past all such superficial and cheating identifications while beckoning us on to a new sense of the freedom and multiplicity of the self. And this is familiar enough, too. What is really interesting, however, is what happens after that: the abrupt flinching recoil from that very prospect, dismissed as yet another falsification, a generalization, a power play or a kowtow to power—"worthless." Everything is called into question again, and this is unsettling, but not as unsettling as the further realization that its being called into question reflects a desire or determination to account for nothing less than everything. In the mark on the wall, as in the vanishing point, a whole world is supposed to come into perspective, and it's not wrong to see the mark of madness in this impulse to find a supreme significance in something completely accidental. Yet the madness is under control here: at the end, the mark on the wall is revealed to be a snail, a conventional twist that makes fun of the conventional requirement that fiction show things as they really are. Then again, the revelation, made by a companion who is on his way out the door to buy a newspaper—another kind of account of things, ostensibly as true as they come—arrives like this: "Curse this war; God damn this war! . . . All the same, I don't see why we should have a snail on our wall." This is inadvertent, humorous, tending to put things in proportion, but at the same time it turns the mark on the wall into the biblical writing on the wall. In "The Mark on the Wall," seemingly a mere sketch, Woolf finds a way to bring out the biggest questions, the life and death questions, of her day.

"The Mark on the Wall" is a little coup de théâtre, and Bell gratified Woolf by calling it "the best prose written in our day." Woolf had found a way of writing that was her own—she was no longer fitting her and her friend's lives into the starchy outfits of a bygone generation—and she could also say to herself that what she was working on was nothing like the endless inventory of the contents of consciousness—what she dismissed as the interminable havering of the "damned egotistical self"—that made Joyce so tedious to her. "The Mark on the Wall" and the other similar sketches she was working on were full of concentrated life, but was this new kind of writing good for a whole novel? The same entry in which she disparages Joyce goes on to ask, "Suppose one thing should open out of another . . . only not for 10 pages but 200 or so—doesn't that have the looseness & lightness I want: doesn't that get closer & yet keep form & speed, & enclose"—what else?—"everything, everything?" She would try to do that in her novel *Jacob's Room*.

Everything had also been altered by Woolf's encounter, in the fall of 1918, not long after she finished *Night and Day*, with T. S. Eliot. Eliot fascinated her. She described him on that first meeting as "a polished, cultivated, elaborate young American, talking so slow, that each word seems to have a special finish allotted it. But beneath the surface, it is fairly evident that he is very intellectual, intolerant, with strong views of his own, & a poetic creed." He showed his poems to the Woolfs—"I became more or less conscious of a very intricate & highly organised framework of poetic belief"—who went on to publish his first book, *Prufrock and Other Observations*. (They would also publish *The Waste Land*.) To Woolf, Eliot seemed representative of a younger generation, his mind "not yet blunted and blurred," "his views dominant and subversive," though she also suspected that "if anyone asked him whether he meant what he said, he would have to say no, very often." His reticence and his assurance provoked and attracted her. She feared his judgment, and she wanted his approval. He was a touchstone, not easily touched.

And Eliot, from the moment she met him, was emphatic that *Ulysses* was the new novel that really mattered, presenting "the life of man in 16 incidents, all taking place (I think) in one day. This, so far as he has seen it, is extremely brilliant," praising it and touting its importance in such a way that he succeeded in getting the Woolfs to consider publishing it again. To Virginia, his admiration for Joyce was all the more striking because of his seeming indifference to her work. "Will he become 'Tom'? . . . Not that Tom admires my writing, damn him." Some months later, however, she records, "Eliot astounded me by praising Monday & Tuesday!"—the slim new volume in which she had collected "The Mark on the Wall"—"This really delighted me." Then again, this very same entry ends "Ulysses he says is prodigious."

She continued to wrestle with the book herself. In 1918 and 1919 she read the chapters that had come out in *The Little Review*, and then she published an essay, "Modern Novels," in which she described Joyce as the "most notable" of the young writers. (Woolf seems to have had a fixed idea that he was a good deal younger than she was, and she noted with surprise, after his death in January 1941, not long before her own in March, that he was almost exactly her age.) Privately, however, she continued to feel that his writing, however beautiful it could be, failed to compensate for the self-centered and self-consciously shocking character of the book. Then, in 1922, after *Jacob's Room* was finished and she had started work on a story that Eliot had gratifyingly said he might like to publish in *The Criterion*, the new journal he was editing, she decided to give *Ulysses* another go. The whole book had at last been published in permissive Paris, and though she begrudged the priceyness of the volume, she bought a copy and set out to read it through.

She didn't have mixed feelings this time. She hated it:

> I should be reading Ulysses, and fabricating my case for & against. I have read 200 pages so far—not a third; & have been amused, stimulated, charmed, interested by the first 2 or 3 chapters—to the end of the Cemetery scene; & then puzzled, bored, irritated, & disillusioned as by a queasy undergraduate scratching his pimples . . . An illiterate, underbred book it seems to me; the book of a self taught working man, & we all know how distressing they are, how egotistic, insistent, raw, striking, & ultimately nauseating. When one can have the cooked flesh, why have the raw?

A cry of condescension and disgust that is interrupted by a second cry, "And Tom, great Tom, thinks this is on a par with War & Peace!" She added later, "But I think if you are aneamic, as Tom is, there is glory in blood. Being fairly normal myself I am soon ready for the classics."

It is easy—it has long been a favorite ploy of Woolf's detractors—to deplore her snobbery. It's also easy—and common too—to point out that elsewhere she offered a more measured assessment of Joyce. The important thing here, however, is to respect the energy of her aroused indignation both at *Ulysses* and at Eliot's championing of the book—to recognize the almost desperate urgency behind this sneering and furious response.

What was at stake? Well, here was this immense book that was certainly immensely new and that had made an immense impression—

for years it had been the talk of the town, and it had even been put
on trial. But it was also, as countless readers, admiring or not, have
faced over the years, a trial to read, and Woolf was not wrong about
that. Certainly the book matched *War and Peace* in bulk, and its title
courted comparison to a foundational work of Western literature. To
Woolf, however, the book seemed both schematic and shapeless, and
its physical size and the size of its ambition only underscored what
she saw as the puniness of the actual accomplishment. But then, next
to *Ulysses*, wouldn't her *Jacob's Room* appear not just slim but small?
Woolf was forty years old. In the spring she had been seriously ill,
enough that she had drawn up her will. Her mental health was always
shaky. On finishing *Jacob*, she had written in her diary that at least she
had found her voice, but perhaps that voice was too faint, too small, to
hear?

  This was not just a question of competitiveness. Yes, her sense of
her own self-worth, as a writer, as a critic, was threatened, but more
than that, her sense of—and this was something she said had mattered
more to her than anything—"literature itself." Woolf—this was another link to Eliot—was rebellious out of a love of tradition, looking
back to Defoe and Austen for inspiration rather than to the established
celebrities of the day. She had inherited this love, worship even, of literature from her father, with whom she had so many quarrels, from
whom she had also inherited a concept of literary greatness: literature
was all well and good, but nothing much unless it aspired to greatness, though greatness took always surprising forms. Was *Ulysses*
great? If it was, then her very idea of literature was wrong.

  I think, too, that Woolf may well have been sensitive to and scared
by the madness of *Ulysses*. Because if the book puts everything together, it does so with a mad single-mindedness, playing as it were by
nothing but its own rules. Joyce himself was alert to this aspect of his
book: each chapter, we have seen him remark, left a scorched field behind. Woolf, for her part, had personally experienced how the mind
consumes itself in madness. What held Joyce together threatened to
tear her apart.

  On the sixth of September, Woolf wrote that she was finished with
Ulysses; it is "a mis-fire." Just then she was also reading the proofs of

her own *Jacob's Room*; her judgment of her own work was also dismissive: "The thing now reads thin and pointless . . . and I expect
to be told that I've written a graceful fantasy, without much bearing
on real life." This is an author hedging her bets, but also an author
who wants to move on. "Nature," she continues, and in spite of the
guarding irony, she means it, "obligingly supplies me with the illusion
that I am about to write something good: something rich, & deep,
& fluent & hard as nails, while bright as diamonds." There was, for
example, the story Eliot had expressed interest in publishing. Back
in June, she had written, "If they say this [*Jacob's Room*] is all a clever
experiment, I shall produce Mrs. Dalloway in Bond Street as the finished product." By the fourth of October the story was finished, and
though Eliot rejected it, the story was not the end of the story. Some
ten days later she notes that "Mrs Dalloway has branched into a book;
& I adumbrate here a study of insanity & suicide; the world seen by
the sane & the insane side by side," and as the reviews of *Jacob* came
in (respectful, but not awed, and the sales were poor), she worked fe-
verishly on the new book. "I want to think out Mrs Dalloway. I want
to foresee this book better than the other, & get the utmost out of it."
In the meantime, she was reading Proust, and she had been shocked
and unsettled by the death of Katherine Mansfield, who, she wrote,
had produced the "only writing I have ever been jealous of." Always, she
is working on the new novel, which, in May 1923, she notes that she is
thinking of calling *The Hours*.

She would rewrite *Ulysses*—and exorcise it.

Mrs. Dalloway is a book in twelve sections that takes place between
the morning and night of a single day. The setting is in Central London, the day is an exceptionally hot one in June, June 1923, we eventually learn, though at the start of the book we are simply told "the War
was over." How things have changed after the war will be one of the
themes, but more important than that is the passage and toll of time
itself. Big Ben strikes at the beginning of the book and then regularly
throughout (at the exact center it strikes noon), and the striking of
its great bells is associated with a motif—"the leaden circles dissolve

in the air"—that remains constant no matter who, in the book's not insignificant cast of characters, happens to hear it. *Mrs. Dalloway* is a book without an identifiable narrator, but Woolf's use of this poetic phrase not only establishes a specific authorial voice but sustains authority: what you are reading, we're to infer, is as undeniable and mysterious, as real, as the passage of time.

The main character is, of course, Mrs. Dalloway. We see the world through her eyes even as we also see her through the eyes of a number of subsidiary characters, some who have known her for years, some who just catch sight of her passing on the street. Clarissa Dalloway is fifty-one years old, the wife of a wealthy conservative MP, Richard Dalloway. He's dull but dependable, a classic dogs and horses sort of English gentleman. She's beautiful, charming, waspish, wound a little tight. People wonder that they're married, and so at times does she. Still, she recognizes the larger social claims her husband's career makes on her, and she loves to throw parties. There is in fact a party scheduled for the evening of the day on which the story takes place: important people will be there, the prime minister himself.

The book's famous opening line—"Mrs. Dalloway said she would buy the flowers herself"—plunges us into the midst of things but also tells us something specific. We see Mrs. Dalloway in her official social capacity, through her own eyes but also through the eyes of the servant she is addressing, but we also see her stepping away into the—to us, perhaps to her—uncharted wilderness of "herself." The first section of the book shows her making her way through the busy streets of the fashionable neighborhood of Westminster, crossing paths with various acquaintances, some of whom will appear again, observing the bustle of the city, the prettiness of St. James's Park, delving into memories of the past: it unfolds, in other words, in the contested no-man's-land between the inner self and the world at large. (The war is over, but this battlefield is never conquered.) Mrs. Dalloway steps out the door—immediately she is invested with her first name, Clarissa—to exult in the fine day and to remember the summer mornings of her youth. (Morning returns us to the morning of life; Woolf's book is from beginning to end meticulously staged.) She recalls too how back then a friend, Peter Walsh, would break in on her elation, troubling and yet intriguing her. His words still stick in her mind. Not just a friend, we soon learn, but a suitor whose proposal she rejected, the man who represents the life that might have been. (He is quick, restless, unconventional, not your garden-variety male; he wanted to write; he is utterly unlike her husband.) He disappeared into India, but she hears from him from time to time, dull letters she doesn't respond to. He is supposed to be back in London one of these days.

He has in fact just returned, and will be one of two major subsidiary characters in the novel. He is still in love with Clarissa, still smarting from her rejection, though what brings him to the city is an affair he has been having with a married woman. He needs advice about divorce; he will need a new job to support his new wife. Unexpectedly, Peter decides to pay a visit to Clarissa, and her servants admit "the elderly man at the door." They talk woodenly. They touch on the past. She invites him to her party. Suddenly he seizes her by the shoulder—is she happy, he wants to know—at which point her teenage daughter comes in: "'Here is my Elizabeth,' said Clarissa, emotionally, histrionically, perhaps."

And so the book proceeds through the day to the party in the evening, artfully interweaving the impressions and reflections of Clarissa and Peter and other lesser figures to fashion a picture of their pasts and of the present day. Clarissa and her contemporaries are survivors from a vanished world, and the changes that have taken place in their lives, ever more rapidly in the aftermath of the war, continually strike them. Clarissa thinks how an uncle held that you knew a woman's worth from her gloves, while her daughter wouldn't think of wearing gloves. Peter, absent from London for so long, returns at the end of the day to sit on the terrace of his hotel, taking in the "great revolution" of daylight saving time:

> The prolonged evening was new to him. It was inspiriting, rather. For as the young people went by with their despatch-boxes, awfully glad to be free, proud too of stepping this famous pavement, joy of a kind, cheap, tinselly, if you like, but all the same rapture, flushed their faces. They dressed well too;

pink stockings; pretty shoes. They would now have two hours
at the pictures. It sharpened, it refined them, the yellow-blue
evening light.

And then the party. Everyone is there, or at least a good many of
the people we have met in the pages of the book and in the course
of the day. The prime minister and other dignitaries and Peter Walsh
and, surprisingly, another friend from the past, Sally Seton, who
had a crush on Clarissa and to whom Clarissa was drawn, and the
thought of what might have come of that is in the air, though of
course it was unthinkable, or perhaps, we imagine, because the attachment remains too strong. Now, after the war, the fact that they
were is becoming admissible, and perhaps to be openly gay is now
possible. Sally, however, has gone on to have six children and live in
the country, where Clarissa has never visited her—out of snobbery,
Sally supposes, or, we may imagine, perhaps Sally means too much
to Clarissa.

The party shows us a particular class of people socializing, but,
more important, it functions as a metaphor for the "life" that means
so much to Clarissa and that is continually cropping up in Woolf's
criticism of the time as the ne plus ultra of the novel: it represents the
abiding ties of community and friendship; it brings out the solitude
and fear of being loveless that we can never escape. It is a microcosm
of the larger macrocosm that is London and the world at large. So
everyone is there, and at the same time all the questions that have
arisen in the book—about youth and age and identity and love and
what, finally, it is to live a good life—are there too, hanging in the air,
to be taken up or forgotten as may be. But the book is over.

Everyone is there, but no, the reader is very aware that one person
is not. We all know just how many people the "everyone" in "everyone
was there" excludes, and in recognition of that, Woolf's book is carefully designed to accommodate the other, the one who is always left
out, whose identity is to be no one. For though Mrs. Dalloway is the
main character, the book complements and contrasts her with another
character very much not of her world, of whom she knows nothing—
Septimus Smith. In her diary Woolf wonders if that is a good name,

and it is certainly a notable one, Smith the seventh, at once hopelessly nondescript and pompously grand, its royal pretensions making its common derivation that much more wincingly obvious (and there's that whiff of the septic). Septimus is a medaled war veteran, an office worker, and an earnest autodidact suffering from a terrible case of shell shock. He is married to an Italian woman who, with her sick husband, is quite out of her depth in the big, alien city, though doing her best (she trims hats) to keep the two of them afloat. Septimus is terrified by backfiring cars, hears voices, scribbles urgent messages to mankind, and on the day of the party his wife has decided to take him to a celebrated medical specialist, who proposes institutionalization. What else is left to do, she wonders helplessly, but when attendants come for her husband in the evening, he throws himself out the window, his body impaled by an iron railing below.

Septimus is a nobody who imagines he is the center and savior of the world: "the whole world was clamouring: kill yourself, kill yourself, for our sakes." He is somebody who feels himself nobody, whose greatest terror is that he cannot feel; he is a nobody who feels driven to become somebody by erasing himself. He is all desperate contradictions, and he is, Woolf implies, an everyman. He is certainly in part her—his delusions and experience with the doctor were drawn from hers—and at one point or another everybody who is anybody in the book experiences Septimus's sense of isolation and despair, just as throughout the book his path has crossed with theirs. They know nothing of him, nor he of them, but now that he is dead, news of his death begins to circulate: Sir William Bradshaw the doctor is at Clarissa's party, and he mentions it. The death of Septimus challenges Clarissa's love of life—"life, to be lived to the end, to be walked with serenely," exposing "in the depths of her heart an awful fear." At the same time, Septimus's death has about it a peculiar integrity: "A thing there was that mattered; a thing, wreathed about with chatter, defaced, obscured in her own life, let drop everyday in corruption, lies, chatter. This he had preserved. Death was defiance. Death was an attempt to communicate." And death is freedom: Septimus no longer has to "fear . . . the heat o' the sun / Nor the furious winter's rages"—the song from Shakespeare's *Cymbeline* that has echoed in Mrs. Dalloway's thoughts all day. Then comes the book's boldest and coldest moment: "She felt somehow very like him—the young man who had killed himself. She was glad that he had done it; thrown it away." At which point Big Ben strikes, and once again "the leaden circles dissolved in the air."

Mrs. Dalloway is a slim book of huge ambition, a book that, fluidly, fluently, subtly, distinctly is about a lot of things; you can practically make a checklist of them. It is a book about how it feels, moment by moment but also year after year, to be alive, how past and present and inner and outer worlds continually impinge upon one another, whether to frustrate or stimulate, in the course of that felt life. It is a book about the self—the tyrant self, the lonely self, the self that is blind to itself, the self as free agent, the destroyed self, the mystery that is the self—but no less about the other: the other as the beloved; the other we always let down, neglecting, avoiding, ignoring, betraying, and then again the other that is the self. It is about those things and also about the world at large—this is a picture of now, the book says—planes and trains and automobiles, men and women, the young and old, clothes and habits and differences, and so on. It is full of the brightness of life—"what a morning ... What a lark! What a plunge! ... How fresh, how calm," Mrs. Dalloway thinks, exclamations that are both the shiny currency of the certain sort of lady she is but are true to her way of feeling too. Then again, it is about the darkness of life: Septimus takes his own plunge. The book is also about the beauty of life and is itself beautiful: "how fresh like frilled linen clean from the laundry laid in wicker trays the roses looked."

"In this book I have almost too many ideas. I want to give life & death, sanity & insanity; I want to criticise the social system, & to show it at work, at its most intense ... I think it most important in this work to go for the central things," Woolf confides to her diary. A book about everything—this was the project that had first taken shape as "The Mark on the Wall"—and this was it, pretty much, written fast, finished in the excited assurance that she had been able to turn sketch into novel. This also could be said to be everything an ambitious book should be. Daring, fresh, true, it possessed the comprehensiveness of the great English novels that she admired and loved, even as it responded to the new concerns and techniques that linked her to her most adventurous contemporaries. Here Woolf takes over Joyce's day-in-the-life framework and his urban setting—why not?—and she of course uses stream of consciousness, but her use of it is not, as she felt his was, rigid and erratic—"raw" she had called it—but of a considered flexible consistency. She uses it to convey the intimacy, immediacy, and character of the self and to establish point of view, while also counterpointing the active mind with the worldly activity around it. Even more important, however, is the moral charge Woolf gives to stream of consciousness. It allows her to displace the omniscient narrator of the nineteenth-century novel, that famous false authority—after all, we are all, writers very much included, only ourselves—while, by virtue of the attention she devotes to those lonely selves, launching an appeal to all of us that in our common loneliness, we respond to one another with as much sympathetic imagination as possible. She uses it to depict character but also to show what it is, she believes, to have character and indeed humanity—or, as in the case of some of her characters, not. These are what she means by "central things," by contrast to the egotistic, eccentric performance of Joyce.

A book of immense ambition, but channeled, concentrated, done in a way of her own, in her style. The book is bold, but it is not, designedly not, the willful boldness but the accomplished style of it that strikes the reader. *Ulysses*, Eliot had said, had no style, and that is a mistake Woolf was not going to make. Her style, her voice, her vision is everywhere unmistakable in *Mrs. Dalloway*, like the tolling of Big Ben. Style was something Woolf gave a lot of thought to. "Style," she says in "Phases of Fiction," an overview of the history of the novel that she wrote in 1929, is the same thing as "arrangement, construction . . . [It] puts us at a distance from the special life and obliterates its features." It is, she says, a kind of "barrier," and "the first sign that we are reading a writer of merit is that we feel this control at work on us." Style in other words must have a certain impersonal authority—it especially forbids the easy satisfaction of conventional storytelling and, along with that, the bad taste of just showing off, which is the opposite of style—and yet for all that, its ultimate attraction and power are deeply personal and generous, a revelation of the creative individuality of the writer that may serve to give readers a glimpse of their own individuality, their own true selves. In the work of a great author, Woolf writes, "from the first page we feel our minds trained upon a point which becomes more and more perceptible as the book proceeds and the writer brings his conception out of darkness." It is, in effect, the vision of Mrs. Dalloway with which *Mrs. Dalloway* ends: "For there she was."

In the years she was working on *Jacob's Room* and *Mrs. Dalloway*, Woolf had written a number of lively and thoughtful essays about the state of contemporary fiction. In 1925, more or less in tandem with *Mrs. Dalloway*, she collected them in a volume she called *The Common Reader*. She wanted to affirm her authority not only as a novelist but as a critic; she wanted to aid in the construction of a new, enlightened audience. In one of these essays, "Mr. Bennett and Mrs. Brown," she takes issue with the veteran novelist Arnold Bennett, who had criticized his juniors for lacking the ability to create memorable characters on the order of Dickens's Mr. Micawber. The new writers, Bennett felt, were so involved with the flux of thought and feeling as to miss the human being. And Woolf doesn't disagree with Bennett. She concedes that modern fiction has a problem with character, but it's a problem, she says, that originates with writers like Bennett, so intent in their work on the material and sociological dimensions of life, so indifferent to individual thought and feeling, that their characters are indistinguishable from the buttons on their shirts. A true sensitivity to character, Woolf argues, was indeed needed, not only in fiction but in life, and to illustrate her point, she creates a character on the fly. Take, she says, a woman glimpsed on the bus. Call her Mrs. Brown. How are we to imagine her not as a person in passing, but as the person she is? How is the writer to give her her own life?

Mrs. Dalloway is Woolf's answer to that question. It is a book in which everyone is glimpsed in passing. It is a book centered on an individual woman. She is not Mrs. Brown (she is certainly not Mr. Bloom); she is Mrs. Dalloway, representative of a certain sort of woman, of

woman in a man's world, and of a woman, at least a good woman—
because *Mrs. Dalloway* is very much a book about what it means to
be a good woman—being more than the sum of her social parts and
feeling that keenly and deeply. She is representative, too, of Woolf's
desire—in a postwar world that is trying to assimilate catastrophic
change along with all sorts of innovations while also seeking to construct a new, better world—to strike a balance between our common
humanity and our common individuality.

An image of what could and should be, not unlike the League of
Nations, *Mrs. Dalloway* is representative of Woolf's utopian wish to
recover the balance and scope of the nineteenth-century novel in a
form appropriate to our times, a wish that of course only a twentieth-
century novelist could have. She was very right that that was not what
Ulysses was about, even if her own sensibility and commitments kept
her from seeing what it is about. Struggling to find a way to do better
than Joyce's book, to go beyond Joyce's book, she perfected a style and
wrote a novel that still speaks with authority to what should be our
common yearning, close to a hundred years later—all too many of
those years memorable for disaster—for a better world, a better life.

10. NICK STANDS UP

ERNEST HEMINGWAY'S *IN OUR TIME*

"The strange thing was, he said, how they screamed every night at midnight."

In the same years that Virginia Woolf was working on *Mrs. Dalloway*, Ernest Hemingway, a young American journalist living in Paris, was reworking a series of short texts that he would eventually call *In Our Time*, in an ironic postwar echo of the Book of Common Prayer, "Give us peace in our time":

> I do not know why they screamed at that time. We were in the harbor and they were all on the pier and at midnight they started screaming. We used to turn the searchlight on them to quiet them. That always did the trick.

Somebody is speaking, we're not told who, but before long he identifies himself as a "senior officer." His speech is slightly mincing, full of polite turns and routine superlatives—"frightful rage," "most insulting," "most severely punished"—that give him away as British, and he seems reluctant to contemplate the catastrophe that is in the offing. Called "On the Quai at Smyrna" this piece of writing—like Woolf's "The Mark on the Wall," it deliberately falls short of a story—would have been recognizable to its original readers as a scene from the Greco-Turkish conflict of 1919–22, one of the continuing aftershocks of the Great War. The Greeks, encouraged by the British government, had sought to take advantage of the collapse of the Ottoman Empire by seizing a chunk of Asia Minor, where a substantial Greek population lived. Initial success had, however, turned into a rout as the forces of the new nationalist government of Turkey, the nascent secular state founded by Mustafa Kemal Atatürk, drove the Greek forces back and pinned them down in the harbor town of Smyrna. The Turks attacked the Greek population of the country, as well as the Greek army, killing those who failed to flee. The scene the officer is describing is, in other words, a scene of genocide, a word that at the time had not yet come into existence. It is a scene of efficient massacre and embarrassed mismanagement, since the officer is no doubt aware that it was British chicanery as much as Greek opportunism and Turkish brutality that brought about the crisis he describes to an interlocutor, who, we eventually glean, had been there too. The men are reminiscing:

> The worst, he said, were the women with the dead babies. You couldn't get the women to give up their dead babies. They'd have babies dead for six days. Wouldn't give them up. Nothing you could do about it. Had to take them away finally.

Even as new babies are being born:

> They had them all right. Surprising how few of them died. You just covered them over with something and let them go to it.

It is a scene of panoramic cruelty as observed and recounted by professional actors in such scenes. No cause is invoked, and there is no effort (on the speaker's or the author's part) to explain the whys and wherefores of the situation. It is assumed that the addressee, the reader, knows all about it already, and perhaps the reader is as complicit as anyone. There is blame to go around, though responsibility is covered in irony: "The Greeks were nice chaps too. When they evacuated they had all their baggage animals they couldn't take off with them so they just broke their forelegs and dumped them into the shallow water. All those mules with their forelegs broken pushed over into shallow water." If casual readers of the time would have known something about the background of the scene, casual readers of a hundred years later will almost certainly be in the dark. That, or the reader will say, "But this is going on right now," and of course it is, even as I write.

"On the Quai in Smyrna," the piece with which *In Our Time* as it now appears begins, was the last piece in the book to be written. The book first came out with a small press, then, in 1925, in modified form, with a trade publisher, before being definitively revised in 1930, which is when "On the Quai" was added. In the first two editions the book had begun with a scene from the Great War, not yet World War I. Putting this brutal story up front was a considered gesture: war, it makes clear, figures here not as yesterday's news, but as an ongoing phenomenon: our time is a time of generalized war. This inconclusive story—or, as one says in the news business, in which Hemingway cut his teeth as a writer, this piece—is both blunt and elusive, and the question of what kind of thing it is, what to call it, and the question of what the relationship of language is to atrocity are very much part of it, not that it offers any answers.

The book begins, then, by placing the reader in confusing, threatening terrain, and the sense of uncertainty only grows as it goes on. The wartime scene with which the earlier editions had begun now follows. A mere paragraph on the page, it opens: "Everybody was drunk. The whole battery was drunk." Then, turning the page, we are in upstate Michigan, a little before dawn. "Indian Camp" is the title of the story, and it concerns a young boy named Nick Adams who is accompanying his father, a doctor, on an emergency medical call. The boy sits close to his father as an Indian rows them across the dark, misty lake. The language is spare, muted. "They walked up from the beach through a meadow that was soaking wet with dew . . . They went into the woods and followed a trail that led to the logging road that ran back into the hills." This story seems remote from "The Quai at Smyrna," but then perhaps not. Again a woman is giving birth. Nick doesn't know what is going on and why he is there. "Oh Daddy can't you give her something to make her stop screaming?"

These events and the rest of *In Our Time* were derived more or less directly from Hemingway's own experience. He had reported for the

Toronto Star from the front of the Greco-Turkish conflict, and had attended the Lausanne Conference of 1922–23, where peace of a sort was hammered out. He was a hardworking young journalist who in the course of a year traveled thousands of miles by train, crisscrossing Europe, and among the interviews he conducted was one with Benito Mussolini, newly installed as dictator of Italy after his March on Rome, the exegete of an aspiring new ideology, fascism. Hemingway, born in 1899, hailing from the prosperous, primly respectable Chicago suburb of Oak Park, came from a good upper-middle-class American family, not rich but with resources. One grandfather was a wholesale dealer in cutlery. His father, Ed, was an obstetrician, a devout Christian with a passion for hunting and fishing. His mother, Grace, had a fine voice—she considered a career in the opera—and gave voice lessons. After her father died and she collected an inheritance, she designed a big new house for the family, with a spacious room for her to put on concerts. Hemingway's parents were the personification of polite American culture, good, active citizens who subscribed to a robustly muscular brand of Protestant piety.

Grace had hoped that Ernest, her first child, would be a girl, and for some years she dressed her son in girl's clothes. He became a boy's boy, however, outgoing, athletic, hunting and fishing with his father, but also avidly studious, reading under the covers at night. He loved Kipling, Ring Lardner, and Mark Twain; he knew his Bible and Shakespeare too. In high school he took up boxing, enrolled in school clubs, and, with his sights set on being a writer, edited the school newspaper. When he graduated, he went to work, courtesy of a relative, on a Kansas City paper, where he was put on the police beat. By this time, America had entered the war, and Hemingway was determined to see the action. Poor eyesight disqualified him as a soldier, so he enlisted in the Ambulance Corps, and he arrived in Italy at the start of a major offensive against Austria. "The big Italian guns are all back of us and they roar all night," he wrote to a girl he knew from high school. "What I am supposed to be doing is running a posto di recovero. That is I dispense chocolates and cigarettes to the wounded and the soldiers in the front line . . . I sure have a good time but I miss their [*sic*] being no Americans . . . Gee but I do get lonesome for the sight of a real Honest to Gawd American girl." One night, Hemingway and a group of Italian soldiers were hit by a mortar shell. One man was blown to pieces ("When there is a direct hit your pal gets spattered all over you. Spattered is literal," he wrote), another fatally wounded. Hemingway's legs were lacerated by shrapnel, but he lugged the wounded man to safety before collapsing himself. It took him months to walk again.

This brush with death was like a second birth for him. It was "the next best thing to getting killed and reading your own obituary," he wrote to his family. He was pleased to see it reported in the Oak Park paper (as the first American wounded in Italy, Hemingway was news not only at home but at large, as was his winning an Italian medal for bravery), but it also helped to liberate him from the stifling conventionality of Oak Park. The nearness of death, so intimate and cold, abolished all that; it left just him. Then again it was also terrifying. He had feared—he now knew—that he really would die; he also feared, perhaps, living on in a state of sexual incapacitation (as Jake Barnes does in *The Sun Also Rises*). The experience certainly gave him something to write about. It is central to *In Our Time* and central to the two novels that followed, *The Sun Also Rises* and *A Farewell to Arms*, but it also—and this is the most important thing for the writer he would become—gave him a new, more direct connection to language. "Spattered is literal." To be a writer would be to find words for that kind of experience, to make it actual, to hold on to it, to survive it. Words were a weapon and a lifeline; you had to know both how strong they were and how weak.

In Our Time—written after Hemingway and his first wife had moved to Paris and met Gertrude Stein and Ezra Pound, both of whom took to him and to his writing; written, also, with Joyce's *Dubliners* in mind—might be said to be an exploded book. It contains sixteen substantial stories with conventional titles that alternate with sixteen numbered chapters: each of these, like the original opening described above, is confined to a single page and, in early printings, set in italics; each is fitted out, formally, solemnly, a little inscrutably, with a roman numeral overhead. The book, in other words, appears both as a series of discrete pieces and a sequence of linked chapters, and it confronts the reader with an immediate challenge: How do these things hold together? What kind of book is this?

Each of the book's two strands has a consistency of its own. The chapters depict scenes of violence: scenes from the Great War, from lesser wars, but also of revolution, execution, and American gangster life. Bullfighting, violence as spectacle, is also there. The chapters are sometimes in the first person (singular and plural) and sometimes in the third person; characters, reduced to a bare passing name or entirely unnamed, come and go. The stories, by contrast, are largely about a single character, the Nick Adams we met in "Indian Camp" as a young boy. We watch him grow up, in scenes mostly set in an upstate Michigan that is wild and beautiful but also full of abandoned mill towns and burned-out vacation camps. We see Nick gassing about books and getting drunk with his best high school friend, breaking up with his girlfriend, bumming around, married and in Europe, skiing and fishing. There are a few stories too that have nothing obvious to do with Nick, which we take to be stories he has heard, stories encountered along his way. Then Nick appears in one of the intervening chapters. Almost as an aside, we learn that he fought and was wounded in the war.

A last long story, "Big Two-Hearted River," is set in Michigan again—we come around to where things began—and it is in two parts. In the first, Nick is back in Michigan "after a long time," back in the wild and on his own. He walks through a landscape at first scorched by fire, on his way to the river that gives the story its title, where he means to set up camp and do some fishing. He walks away from the past. "Nick felt happy. He felt he had left everything behind, the need for thinking, the need to write, other needs. It was all back of him." So he is a writer now, and we are led to suppose that the chapters that we have read are his work. That realization is, for the reader, the main event of the first part of "Big Two-Hearted River," in which otherwise little happens, except that Nick does make it to where he meant to go and then pitches camp. What happens is, in fact, as close to next to nothing as a story can get:

> While he waited for the coffee to boil, he opened a small can of apricots. He liked to open cans. He emptied the can of apricots out into a tin cup. While he watched the coffee on the fire, he drank the juice syrup of the apricots, carefully at first . . . , then meditatively, sucking the apricots down. They were better than fresh apricots.

"He liked to open cans"! Then he crawls into his tent and goes to sleep.

"They hanged Sam Cardinella at six o'clock in the morning in the corridor of the county jail": the chapter that interrupts the story begins—a jarring note, one that, on turning the page to see that the story we were reading has a second part, further jars us into the decisive realization that just as this story continues after it, so all the stories in the book, titled and untitled, should be seen as a continuity. (You could put it differently, however, saying that this story, like the book itself, is broken into pieces.) The story as it resumes, then, is already a new thing: the continuation of the story of Nick's fishing the river that we have begun, yes, but also and equally the story of *In Our Time*, this splintered book, finally coming together, and how will that be? It is morning when they hang Sam Cardinella, and it is a peaceful and sunny morning on the river where Nick is. He has just woken and is looking forward to the day's fishing. He catches grasshoppers for bait, makes breakfast, assembles his line and rod, wades into the river. He almost catches a big trout, shockingly big, but it gets away. He catches three other trout that are good enough. Again the story is close to nothing. And as if to confirm that suspicion, the main thing that does happen before the end of story, the main thing after the failure to catch the big trout, is another thing that doesn't happen. Wading downstream, Nick arrives at a swampy stretch of the river, forbidding, not unlike the scorched landscape he'd hiked through the day before at the start of this story, and he considers fishing there. But no:

> In the swamp the banks were bare, the big cedars came together overhead, the sun did not come through, except in patches; in the fast deep water, in the half light, the fishing would be tragic.

Tragic is a strange word to come after so much mundane detail, almost humorously exaggerated, yet it feels right. Waterside, are we back on the quai at Smyrna? In any case, Nick will not fish there now. There should be time for it later, and so the last story in *In Our Time* ends.

Ends decisively yet uncertainly. Back in Michigan, Nick is back in the world of his childhood, to which he cannot really return; he is also back from a war that he will not ever escape. Implicitly, in other words, the story contains everything we know about Nick's life from that first story we read about him, "Indian Camp." There Nick was exposed not only to the trauma of birth—the mother's terrible screaming—but also, even more terribly, to the trauma of death: the story ends with the discovery that the father of the child has slit his throat during the night. That was the beginning, and we have seen what came later: war, work, marriage, and so on. All that is in the background of "Big Two-Hearted River," so that its two parts could be said to bracket the action of the book, everything that has passed, even as the completed book will bracket this final story, opening up a distinct space, a moment where the reader is, with immense delicacy, led to share an unspoken, unspeakable sense of what is at stake for Nick. He is alone, not so much because his marriage has failed or his friends have drifted off or died and all the parties have ended, though we might surmise all that, but because this is what we all are: alone. Still he is holding it together, just:

> Nick stood up. He leaned his back against the weight of his pack where it rested upright on the stump and got his arms through the shoulder straps. He stood with the pack on his back on the brow of the hill looking out across the country toward the distant river and then struck down the hillside away from the road. Underfoot the ground was good walking. Two hundred

yards down the hillside the fire line stopped. Then it was sweet
fern, growing ankle high, to walk through, and clumps of jack
pines; a long undulating country with frequent rises and de-
scents, sandy underfoot and the country alive again.

Writing like that is as much as anything about writing like that.
It paces itself, and it minds its paces, the play of sounds—back, pack,
stump, struck—its symmetries and repetitions, checking and testing
its progress as Nick does the straps of his pack or the ground underfoot. It is writing that works through and exemplifies attention, concentration, precision, and control. It is all about self-awareness. It is
all about discipline. It observes the outer and inner worlds with equal
care, maintaining a balance that might remind us of the nineteenth-
century novel's balance of the claims of self and society, only this balance is not a prospect or an outcome, but an ongoing challenge: the
novel, you could say, has shrunk to sentence after sentence, and this
awareness of the sentence as the essential open-ended unit of actively
making meaning reflects, as I mentioned before, the influence of Gertrude Stein. The story's subject is the question of its own going on.

In Our Time is a book about growing up, encountering the violent nature of life, and growing out of any sentimental or moralizing
preconceptions you may have had to begin with. It shocked Ed Hemingway, who admonished his son, as if from the pulpit, "The brutal
you have surely shown the world. Look for the joyous, uplifting, and
optimistic, and spiritual in character." Grace for her part never had
a good thing to say about her son's work and even banned his books
from her house. *In Our Time* is also a book about becoming a writer,
about the twentieth century, and about language. If the form of the
book is from the beginning presented to the reader as something to
puzzle over, the right and wrong use of language is also a subject from
the start. It is present in the little sprays of superlatives with which the
British senior officer sanitizes the horror on the quai at Smyrna, in a
punch-drunk old boxer's sudden lurch from friendly recognition to
blind, bellowing rage (he is silenced by a discreet tap on the head with
an iron frying pan), in dialogue like this:

"What's really the matter?"
"I don't know."
"Of course you know."
"No I don't."
"Go on and say it."
"It's not fun anymore."

Speech in *In Our Time* is largely lacking or failing, failing in the face of violence or succeeding only in inviting violence (failure and success being what Hemingway's middle-class American milieu talked about all the time). Violence silences speech, and Hemingway respects it for that, so much speech being a travesty, and capturing violence on the page is what, as his reputation grew, he was more and more praised for, notwithstanding his work's no less evident finesse.

"The movies ruined everything. Like talking about something good. That was what made the war unreal. Too much talking . . . Talking about anything was bad." In the original version of the second part of "Big Two-Hearted River," Nick, relaxed after reeling in a "good trout," sinks back into the stream of consciousness. We hear about how important fishing is to him, and about his friends and his marriage and Paris, bullfighting and boozing, and how hard it all is. Then he turns to writers and writing, name-checking all the important—many already legendary or notorious—modern writers Hemingway had come to know in Europe: "It was easy to write if you knew the tricks. Everybody used them. Joyce had invented hundreds of new ones. Just because they were new didn't make them any better. They would all turn into clichés."

Nick, by contrast, wants to write

like Cezanne painted. Cezanne started with all the tricks, Then he broke the whole thing down and built the real thing. It was hell to do. He was the greatest. The greatest for always. It wasn't a cult. He, Nick, wanted to write about the country like Cezanne had done it in painting. You had to do it from inside yourself.

Write like Cézanne, which you might rephrase as write sentences free of pomp or chatter, sentences that possess the authority of a painting's silence. A curious feature of "Big Two-Hearted River" as published is that it includes almost no auditory detail. Twigs don't snap underfoot, wind doesn't whisper, water gurgle, what you will. The whole story is enveloped in a hush, like someone holding his breath.

In the draft, however, saying at length all the things that go unsaid in the published story and underlining like a student the fact that this book is Nick's book, Hemingway is doing anything but holding his breath, and we have to be grateful to Gertrude Stein for prevailing on him to cut these pages. Because it is by virtue of this cut that this last story, so acutely focused on the present moment, puts the book as a whole in perspective, making it a whole and making it clear that this book, about war and words and writing, is above all about making—or trying to at least—things whole. It is an exploded book, I said: it shows its guts. It is also a book that defies description, splitting the difference between part and whole. And it is, as D. H. Lawrence immediately perceived, very much a novel, a new kind of novel, a better one in many ways than any that Hemingway would subsequently write. A small proof of the book's ultimate integrity and originality: it's impossible to separate "Big Two-Hearted River" from the book as whole, as in an anthology, without reducing it to meaninglessness or sentimentality.

How to characterize Hemingway's achievement, his place in the life of the twentieth-century novel? Hemingway became Hemingway, a bestselling American writer all over the world, a man who had set a new tone for fiction high and low, and, more important than that, for the movies. (Without Hemingway, no Bogart.) And yet, as a writer of the novel, he struggled. He wanted to write truthful, thoughtful, immaculately wrought novels of broad appeal, novels that would be of the time—their manners uncompromisingly modern—telling stories of the day, and he did. He did, and the novels were enormously successful, but as novels they depended to one degree or another (and more and more with time) on what, in *In Our Time*, he had gone out of his way to avoid: plot and character, those building blocks of the nineteenth-century novel. The problem was that his characters were one-note, their predicaments sentimental, and the plots that tied them together a loose string of incident. Hemingway was not the novelist he now committed to be, but rather a Steinian inventor of sentences and a Gidean novelist of voice with an extraordinary strength and elegance of his own, and the simplest way to describe his achievement— as distinct from his popularity—is to say that he wrote like no one else and wrote beautifully, in a style that was tense and tenuous, sensitive to its own effects but not the least attention-grabbing, delicate, direct, astonishing. Ezra Pound, who famously stipulated that poetry should be at least as well written as prose, said of Hemingway that he wrote the best prose of his time—and the best of his prose has the concentration of poetry.

What Pound said of Hemingway is of course what Clive Bell said of Woolf, and that overlap tells us something about postwar taste, in which writers, like the great painters of the late nineteenth and early twentieth centuries, are admired for the individuality of their paint handling rather than for the recognizability of what they paint. *Le style c'est l'homme*, and the quality of your style, the courage with which you pursue and maintain it, is the quality of your character—not just an aesthetic achievement but a moral index. The great inventions of Woolf and Hemingway are Woolf and Hemingway, and there is, I think, much in common between these two writers who may superficially seem so unlike—adventurous, manly Ernest (a name he hated) and introspective, supersensitive Virginia, yang and yin. As with Gide and Wells, apparent opposites share a good deal, and what they share helps define the particular set of challenges that face the postwar, post-Joyce novel as it sets out to be of the moment (though the great big books of Proust and Mann and Joyce, however transformative, are all backward looking)—documenting, taking stock of a world of changes that can be everywhere observed—but also of moment, momentous. Hemingway and Woolf set out to be consolidators as much as innovators, seeking to fashion a novel that is tough enough for the times but tough enough, too, to outlive them, not eccentric and tricksy, however brilliantly so, as they both deemed Joyce to be, but central.

Hemingway and Woolf, then. They are both sensual artists, sirens of appetite, outright gourmandizers. (Forster wrote of Woolf, "It is always helpful, when reading her, to look out for the passages that describe eating. They are invariably good . . . She had an enlightened greediness." Hemingway's novels can seem to be nothing so much as a count of bottles of good wine and omelettes aux fines herbes.) They are both public figures and political to boot, on the left though not doctrinaire, but aligned with people—like Leonard Woolf—who are taking an active role in current events and, with the rise of fascism and the advent of the Spanish Civil War, increasingly are doing so themselves. And they are both—this is perhaps the most thought-provoking resemblance—deeply engaged with the question of sexuality. They wrote at a time when sex roles were very much up for redefinition, as women in the UK, the US, the USSR, and Germany went to the ballot box and—after the deaths of so many young men in the war—went to work, too; young men and women went to the dance hall, to the cinema, and, with sexual mores loosening, they went to bed. From experience, Hemingway and Woolf were both acutely aware of how disfiguring the old sex roles could be. Woolf may well have been sexually abused by an older half brother; she had seen her bereaved father lay to waste the lives of his children. For Hemingway, his mother was the vengeful, life-destroying embodiment of the fetishization of feminine virtue and taste that has always been a distinct feature of bourgeois life. (It takes on, as the historian Ann Douglas documents in *The Feminization of American Culture*, a unique virulence in America.) Then again, Hemingway would also bear the burden of a no less American, no less destructive idea of masculinity, of which his father's suicide, in 1928, after blowing through the family's small fortune, may be seen as an example. Woolf, saying that Mrs. Brown embodies human nature, is making a corrective point about the centrality of feminine experience to being human. Hemingway pits true manliness not only against domestic propriety but against brittle masculine posturing and the warmongering of the men in power. The two writers outline new models of feminine and masculine deportment; they also go so far—very far in their day—as to blur or erase the lines between the sexes. In Hemingway's unfinished, long-labored, only posthumously published *The Garden of Eden*, the hero and his girlfriend swap sex roles in bed and beyond. Halfway through Woolf's *Orlando*—her most popular book—the protagonist is transformed from a man to a woman.

The new postwar world was full of new possibilities for living and writing, exciting, unnerving, appalling, and Hemingway and Woolf sought to be alive to them all in their work. The sense of promise is also a sense of portent, further overshadowed by a fear of failing to see, falling short, or selling out. Trapdoors are everywhere. The new postwar world is among other things a self-consciously fashionable world, and in it they were fashion plates, *Vanity Fair* running an issue with an Ernest Hemingway cutout, *Vogue* a Virginia Woolf photo shoot in which she posed in a dress of her mother's while puffing on a cigarette. Bloomsbury and Hemingway's Lost Generation take part in an international scene that extends from the New York of the Jazz Age to the London of the Bright Young Things to Paris and Berlin and even Moscow (where Stalin, cementing his power in the early thirties, propagandized that "Life has become happier! Life has become merrier!") and Tokyo, leveled by the 1923 earthquake but rapidly rebuilt bigger and better. And all the while Hollywood is beaming out over the globe, flickering images of this brash new world. Hotel World, you could call it, in which everyone and everything is tossed together and everybody is casting an alert, assessing eye at the neighbor who is nothing but a stranger after all. A world of transient satisfactions that always come at a cost, good for a night but how much longer, and can it last?—a scene that even spawns a new genre, the hotel novel. The hotel novel par excellence is Vicki Baum's *Grand Hotel*, published in 1929 and set in Berlin—an international bestseller, then Broadway show, then movie (featuring Greta Garbo and her most famous line, "I want to be alone"), its stock characters circulating around the front desk and through its pages as efficiently and effectively as the revolving glass door that is a recurrent image throughout. Look closely at the art on the walls in the movie and you'll see that it consists of so many pastiche Picassos and Cézannes.

How do you hold your own in this hard new world? How do you stick up for the real, not the fake, goods? Woolf and Hemingway have

in common a heroic image of the writer as the trailblazer through rubble and glitz, and though I am making a case for ways they are alike,
they didn't like each other's work. In 1927, Woolf reviews Hemingway's short story collection *Men Without Women* with condescending
circumspection, chastising its stripped-down style as symptomatic
of the hollow, shallow, bragging, brazen American youth of the day.
The work, she said, is faked. Hemingway read the review (maybe the
only thing of Woolf's he ever read) and in response wrote to his editor
dismissing the Bloomsbury people as effete and—what else?—fakes.
Another thing the two writers would turn out to have in common
over the course of their careers is the propensity to inadvertent self-
parody, as in the self-serious prose poetry of Woolf's *The Waves* or the
bathos of Hemingway's pillow talk.

Still, one hundred years after they wrote, the words of these prophets of the fully lived life and the completely realized sentence still
live on the page. Mrs. Dalloway's day is as close to right now in the
reader's world as Woolf can make it. *In Our Time* takes place in our
time. The books are full of life, not least because they are full of fear.
"Fear no more the light of the day," Mrs. Dalloway keeps thinking.
"Allow yourself to fear the swamp," Nick tells himself. Fear is real,
as death is real, and both writers fear that nothing else is as real—a
matter of private demons, no doubt, as the writers' deaths attest, but
private demons that also spoke to widely shared public anxiety. And
against fear and death, what can good writing do? (Can a Cézanne
stop the screaming?) Well, it does what it can to assert its presence, to
prove itself as writing, to figure. Woolf's next novel after *Mrs. Dalloway*, her greatest, *To the Lighthouse*, ends with Lily Briscoe, a painter
of course—because painting is for Woolf, as for Hemingway, the exemplary art—finishing the composition she has worked on for years:
"Yes . . . I have had my vision," she thinks, work and life achieving an
equipoise. Then there is the terrible, stark pathos—or simple make-
believe—of the end of "Indian Camp," with Nick, a boy who in the
course of the night has witnessed both childbirth and suicide, back
out in the open: "In the early morning on the lake sitting in the stern
of the boat with his father rowing, he felt quite sure that he would
never die."

11. CRITIC AS CREATOR
ROBERT MUSIL'S *THE MAN WITHOUT QUALITIES*

"A novel," the poet, critic, and novelist Randall Jarrell nicely said, "is a prose narrative of a certain length with something wrong with it." It is a very twentieth-century adage, an appreciation, however ironic, that contrasts with the nineteenth century's suspicion of the novel as merely superficial. A sense of the novel as both mattering immensely, as being a crucial way of getting certain things right, but also being misbegotten, inspires and haunts the novelists of this book. To read them is to catch them in the act of thinking about the novel in the midst of writing a novel, mindful that their endeavor is as critical as it is creative and that this presents a problem in its own right. They write both as novelist and as the critic looking over the novelist's shoulder, and how are they to make a book that accommodates such a split consciousness? Should it be exercised? Should it be exorcised? One way or another, the problem of approaching the problem always lurks in the background—we have seen it in Gide and Wells and again and again—and as the century wears on, the critic has more, not fewer, questions for the novelist. What is the relation between part and whole, between writer and reader, between the twentieth-century novel and its forebears, between self and society? And the beleaguered novelist who can't make the questions go away may be tempted to as-sume the critic's role herself, as we have already seen Woolf do.

The most sustained, astonishing, and inventive effort to combine the critical intelligence, in all its disabused analytic rigor, with the creative spirit, in all its lavish plenitude, is the vast, microscopically observed, uncategorizable work in progress *The Man Without Qual-ities* by the Austrian writer Robert Musil. The book is as much dis-quisition as it is novel, and what is perhaps most impressive in this shape-shifting work—social satire, (anti-)philosophical treatise, spiri-tual quest and inquest—is the surgical ply and gleam of Musil's verbal intelligence. Along the way, he is continually considering and recon-sidering the nature of what he is up to; at one point, he coins the term "essayism" to describe it. By essayism he means more than an aes-thetic program. Like fascism, like communism, the political move-ments that sought to reshape the world after the war, it is a matter of life and death.

Musil, born in 1880 (and so part of the same generation as Woolf and Joyce and Kafka, and Kafka he knew), was a restlessly intelligent man who pursued careers in the military and engineering (his father was also an engineer) before taking a degree in psychology at the Univer-sity of Berlin. As early as the first years of the new century, he had an ambition to write a novel—he called it simply *Novel*—that would con-tain and explain his life and his times as a whole and somehow serve to make them whole, and toward that end he began to keep notebooks full of detailed observations of his own changing and contradictory moods and attitudes, as well as those of his friends and lovers. Musil had a critical and analytical turn of mind, and at this stage of his life he styled himself as the Vivisector (had he read *Moreau?*). Per-haps because he was so gifted at taking things apart, his big, densely worked novel refused for many years to come together, though he wrote a small, vivid tale of sexual and psychological abuse in the hot-house of a military school, *The Confusions of Young Törless*, which came out in 1906: a book full of fin de siècle anxiety that is still worth reading.

His studies complete, Musil balked at an academic career—psychology was no more to his taste than engineering or the military—and chose instead to freelance as a writer and editor. (As an editor, he sought to publish Kafka's *Metamorphosis*, but was overruled.) He was adrift, but then the war solved the problem of what to do, and

Musil responded to it with the mystical enthusiasm of so many on both sides. In a notebook from the 1920s, he speaks of "the human being" being "subjected to surprise attack by the war," but also of "all people" being "touched by something irrational and gigantic . . . for the first time everyone had something in common with everyone else. Dissolution into an impersonal happening." Though disillusioned by his experience on the Italian front (opposite Hemingway), Musil kept the moment in mind, as he kept in mind the comparable "Easter world-mood" at the end of the war, when once again he took up the idea of his big novel. Now he envisioned it as a book in so many volumes, a novel that would encompass everything while also serving as a critique of the novel. Soon, however, he abandoned this scheme and set to work on a book he called *The Man Without Qualities*. A first volume appeared in 1930, the second three years later. Together they added up to some thousand pages, and Musil was by no means done.

The Man Without Qualities is a teasing sort of title. The word *Eigenschaften*, translated as "qualities," means characteristics or features, and to characterize the main character of a novel as being without character—well, what can that be about? In light of it, the reader might expect a book bearing some resemblance to, for example, Heinrich Mann's *Underling*. Then again—though how many readers would have known this?—the phrase to be "without qualities" derives from Musil's extensive reading in mystical literature, from Buber's anthology *Ecstatic Confessions* to the medieval German philosopher Meister Eckhart, and designates a state of selflessness. The title, in other words, can be taken in quite distinct ways, worldly and otherworldly, while also raising the question of what are the qualities or characteristics appropriate to the protagonist of a novel, or indeed a human being. (The critic steps in!) And once one starts reading the novel, it rapidly becomes clear that the title's ambiguity reflects a general interest on Musil's part in the various meanings a single phrase or word may contain and in the whole complicated, even tortuous, process of meaning-making, in which opposing concepts often reveal themselves to be kin. "I think in an 'other' way," Musil writes in his notebooks. "This comes from my being an engineer." This other-thinking continually spurs him on to think across given categories and meanings. Thus, "From the time of my youth I have considered the aesthetic to be ethics."

It will hardly be a surprise, then, that Ulrich, the man without qualities himself, in fact has lots of qualities. The son of an esteemed, politically influential jurist, he is, socioeconomically, recognizable as the pure product of the *Bildungsbürgertum*, or educated upper middle class, highly cultivated and fully inculcated with the bourgeois precept that it is a man's job to make something of himself, to develop his character and to show character. And so he has, and quite successfully, it would seem. Ulrich is clever and strong—*mens sana in corpore sano*—and from an early age he has felt himself called to nothing less than greatness, that perennial nineteenth-century preoccupation. As a child, his conception of this calling was military: Napoleon was his hero and model. But then, growing up as he does at the end of the nineteenth century in the long lull of European peace and prosperity, he realizes that the "heroic conviction of lordliness, power, and pride" is obsolescent. (The action of *The Man Without Qualities* begins in the summer of 1913, and when it does not end, more than a thousand pages later, it has still not reached the summer of the next year; no one reading the first volume on its publication in 1930 would have missed the multiple ironies of Ulrich's youthful complacency about both peace and power.)

Having ruled out the military option, Ulrich's ambitions take a more practical and constructive turn. The slide rule and the turbine become his bellwethers; he will excel as a civil engineer. But before long, the unreflective and inelegant character of his fellow professionals puts him off. They look at things only from the outside—they lack soul—and display the oddest of outsides, at that. Ulrich wonders

> Why for instance do they so often wear a watch sling on a steep, lopsided curve from the vest pocket to the button higher up, or across the stomach in one high and two low loops, as if it were a metrical foot in a poem? Why do they favor tiepins topped with stag's teeth or tiny horseshoes? Why do they wear suits constructed like the early stages of an automobile? And why, finally, do they never speak of anything but their profession?

They lack soul and they lack style, and Ulrich, forsaking bridge building as much as empire building, turns to the pure and difficult and slightly inhuman study of higher mathematics. It is a field in which, we are told, he has done good work.

Yet when we meet him at the start of the book, he has given it up. Ulrich is thirty-two, straddling the border of youth and full maturity, and he has decided, as he puts it, to take a holiday from life, to do nothing. His education—which can be read as an allegory of the world of the nineteenth century yielding to the corrosive power of modern skepticism, until the nature of the world itself is called into question—has led him nowhere, and now he has decided to return to the world of play, of active inactivity, that is childhood, even as he begins to foresense the world of achieved or enforced inactivity that is old age (at the time the novel was written, thirty-two, the age of decisive maturity, would have also figured as the moment of incipient middle age). He is suspending himself in the midst of life. Ulrich is lean, athletic, attractive (the Viennese ladies line up at his door), sensual though not in the least sentimental, conspicuously intelligent, quizzical, reserved, ever ironic, and it is his friend Walter, a musician, who dubs him the Man Without Qualities. He does not mean it as a compliment. In Ulrich he sees a typical twentieth-century man, smart but without depth or passion, bloodless, bereft precisely of greatness or any idea of greatness, and the high-minded, highly romantic, and deeply frustrated Walter is desperate for greatness—though his life, spent quarreling with a wife who is no less hungry for transcendence than he is, is mired in pettiness.

Ulrich, who has gotten over his own cult of greatness, would not dispute Walter's characterization. To the contrary, he embraces it, the better to train on his own existence, his own being, the exact attention found "not only in the scientist but the businessman, the administrator, the sportsman, the technician"—prototypical twentieth-century figures—though Ulrich is quite aware that these types who are otherwise "so thorough and unprejudiced in everything [abhor] nothing so much as the idea of being thorough where [they themselves] are concerned." Ulrich's new quest to identify what he thinks of as "the Utopian idea of himself" would, he realizes, seem to them nothing more than "an improper experiment" unworthy of men "occupied with serious business." It is, however, just this improper experiment that Urich is intent on conducting. Can the sterile environs of the laboratory that is the twentieth century produce soul? Happiness, the French revolutionary Saint-Just had said, is a new idea in Europe. Not greatness but happiness, Ulrich has come to see, is what he is looking for, and always has been. Happiness is his utopian idea, though strangely it is just this commitment to happiness that all through his life has left him "more or less alone."

Gradually it becomes clear that Ulrich's holiday from life is actually "the worst state of emergency of his life." Musil's plan was for *The Man Without Qualities* to end with the outbreak of the war; and Ulrich's personal emergency and utopian project represent an effort to grapple with the underlying malaise of the time that would lead to the war. To no avail, we know. But what does it tell us about its own time, the growing emergency of the twenties and thirties? Though set at the start of the century, the book will suggest to the alert reader that the crisis of the time, after leading to one war, has only become that much more critical.

When Ulrich sets out to conduct his experiment, he is at the same stage of life as Jesus was when he took to preaching the gospel, as Dante was when he embarked on his pilgrimage, and naturally he must be tempted. No sooner does he retreat from the world than he finds himself plunged into worldly business. Temptation comes in the form of his cousin, a beautiful society hostess and patron of the arts who goes by the exalted (Platonic and poetic) name of Diotima. Diotima, the wife of an aristocrat high up in the imperial administration, is, like Ulrich and his unhappy friend Walter, hungry for meaning and purpose, and in the upcoming thirtieth anniversary of the Dual Monarchy of Austria-Hungary she sees a historic opportunity to redress the sense of apathy that has overtaken both private and public life and at the same time to confirm a new commitment to the common good. Providentially, inspirationally, this thirtieth anniversary happens to coincide with the seventieth anniversary of the ascent to the imperial throne by the venerable Franz Joseph, and

Diotima wishes to launch a great "parallel campaign" to celebrate what she effusively dubs "Global Austria" (the Dual Monarchy's wondrous unity standing as an example to the world at large) as well as the long, prosperous reign of "the emperor of peace." So great and significant a project will take thought and require vision and much hard work to pull off properly, of course, but there is time for that: the two anniversaries will not take place until 1918.

Kaiserlich and Königlich: for the two-headed sacred monster that was the Austro-Hungarian Empire, Musil cooked up the mocking sobriquet Kakania ("Shitland"), and of course by 1918, after parallel campaigns of a different order than any envisioned by Diotima, the place had been wiped from the face of the earth. We know this, Musil knows this, and though Ulrich cannot know this as the designated secretary to the parallel campaign, he is able from the start to savor the ironies that attend this world-improving endeavor: the bureaucratic snags, the political considerations, fundraisers, innumerable interminable meetings, self-important talk. There is all this, and then there are the sexual interests and tensions that fine feelings so often arouse. Diotima is taken with Ulrich, and he feels drawn to her, but soon she falls completely under the spell of the German industrialist Arnheim, a man who has every quality anyone could ever imagine: he writes books, he prognosticates, he philosophizes, he schmoozes, he sits on boards, he advises heads of state, he is made of money. Arnheim, modeled on the German industrialist and statesman Walter Rathenau (assassinated in 1922, after being brought into the government of the Weimar Republic as the minister of finance in order to stabilize Germany's economy), exists in the novel as an illustration of contemporary superficiality in its highest form. Arnheim is, in a sense, what Ulrich might have been if he had not known better—or might have been had he not had the courage to know less than the everything that Arnheim feels continually compelled to make an appearance of knowing. That said, Arnheim fascinates Ulrich almost as much as he does Diotima, perhaps because Ulrich is not as indifferent to worldly success (or Diotima) as he affects to be; perhaps because he recognizes that knowing better than the likes of Arnheim is not much, and when push comes to spiritual shove, no better.

The satire that takes up much of the first part of Musil's novel is very funny and brilliantly executed, and the types he describes remain familiar—Arnheim, for example, is the spitting image of what at the end of the twentieth century came to be called Davos Man—but it is fairly conventional in form, and Musil the novelist is as restless within those conventions as Ulrich is in the face of the conventions of Viennese society. The modern muddle of Diotima and Arnheim (and Musil is careful to implicate Ulrich and us in it as well) is matched in Musil's mind by the muddled and unsatisfactory form of the novel. Musil's novel is full of detail and incident and attitude and humor and life, as a good novel should be, but it is from the start also full of a certain suspicion, even disdain, for its own effects. Musil participates in his growing novel as incredulously as Ulrich does in the parallel campaign, even as his novel often delights us with a sense that, caught up in appearances as it may be, its transparent factitiousness makes it the perfect (perfectly facetious) instrument for taking the measure of our factitious times. The first book of *The Man Without Qualities* is called "The Like of It Now Happens"—Sophie Wilkins translates the original German more interpretively as "Pseudoreality Prevails"—and in it Musil's ambition to write a new kind of novel and the prejudice of none other than Arnheim against the novel (it is unserious!) converge marvelously to send up the bogus pretentions of a very serious man like Arnheim and to whet our appetite for something else.

And Musil, like Ulrich, wants something else, wants to do more than merely flout and send up existing conventions. *The Man Without Qualities* can only be realized as a novel without qualities. In another sense then, this first satirical part of the novel can be seen as a kind of striptease. What happens next? That's a good old-fashioned novelistic question standing naked on the stage!

There is another man without qualities in *The Man Without Qualities*, Moosbrugger, a carpenter, a half-wit, a brute, a sex maniac, a murderer—he picked up a prostitute on the street and cut her throat—a prisoner awaiting judgment now. Moosbrugger fascinates Vienna, his trial filling the pages of the newspapers and the pages of Musil's novel, a dark parallel to the sunny parallel campaign. Ulrich too is fascinated by Moosbrugger, and wonders at the man's state of mind or mindlessness, his malevolence, his malignity. Moosbrugger is the Jack the Ripper figure who haunts the literature and art of the first part of the century (Berg's Lulu; the sex murder scenes of artists like Sickert and Grosz). In Musil's novel, Moosbrugger is a grotesque, brooding conundrum and the problem of evil incarnate, a problem that the wheels of justice—remember that Ulrich's father is a distinguished jurist—can hardly resolve. For one thing, Moosbrugger is plainly out of his mind and so as innocent as not, and Ulrich is bitterly amused by the legal and medical hoops and half-truths that the assembled experts leap through in order to justify a judgment that they have never for a moment doubted: Moosbrugger the murderer must be murdered by the state—a charade that only makes Ulrich much more aware of Moosbrugger as the dark shadow of our common humanity, the depravity that is continuous with legality and civilization itself and that will become newly manifest, the reader knows, in the war to come. What I want, Ulrich says early in the book, is to stop and think, at which point it strikes him that stopping to think can be dangerous. (It is the same need to stop and think that strikes Nick on the Big Two-Hearted River.) Thinking can bring you up short before the unthinking violence of Moosbrugger and his fate.

Moosbrugger represents a challenge, a moral one, to conventional morality but also a challenge to Ulrich and the novel: How are they to make sense of this aberration and abomination, which is, for all that, unmistakably human? All his adult life, Ulrich has had little patience for received morality, precisely on moral grounds: morality "was no more than the senile form of a system of forces that cannot be mistaken for morality without a loss of ethical force." His own endeavor, formed in the full "self-confidence of youth," had instead been to "live hypothetically," and of course his holiday from life, even as it reflects a crisis of that early confidence, continues this experimental, quasi-scientific approach to his own existence and his relations to other men and women. The idea of a hypothesis, however, has become a suspect notion to him, designed as it is to arrive in the end at proof.

It's in this context, with Diotima's superficial pursuit of the good and Moosbrugger's unfettered depravity in the background, that Ulrich formulates and embraces what he calls "essayism": "It was approximately in the way that an essay, in the sequence of its paragraphs, takes a thing from many sides without comprehending it wholly—for a thing wholly comprehended instantly loses its bulk and melts down into a concept—that he believed he could best survey and handle his life." Essayism resists any final definition and, in Musil's articulation of it, paradoxically goes against the grain of precisely the pragmatic open-endedness so often associated with the form of the essay; Musil's restlessness is a restlessness that is not content to stop at mere reflection and reconsideration and what might be called just thinking about things (the very thing Montaigne values above all); it calls into question dogmatic truths but equally resists any sort of provisional accommodation with uncertainty, any form of just making do. Its issue must in the end be action, whether on the soul or in the world: "An essay is not the provisional or incidental expression of a conviction that might on a favourable occasion be elevated to the status of truth . . . An essay is the unique and unalterable form that a man's inner life assumes in a decisive thought. Nothing is more alien to it than that irresponsibility and semi-finishedness of mental images known as subjectivity; but neither are 'true' and 'false' . . . terms that can be applied to such thoughts." Essayists are "masters of the floating life within" and essayism a radical refusal of moral fixity.

And yet Ulrich, the master of the floating life within, keeps bumping up against the question of Moosbrugger and murder and punishment and law. How is he, the essayist, to accommodate his freedom along with the requirements of society? How is society to maintain order when it contains the likes of Moosbrugger? How is the essayist's unregulated decisive action different from Moosbrugger's murders? And where does the aesthetic world of the novel connect with the ethical (if extra-moral) world of the human? From the floating perspective, from the perspective that floating is the thing to do, the criminal Moosbrugger, driven by sexual fixations and the need to punish what attracts him, could be seen to embody the explosive dangers of repression—set afloat, the spirit would find its level—but perhaps not: perhaps Moosbrugger is the perfect illustration of why the spirit needs to be bound. What underwrites the commandment not to kill (a question that might be rephrased as why is the war bad?), especially since, for Ulrich, "the linking of anything with a law above or within arouse[s] criticism from his intelligence"? There is no way to know in advance of taking action; it is only in action that the rightness of an action becomes clear, though no general understanding is to be derived from what is a unique situation. "In some way his decision might coincide with his happiness. He might be happy that he did not kill, or happy that he did kill, but he could never be an indifferent fulfiller of a demand made upon him." What essayism points to, beyond the "pure exactitude" of mathematics in which Ulrich had taken refuge, is that "there is only one question really worth thinking about, and that is the question of right living."

Not not killing, then, but right living; not prohibition, but permission—permission to grow into ever greater vitality. As Musil ventures on to the field of essayism, his novel sounds less and less like a novel, even if his writing is always underpinned with metaphor, like that "thing wholly comprehended" rendered, above, as a piece of butter or lard, melting into conceptual nothingness on a griddle. It is by turns philosophical, analytic, theoretical (what is essayism but a theory?), but above all therapeutic. The book is not an experiment, but an exercise, the spiritual equivalent of the push-ups and jumping jacks that were as much a routine for Musil as the cigarettes he chain-smoked. The book is an exercise and an ongoing emergency, the question of what kind of book it is and if it will ever end being ever more central to the book that it is. *The Man Without Qualities*, which from one point of view looks so much like *Ulysses* and *In Search of Lost Time* and *The Magic Mountain*, is something else altogether—a freakish twentieth-century offspring of Loyola's spiritual exercises, a self-help book too big to be of help, an endless essay to no end.

And yet it remains a novel, and in the novel what happens next is that Ulrich's father, the aged, universally esteemed expositor of the law, dies, obliging Ulrich to return to his rural hometown and childhood home to attend the funeral and to settle the will. There he encounters—have we heard of her before? only in passing if at all—his younger sister Agathe, and the book is transformed, or rather, a new book begins. From here on, the Viennese scene, and Diotima, will recede into the background while the very different story of brother and sister moves to the fore. Agathe, still in her twenties, is also facing a crisis in her life. Married early to a man she loved deeply who died almost immediately, she succumbed to a grief that has, in a sense, never lifted, even though to get over it, she married again. Hagauer, a professor of education, is Agathe's husband, and he is not only distinguished and learned, but intelligent and good. Agathe despises him. She despised him from the start, and perhaps even more herself for marrying him. Having come to bury her father, she has decided that she will never go back to Hagauer. She is dead to these two figures, who represent learning and justice as conventionally understood.

Agathe was no closer to the departed father than Ulrich was, and though brother and sister have pretty much been strangers to each other, Musil's description of their first encounter, each by coincidence dressed in an androgynous Pierrot-like pajama costume, immediately establishes the one as the reflection of the other in the mirror space of sex. (Being two in one, they also bear a notable resemblance to Kakania.) And so, at first over their father's bier and continuing in the course of excursions to the surrounding country and while sorting their father's papers in his handsome library, Agathe and Ulrich begin a series of intense conversations—holy conversations, Musil calls them, and he is not being ironic. Agathe may be even more spiritually famished than Ulrich, and not having been malformed by the burdens of education and occupation that men bear, she is quicker than he is not just to question but to break the rules. Agathe, whose name means "good," is willing to be bad. Like that, she bends down and slides off her garter and slips it into her dead father's pocket—how scandalized he would have been!—and before long she has made up her mind to alter his will, which, by law, would consign her part of the estate not to her, but to Hagauer.

Ulrich is aghast and enchanted, and as brother and sister continue to talk, their discussions circle back to the topics he has entertained from the start of the novel while moving outward (and inward) toward states of contemplation that verge on the ecstatic and erotic. These conversations, modeled in part on those between Dante and Beatrice in "Paradiso," also reflect on the moral and spiritual travails of the twentieth-century novel. Rejecting moralism and, pointedly, the good judgment of his nineteenth-century father, Ulrich is no less dismissive of the immoralism of Gide's Michel; decadence and bohemianism are after all only alternative conventions. Admiring, as we have seen, scientific exactitude, Ulrich nonetheless disdains the scientism of Wells. And though Agathe and Ulrich do not of course know that they are characters in a novel, Musil the novelist gives them the task of breaking that frame of understanding as much as any other. Musil—this is another way in which he is unlike Mann, Proust, and Joyce—was not finally invested in writing a big book, an encyclopedic book, even as his book got ever bigger. Interested in taking note of every fine distinction, he's as happy to see the balloon pop as he is to see it swell and take flight, and if anything, expansion constitutes a form of asceticism here: the rigor of the quest demands that it continue indefinitely.

In Agathe and Ulrich's duet over the body of their dead father, Ulrich takes the conceptual and Agathe the sensual and willful part (who then is more active?), so it is left to him to articulate the realization that the question of right living that haunts the novel hinges on a question of belief. Ulrich's predicament is, he says, that he is a believer who doesn't believe in anything. This allows for a possibility of a *via negativa*, an apophatic approach to knowledge, not unrelated to the earlier disquisitions on essayism, though it was not clear if those actually led anywhere. Agathe, in any case, wants something more. Often at a lack for words to say what she feels and wants, she yearns for, we come to understand, something deeper than Ulrich's torrent of words and Musil's multiplying scenes and chapters. What can it be? How can it be shown? The book about stopping to think—about the pursuit of happiness and the triviality of modern life, about right living, about the interdependence of ethics and aesthetics and the question of evil—has evolved, or simply shifted, since evolution is too unidirectional to suit Musil's octopoid mind, into a book in which belief is to find its embodiment—transgression meeting transcendence—in the incestuous union of brother and sister and the creation of a new woman/man. Ulrich and Agathe's dead father can be taken as a figure for Jehovah, but who expected the novel to turn into Genesis?

Ulrich and Agathe do have sex in one of the many chapters and sketches of chapters of *The Man Without Qualities* that Musil left behind after his death; then again, in the notebooks he also records that there will be no need for them to have sex. Both ends were conceivable, but neither was satisfactory, since the form of the novel, and the form of brother and sister's and man and woman's relationships, was essentially asymptotic, a continual approximation of what cannot be said. Like Zeno's arrow, *The Man Without Qualities* perpetually approaches a target that it can never reach, or perhaps perpetually defers the inevitable disaster, the war, of which it is the product, even as a new war broke out before Musil died and left his finally unfinishable book finally unfinished.

Musil's book, I've suggested, is a novel in which the critic looking over the novelist's shoulder steps into the action, and the action here is, essentially, the writing and rewriting of the book over the course of a century of crisis. The critic at the shoulder might disapprove of this book all the more for his having been drawn into it; his involvement—Georg Lukács would have said something like this—means that it not only never ends but also could be accused of never taking form. Then again, the critic might also see in it the delirious realization of the critical principle itself, tirelessly questioning any and all given forms, an apotheosis. The reader, in any case, encounters a book that is funny, riddling, enigmatic, and quite beautiful at times, a social satire, the world's longest feuilleton, a philosophical digression, a pilgrim's progress. This product of Musil's other-mindedness is a book unlike any other, and one of the things that sets it apart is that, as it goes on, one senses, quite strangely, that it might have been another book altogether. In that sense, the experience of reading it is a little like the experience of contemplating one's own life, its events coming to mind both as what they are and as what they might have been, and also as what might still be transformed—at least until time runs out—and it's worth noting that at one point *The Man Without Qualities* was to have been called *Agathe* and that one of Musil's notes sees the beginning of the book in the meeting of brother and sister. It's also unsettling, as the whole book is, to think that their coming together at what now passes for the end of the book might well be seen as that mainstay of the nineteenth-century novel—marriage.

It comes with the territory, of course, that this book, which in its shapelessness can only be considered the most improbable of successes, is also a failure. A failure because, even as it seems to shed the skin of the novel and emerge as some glittering new serpent of wisdom, it remains a novel. A failure because, even as it seeks to call into question the abstractions of philosophy, it cannot—except in the thoroughly symbolic form of incest—embody them in a novel. Certainly it does not succeed in giving birth to the new era in the history of the spirit announced in the title of the second book of Musil's novel. *Into the Millennium*, it's called, and the word and the hopes Musil invested in it and in his book could only have resonated with growing strangeness as the Nazis pursued their Thousand-Year Reich, Austria was absorbed into Germany, and Musil himself was prevented from publishing and then driven into the Swiss exile in which he died. We feel the urgency of the work and its immense, sad brilliance and how finally it too must fall prey to the irony it everywhere displays, even as it dreams of some final candor, and so at last we see it: an infinite scaffolding around an unbuildable house.

12. THE HUMAN AND THE INHUMAN
ITALO SVEVO'S *CONFESSIONS OF ZENO* AND
JEAN RHYS'S *GOOD MORNING, MIDNIGHT*

"Over the last few days both Martha and I have had a good deal of pleasure reading Zeno Cosini by Italo Svevo," wrote Robert Musil in one of the forty notebooks he maintained on various subjects, notebooks he even envisioned publishing one day as *The Forty Notebooks*, with that definite article very much to the point. For Musil, everything he did was part of the great work, and in that, he is like the other postwar writers I have been talking about here, all of whom have something to prove—and, bringing a certain hindsight to bear at this point, you could say that this has been a defining feature of the twentieth-century novel from the start: it has been on a mission to find out what it is, to show itself for what it is, and to tell all the world, and that this is important, all important, a matter of life and death.

Then again, there are writers who look askance at all that, who are mercifully, or mercilessly, free of the impulse to convert the reader, moved by their own peculiar concerns and quirky talent more than they are by big questions of art and the big questions of the day. These unapologetic writers contribute as richly and strangely to the fabric of the twentieth-century novel as do those who set out to serve as its masters. These writers may also be said to have learned a lesson from Proust and Joyce, but a rather different one, admiring in them not so much their greatness, as the greatness of their self-absorption, their unfettered devotion to their own sensibility, the absurdity of the inspiration that we can't help but catch occasional glimpses of between their lines.

Svevo, who gave Musil and his wife such pleasure, is very much one of these writers, and it's a matter of fact that without Joyce, we would not have Svevo as we now know him, which is to say as the author of the novel translated into English as *Confessions of Zeno*. Ettore Schmitz (Svevo's given name), born in 1861, so of the same generation as Wells or Gide, was a Triestine Jew from the business class who was educated in Germany. His early dreams of writing were dashed by his father's financial misfortunes. He worked in a bank and in 1892 published a novel, *A Life*, and in 1898, a second one, *Senilità* (translated as *As a Man Grows Older*). Both books are close studies of psychological frustration, and their protagonists might be described as Svevo described himself in a letter to his wife-to-be, Livia: the "end product of a century's ferment—a creature that cannot continue because all it knows how to want with any intensity is peace or hasty satisfaction." Both books were hardly noted, poorly received, and immediately forgotten. Livia Svevo's memoir tells us that her husband was especially wounded by critics who "reproached him for the poverty of his language." This Jewish writer's Italian was not only not the literary Italian taught in schools, but also his regional Triestine dialect, and for some Italian critics this meant that his work could only be deemed provincial.

Schmitz/Svevo gave up any dreams of being a writer, devoting himself to working in his father-in-law's business, for which he traveled frequently, sometimes as far as London. Wanting to improve his English, he hired James Joyce, "at that time . . . a fashionable teacher of Trieste's rich bourgeoisie," as a tutor. The two men hit it off. Joyce read his stories to Svevo. Svevo gave Joyce his novels. Joyce admired them. "Some pages of *As a Man Grows Older* could not have been done," Joyce said, "by the great masters of the French novel." The two men remained in touch, and by the end of the war, Svevo had a new novel in mind. Finished by 1922, he self-published it the next year, and in Italy once again it attracted little attention or praise. But he sent it to Joyce, who, following the publication of *Ulysses*, had become a European figure. "As far as the Italian critics are concerned," Joyce wrote back, "I don't know. But have review copies sent to M. Valery Larbaud, M. Benjamin Crémieux, Mr. T. S. Eliot, Mr. F. M. Ford. I shall speak with or write to these literary men about it." Chapters of *Confessions of Zeno*, and soon of his earlier novels, appeared in France, and Svevo was "called the Italian Proust." *Zeno* was rapidly translated into other European languages, and at last Svevo found admirers even on home ground, among them the brilliant young poet Eugenio Montale, who later won the Nobel Prize. Svevo was eager to write a new book, though his health was failing. In 1928, he died after a car crash.

Confessions of Zeno might be described as a descendant of *Notes from Underground*—in his youth, Svevo was a keen reader of Dostoevsky—but it is more genial than nerve-wracking. Zeno Cosini is a smoker, a compulsive smoker, and—this is the initial humorous conceit of one of the world's great comic novels—a compulsive quitter of smoking, as addicted to the latter as to the former. In fact, every single cigarette Zeno has ever smoked, starting with the first—from a package bought as a boy with money pilfered from his father's pocket—has been his last cigarette, a pattern that he would be the first to call pathological. (He is as devoted to, and entangled in, infinite regression as his paradox-mongering namesake, or, for that matter, Musil's Urich.) Now, however, he is getting old, and he has decided, at last, to address his predicament seriously, signing up for a course of—what could be more twentieth century?—psychoanalysis. Yet even as we begin his first-person account of his lifelong struggle, we know that this latest effort has already ended in failure, since Zeno's narrative is preceded by a note from none other than Zeno's analyst: "I must apologize for having persuaded my patient to write his autobiography," he says, and with an inconsistency that rivals his patient's, he continues: "I still think the idea was a good one," if only "the patient had not thrown up his cure just at the most interesting point . . . I take my revenge by publishing [these memoirs], and I hope he will be duly annoyed. I am quite ready however to share the financial spoils with him on condition he resumes his treatment."

The only product of Zeno's unavailing therapeutic labors is the book in hand, which proves to be an interminable self-reckoning that never really adds up, or adds up to something quite different, perhaps, from what he meant. (Zeno, we will discover, bears a distinct resemblance to T. S. Eliot's J. Alfred Prufrock, muttering, "That is not what I meant at all. That is not it, at all.") Zeno is a well-heeled citizen of Trieste, an Italian city that, at the time of the story, was a possession of the Austro-Hungarian Empire, and the story he has to tell is, on the face of it, spectacularly ordinary: Zeno studied without conviction or direction, inherited hard-earned savings from his father, married, had a child, prospered. Behind the scenes, however, there is quite another story. Did his father—they had nothing in common; Zeno considered him a stuffed shirt and a bit of a joke; the father took Zeno for a waster—deliberately strike his son as he fell dead from a stroke, the scene Zeno describes, or was it rather that Zeno knows he turned a blind eye to his ailing father's health? What is the nature of Zeno's marriage to Augusta, to whom he proposed, he admits, only after and because her sisters Ada and Alberta had successively refused him? (He still has a crush on both of his sisters-in-law.) He cheats on his wife (we learn about his first love affair, not that he ever had the least intention of getting involved in a love affair), and he cheats his brother-in-law and business partner, Guido, the unforgivable recipient of Ada's hand, and somehow or other the unsuspecting, rather dreamy Guido speculates himself into bankruptcy while Zeno's assets, carefully secured, accumulate inexorably. But Zeno, lighting another last cigarette, is of course distraught about all these entirely unforeseen eventualities, as he sees them, and that is why he has sought help. And then there is, always, his health. Since his honeymoon, he has been on his last legs: it was "a light illness" that attacked him, he says, though he "was never to recover . . . A mere trifle; the fear of growing old and above all the fear of death." And so he pursues an endless "series of cures." "I love my medicine," he admits, and having studied chemistry at university, he is able casually to expatiate on the lethal results of combining certain medicines to Guido, the very combination—who would have expected it?—the disgraced brother-in-law employs to end his own life.

The title of Svevo's book in Italian is *La coscienza di Zeno*, and *coscienza*, though related to English "conscience," also carries connotations of self-awareness and even wisdom, and if Zeno's conscience might be seen as the critic at the shoulder of my last chapter, Zeno's wisdom is to pay him no heed. Zeno is forever blaming himself for his behavior or wringing his hands over its results, but he forgives himself for everything and then does it all over again. He can hardly be said to have a conscience, but he certainly does have his ways of getting what he wants, and they serve him very well. For his part, he is happy to present himself as the most unattractive of men, stooped, balding, sickly, a layabout and old now, and only getting older, all of which surely excuses everything. When you get down to it, Zeno has no conscience at all. He is a monster of pettiness, selfishness, even ruthlessness. He is odious, appalling. And yet, for all that, he is funny, he is charming. Like Augusta—notwithstanding all his infidelities, his wife is forever faithful to him—we love him.

What makes Zeno, in spite of himself, so charming, and his story funny? Partly it is that he is, quite unabashedly, everybody's worst self. Shameless, he is the token of our innocence, which of course is precisely how he sees it. The main thing, however, that makes Zeno exercise such a hold on our imagination and heart is that he is the almost mythical being whose uncertain toehold in the twentieth-century novel prompted that famous critical dispute between Arnold Bennett and Virginia Woolf: a character. (Bennett would review *Zeno* in a popular London paper, writing "take out your map of modern literature and mark on it the name of Italo Svevo.") Character, Heraclitus said, is fate, which is to say the character is a figure whose true nature will be revealed no matter what he does or doesn't do, the way Oedipus simply is the man who will kill his father and sleep with his mother. He has no other being to be, and to pretend otherwise will only make his predicament that much more plain. (Zeno's shrink diagnoses him as having—what else?—an Oedipus complex, and his patient is predictably indignant; that said, Zeno, like Oedipus, always ends up doing what he protests he never meant to do.) Character is a human type given memorably individual form, memorable because we recognize in the individual a defining form of the human, a specific dimension of what we as human beings have it in us to be. Character gives life to our sense of what it means to be human, which is the reason real characters often turn into adjectives. Falstaff is a character. Mr. Micawber and Mr. Podsnap are characters. So is Emma Woodhouse and, pathetic as she is, Emma Bovary.

Not all fictional characters are characters in this sense, and Bennett was prescient when he diagnosed the twentieth-century novel as more often than not lacking them (perhaps, we could say, because in it the character of the novel becomes more important than its characters). As E. M. Forster noted, whatever Mrs. Dalloway is, and remarkable as she is, she is not a character. Nick Adams is not a character; nor is Kafka's Joseph K. We would not recognize their like on the street. They are luminous presences—through them we see something new about the world and, perhaps even more important, about language—but they themselves don't cast much of a shadow, or, you could say, they exist largely in the shadow of their makers, whose sensibility and perhaps even fate they seem to reflect. Leopold Bloom, by contrast, is a character, *l'homme moyen sensuel*, though it is oddly disconcerting to think about the immensity and complexity of the fictional architecture Joyce required to realize so straighforwardly human a being. Bloom as it happens is in part modeled on Italo Svevo, and Zeno in turn—Jewish like Schmitz himself and, of course, Bloom—is in part a reflection of Joyce's creation. *Zeno* is marked throughout—this is also part of the pure pleasure of the book—by a very Jewish sense of humor, unfailingly, unflappably fatalistic.

Zeno is a character, and one of the great characters of twentieth-century fiction, along with Bloom and the good soldier Švejk and Baron de Charlus and Bertie Wooster. As a character, Zeno is an avatar of the hypocrite (though he updates this Victorian and medieval mainstay) and a precursor of the likes of Portnoy (Roth's psychoanalytic mise-en-scène bears the mark of Svevo). Zeno, born in the nineteenth century, is something of a throwback; he may make fun of his father's steady habits and high ideals, the pomposity of his self-presentation, and we laugh along with him as he does, but at the same time he goes on enjoying every patriarchal perk in the book, free, however, of the associated responsibilities. Zeno, in any case, is the hypocrite as immoralist rather than moralist, who goes on benefiting from all the stable arrangements he claims to find no comfort in. "Complete freedom consists in doing what you want on condition that you do something else as well which you like less," he says at one point, while, mortally ill as he always deems himself, he happily signs up for new illnesses in the interest of getting on with life: he is crushed with depression, he tells Augusta, "invent[ing] a disease that was to enable me to do whatever I wanted without feeling guilty." (Zeno bears a good deal of resemblance to Machado's Brás Cubas, by the way.) Old-fashioned man of substance, newfangled creature of countless complexes, he is transcendentally and transparently two-faced, and he makes the therapeutic nostrums of Freudianism seem as absurd as everything else he touches. Unapologetically unreliable narrator par excellence ("I myself could not open my mouth without misrepresenting things or people" he admits), a monster of egotism who perpetually betrays himself, Zeno makes a game of everything, just as his father complained, and yet his gift to us, Svevo's gift of him to us, is to expose the endless fictions of which what passes for reality or identity is composed. Character, humanity itself, is revealed as the irreducible remainder of all our good intentions and self-justifications. The gift of the absurd. We feel the happier for it.

So the book lives up in its way to its therapeutic conceit, a cure for the sorrow and frustration it records, and at the end Zeno pronounces himself completely cured, thanks perhaps to the writing of it, rather than to the shrink, now dumped. (Not that he is not still smoking.) But really, Zeno is cured thanks to having made a bundle on currency speculation in the Great War, which has started as his book comes to an end, and even more money on what sounds like the black market. *Zeno* is in fact a war book, undertaken by Svevo because the war had idled his business, and at the end, almost breaking character, he allows the darkness underlying it to emerge. In his new condition of well-being, facilitated by the disaster of war, Zeno's thoughts turn to universal destruction. He has a vision, an H. G. Wells moment:

> When all the poison gases are exhausted, a man, made like other men of flesh and blood, will in the quiet of his room invent an explosive of such potency that all the explosives in existence will seem like harmless toys beside it. And another

man, made in his image and in the image of all the rest, but a little weaker than them, will steal that explosive and crawl to the center of the earth with it and place it just where he calculates it would have the maximum effect. There will be a tremendous explosion, but no one will hear it and the earth will return to its nebulous state and go wandering through the sky, free at last from parasites and disease.

The vision of universal destruction is a vision of the universal return to health, Zeno's ultimate paradox. Of course, within a quarter century of the publication of *Zeno*, the vision (in no way unique to Svevo) was proved prophetic—we now really can blow up the world and cure all our problems—and one of the reasons Svevo's novel still makes us laugh is because it is so riddled with a darkness that is our own, ever more our own. Puffing away all the time, Zeno the conniver and destroyer is also the ultimate survivor (unlike the hapless Guido). Zeno the amateur chemist might be the inventor of the bomb. Zeno the obsessive nurser of grudges could also easily be the person who climbs into the hole with it clutched to his breast and detonates it. Zeno would certainly be its victim. Can Zeno survive Zeno, or any of us ourselves? It is, Svevo makes it clear, only as the likes of Zeno—hardly as the new man/woman of Musil—that we will survive, and in all conscience, let us recognize and even embrace our hopeless characters.

Human failings and human cravings: Zeno's endless cigarettes and endless excuses, his appetite for cigarettes and excuses, ally his story with a small but notable subgenre of the twentieth-century novel, the alcoholic novel. This is not to be confused with novels about the perils of alcoholism, a venerable storyline and a flourishing moral property of the Victorian era, even if, unsurprisingly, some alcoholic novels are written by and about alcoholics, nor is it the same thing as a novel written by an alcoholic. Hemingway was an alcoholic; Fitzgerald, Faulkner, Cheever, Kingsley Amis, etc.: none of them are writers of the alcoholic novel. The true alcoholic novel is not so much about drinking as it is steeped in the power of the bottle both to concentrate and freeze the attention and to let it wander. It is a variant, typically, of the Gidean high literary novel of voice in which the writer taps into the self-awareness that may come with self-indulgence and, in the best of such books, finds the stylistic resources to slur and brawl and black out with precision. And to go on, because the alcoholic novel is essentially a heroic (and comic) construct. Among such books are Gyula Krúdy's Sinbad stories, Malcolm Lowry's *Under the Volcano* and Venedikt Erofeev's *Moscow to the End of the Line*, and the late novels of Joseph Roth, like *The Emperor's Tomb*, overgrown with metaphor. Henry Green is perhaps the purest of alcoholic writers, modeling in his sentences the slippery fishbowl distortions of ordinary speech, meaning and intent drifting in and out of sight amidst the wobbly weeds and the shimmer of words. Green has the gift of falling asleep at the start of a sentence and waking up in some entirely other place without batting an eyelid, and after writing nine novels of perfect originality, he lapsed in his last decades into alcoholic silence.

Jean Rhys is another master of the art. Rhys was born on the Caribbean island of Dominica, the daughter of a doctor who had emigrated from Wales. Sent as a teenager to study art in England, she found a gig as a chorus girl in a touring theatrical troupe and fell in love with a rich young Englishman who broke her heart and left her a small, irregular stipend for her pains. She never really got over the experience. She married a shady Dutch journalist, drifted from Amsterdam to Vienna to Paris, had two children, one of whom died, and started to write. In Paris, Rhys came under the sway of the eternal and ubiquitous Ford Madox Ford, who spotted her talent. He also moved Rhys in with his wife in a ménage à trois, an unhappy situation that inspired Rhys's first novel, *Quartet*.

Rhys wrote four novels in total between 1928, when *Quartet* came out, and the advent of the Second World War: the first, *After Leaving Mr. Mackenzie*, was followed by a novel about a kept and forsaken woman, and another, *Voyage in the Dark*, drew on her music hall years; in 1939 came *Good Morning, Midnight*. The heroines of these novels, Marya, Julia, Anna, Sasha, are all the same woman—pretty, a little giddy, self-conscious, passive, romantic, disabused, depressed, self-destructive. They are all mood, condemned neither to outgrow their dreams nor ever to put much faith in them. They know perfectly well, and, really, haven't they always known, that money makes the world go round, and if they continue to live *la vie de bohème*, or rather to slip ever deeper into social limbo and their personal hell, it's not because they feel much of an attachment to it, but because they can't help it. Someday, they suppose, their man will come, money in hand; someday love may transform their lives entirely; something, as Mr. Micawber says, will turn up. Yes, someday. Why not? In the meantime, they drift among jobs and cafés and hotel rooms and men, or they fall into depression and decide to drink themselves to death, but never quite succeed at any of it. They drift and drink while popular songs play in the background, they kill time in the movies, and sometimes they slip into prostitution, and when they have a little money, they may go on a small spree. "Money, for the night is coming," thinks Sasha in *Good Morning, Midnight* ("Work, for the night is coming," says the Bible), and she imagines going to the department store Au Printemps the next day "to buy gloves, buy scent, buy lipstick . . . buy anything cheap. Just the sensation of spending, that's the point." In all this, the Rhys character is the opposite of Colette's Claudine, as Rhys is of Colette. Claudine and Colette are women who take their lives firmly in hand, while Rhys's protagonists slip determinedly out of control. Who they do resemble is the beautiful, clueless, booze- and drug-addicted young man, a pure product of a twentieth century in which he feels completely at a loss, who gives his nickname to Colette's great Cheri novels—though, unlike Rhys's women, Cheri at least is rich.

Of Rhys's novels, *Good Morning, Midnight* is certainly the bleakest: as bare as bones. On the advice of a friend, Sasha has come to Paris to take a vacation from the void her life in London has become, and that friend, one can only suspect, just wants to get Sasha out of her hair. It is 1937, Sasha is not getting younger, and her hotel, she notes wryly, is located on an impasse, as dead-end streets are named in France. What is crucial, she says to herself, is to organize her days around a "program," but everywhere she goes there are ghosts—of old jobs, old lovers, of the child she lost—and all she can bring herself

THE HUMAN AND THE INHUMAN

to do is try to remember and try to forget. *Good Morning, Midnight* is written in the present tense, at that point still an unusual narrative tense in English, to devastating effect. Sasha lives in the perpetual present of someone with no past and no future, the perpetual present of the afterlife:

> Eat. Drink. Walk, March. Back to the Hotel. To the Hotel of Arrival, the Hotel of Departure, the Hotel of the Future, the Hotel of Martinique and the Universe . . . Back to the hotel without a name and the street without a name. You press a button and the door opens. This is the Hotel Without-a-Name in the Street Without-a-Name, and the clients have no names, no faces. You go up the stairs. Always the same stairs, always the same room.
> Then again:
> My life, which seems so simple and monotonous, is really a complicated affair of cafés where they like me and cafés where they don't, streets that are friendly, streets that aren't, rooms where I might be happy, rooms where I never shall be, looking-glasses I look nice in, looking-glasses I don't, dresses that will be lucky, dresses that won't, and so on.

"What is she doing here, the stranger, the alien, the old one?" she imagines a park attendant thinking. She goes on, "I have seen that in people's eyes all my life. I am asking myself all the time what the devil I am doing here. All the time." Then again she also has her answer (a knowing echo of Stein's "Rose is a rose is a rose"): "I'm here because I'm here because I'm here."

This is post–World War I Paris, which is to say the world capital of art and style, the capital of what I called Hotel World earlier, with the usual cosmopolitan traffic of tourists: Americans, Arabs, others from elsewhere. Sasha may once have been part of all that. She isn't really anymore. She meets a melancholic young Russian. He spends money on her and she feels bad, so she spends some of the little money she has to buy a so-called African mask from a friend of his who makes a living off forging such things. She meets another young man whom she immediately sizes up as a gigolo. He flirts with her, and she flirts back, since she likes the thought that he thinks she is rich enough to support him, and when it becomes clear that she is not, she likes him because he wants to seduce her even so. After a drunken evening they go back to her hotel room, but when he wants to have sex, her mood abruptly turns against him. They struggle, and he leaves. She is very drunk and suddenly distraught that he is gone. Her next-door neighbor, often encountered on the landing in his white nightshirt, a sinister man who has accosted and yelled at her, breaks into her room. "I look into his eyes and despise another human being for the last time." In his white nightshirt, he had first impressed her as looking like "a priest, the priest of an obscene, half-understood religion." Not wanting to have sex, she submits to it, saying, Molly Bloom–like, "Yes, yes."

Like the early novels of Svevo, Rhys's books were not much remarked when they came out and were quickly forgotten. Only in 1966, when, after long silence, she published *Wide Sargasso Sea*, imagining the Caribbean backstory of Jane Eyre's Mrs. Rochester, did she begin to get the attention she deserved. Her early novels were revived and, in the 1970s, given a feminist reading. You could say that Rhys's discarded women illustrate the traditional subjugation of all women in bourgeois society; in their settled indolence and moody sensitivity, they are in fact not unlike old-fashioned Victorian "ladies," the ladies who at the same time they very much aren't. But though Rhys's women are keenly aware of themselves as women in a man's world, they can't finally be said to put up much fight against it, not just because they hardly can, and in their own minds could hardly be expected to, but because they don't care to. Cast off and degraded though these women may appear, that is not their story. Their story is that in spite of everything, they are in the end entirely themselves, and they are not sorry for it. They do not need your pity or a helping hand, and they will not have their consciousness raised. They have a job to do, a "living to fail," as one of John Berryman's poems memorably puts it. In the end, they don't need money, a man, or worldly position or recognition. They don't need anything or anybody, and besides, nobody could help them anyway. They don't need themselves. They have a

date with death, the figure of the man in the white nightshirt, hardly
to be distinguished from a woman in a nightgown—death, in which
the self is at last lost and found.

Is this a kind of self-deceiving fatalism? Naturally. Could there
have been another outcome in a better world or if they had played
their cards differently or shown more gumption? Yes, of course. There
is a nineteenth-century novel in everybody's life, and hope, as Kafka
said, is infinite, but not for us. I can't think of another writer of the
1920s and '30s who is as tough-minded, not least in courting the accu-
sation of a kind of desperate sentimentality. Rhys's world is the world
of Vicki Baum's *Grand Hotel* and Hemingway, but she doesn't take
Baum's bird's-eye view of it, nor does she confront and condemn its
inauthenticities with the high style of Hemingway. Rhys doesn't need
to prove herself; she doesn't expect you, the way Woolf and Hemingway do, to admire her poise and acumen and guts, though she has
plenty. Which is not to say that Rhys was not as hungry for recognition as any writer, but that she doesn't ever compromise the perfect
sangfroid of her depiction of her characters or the pitiless simplicity
of her prose. Her novels are less novels than acts of ritual violation
and purification in which her characters, vowed to abjection as a nun
is to God, resist every temptation of the good life or of setting themselves up at all. (If they seem like waifs and naïfs, that only shows that
their author is as hard as nails.) Rhys's characters are among what
Simone Weil, who bears a surprising resemblance to them, called the
afflicted. Weil wrote, "In an epoch like ours when affliction is suspended over all of us, bringing help to the soul is only effective to the
point of preparing it for affliction"; Rhys, more rigorous, would not
have permitted herself the consolation of an epoch.

Shortly before Sasha is raped, overcome with regret about driving
off her Russian gigolo, hopelessly drunk, she has an out-of-body experience, a vision:

> A hum of voices talking, but all you can hear is "Femmes,
> femmes, femmes, femmes . . ." And the noise of a train saying:
> "Paris, Paris, Paris, Paris . . ." Madame Venus is angry and

Phoebus Apollo is walking away from me down the boulevard
to hide himself in la crasse. Only address: Mons P. Apollo, La
Crasse . . . But I know quite well that all this is hallucination,
imagination. Venus is dead; Apollo is dead; even Jesus is dead.
    All that is left of the world is an enormous machine, made
of white steel. It has innumerable flexible arms, made of steel.
Long, thin arms. At the end of each arm is an eye, the eyelashes
stiff with mascara.

"I have another drink," that passage ends, Sasha coming back to her
senses. If Svevo gives us a glimpse of the incorrigibly human, Rhys embraces the inhuman, each, notably, against a backdrop of the end of the
world. This vision, of a vision machine staring out through made-up
eyes (which is to say eyes intended for another's observation, the other
who is nowhere to be seen) at a world it can never fully envision, since
all that is left of the world is itself, is a vision of woman as both victim
and predator, a monster secured at last in her monstrous aloneness.
It is very much not the vision that Mrs. Dalloway presents at the end
of Woolf's novel—"for there she was"—of a woman realized, which
is why Rhys's work remains unassimilable to feminism, or for that
matter any of the isms that the twentieth century paraded (apart from
alcoholism, perhaps). But that vision could be seen as a figure of the
novel, brandishing in vain—here a woman's vanity but also, because
Rhys is in the end a moralist, the vanity of human understanding—its
countless points of view.

13. THE EXCEPTION

D. H. LAWRENCE'S *SONS AND LOVERS* AND
THE RAINBOW

Such an improbable figure! Improbable, first and foremost, that he should even have become a novelist, leaping over all the obstacles that in his day barred a working-class English boy from the so-called world of letters. D. H. Lawrence was nothing if not working-class: his father a coal miner, his mother a woman of some education but little social standing who bitterly resented the marriage she'd made. Lawrence, born in 1885 and spurred on by his mother's vicarious ambition, was able to benefit from the expanding social state at the turn of the century, along with the expanding market in cultural goods. He was well-schooled (ferociously self-taught), and though unable to take a university degree, he qualified as a schoolteacher, and by the age of twenty-three had found a position in a school outside of London. He wanted to be a writer, though, and his literary talent was quickly recognized: a girlfriend sent off some of his poems to Ford Madox Ford at *The English Review*, and Ford liked them, published them, and helped Lawrence find a publisher for the novel he was working on, *The White Peacock*. The book came out in 1911, receiving respectable reviews.

He was launched, and before long he was regularly placing poems and stories in periodicals and had had a second novel accepted for publication by Edward Garnett, the influential editor who was the husband of the celebrated translator from the Russian, Constance Garnett. Soon, too, he was able to quit his teaching job and devote himself to writing. His gift was acknowledged, yet at the same time he would always remain a freak. Ford wondered before meeting him, "if he was really the son of a working class coal-miner, how exactly how was I to approach him in conversation?" After all, he came from "a race as sharply divided from the ruling or even the mere white-collar classes as was the negro from the gentry of Virginia." Garnett's son, David, whom Lawrence befriended, described the writer's hair as "bright mud-colour, with a streak of red in it, a thick mat, parted on one side. Somehow it was incredibly plebeian, mongrel, and underbred," while the man himself was "the weedy runt you find in every gang of workmen." Animal metaphors proliferate around Lawrence; he retained his Midlands accent, and Rebecca West thought his voice sounded "curious, hollow, like the soft hoot of an owl." Lawrence himself made the best of it: "I'm afraid I'm incorrigibly ill-bred."

An unlikely novelist, he led an even more unlikely life. As a child, he was a mama's boy, sickly, studious, quizzical, ever alert; he would grow up preferring the company of women to that of men. Sympathetic in many ways to the cause of women's rights, he saw more of himself in women: like him, they stood outside the established order of things, eager to be free of it but uncertain of what shape that freedom should take. As they wondered what it was to be a woman if it was not to be merely a wife, Lawrence, anxiously, obsessively, wondered what it was to be not a workingman or a gentleman, but a man.

Then there was the transformative encounter at age twenty-seven with Frieda Weekley, née von Richthofen, a German aristocrat who was married to a sometime teacher of Lawrence's. Six years his senior and a mother of three, she took Lawrence aside for sex when he was waiting to meet his former professor. In 1912 they eloped, beginning a career of public scandal that would last for the rest of Lawrence's short life. Frieda eventually secured a divorce; the couple married. But Frieda was from the start chronically unfaithful to Lawrence (a man more sexually fascinated than active), and the two were notorious among friends for their bitter, violent, hair-trigger fights and morning-after rapprochements.

Lawrence and Frieda were continually on the move: Germany, Italy, England again, Australia, New York (Lawrence hated New York), New Mexico, Mexico, Italy again, until Lawrence died of TB when he was forty-four. They moved for his health; they moved because Lawrence couldn't imagine possessing something as confining as a home. All the time, however, he was writing: poems, stories, novels, criticism, polemics, prophecies, psychological tracts, a book-length interpretation of the Book of Revelation, countless letters. (He is a wonderful letter writer.) He wrote, he made a living writing, but what he wrote repeatedly ran into legal obstacles. *The Rainbow*, one of his greatest novels, was withdrawn from publication for obscenity. For the same reason, *Lady Chatterley's Lover*, his final novel, could only be published privately on the Continent, and the book remained banned in England until 1960. Even so, his work was in demand.

Utterly charming when he chose to be, attentive, sympathetic, funny, an amazing mimic, Lawrence was also moody, paranoid, pedantic, prickly, scolding, prone to violent outbursts and permanent breaks. If he liked you, he would probably write about you, but you were unlikely to like what he wrote, while he was always taken aback that his former friends should have discerned any resemblance to them in the characters in his books. He could see uncomfortably deeply into people; he could also see only what he wanted to see. E. M. Forster had been an early admirer of Lawrence's work, and Lawrence and Frieda eventually invited him to stay with them in the country. "Forster is here," Lawrence writes in a letter. "He is very nice. I wonder if the grip has gone out of him . . . We have talked so hard . . . at least I have talked—it is my fate, God help me." What had they talked about? Lawrence spent the weekend hectoring the gay Forster, pressing him about his need to "take a woman and fight clear to his own basic, primal being." Unedified and unamused, Forster left. A few weeks later Lawrence revisits the episode in another letter to another new friend, Bertrand Russell. Is he being sheepish when he writes, "He was very angry with me for telling him about himself"? Perhaps, since he continues, "I feel you are tolerant when you listen . . . I wish you'd tell me when I am foolish and overinsistent." It didn't take long for the relationship with Russell to crash and burn too.

How to think of Lawrence's achievement? In his own day, he was seen as both prophetic and preposterous; looking back, he may seem the quintessential twentieth-century novelist: a writer who reveals things once kept under lock and key—domestic misery, manual labor, sex—a writer determined to set himself and everyone else free. He denounces the hypocritical world that was; he denounces the new century no less relentlessly—this too is of the essence of the twentieth-century novelist's role. The new fashions are even phonier than the old lies. He despises politics, and he fantasizes about politics—a proponent of revolution, or perhaps it is reaction. Novels from the 1920s, such as *Kangaroo* (set in Australia) and *The Plumed Serpent* (Mexico), are about strongmen heading popular movements in which the people are to heed the call of their blood and return to a state of pre-political ritual observance; there is more than a whiff of fascism here. Man must be remade, woman must be remade, the world must be remade, the novel must be remade. Something newer, older, deeper, lighter is needed if we are—and here the great postwar commonplace duly appears—to recover the "Absolute we are all after, a statement of the whole scheme" (this from a letter written to Lady Ottoline Morrell, a fashionable aristocratic patron of the arts).

Lawrence, in other words, may almost seem a sort of ventriloquist's doll, perched on the century's knee and giving voice to its sexual hunger and terror, political and aesthetic extremism, bloodlust, its self-involvement, self-aggrandizement, self-hatred, and perhaps above all its propensity to self-parody. And yes, he can be accused of all those things. And then again, not. Because no one is more conscious a critic of just these proclivities than Lawrence. So perhaps I should have written that he embodies above all the century's sheer dreadful confusion. But no, that is not true either: no one more persistently seeks clarification. There is a logic and shape to this most restless of writers, more resistant than susceptible to the siren song of "the Absolute," a will to go on thinking and feeling and living no matter what, that sets him apart. He is both the quintessential twentieth-century novelist and the great exception.

Consider *Sons and Lovers*, Lawrence's third novel, finished when he was twenty-seven. *Sons and Lovers* is a big book, written, as Lawrence always wrote, fast. Just before he started it, he was unhappily slaving away as a schoolteacher in a suburb outside of London, hoping to gain the means to marry the woman he had impulsively become engaged to. He wanted to be a writer, and he was writing tortuously about sex, of which he had had hardly any real experience. He also wanted to live a normal middle-class life. Then his mother died, and suddenly it seemed possible and necessary for him to write about a relationship that up to then had dominated and defined his life. He came down with pneumonia, was close to dying, and on recovering, he decided to give up teaching and break off his engagement. Soon after came his decisive encounter with Frieda, and soon after that the lovers' elopement, and suddenly *Sons and Lovers*—at that point called *Paul Morel* after its main character—took flight. The book was an act of emancipation—from the world of his childhood, from his mother, from the girlfriends of his teens and twenties who had formed his sensibility, from his own old self. When he sent the completed the manuscript to Edward Garnett, he included a letter saying, "I have written a great book." He had.

Not, however, a book about great people or great deeds. It's a book full of scenes of people walking, going to and fro from home to work, from town to country, upstairs and downstairs, room to room, by rivers or through woods; it is, you could say, deliberately pedestrian in its gait, about nothing so much as getting through and going on but also noticing all the things that are going on around you as you do. It is set in a coal town in the English Midlands—Lawrence's hometown of Eastwood disguised as Bestwood—and it starts out as the story of the unhappy marriage of Gertrude and Walter Morel: Gertrude, like Lawrence's mother, is an intelligent woman with social aspirations who is married to a workingman. Walter is a handsome fellow she met at a country dance whom she took to be a manager, a man on the rise, not the mere miner he is, her mistake and one she will never forgive him for. Instead Gertrude seeks to realize herself through her boys.

The outgoing older William dies young, which leaves Paul, sensitive, even girlish, very much a mama's boy, and the book now becomes—this is the greater part of Lawrence's novel—the story of Paul's efforts both to satisfy his mother and strike out on his own.

Paul goes to work in a factory at an early age—turning over his earnings to his mother while also studying to become a commercial artist.
As he graduates from his teens to his early twenties, he struggles to
make sense of girls, his feelings for them, theirs for him. Two relationships are especially important, one with the spiritual and artistic
Miriam, who comes from a farmer's family but, like Paul, is a reader
and wants something different from what she knows; the other with
the somewhat older Clara, married but separated from her husband,
carnal and political too: she is a feminist. And always there is his
mother.

All ordinary enough, and it would seem like the ordinary stuff
of the novel by this time—except, that is, for one thing: this novel
of everyday life (and the dailiness of life is stressed again throughout its four hundred or so pages by a succession of formulaic *the next
day*s, and *sometime later*s, and *at that time*s, so that the reader is as
continually aware of the coming and going of the days as he is of the
characters) is a novel of working-class life. Working-class life is just
the kind of life that, for the bourgeois novel, is not ordinary, allowing
neither for self-development nor social advancement, dooming you to
the sort of mute, baffled existence that Walter is shown to lead, to the
bitter, fruitless complaints of Gertrude. Walter in particular figures
in the novel as the man about whom a novel could never be written,
who has no words worth speaking of nor any story to tell, only coal
and coins.

Lawrence will find a place for Walter and Gertrude in his novel,
the better to show that his novel is not confined to that place, or to
pitying or picturesque evocations of the life of the laboring poor.
Lawrence describes the look of the coal town, little brick houses lined
up all in a row, the black-faced men coming home at the end of day—
"all along the road to Bestwood, the miners tramped, wet and grey
and dirty, but their red mouths talking with animation"—the physical risk of the work and the financial precariousness of it, the mine
owners simply shutting operations down when they can't pay and
the workers left to shift as best they can. He describes Walter sitting
with a basin by the stove in the parlor and washing himself; describes
Walter drunk and stupidly belligerent, Gertrude's terrible contempt

for her husband, domestic squabbles, broken plates; describes Paul's awkwardness in going to fetch his father's pay and his meek, childish pride in having a bus ticket of his own and a job of his own, carefully enumerating his modest earnings. He describes Paul making out with Clara in a field by a canal, with "the other lovers slipping behind the hedges," all without a hint of the embarrassment and pity of, for example, Woolf's depiction of Septimus Smith in *Mrs. Dalloway. Sons and Lovers* describes working-class life but in such a way as to make it plain that it is in no sense a novel of working-class life, a genre piece. It is written without a trace of "cultural cringe," even though the things it describes were sure to raise the eyebrows of well-bred readers, and did.

Clara, working-class herself, but a city girl, visits Paul in Bestwood. "What a pity," she says to Paul, "there is a coal-pit here where it is so pretty":

> "Do you think so?" he answered. "You see I am so used to it, I should miss it.—No, and I like the pits here and there. I like the rows of trucks, and the headstocks, and the steam in the daytime and the lights at night.—When I was a boy, I always thought a pillar of cloud by day and a pillar of fire by night was a pit, with its steam, and its lights and the burning bank—and I thought the Lord was always at the pit-top."

This is a surprise, to Clara and to the reader, too. The novel up to this point has shown no inclination to whitewash the black mark that is the pit. One of the things that is going on here is that Lawrence, who was endowed with a preternaturally keen sensitivity for mixed feelings, is showing Paul to bristle a bit before Clara—you won't patronize me, Paul is letting her know; you won't feel sorry for me or see through me—but in letting that understandable if somewhat mean emotion come to light, I think Lawrence also shows Paul—very likely to Lawrence's own surprise—surprising, astonishing himself. Paul, defensive, realizes that the beauty of the pit that he was claiming to score a point is in fact real. He is opened up. To the awakened imagination, even the pit is alive.

And this kind of ordinary actual astonishment is registered throughout *Sons and Lovers*. It's what the novel itself lives for; it's what sets it apart as a novel from those that came before it and others of its time. What Lawrence is struggling to do, and will continue to struggle to do in all his work, is to recover what is perhaps best described as a reawakened sense of innocence, innocence not as a lack of experience or as an escape from the consequences of one's actions—but as an alertness and receptiveness to the full variability of experience, in oneself, in others; innocence as a sense of possibility, lighting our way into and through the darkest, most difficult and inadmissable of feelings. Innocence, not judging, as the necessary ground of life and love, as the escape from the uncertainty and fear and hate that preoccupy us so much of the time, because about this—the pit, you might say, within the human breast—Lawrence makes no bones. He was afraid; she hated him; he hated her: such flat statements resound again and again in *Sons and Lovers*, a novel that is in its way quite fearless in taking the measure of ugly and unhappy and unresolved emotions.

Fearless, too, is its recognition of the power of sex, not just as something people get up to, but as a kind of ever-present confusion of the will and the senses. There is a wonderful scene where Paul and Clara are trying to find some place to make out—for them, given their youth and class, these places are almost always outdoors—and they excitedly stumble and slip down a muddy riverbank only to find themselves dangerously trapped at the river's edge. There is no place for them; the search for one lands them in a muddle, a thrilling one. There is the night that Paul is allowed to stay over at Clara's mother's house in town, though of course he must sleep apart from Clara. Her room is turned over to him—she will sleep in the parlor—and he wakes in the middle of the night wanting her desperately. Seeing a pair of her stockings on the back of a chair, he climbs out of bed and slips into them. Wearing a lady's stockings, he sits up straight—"erect," Lawrence writes—on the edge of the bed; finally, timidly, desperately, he creeps downstairs to her. The passage was cut by Garnett when the book first came out, but that Lawrence submitted it in the first place, that he wrote it at all, is extraordinary, all the more so because—you can feel it in the texture of the writing, its unapologetic matter-of-factness—he actually considered it entirely ordinary. He isn't making a point. This just is how things are.

And the denouement of the book—that too is fraught with both fear and fearlessness. Paul's mother becomes painfully and mortally ill. Paul and his sister tend to her, watch her waste away—Walter looks on helplessly—suffering for her as the pain becomes an agony. They watch in fact with the same riveted attention that comes with sexual desire. But at some point they can no longer bear it, and by tacit agreement they spike their mother's evening cup of warm milk with morphine. She dies that night. Here the pat, quasi-Freudian reading that Paul must kill his mother to be born into his own life, though unavoidable, is tritely reductive, missing the plain actuality that Lawrence brings to bear on the situation. It is not simply that the son must kill his mother: it is both that love is murderous, and that murder can be love.

Sons and Lovers is a book of fear and pain and sex and frustration and death, but also of wonder. The events of the novel play out against a background of observed life, and Lawrence is a wonderful observer of human presence—"he sat with his shirt turned back, showing his young throat almost like a girl's, and the towel in his hand, his hair sticking up wet," a sentence as perfectly paced as it is seen—and of the natural world (take, for example, a "quiet lawn surrounded by sheaves of shut-up crocuses"). He is in fact one of the great nature writers, glimpsing the shine and shadow of the woods, peering into the calyx of a flower, and if people walk back and forth endlessly in this book, everywhere they have the ground beneath their feet, the sky overhead. The lives described may be physically and emotionally cramped, but the book is full of the energy of noticing, of not settling, of seeing and seeing again. *Sons and Lovers* is a book of splendid shifting weather, both inner and outer.

Part of this energy and weather comes from the double or multiple viewpoints from which Lawrence views his characters. Formally, he is forever moving in and out of or circling around his characters and their thoughts with confident nonchalance toward the niceties of point of view. Paul, for example: much of the time we see things through his eyes, yet sometimes, abruptly, Lawrence pulls back and refocuses so that we see him not as he feels himself to be, but for the type of young man he is: "'I think, my friend,' said Clara very coldly, 'that I have met your sort before: the young man who thinks he knows everything,'" and we know she is right. And if the book is ultimately about Paul's coming of age, it is not about his coming into any great talent; his art is nothing special, and at the end he hasn't so much grown up as grown out of others' expectations for him, as well as his own expectations. What he arrives at is the full uncertainty of his own self, an uncertainty the novel resolutely refuses to resolve for us or for him: Paul, a quantum of life. He is not quite like us; he is in fact not quite to our liking—Lawrence makes it clear that he can be mean and small—or for that matter to his own liking; in all of which, we realize, he is no different from us. His life is not our life—it is distinctly his—but it is made present to us in such a way as to lead the individual reader to wonder in turn, What is mine?

Not only has Paul not found himself at the end, but he is said to be—this is the title of Lawrence's final chapter—derelict. It is night, and, as so often, he is on the road:

> Who could say his mother had lived and did not live. She had been in one place, and was in another, that was all. And his soul could not leave her, wherever she was. Now she was gone abroad into the night, and he was with her still. They were together. But yet there was his body, his chest that leaned against the stile, his hands on the wooden bar. They seemed something. Where was he?—one tiny upright speck of flesh, less than an ear of wheat lost in the field. He could not bear it. Night in which everything was lost, went reaching out, beyond stars and sun. Stars and sun, a few bright grains, went spinning around in terror and holding themselves in embrace.

Terror and embrace; "he could not bear it": we are in the presence of first and last things, where personal or collective histories run up against the limits of the knowable; we are walking down a country road. Paul is derelict: he has come to the place—he has become a place

and for now is nothing else—where life and death meet and everything is up in the air. Here innocence encounters the grief that is the
inevitable burden of our limited lives. Paul is grieving, left as he is at
this last moment only with the hopeless love for his lost mother, and,
Lawrence allows us to suppose, it may be that it is only in grief that we
can at last open up to ourselves and to others. "Grief, grief and suffi-
cient grief makes us free," Lawrence wrote in a poem for Frieda that
he composed while working on *Sons and Lovers*, "to be faithful and
faithless as we have to be."

Faithful and faithless describes Lawrence's relationship to literary
form too. *Sons and Lovers* may look like a bildungsroman, but it's not
really: it's more of a stripping away. And faithful and faithless also
describes how Lawrence's successive novels are related to each other,
each one reacting not so much against as away from the last. "All vital
truth contains the memory of all that for which it is not true," Lawrence wrote to a friend, and he was nothing if not a connoisseur of
contradiction. *Sons and Lovers* is about breaking away from the family and assuming the burden of individuality. *The Rainbow*, begun almost immediately after the earlier novel was finished, is by contrast a
book about, precisely, the life of a family in which Lawrence searches
for a sense of human coherence above and beyond the individual self.

The book begins in the mid-nineteenth century, when Tom Brangwen, a twenty-eight-year-old yeoman farmer from an old, well-
established farming family, falls in love with Lydia Lensky, the Polish
widow of a Polish doctor and political refugee. (The couple have had
to flee Poland after supporting that same ill-fated Warsaw uprising
that led to the banning of the Dostoevsky brothers' magazine.) Lydia,
some six years older than Tom, is a single mother with a four-year-old
daughter, Anna. Lydia speaks halting English and is from a background (she is a trained nurse) that is not remotely similar to his, but
of course it is her strangeness that draws him to her, as Lawrence in
turn is fascinated, here and throughout the novel, by the strangeness
that exists and persists between men and women, drawing them together and keeping them apart. The title of the first chapter, "How

Tom Brangwen Married a Polish Lady," tips us off right away as to how things will turn out, but how they take that turn is described with the same tight-focused intensity that Lawrence perfected in *Sons and Lovers.* The reader shares in Tom's hesitations, uncertainties, awkwardnesses, his showing up at the door with a "gripped fist of flowers," the inklings, blanks of consciousness, and other tropisms that move him toward Lydia. We are right there, in what might be called the unstoried space that always surrounds what happens, the space of wanting and waiting, full of desire and dread and ignorance of what is to be. Then Tom and Lydia are married. The story is told, and in the way of things, there is nothing left to say. Briskly, the book moves on to a new generation.

Finality and continuity: the story moves on and the story repeats itself, because here now is Will, an apprentice draftsman and designer in a lace factory, and here is Anna, Lydia's child, a slip of a girl, and though they are different of course from their parents and people of a different time, they are, Lawrence means us to see, also much the same, alike especially in that same quality I am calling wantingness. Will and Anna will marry and have nine children, and the first of the nine, Ursula, will be the novel's final subject, and Ursula will not marry. At the end of the book, after love affairs with women and men and after conceiving and miscarrying a child, she emerges, you could say, as the new subject for a new century, a single woman responsible for her own experience, yet still very much part of a larger family, and still wanting in that Lawrentian way that makes any one of us both more and less than him- or herself.

Lawrence worked on *The Rainbow* over the course of three years, beginning it while he and Frieda were still traveling in Germany and Italy, finishing it after she had obtained her divorce and they had married and moved back to an England now at war, his German wife suspected of being a spy, his own sense of the world transformed by the war into a bitter, sometimes frantic pessimism. It does not show in the book, however, which he wrote with great excitement and the sure sense that he was doing a great new thing, for himself as a writer and for the novel. Garnett, however, didn't see it that way—he was dismayed from the moment Lawrence sent him the first draft of the novel, then called *The Sisters*, and Lawrence's revisions didn't change his mind. (Garnett would eventually turn the book down.) He felt the novel wasn't on a par with *Sons and Lovers*, and to this criticism Lawrence responded that it was simply another kind of thing; it was what he was after: "I shan't write in the manner of *Sons and Lovers* again, I think—in that hard violent style full of sensation and presentation," he insisted, and then, "I have no longer the joy in creating vivid scenes that I had in *Sons and Lovers*. I don't care much more about accumulating objects in the powerful light of emotion, and making a scene of them. I have to write differently."

Lawrence, however, sells himself short here. *The Rainbow* is full of great scenes that stand out all the more because the book as whole, with its elongated time frame and shifting cast, is episodic in structure. "The powerful light of emotion" is, if anything, intensified, the style as vivid and violent as ever, but also capable of a new tenderness. Early on there is, for example, the birth of Tom and Lydia's first child, which of course takes place on the farm. Anna, still a young child, is alarmed by the whole mysterious business going on around her: something is clearly wrong with her mother. "I want my mother," she says to her stepfather, to her still very much an interloper:

> "Ay but she's badly," he said mildly, unheeding.
> She looked at him with lost, frightened eyes.
> "Has she got a headache?"
> "No, she's going to have a baby."
> The child looked round. He was unaware of her. She was alone again in terror.
> "I want my mother," came the cry of panic.

Tom is a calm and deliberate person, but under the circumstances the girl irritates him. He undresses her to put her to bed and get her out of the way, but she keeps crying, turning his irritation to anger, all the more so as the labor drags on without news from the midwife. But then Tom has an idea. "Come," he says, "we'll go an' supper-up the beast," and so he takes Anna out through rainy darkness to the barn full of cattle. He carries the child in his arms as he feeds the cattle in their cribs, and she is freed of panic:

> The two sat still, listening to the sniffing and breathing of the cows feeding in the sheds communicating with this small barn. The lantern shed a soft steady light from one wall. All outside was still in the rain. He looked down at the silky folds of the paisley shawl. It reminded him of his mother. She used to go to church in it. He was back again in the old irresponsibility and security, a boy at home.
> The two sat very quiet.

Before taking the child out in the rain, he has wrapped her in the paisley shawl that reminds him of his mother—he has taken it on himself to be a mother himself, and a child again—and now the birth of the new child becomes the occasion of the birth of a new relation between stepfather and stepdaughter (and he will always be closer to her than to the son who is about to be born). Man and child, sitting among the beasts with the wind blowing and the rain falling outside, are more than man and child; they exist in a space at the edge of male and female and the generations that were and the generations to come, immersed in animal life. Our various ways of being creatures are somehow brought into equilibrium here, and after a while the girl falls asleep and Tom carries her back to bed, able now to tend to his wife, still in labor. There are symbols here—the wet darkness is the element of life; the manger is a sacred space—but they are not overbearing: after all, wet darkness matter-of-factly is where life begins, and these cows are cows. The whole scene is delicate and exact and true. It is very moving as well.

But rain and darkness will reappear before long as the occasion of death, not birth. Tom has prospered—he is a gentleman farmer—while his two sons have studied and left the farm and the world of manual labor, becoming gentlemen for real. Tom has grown a little lazy, developing a "luxuriant ease," drinking "in the hotels and inns with the better-class farmers and proprietors" (Lawrence deftly deploying the given language of the type of men he's describing). One night, in drenching rain, after going to market and drinking at a pub, he drives home drunk in his horse-drawn trap and along the way falls asleep. The water around his house has risen, and he has trouble stabling his horse, but so much rain makes him drunkenly curious to check out the farm pond:

> He went on . . . shakily. He rather enjoyed it. He was now knee deep, and the water was pulling heavily. He stumbled, reeled sickeningly . . . As he staggered, something in the water struck his legs, and he fell. Instantly he was in the turmoil of suffocation. He fought in a black horror of suffocation, fighting, wrestling, but always borne down, borne inevitably down. Still he wrestled and fought to get himself free, in the unutterable struggle of suffocation, but he always fell again deeper. Something struck his head, a great wonder of anguish went over him, then the blackness covered him entirely.
> In the utter darkness, the unconscious, drowning body was carried along, the waters pouring, washing, filling in the place. The cattle woke up and rose to their feet, the dog began to yelp.

Again a simple scene, precise and recognizable in the progression of feeling and event to its frightening but at the same time unsurprising end. Still, we are shocked by the almost offhand way that Lawrence disposes of Tom, a character we have come to count on to be there, much as we rely on our own selves to go on being there. At the same time we know how these things happen and that they do happen; we know—Lawrence reminds us—that one way or another, one day death will happen to us. ("Unutterable," Lawrence writes, a sounding word, but exact here; what he is describing is just that.) Lydia, in the farmhouse waiting for her husband to come back, is worried that he has not; anxiously discussing the situation with her son, she lets out a cry, and it is, across the pages and as incidentally as symbolically—people cry out at such times—an echo of her earlier birth cries. Lawrence also repeats the words he used about Tom before—"The unconscious, drowning body was pushed past the house in the deepest current"—and the imagery of birth is unmistakable, though it is birth into death this time, as in the end any birth is. In this great, dark scene—the first and only death in the book—*The Rainbow* as a novel comes alive in a new sense too. We see that the subject of the novel is less a specific family, much less Tom and Lydia and Will and Anna and Ursula, than this almost featureless, unindividuated body pushed through time and the elements that is both none of us and all of us.

Writing to Garnett with the book done, Lawrence tried to describe his new sense of embodied personhood, as distinct from character. (There's a resemblance to Joyce telling Pound at about the same time that Stephen Dedalus was no longer of interest to him.)

> You mustn't look in my novel for the old stable *ego*—of the character. There is another *ego*, according to whose action the individual is unrecognisable, and passes through, as it were, allotropic states which it needs a deeper sense than any we've been used to exercise, to discover are states of the same radically-unchanged element. . . .
>
> That which is physic—non-human, in humanity, is more interesting to me than the old-fashioned human element—which causes one to conceive a character in a certain moral scheme and make him consistent. The certain moral scheme is what I object to. In Turgenev, and in Tolstoi, and in Dostoievsky, the moral scheme into which all the characters fit . . . is, whatever the extraordinariness of the characters themselves, dull, old, dead.

Hence this family novel which, as much as *Sons and Lovers* is not the bildungsroman it looks like, is not really a family novel. (Writing things that turn out to look different from what they look like at first—and make us look at things differently: Lawrence's genius lies in that.) Typically, the family novel tracks the changing fortunes of a certain sort of family, aristocratic, bourgeois, working-class, and how different members of that family, subtypes of the social type, respond to those changes against a recognizable stretch of history. They serve as intercalibrations of self and society, and the pleasures of the great ones (Mann's *Buddenbrooks* being the greatest) are musical, the characters and themes rising and falling, the passage of time made sensible. Lawrence's novel begins, by contrast, with the formation of a distinctly atypical family unit: Tom and Lydia having neither class nor country nor even language in common. (What, more than anything, they share, in fact, is an unease with language.)

Here Lawrence could be said to be making the historical and sociological point that such old distinctions are increasingly obsolete. And no doubt he is registering that fact, yet that isn't the main thing his book has in mind. In *The Rainbow*, social and historical change exist in the background, and matters like class are incidental to the ordinary, yet always staggering, mystery of whatever it is that brings a particular man and a particular woman together to form a particular family. This doesn't prevent him from situating his characters in the world. As in *Sons and Lovers*, where they come from is made quite clear, along with such developments as the growth of the social state and the expansion of industry and the new towns that have come with it, things that make it possible for Ursula, in the third generation of Brangwens, to train and work as a schoolteacher. Meanwhile, her lover Skrebensky goes off to the Boer War to make a man of himself. But such public developments and events are essentially a foil for the psychological and somatic continual present in which the main action of *The Rainbow* takes place. This is a novel that determinedly goes nowhere, its plot little more than the biblical one generation cometh and another falleth away, its world at once mythic and immediate.

And sexual. It is in *The Rainbow* that Lawrence gets down to the business of writing about sex with an emphasis no one had brought to the subject before.

He describes for example the sexual arc of Will and Anna's marriage. The couple marry young, and they know so little about life that they may as well be Adam and Eve in the garden. (Will is in fact described as carving a relief of the first parents shortly after he first meets Anna.) They have everything to find out, and Lawrence

describes the rapt intensity with which they go about it, losing themselves in each other's bodies. They have sex, wake hungry, fetch food
to bed, and "when the meal was over, she wiped her mouth on her
handkerchief quickly, satisfied and happy, and settled down on the
pillow again, with her fingers in his close, strange, fur-like hair." This
goes on for a while, but then Anna tires, as people do, of this feverish engagement; she wants the exteriority of everyday life, and before
long, Ursula (the first of many children to come) is born, and Anna
becomes absorbed in motherhood. Feeling abandoned and resentful,
Will withdraws into himself.

Will's work is in Nottingham, and now, after work, he starts to go
out. One evening he picks up a girl, and when he gets home, he sees
Anna with new eyes, and she, for the first time in a long time, sees him:

> She watched him undress as if he were a stranger . . . and she
> roused him profoundly, violently, even before he touched
> her . . . They abandoned in one motion the moral position,
> each was seeking gratification pure and simple . . .

The couple's sex life is transformed:

> He would say during the daytime:
> "Tonight I shall know the little hollow under her ankle,
> where the blue vein crosses." And the thought of it, and the
> desire of it, made a thick darkness of anticipation . . . This is
> what their love had become, a sensuality violent and extreme
> as death. They had no conscious intimacy, no tenderness of
> love . . .
> He had given way, and with infinite sensual violence gave
> himself to the realisation of this supreme, immoral, Absolute
> Beauty . . .
> The thing terrified him . . . even whilst he gave himself to
> it. It was pure darkness, also. All the shameful things of the
> body revealed themselves to him now with a sort of sinister,
> tropical beauty. All the shameful, natural and unnatural acts of

sensual voluptuousness which he and the woman partook of together, created together, they had their heavy beauty and delight. Shame, what was it? It was part of extreme delight. It was part of delight of which man is usually afraid. Why afraid? The secret, shameful things are most terribly beautiful.

Their outward life was much the same, but the inward life was revolutionised.

As it happens, this new abandon, this testing of the limits of sexuality that sees the couple forsaking the "natural" missionary position for the "unnatural" pleasures of sodomy, revolutionizes Will's outward life as well. He gains in confidence, in willfulness, you could say, and starts a popular woodwork class in the village.

What is going on here? Why does Lawrence lavish such attention on this couple's sex life? Lawrence is of course building on the greater realism about human sexual behavior that had been pioneered by Flaubert and Maupassant and Zola and had become more or less commonplace in continental European novels, if still rare in England. (Published in 1915, *The Rainbow* was immediately denounced by the press and Parliament as obscene, and Lawrence's new publisher, Methuen, soon had the book withdrawn. There was particular concern about the effect it might have on the morale of the troops in the trenches.) Freud and Weininger and Havelock Ellis and the whole turn-of-the-century vogue for prying into and theorizing sex made a mark on Lawrence too, as did such activists for sexual freedom as Edward Carpenter and Walt Whitman and, as we have seen, the work of Lawrence's contemporaries—Gide, Wells, Colette, Stein, Proust, Joyce, Hemingway—was also shaped by (and helped to shape) the quest for sexual freedom and the freedom to describe sex in the pages of the novel.

Lawrence is a man of his time, then, yet as a novelist his interest in sex is quite different from that of other contemporaries. He is not really interested in what could be called realism for realism's sake, impressive scenes of squalor, or, notwithstanding the "unnatural" sexual acts above, in sex as transgression. He is not interested in what sex drives people to—the madness of infatuation, Charlus begging to be whipped. Nor is the erotic or the sensual much on his mind, unless perhaps it involves birds, beasts, or flowers (that he loved flowers and animals is evident on almost every page of his work). As to the bawdy and the pornographic—the most ancient and venerable forms of depicting the sexual—though he speaks admiringly of Boccaccio, bawdiness is little in evidence in his own work, while the pornographic is for him only the Janus face of sexual repression.

What is it he is after? For Lawrence, sex is the lived center of human experience, a supremely ambiguous power that both defines and defies everything we are, something that both leads us on and eludes us and something, comparable to a certain mystical picture of God, best characterized by everything it is not. It is not, for example, about individual identity or self-expression or even pleasure, the things that we take to set us apart or make us feel good; to the contrary, sex awakens an unknown part of ourselves (another self) that drives us out of ourselves and toward the unknown other. (Sex, to return to a word I used above, finds us wanting.) Sex is not about individual identity, and it is not about sexual identity, maleness or femaleness or what you will, and as for sex roles, those can be nothing but travesties. Lawrence does carry on at times (though not in *The Rainbow*) about the male and female principle, but at the same time he is keenly aware that both exist in all of us. He is phobic about homosexuality, but that a strong sexual current flows between men and men and women and women— in other words, that any and all relations between human beings are sexualized—he took for granted and considered a great good. Indeed, the homophobia in his work is partly born of his fear that to engage in homosexual acts would be to fix one's identity as a homosexual, a label prejudice made him dread (and no doubt, too, the fear that he was one: Lawrence may have had a male lover; he certainly fantasized one), but also a fixity he rejected in principle: to fix sexual identity was to betray just that sovereign fluidity that the sexual stirs within and among us. Sex calls into question set ideas of selfhood; sex challenges the social order too: just look how the powers that be—the "machine" in Lawrence's words—seek to control and suppress it. Sex transcends class; sex overrules morality; sex exhausts character and psychology;

sex, as humanity has immemorially known, even breaches the division between life and death. In the novel, the covenantal and recurrent image of the rainbow, stretching between earth and heaven, opening a doorway into the unknown, ungraspable in its essence, is the symbol of the sexual, the sexual as something finally unidentifiable, neither female nor male. The sexual in Lawrence finds expression not in licentiousness, but in marriage, in a new conception of the married couple that bears comparison with Woolf's and Hemingway's transsexual forays, not to mention Musil's Ulrich and Agathe.

"It is no use thinking you can put a stamp on the relation between a man and a woman, to keep it in the status quo. You can't. You might as well try to put a stamp on the rainbow or the rain," Lawrence writes in an essay from 1925—the metaphor of his novel of a decade before still significant for him. I imagine he would have also said that it is no use trying to put a stamp on the relation between anyone and him- or herself. The sexual reveals the fact that a human being is not a unit, a given simple self, but is a being in relation to, potentially, an infinite number of other beings.

"The business of art is to reveal the relation between man and his circumambient universe, at the living moment," Lawrence writes in "Art and Morality," another essay published in 1925. He continues:

> Morality is that delicate, for ever trembling and changing balance between me and my circumambient universe, which precedes and accompanies a true relationship.
>
> Now here we see the beauty and great value of the novel. Philosophy, religion, science, they are all of them busy nailing things down, to get a stable equilibrium . . .
>
> But the novel, no. The novel is the highest example of subtle inter-relatedness that man has discovered. Everything is true in its own time, place, circumstance and untrue outside its own place, time, circumstance. If you try to nail anything down, in the novel, either it kills the novel, or the novel gets up and walks away with the nail.
>
> Morality in the novel is the trembling instability of the balance.

"Trembling instability" describes the mobile perspective of Lawrence's novels (if they were films, the camera would be handheld). Lawrence writes, as I have said, with an almost somatic immediacy from the point of view of his characters. He also and equally writes from his own point of view. As his books unfold, you feel his character and interests, the urgency of the story for him, as much as his characters' characters and interests. This could be described as free indirect discourse, but in practice it's quite different. Free indirect discourse typically constructs a neutral narrative space that allows writers to pivot conveniently from the view from within to the view from without, permitting them to present characters' motivations and actions in what appear to be their own terms. Lawrence is comfortable with this convention of the late-nineteenth-century novel, he sees its uses, and this sets him apart from many of his contemporaries—Woolf, for example—for whom its reliability, its affectation of evenhandedness, seems deeply suspect, coercive of individual experience, closed to the marvelous. But if Lawrence depends on what might seem a clapped-out narrative technique, in doing so he transforms it. Neutral space? There's not an inch of it anywhere in Lawrence's work—the space of his books is charged through and through—just as there is nothing like old-fashioned omniscience. Far from knowing what's going on, Lawrence the writer, like his characters, is perpetually in the thick of figuring something out. In a broadside from 1923, "Surgery for the Novel—or a Bomb," he wrote, "It seems to me the greatest pity in the world, when philosophy and fiction got split. They used to be one, right from the days of myth . . . The two should come together again—in the novel." This remark conveys Lawrence's open-ended commitment to feeling as thinking and vice versa. Even more characteristic is how this explosive essay ends with an image of the modern novelists tentatively slipping like sheep from one field to another through a gap in a wall to discover a new world. The image is not derisive—to the contrary—and its muted, modest ordinariness serves to make a point of its own: though the world beyond the wall may be new to the sheep, it is really just a field.

Trembling instability is also apparent in Lawrence's very sentences. Lawrence, notoriously, repeats. As he writes in his foreword to *Women in Love* (the novel that followed and grew out of *The Rainbow*), "In point of style, fault is often found with the continual, slightly modified repetition. The only answer is that it is natural to the author: and that every natural crisis in emotion or passion or understanding comes from this pulsing, frictional to-and-fro, which works up to culmination." Well, the sexual metaphor is clear enough here, and yet the statement is in tone rather dryly descriptive, reflecting Lawrence's unwavering commitment to *both* and to *and*. Nothing orgasmic about that "work[ing] up to culmination." Repetition is how Lawrence both develops a situation and how he introduces a reflective dimension into what he's described: like this, but not quite, his sentences suggest, and indeed it's always like this, but not quite; we are always trying to figure out what it's like. Stylistically, his use of repetition is no less complex and ordinary. It echoes the paratactic simplicity and swelling rhythms of the Bible. It points at the same time to something quite different, a world apart from the severities of Genesis: impressionism, with its way of bringing daylight into focus by countless discrete little touches. And that Lawrence finds a way to mix these things up, just as he proposes to infuse philosophy with the novel—that is part of the ongoing surprise of his work. And here it is worth bringing up all the different forms that Lawrence worked in, not only the novel and the short story, but the essay and poetry, his poetry being as fine as his fiction, and as I have already mentioned, his wonderful letters.

"Morality in the novel is the trembling instability of the balance." To which Lawrence adds:

> When the novelist puts his thumb on the scales, to pull down the balance to his own predilection, that is immorality. The modern novel tends to become more and more immoral, as the novelist tends to press his thumb heavier and heavier in the pan: either on the side of love, pure love, or on the side of licentious "freedom."

Excoriating the immoral licentiousness of modern novelists, Lawrence sounds of course like his own persecutors, as his insistence on balance would seem to align him with the novelists of the nineteenth

century. He sounds like Henry James! And Lawrence does share with
James a deep respect for his characters' independent being. There is a
difference, however: Lawrence never settles. Balance is not a result, it
is an action, and balance is continually in question, "trembling" (and
we need to hear the fear there, and the desire).

In Lawrence, writing is inseparable from love and sex and morality, and reading his work allows us to see how love, in the novels of his
great contemporaries, tends to pull away from particular personal or
social relations and come to figure as a strange absolute, more philosophical than actual, a Kantian category almost, and something similar has happened to sex. Mother love is undying in Proust, but mothers
die, and all other love is a deception, or just plain old sex; what is left to
the narrator is the great truth of the work of art in which all will at last
be gathered together. Mann and Joyce both recognized the weirdness
of sex and the binding force of love, and Joyce, confident in comedy,
even has Mr. Bloom rescue the honor of the institution of marriage.
Woolf and Hemingway share a sad foreknowledge that love will fail;
love figures as a supreme conundrum in Musil. Lawrence is certainly
at large in the same territory, but his conceptual flights are never separate from a matter-of-fact appreciation of the concrete character of relationships, which is what makes him such an unequaled chronicler of
irritation and hate. His characters chafe against each other and themselves, and no one better shows how two people emotionally deface
each other, or how the self preys upon and maims itself. Lawrence's
focus on human connection can seem adolescent and embarrassing—
even now he can embarrass his readers as much as his uncouth presence threatened Ford in his office—and that embarrassment may
account for the persistent critical impulse, whether in the trial of *The
Rainbow* or by progressive critics later, to put him in his place, to denounce him as unacceptable, or, a refrain that has accompanied his
work from surprisingly early on, to declare him "unfashionable" (fashion being an odd authority for critics to embrace). He goes on being
read, though. Love, Lawrence writes in an essay of the same name, "is
strictly a traveling."

He goes on being read because the urgency and concentrated energy, the speed, but also the luxuriance of his own traveling—in the

world, on the page (yes, he is also a great travel writer)—continue to astonish. A man with no way back to the world he'd come from, accepted only on sufferance in the literary world, a man who spent most of his working life on the move, some of it on the run, and much of it dying, Lawrence fashioned a body of work that lives as a continual act of attention to life. The work is essentially relational—Lawrence's power is the power to make connections and to make objections, too—and gestural in form, a work that served to place himself in a world where he was nothing if not displaced. That displacement marks him as of his time, as does the effort to make sense of it, but he seems to me exceptional in his determination to embrace it and challenge it. His work is essentially provisional, unfinished. The glory of his style is its openness, its steady pulse, its hectic flashes, its power of noticing—to echo Saul Bellow, who learned a lot from Lawrence—and the slightly puritan sound of the judgment that he left his work unfinished would, one imagines, have pleased him. But there remains the exhilaration of what he did do. The last line of *Sons and Lovers* is, "He walked down the road, quickly." In that comma, that pause before moving on to the abrupt period at the end, we see Lawrence's art. Life continues. The novel stops.

14. THE END

HANS ERICH NOSSACK'S *THE END* AND
VASILY GROSSMAN'S *LIFE AND FATE*

New ways of living, new ways of understanding oneself or others or
what it means to be a man or woman, new forms of the novel—and
now a new war. It was a setback for H. G. Wells's scheme of world government. It was a setback for Mrs. Brown.

The Germans invaded Poland on September 1, 1939, and England
and France declared war in response. There was none of the exhilaration of 1914, at least not among liberal democracies, and the military alliance that finally defeated Nazi Germany and the Axis powers
would not take shape until the end of 1941, after Hitler had discarded
the Molotov-Ribbentrop nonaggression pact to invade the USSR and
after the Japanese attack on Pearl Harbor brought the United States
into the war. Even before it was over, the new war would be broadly
seen as the consequence of, on the one hand, the punitive terms imposed on a defeated Germany at the end of the First World War and,
on the other, the timidity of politicians unwilling to confront Hitler's
aggression for fear of causing a new war. The ironies of the situation
were obvious enough, which didn't make them less cruel or alarming.
In any case, what would henceforth be known as the interwar years
had been marked by plenty of wars: the Italian invasion of Ethiopia,
Japan's invasion of Manchuria, the Spanish Civil War, many others.

Catastrophic violence had figured in the novel for some time. André Malraux's *The Human Condition*, published in 1933, is about a
failed revolutionary uprising in Shanghai in 1927, but is in a larger
sense—and the book's title could hardly be more expansive—about

the tragic centrality of violent political struggle in human life. Two books from 1939 capture the mood of apprehension that had only grown in the course of the decade. Nathanael West's *The Day of the Locust*, set in LA, the western dead end of America, concludes with a riot and a vision of "the burning city, a great bonfire of architectural styles, ranging from Egyptian to Cape Cod colonial," a vision of Hollywood stage sets collapsing into real life and history. *On the Marble Cliffs* by Ernst Jünger—whose ferocious and ecstatic account of combat in World War I, *Storm of Steel*, had made him a right-wing celebrity intellectual in Germany—allegorizes the destruction of Europe and its classical heritage by marauding bands of warriors under the command of a murderous Head Forester, a character modeled on Göring who exists implicitly as a criticism of the whole, savage Nazi project. The book had a brief success in Germany before it was decisively put out of print.

Thomas Mann, once Germany's champion, was now a refugee, and he was not alone. Mann had fled Germany in 1933, after the Nazi electoral victory, and in his homeland his books had been condemned and burned. By 1939 he was in Hollywood. Most of the writers who have figured in this book were alive to see the new war that the no-longer-new century had brought. Colette remained in German-occupied Paris, busily writing and with enough social pull to protect her Jewish husband. Gertrude Stein, in the South of France, accommodated herself to the Vichy authorities, who turned a blind eye to this American Jew; she survived, as did her art collection in Paris. Gide retreated to North Africa. Joyce left Paris for Zurich, where he died early in 1941. In London, both the London house Virginia Woolf had lived in when she was writing *Mrs. Dalloway* and the new one she had recently acquired were destroyed in the Blitz, events that contributed to her final depression and suicide. Woolf and her husband, Leonard, were on a German list of people to be detained in an occupied Britain. So was Wells. Hemingway, as a reporter, observed the invasion of Normandy from the sea and took part in the liberation of Paris. Musil stayed in Switzerland, hard at work on his private millennium until his death, in 1942.

Reality has become violent, the American poet Wallace Stevens declared in a 1942 address at Princeton University, "not yet physically violent, as yet, for us in America, but physically violent for . . . our friends and . . . our enemies and spiritually violent for everyone alive."

The Second World War would far exceed the first in its scope, violence, and lethality. It would be a total war. How could the novel answer to that?

As fiction, novels inevitably raise the question of truth—more so, paradoxically, than nonfiction does, just because the truth of the novel is imaginary and can't be checked against anything except the reader's reckoning and pulse. It's not suspension of disbelief the novel demands so much as an attitude of inquisitive credulity—and an awareness, happy or unhappy, that truth as it appears to us is always subject to further consideration. The novel's business lies with precisely that domain of the truth, the truths that exist for and between people, those points of view of which James made so much and which writers like Wells and Gide would put into perspective in turn, the truth that Musil seeks in action and Lawrence in relation, the uncertain truths we know for certain that we live by. I have described the nineteenth-century novel as practicing a judicious realism. As to the ferment of questions about the world at large and the world within and the nature of the novel that gave rise to the twentieth-century novel, that might be called emergency realism. For novelists old and new, however, the novel is at heart a form of reflection (whether or not it tells a story), and reflection, to be engaged and enjoyed, takes time.

Under attack, there is no time. When war engulfs the whole of life and destruction has become the order of the day, when the world becomes unrecognizable, the fiction of fiction—of a world existing in reserve from the world we exist in—is no longer sustainable. There is neither time nor space in which to entertain the possibility of other realities. How does a writer of fiction write in response to the unrecognizable and unutterable catastrophic moment? This is what the German writer Hans Erich Nossack sought to do in an account of the bombing of Hamburg, which is called simply *The End*.

———

The Allied code name for the bombing of Hamburg was Operation Gomorrah, and the name concisely identifies the purpose of the operation: divine vengeance and total destruction. It was the first Allied bombing of a German city deliberately to abandon, as the German Blitz already had, the distinction between military and civilian targets, and it took place over the course of eight days in July 1943. From the start, British planners had hoped to ignite a firestorm in the city, and on a hot summer evening they succeeded. Much of the city of Hamburg was destroyed. Some thirty-seven thousand people died. There were more than 150,000 casualties. Neither this nor any of the subsequent firebombing of German cities actually did much to impede the German war machine, but then considered judgments of what did or didn't work were hard to come by at the time. Total war was a new undertaking.

As it happened, Nossack and his wife, Misi, were out of Hamburg when the city was bombed. The couple had left the city, already under aerial attack as one of Germany's industrial centers, to spend a few days in the country. They had just settled in when the attack began, a dull, vibrating, unignorable roar—"the sound of eighteen hundred airplanes approaching Hamburg . . . at an unimaginable height . . . a sound that made a lie of all talk, [disarming] every word and [pressing] it into the ground." The sound filled the house and penetrated the earth. There was no escaping it in the cellar, where the couple ran to hide, and after a while Nossack went back upstairs and out to the garden to see what he could see:

> There wasn't much . . . and it was always the same . . . Numerous flares hung in the air above Hamburg; they were popularly known as Christmas trees . . . Many disintegrated as they sank, and it looked as if glowing drops of metal were dripping from the sky . . . Later they vanished in a cloud of smoke . . . A few airplanes caught fire and fell like meteors into the dark . . . Where they crashed the landscape lit up for minutes.

"There wasn't much and it was always the same"—notwithstanding the almost pretty stock images that Nossack the writer conjures up. It was the sound, in any case, that dominated, he insists, a sound that "was something completely new. And yet there was an immediate recognition: this was what everyone had been waiting for, what had hung for months like a shadow over everything we did, making us weary. It was the end."

The words *the end* will continue to sound, like a dying echo of that unbearable roar, throughout Nossack's short narrative, changing their meaning with each repetition, as if so many things had come to an end—or needed to end—that there's no getting to the end of them. It is the end of the great port and city of Hamburg as Nossack has long known it, growing up there. The son of a prosperous merchant family, he had flirted with communism before settling down to work in the family firm—and that too has come to an end, as has his and Misi's life together there, though they are alive, while countless other people's lives have come to an end. Within days of the first air raid, Nossack hears that his apartment has been destroyed, and when he and Misi make a foray into the city, they find a scene of devastation where the "very concept 'street' had ceased to exist." Their apartment is gone, and everything they owned and cherished—and coming as they did from a "good family," they had things, old things, nice things, paintings and books, things that mattered to them and, one imagines, insulated them from the ugly Nazi world around them—all those things are gone too, with the exception of one suitcase of dirty laundry salvaged from the cellar. It is the end of having such things and of taking them for granted, and it is the end of Nossack's work as a writer. He was not a published writer, but he wrote for himself, poems, plays, a journal, which he suggests was the place where, in an otherwise alien and indeed evil world, he could be himself, and that is now gone too. The material shelter of the house and the spiritual shelter of the journal—these have both been destroyed. It is the end of making private arrangements with history, of making excuses, of being who he was.

Can the end be the occasion of a new beginning? Nossack and Misi walk through the destroyed city looking for something to hold on to, some message or lesson, and in them we can see another incarnation of those inveterate walkers who figure repeatedly in the

twentieth-century novel, Aschenbach, Bloom, Mrs. Dalloway, Nick
Adams, Jean Rhys's ladies, Paul Morel among them. They are all looking and waiting for something. Nossack says that in the midst of the
bombing they "were without exception firmly convinced that the war
would be over very shortly." Later, traveling back to the dead city, he
says he was "hard put not to shout exultantly: Now at last real life begins. As if a prison door had swung open before me and the clear air
of freedom, long anticipated, were suddenly blowing in my face . . ."
And yet confidence and euphoria are soon replaced by qualms and
doubt. Caught between a lost past and an unimaginable future, Nossack wants to give the reader the sense of being suspended above an
abyss—another word that sounds throughout the book—of being out
of stories and even words, of having only this emptiness to hold on to,
a floundering present now disconnected from calendrical or historical time, even as Nossack struggles with the question of hitting the
right note, since every note seems false. But if what he writes rings
hollow or falls flat, isn't that as it should be? Or is that only to stumble
upon the oldest cliché of all—that words fail him? He finds himself
reduced to seeming to shrug the whole business off, vaguely gesturing
at "something like that," "something consoling," the voice of the book
sinking to an appalled apologetic mumble: "As I ride back in memory
down that road to Hamburg I feel the urge to stop and give up. Why
go on? I mean, Why record all this? Wouldn't it be better to surrender
it to oblivion for all time? For those who were there certainly don't
have to read it." And who are his readers? "Those who will come later?
What if they read it only to enjoy something strange and uncanny
and to make themselves feel more alive? Does it take an apocalypse to
do that?" Haunted by that long gone moment of hope, his rumination
concludes: "Or is this a plea to the others that they not judge us . . . ?"

The End is not a novel. Its author is without authority. Its audience is inconceivable. The sense of who and where and when by which
fiction stakes its claim on the imagination has been stripped away
from the story. It is not a novel, but it is a book (though surely it's a
mistake to describe as a book a piece of writing that, at the time of
its writing, could not be imagined as bound and printed under any
foreseeable circumstances) by a man who wanted to be a novelist and

who, after the war, became well-known as one, in which the imaginative energies that have gone into the twentieth-century novel are turned to describing an unimaginable reality. It's a book in which Nossack deploys various novelistic conventions while avoiding the novel's usual sense of consequence. The brute fact of total destruction has exposed the fictions that filled daily life, depriving its victims of any sense that things will work out, and in *The End*, in spite of all the things that have come to an end, there is no end, just the rubble of the stories people used to tell themselves in the rubble of the world they go on, for now, living in. Nossack's text describes the end of a city and the end of one way of life but hardly the end of the war—when he completed it, that was still nowhere in sight. In that perspective, the end, whether happy or sad—one of the promises of narrative form—is something that *The End* cannot promise.

The End is not a novel, but it is not at all a memoir. Novels look forward, projecting an image of possible life; memoirs look back; *The End* has nowhere to look. Written at a time when past and future have both been destroyed, when facts look like fiction and terrible fictions have been promoted to fact, it is writing in free fall. But if there is one kind of fiction it does resemble, or looks to for guidance in spite of all, it is fairy tale. Nossack mentions fairy tales at several points in passing. He even introduces some dark ones of his own:

> There once was a creature that was not born of a mother. A fist struck it naked into the world, and a voice called: fend for yourself! Then it opened its eyes and didn't know what to make of its surroundings. And it didn't dare to look back, for behind it there was nothing but fire.

The fairy tale—in German, *Hausmärchen*, or "household tales," which is to say stories told over bed and hearth—is an important, even foundational genre of modern German literature (the Grimm brothers, who collected them starting in 1812, also composed the first modern German dictionary), and Nossack, in bringing these stories into his story, confronts, as he does throughout his text, the impossible possibility of starting again. I imagine that in the back of his

mind he would have had the beautiful words of the Grimms' preface
to their first collection:

> When a storm or some other calamity from the heavens de-
> stroys an entire crop, it is reassuring to find that a small spot
> on a path lined by hedges or bushes has been spared and that a
> few stalks, at least, remain standing . . . That is how it all seems
> to us when we review the riches of German poetry.

In Hamburg in 1943 the riches of German poetry would have
been hard—or perhaps all too bitterly easy—to discern! How, among
so many devastated households, can the very idea of a household tale
be considered anything more than the most sentimental of tales? The
tropes of the twentieth-century novel—the self-consciousness about
literary form of Gide and Wells, the program of starting a new literature to describe new realities, inner and outer, that writers pursued in
the years before the war—has come to a dead end in the anything but
conceptual mise en abyme of *The End*. They were nothing but fairy
tales, in the pejorative sense of the phrase. But then again—and *then
again* might be the words for the mode in which Nossack's strange,
stripped factual and hallucinatory text is composed—what else do
we have? Nossack ends in any case with a real-life story of someone
who, unlike him, actually went through the bombing, a man who,
after taking shelter from the firestorm in a cellar, fled the cellar before it collapsed in the spreading fire, killing the people within who
had been too terrified to react. "Then we were through it," the man
says: he is a true survivor, and yet survival is not the end of his story.
The end comes flatly: "Some people keeled over in the street then. We
couldn't take care of them." In the end, there are those who survived
and those who didn't, bound by their separation forever. And perhaps
we remember that earlier Nossack had written, "From now on we can
no longer ask ourselves: Will it hold its own, your work, in the presence of the wide countryside and by the edge of the sea? We will have
to ask: Will it hold its own in the presence of this cemetery."

———

The Soviet writer Vasily Grossman also saw the war from up close. Born in 1905 into a nonobservant Jewish family, the son of a chemical engineer with leftist leanings and trained as a chemical engineer himself, Grossman was an enthusiastic child of the revolution. In the 1930s he made a name for himself as an up-and-coming writer with a couple of very Soviet novels—the first a tale of heroic miners—as well as vivid stories, some of which were published not only in the USSR but in English translation alongside work by such celebrated writers as Mikhail Sholokhov. When the war broke out, he went to work as a reporter for the newspaper of the Red Army, *Red Star*, which was read throughout the USSR by both civilians and soldiers. Grossman was on the front lines in the summer of 1941, when the Soviet army, unprepared for the German invasion that everyone—except, it seems, Stalin—had known was coming, reeled from defeat to defeat. Grossman knew that countless Soviet soldiers, forbidden to retreat, had been taken prisoner and killed. He knew that many Ukrainians, in the aftermath of the terror famine of the early thirties, had welcomed the German invaders. He knew that his own mother, in Berdychiv, the heavily Jewish Ukrainian town where he had grown up, had disappeared behind the German lines.

The Germans mounted a siege of Leningrad (the siege would go on for 872 days during which some 1,500,000 people would die, more than half of them civilians) and drew close to Moscow, but come winter, their advance stalled. In the summer of 1942, however, it resumed to the south, and by August the German army was on the outskirts of Stalingrad, an important industrial city on the banks of the Volga. After bombing the city, they were prepared to take it, which would allow them to march east or turn north. But a small number of Soviet troops, defending a sliver of the devastated city on the west bank of the Volga and linked to the main body of the Red Army on the east bank only by ferry, managed, against all odds, to hold off the Germans until Soviet forces from the north were able to encircle the German Sixth Army and, in February 1943, capture it. It was the first decisive German defeat in the war, and it is seen by many historians as the point at which the tide turned decisively against Hitler. After the defeat at Stalingrad, Hitler never made another speech in public.

Grossman was on the front lines in Stalingrad for almost the entirety of the five-month battle, and the stories he filed were read all
over the world. He had already written a novel, *The People Immortal*,
about the Red Army's heroic resistance to the invading Germans, that
had been published internationally. His reporting from the besieged
city was one of very few sources of news available to the USSR's Western allies. At the battle's end, he proceeded to accompany the Red
Army on its westward advance to Berlin. He saw the mass graves
in the Ukraine—his mother, he had long since realized, must lie in
one of them, shot dead or buried alive—and he was present when the
smoldering ruins of Treblinka were discovered: he conducted careful,
on-the-spot research to establish how the death camp operated and
wrote a detailed report that was submitted as evidence at the Nurem-
berg Trials. In the aftermath of the war, he worked with Ilya Ehren-
burg on *The Black Book of Soviet Jewry*, which was meant to serve
as a definitive record of the Nazi Judeocide in the USSR. The project
was at first encouraged by the Soviet authorities, but Stalin soon had
a change of heart. His chief concern now that the war was over was
to reestablish control over the various peoples in the Soviet Union—
Russian, Belarussian, Ukrainian, and so on—and documenting collaboration with the Germans in killing Jews hardly served this purpose.
The project was shut down, and *The Black Book* was not published in
full in Russia until 1991, long after Grossman's death and when the
USSR was no more.

For all that, Grossman saw the Soviet victory as a great moral
victory. It was a moral victory of the Russian people over fascism,
of course, but just as importantly over the demons of the recent Soviet past. For Grossman the Russian Revolution had represented the
revelation and liberation of the power of a common humanity, or at
least the promise of it. That common humanity had been challenged
by fascism and also, Grossman would come to feel, by Stalin, under
whose prewar rule the revolution had descended into an inhumanity
that rivaled Hitler's. In the 1930s, Grossman had seen a favorite aunt
shipped off to the gulag for ideological deviance. He knew about the
Ukrainian famine—the Holodomor—and how its horrors had contributed to Ukrainian collaboration. He knew how Stalin's purge of

his generals had left the USSR unprepared for war. He himself had been caught up in the immense, sticky web of acquiescent complicity that Stalin's serial terrors had cast over the life of the Soviet Union. Terror had left Russia almost unable to defend itself from German evil. The war had been a very close call. Yet in the end it had been won. Russian humanity had emerged anew, and in the aftermath of the war, that renewed revelation stood as a reminder of the true meaning and passion of the revolution.

Having kept notes about what he had seen in the war, Grossman wanted to write a novel that would bring out the true meaning of the epic battle that had just been fought. During the war, he had returned to Tolstoy's *War and Peace* repeatedly. It was, he wrote, the only book he could read under the circumstances. Now, at a turning point of the twentieth century, he consciously set out to write a novel that would mirror Russia's greatest nineteenth-century novel.

The novel was to be about the Battle of Stalingrad and was to be called simply *Stalingrad*. The battle of writing it and finding a way to publish what he had written would take up much of Grossman's remaining life.

He went to work with determination. By 1948 he had readied a first draft of the first volume, about the retreat of the Red Army before the invading German forces, and was showing it to publishers. Confronting and overcoming an impossible challenge is the stuff of an exciting novel, and Russia had certainly confronted a serious challenge in the summer of 1941; Grossman's challenge was to make that plain—without, however, suggesting that the size of the challenge might have owed something to Stalin's lack of foresight. The matter had only grown all the more delicate in light of the worsening international situation and the emerging Cold War. A new crackdown was in the works. Years went by as Grossman negotiated with literary supporters and critics, fine-tuning his novel in various ways—rejecting the demand that Viktor Shtrum, the Jewish physicist who is one of the book's central characters (and in many ways a portrait of Grossman himself), and his family be eliminated from its pages; agreeing to add a whole section about valiant Siberian miners—and it was not until 1952 that at last it was serialized, not as *Stalingrad*, but as *For a Just Cause*, a nod to the defiant speech that Molotov, the Soviet foreign minister and a faithful Stalinist henchman, had delivered in response to the German invasion in 1941. Well-received, the novel came out as a book the following spring—only to be savagely attacked as part of a new campaign of terror launched by Stalin in response to a putative plot by a group of Jewish doctors to kill off the Soviet leadership. Just then, however, Stalin died, quite possibly saving Grossman's own life. *For a Just Cause* remained in print and was reprinted under the new Khrushchev regime, in which the Stalinist cult of personality was denounced and some of the vast population of political prisoners in Soviet camps gained release. New editions of the novel did have to be revised anew to remove any references to Stalin now deemed overly flattering.

For a Just Cause had brought the story of Stalingrad to the outbreak of battle, but had not continued through the resistance to its victorious conclusion. Now, after his brush with death and in the new, more permissive atmosphere of the Thaw, Grossman set out to complete his vast project. *For a Just Cause* had introduced characters from all walks of Soviet life, peasants, miners, engineers, scientists and members of the old intelligentsia, political commissars, officers and soldiers, as well as real-life figures: it included memorable cameos of Himmler and Hitler. It was a total picture of the world of total war, except that Grossman had had to steer clear of the German concentration camps and mass killings. In the Stalinist imperium, such arrangements cut too close to the bone. Nonetheless, in *For a Just Cause*, Grossman had introduced the story of the mother of the Jewish physicist Shtrum. She lives, as Grossman's mother had, in Berdychiv, and like his mother, she finds herself caught behind German lines. Viktor hears nothing from her or of her until, months later, a letter arrives. *For a Just Cause* makes it clear that this letter contains her last words. What they might be, the novel leaves to its readers to infer.

Life and Fate, the title Grossman gave to the second, concluding volume of his great design, picks up where *For a Just Cause* leaves off. Here the text of Viktor's mother's letter is included, Grossman effectively granting words to his own mother to tell a story—of social ostracism and humiliation and final collection for death—she could not tell herself. Here too he goes into the German camps and also into the Russian camps. He compares them. He compares Stalin to Hitler and presents both of them as evil geniuses of totalitarianism. He features a character, an old Bolshevik, who is wrestling with the meaning of his life and of the revolution; it describes his arrest and torture by Soviet authorities and the confession he is forced to make. He shows Viktor awakening to his being a Jew and to the reality of anti-Semitism. In a German camp, an eccentric holy fool named Ikonnikov argues with another old revolutionary, extolling what he calls in a small treatise he has written "senseless acts of kindness" over the revolutionary rigor espoused by his interlocutor. The commissar is strangely shaken. *Life and Fate* also features the disappointments and accommodations of marital, martial, and professional life, those too-realistic details of everyday existence that the censors had sought to purge from the pages of *For a Just Cause*. The book is full of death, yet it is written in defense of freedom and life. Expansive and philosophical, imbued with a mystical materialism, it is in its way heroically modest: Grossman has a style as simple as an outstretched hand, and he has a faultless eye for the minutiae in which human nature is revealed. And that the character closest to Grossman is called Viktor is meant, I don't doubt, to make a point. At once completing the story of Stalingrad and putting it in perspective, *Life and Fate* fills out a record of unspeakable suffering and stands as an exposé of evil. It is also, however, an affirmation of the abiding, transformative, revolutionary power of humanity.

Grossman was confident that *Life and Fate* would be published—he presented his manuscript for publication in a magazine in 1960—but he was mistaken. In the new climate of the Thaw, authors might be free to propose certain new understandings of the revolution, but it remained impermissible to question the authority of the revolutionary state, whether in word or in deed. The authorities had been severely embarrassed by the recent smuggling of Pasternak's *Doctor Zhivago* to the West, and insult was added to injury when Pasternak was awarded the Nobel Prize. At the same time, the liberalizing Khrushchev was under increasing challenge from the Stalinist old guard. In February 1961, agents of the KGB knocked on the door of Grossman's apartment. They seized his novel and interrogated him for hours. They wanted to know who else had copies, and they proceeded to seize the copies they learned of as well. Emotionally wrecked, Grossman continued in the next years to try to get the book published, going so far as to take its case up with the state chief of ideology, Mikhail Suslov, to no avail. Grossman's epic was sentenced to the top drawer for even longer than Nossack's fairy tale. In 1975 Grossman's friend Semyon Lipkin brought a typescript of *Life and Fate* he'd secretly retained to the novelist Vladimir Voinovich, who helped smuggle a mimeographed copy out of the USSR; it was published in France in 1980. An English translation appeared in 1985. Finally, in 1988, just before the collapse of the USSR, the book was published in Russia. Grossman had died in 1964.

The two volumes of Grossman's Stalingrad novel—*For a Just Cause*, subjected to the censor's pen, and *Life and Fate*, sprawling and unedited—can be seen either as a monumental whole or a massive fragment. One way or another, they are a record of Grossman's growing determination, after so many years of lies, to tell the truth, to get it all out there, and though exposing lies and hypocrisy has been part of what could be described as the twentieth-century novel's brief, the positive truth Grossman has in mind has rarely been part of the novel's truth, as I said at the start of this chapter. Grossman's model in writing the novel had been *War and Peace*, a novel that Tolstoy notoriously interrupts in midcareer with a long attack on the great man theory of history. Tolstoy is by no means alone among nineteenth-century novelists in shifting from the dramatic to the didactic (Manzoni's *The Betrothed* includes a long broadside on the inefficiency of price controls; *Les Misérables* is an encyclopedia of authorial opinion), and a live tension between presentation and interpretation remains central to the socialist realist aesthetic that Grossman, as a young writer making his way in the 1930s—mentored by Gorky, admiring of Babel—had been formed by. What is striking about what Tolstoy does in *War and Peace* is that it seems to be deliberately pitted against the onward march of his novel, as if the author had lost patience with his own creation, and later, of course, Tolstoy would wash his hands not only of *War and Peace* but of the whole genre of the novel. The novel lacked moral clarity. It could not be trusted to tell the truth. Grossman, by contrast, largely makes a practice of putting his points—about, for example, what is true revolutionary commitment or a travesty of it; about the true power of art—in his characters' mouths, and though his dialogue can be stilted, he can certainly write memorable characters and train his eye on the details of lived life. The reading of the book, however, is always accompanied by a distinct and unusual feeling that the lived scene it presents so vividly is at the same time a great curtain that, the more we examine it, the more we realize exists to be lifted. And what will we see then? The most important thing: the figure of the writer as living witness and in that image our own responsibility too.

So though the book tells many stories, it is also full of a wartime sense that the time for stories is over—as with Nossack. This comes out distinctly in a feature of the overall design that may in fact have occurred as an accident of composition. Perhaps it was fear of the censor, or even the action of a censor, that led Grossman not to include the text of Viktor's mother's letter to her son in *For a Just Cause* and the prospect of a relaxation of censorship that allowed him to put it into *Life and Fate*. Whether or not that is the case, the letter's double appearance across the two volumes—alluded to in the first, reproduced in its entirety in the second; unheard and then heard—accentuates its centrality to the work as whole, even as it is made to figure as an entirely different kind of writing with a different effect on the reader from the novel that contains it. In *For a Just Cause*, the letter comes Viktor's way when he is embroiled in an adulterous flirtation. He reads it, and we are left to imagine what he has read: the silence resonates and in a sense grows, while Viktor withdraws from his duplicitous entanglement, or so we gather, given that there is no further mention of it. The letter has put an end to lying fantasies of that sort. The unspeakable implied truth—of the mother's death, of how the mother, like so many others, came to meet her death—has silenced them. In *Life and Fate*, by contrast, the letter is there for us to read. We now hear what was before silent and what has been silenced—the mother's voice—even as we recognize that this is just what we do not and cannot hear, since this letter is in fact a contrivance of the author, and then in the history of the novel as a genre there is hardly a hoarier convention than trotting out a letter as a sign of unfiltered veracity. Appearing twice in different ways in the novel, the letter takes precedence, even drowns out the stories the characters in the book are telling to themselves about their lives, as well as the big story Grossman is telling us. It exposes us to another order of the word, another order of experience, from storytelling. This is the truth.

You can imagine Nabokov—who was of a generation with Grossman, who lived through a good deal of death and destruction himself, and for whom, perhaps for that very reason, the artificiality of the novel was an article of faith—dismissing Grossman's devotion to the novel as testimony as a hilarious category mistake. But it is this misunderstanding, or rather different understanding, that makes Grossman's novel stand out. For Grossman, the novel exists as part of a lived world in which it lives and works and serves as a moral agent itself. The truth that emerges from the pages of his books is sometimes terrifying, whether he is describing the slow dispossession of a lone Jewish woman by people she has always considered her neighbors or the chaos of the bombing of Stalingrad, but then there are comic scenes, too. There is pretty much everything we expect to find in a novel, and on top of that, there is something else, an edifying sense of human suffering and obligation. But can the novel really be edifying? Or should Grossman's novel be seen as an antinovel, to use a term Jean-Paul Sartre introduced in 1948, as much a test and critique of the form as an exercise within it, a wrenching response to the spiritual violence that Wallace Stevens saw the times inflicting on everyone alive? There is edification, in any case, in the way Grossman doesn't just record the details of how people look and act, but records them in such a way that close observation becomes a commitment to life. Yes, it is like that: girls doing a nervous shuffle dance in the glare of the bombs that are destroying a city. Life is like that: it needs to be defended from the death in the air and the death of the heart.

One strand of *Life and Fate*, however, leads to the German death camps. In *For a Just Cause*, Sofya Levinton, a surgeon and a single woman who lives in Stalingrad and is as good as family to Viktor Shtrum's in-laws, comes back from a desperate day at the hospital in a car that takes a wrong turn and falls into the hands of the Germans. She ends up in a transport of Jews that also contains a young boy, David, who has been separated from his family. Sofya takes David under her wing, and in *Life and Fate* Grossman follows them on their final trip to the gas chamber:

> David watched the door close: gently, smoothly, as though drawn by a magnet, the steel door drew closer to its steel frame. Finally they became one.
>
> High up behind a rectangular grating in the wall, David saw something stir. It looked like a grey rat, but he realized it was a fan beginning to turn. He sensed a faint, rather sweet smell.

Sofya is holding the boy in her arms "with a peculiar strength familiar to the Germans who worked there—when they emptied the chamber, they never attempted to separate bodies locked in that close embrace." She is waiting for death:

> Her eyes—which had read Homer, *Izvestya*, *Huckleberry Finn*, and Mayne Reid, that had looked at good people and bad people, that had seen the geese in the green meadows of Kusk, the stars above the observatory at Pulkovo, the glitter of surgical steel, the *Mona Lisa* in the Louvre, tomatoes and turnips in the bins at market, the blue water of Issyk-Kul—her eyes were no longer of any use to her.

David, however, continues to look around, to react to his surroundings:

> This world, where a chicken could run without a head, where there was milk in the morning and frogs he could get to dance by holding their front feet—this world still preoccupied him.

All this time David was being clasped by strong warm hands. He didn't feel his eyes go dark, his heart become empty, his mind grown dull and blind. He had been killed; he no longer existed.

Sofya Levinton felt the boy's body subside in her arms. Once again she had fallen behind him . . . This boy, with his light, bird-like body, had left before her.

"I've become a mother," she thought.

The orchestration of this passage is impeccable and almost unbearable. You want to look away. And I suppose that, in a way, I am doing just that when I propose to consider this scene in the dry light of Grossman's handling of point of view, that formal question that has, from the beginning, done so much to shape the twentieth-century novel. And yet, aren't point of view and even its relation to the work of the novel just what Grossman is asking us to consider here—among other things—as he describes with his journalistic eye a scene he could never have seen, entering into the hearts and minds of two people dying together and dying alone, two people who are just like us and, mercifully, not us, though they could be. He shows us Sofya's eyes, the physical organ of vision, and what are we told those eyes have done? They have read. They have tried to establish a point of view on reality, whether from reading the newspaper or an American author. We see, in her final glimpse of herself as a mother, someone still yearning, as well as a not-yet-extinguished sense of irony that we in turn experience as bitter irony and deep pathos. We see David, his mind mixed up to the last moment with the stuff of life, including—those dancing frogs—the casual cruelty that exists on a continuum with the deliberate cruelty of the men who have brought him here to kill him. We see all that, and perhaps also in the background the fairy-tale figures of Hansel and Gretel and Brother and Sister, and it is probably not necessary to point out the allusion to the Madonna and Child.

We see that all points of view end here.

PART III

THE
WITHDRAWAL

15. DON'T CRY

ANNA BANTI'S *ARTEMISIA* AND CHINUA
ACHEBE'S *THINGS FALL APART*

"If you want an image of the future, imagine a boot stamping on a human face forever," George Orwell wrote in *1984*, completed in 1948, a book that is as much about the present postwar world as it is about a world to come. Orwell was not optimistic.

Nineteen forty-eight was also the year in which the Italian film director Roberto Rossellini released *Germany Year Zero*, a movie about life in the razed streets of the capital of the Nazi Reich; it was shot among those ruins and featured a cast in part composed of war refugees. Here, the word *zero* figures as the end—from the Nazi delusion nothing but devastation remains—and curiously, the film bears a certain resemblance to Nossack's *The End*, which was published that very same year, though not long before its publication had seemed utterly inconceivable. Movie and book share a comparable mix of the documentary and the imaginary and a similar lack of finish, a ragged, bony, famished look, a look that makes sense at a moment when the twentieth century has developed, like a suspect individual, a past, something that can't be wished or hidden away, something that can't be forgiven or forgotten or even accounted for. Things have come to nothing. Things have to be rebuilt from the ground up and, one way or another, will be rebuilt; and one way of addressing the damage that has been done will be to work the questions and uncertainties it raises into the new work. Much of that work will be the work of mourning.

In the summer of 1944, the retreating German army tried to slow the northward advance of the Allies through Italy by mining and demolishing the bridges of Florence. The commander of the German forces, a connoisseur of art, saw fit to spare the famous Ponte Vecchio. The jewelers' bridge was preserved. The neighborhoods at either end of it were reduced to rubble.

Anna Banti's *Artemisia*—published in 1947—begins after the dynamiting. The sun is rising on the ruins of Florence, and the narrator, in her nightgown, finds herself "as in a dream" among a crowd of desperate people who have taken refuge in the Boboli Gardens. The narrator is the author of the book we are reading, Anna Banti, the pen name of Lucia Lopresti, a novelist, critic, and translator, the wife of the well-known art historian Roberto Longhi. In the book, in the garden, Banti is in tears. Her own house has been destroyed and with it the manuscript of the novel she has been working on since before the war.

"Don't cry," Banti overhears someone saying. The voice could be addressed to her, mourning her lost novel, but it also speaks to the subject of that novel: Artemisia Gentileschi—the daughter of the celebrated early baroque painter Orazio Gentileschi—who would become a noted painter herself. In 1611, when Artemisia was eighteen, her father asked a fellow painter and sometime collaborator, Agostino Tassi, to give his daughter lessons in painting and drawing. Tassi raped her. Having raped her, he promised to marry her; having promised, he reneged. Orazio sued him. Parts of the lurid transcript of Tassi's trial have survived; it appears to have ended with his conviction, but he was soon set free from prison. From the transcript we also know that Artemisia herself was repeatedly tortured in order to establish the veracity of her testimony. Torture in 1944 was not old history.

"Don't cry"—these are the first words of the novel we have in hand, the new novel written in place of the old, lost one. This book will be very different from the book Banti had written before, she suggests, implying that that one had been a thoroughly researched, properly trimmed and fitted costume drama of the old school, in which the past was not so much re-created as taken for granted, as if one could know just what it looked like and, with a wave of the pen, summon it back to life. That old novel, conceived and executed under

Mussolini's fascist regime, might well have turned to such a past as a convenient refuge from the present. Even if it didn't pay lip service to the powers of the day, it would have been constrained when it came to saying certain things.

The old book, Banti as good as says, deserved destruction: "Don't cry." The old narrative of European civilization, a historical fiction stretching like a great bridge from Greece and Rome and the Renaissance to the modern state, has been blown to smithereens. European history—often taken and taught by Europeans as the only history— has collapsed on itself, and the story that needs to be told now is the story of that collapse, and for that we will need a new kind of novel, though it's hardly clear what good any novel can do for the poor, displaced people now picking their way through Europe's postwar rubble. Still, this new novel is what, in the years following that morning of destruction, Banti has sought to produce in rewriting her old novel, a novel about a historical figure about whom something is known, though not much, and only thanks to the accidental preservation and discovery of an obscure legal document—an artist whose art has long been seen primarily as a footnote to that of her father and a footnote to art history. A lot is missing from the story, and the only way to tell it truthfully will be, paradoxically, to include those omissions. It must be a novel that is alive with that absence, that captures the gaps in the records and our knowledge and the limits of our imagination. If that can be done, then Artemisia Gentileschi—and Anna Banti's novel— will come to life, reminding us at the same time of those other human beings and human works that have not survived: lost manuscripts, paintings, and lives, the innumerable dead of this last war and centuries before, silenced, as Banti and Artemisia might equally have been.

Writing about Artemisia is a question of speaking for the speechless, speaking for the dead, though Banti is quite aware that to speak on another's account, however well-meaningly, is to presume. So her novel, she figures, has to be self-aware, as guarded as it is generous, a novel that continually inspects the grounds of its own existence. This makes *Artemisia* very much a twentieth-century novel, literary and lyrical, in the line of Gide and Proust and Woolf, and Banti had translated Woolf. This also marks a change. In *In Search of Lost Time* or *The Counterfeiters*, protagonist and author are presented as a lot alike, yet not quite alike, and the slight gap between them allows the novel itself to emerge as the triumph of that elusive other entity—distinct from the author's or the protagonist's interests—that is art. "Yes, I have painted my picture," Lily Briscoe affirms at the end of *To the Lighthouse. Artemisia*, by contrast, continually resists and finally rejects this leap into the saving dimension of art. Artemisia after all is not Banti, in a quite different sense from the way Marcel is not Marcel Proust, or Briscoe, Woolf. Artemisia was a real person, and her separate reality must be made clear. To live as a novel, *Artemisia* needs to establish the gravity and opacity of Artemisia's individual life.

At various points in the book, Banti imagines Artemisia stepping forward to reproach her for getting too close, for impinging on her privacy. She responds:

> I now admit that it is not possible to recall to life and understanding an action that happened three hundred years ago . . . I acknowledge my mistake . . . I limit myself to the short span of my own memory, condemning my presumptuous idea of trying to share the terror of my own epoch with a woman who has been dead for three centuries. It is raining on the ruins over which I wept . . . Artemisia's two graves, the real and the fictitious, are now the same, breathed-in dust.

Which, however, far from entailing the abandonment of her project, prompts her to go on:

> We have found out once again that we are poor, and the poor must learn to persevere. For this reason, and not for any more exalted one, but in secret expiation, I will continue the story of Artemisia.

What does it mean to exist? We exist as a set of preconceptions about who we are—worker, peasant, shopkeeper, lawyer, businessman, soldier, German, Jew, Nazi, writer, and so on—that are both ours and others', and often it is a struggle to clarify our own real share in the business. The war made it unmistakably clear how little control we have over our own descriptions, how easily they might be redefined, wrenched from the social surround, come to seem completely unreal, be turned against us. Raped, Artemisia is no longer a "proper woman," which is to say that even when she was "a proper woman" (or rather girl), even before she was raped, the identity she enjoyed was an identity that was not hers, but one that had been conferred on her by another and could equally be retracted by another: by Tassi, her rapist, who then refused to confer on her the title of wife; by a society that may condemn the rapist but condemns the raped woman too. Wounded and wanting, Artemisia discovers that in a sense she was never herself, and now that she is condemned to be nothing but herself—which in the eyes of the world is as good as, or indeed worse than, nothing, the fallen woman, temptress, vamp, or slut that society, abhorring a void, accuses her of being—she discovers too that her life can only be an ongoing struggle not to be defined as one thing or another: to imagine herself freely and anew. Is it even possible? How can Artemisia not desperately desire, as Banti puts it, "an image with which she could identify completely, under whose name she could fight"?

"But," the novel continues,

> she is not a princess, she is not a pawn, she is not a peasant nor a tradeswoman, not a heroine, not a saint. And not even a courtesan . . . As for the rest—her painting, her reputation, her ambitions of fame—Donna Artemisia will have to be content with improvising her own methods and rules, with sowing the seed that will produce, whenever it may be, the fruit which could satisfy her present thirst, but which does not yet exist.

The power of Artemisia's art, then—and Banti would surely say of all art—exists in rejection of any determined identity, those identities in the name of which so many people have been thwarted and killed. To that end, Banti insistently complicates any identification of herself with Artemisia. Similarly, the power of Banti's novel lies in its dramatization of the distance between author and character (between this

book and the lost book) and the reader too. This is a new form of mise
en abyme, a new way of incorporating the frame in the picture, but
here the work of art is incorporated in the work of art as a blind spot.
There is a hole at the heart of the book not unlike the hole blown by a
bomb in the middle of a city.

Artemisia is, you could say, a self-portrait of any and all of us as
an other, and toward the end of it Banti looks at one of Artemisia's
most famous pictures in just this light. The painting is of a woman
painter who is about to put her brush to a blank primed canvas: she
is on the verge of painting the painting of herself that we are looking
at. The picture is commonly seen as an allegory of painting (it is conventionally known as *The Art of Painting*), as Artemisia's self-portrait,
and as an affirmation of herself as a woman artist. Knowing all this,
Banti, however, frames the picture differently: she imagines Artemisia
painting the portrait of a younger painter, an up-and-coming young
woman who may have it in her to be a better artist than Artemisia
is—someone she's a little jealous of and a little smitten by, too. This
other painter is Banti's invention, as of course Artemisia in Banti's
book is Banti's invention, but then we exist, all of us, as inventions of
ourselves and others. The art of painting's struggle to depict someone,
or the world at large, is a struggle to recognize something (a struggle, too, for recognition), and to recognize a person, especially, is to
recognize that there are some things we know about the person and
some things we don't. It is to recognize and admire in that person the
unknown as well as the known—as with Artemisia's painting, which
may or may not be a self-portrait, in which Banti admires the various
ways in which it can be known and yet remain its own and apart.

Here Banti offers a vision of art—and this question of what art is
good for is one that artists and writers keep circling back to after the
war—that is fully ethical, as Musil in his notebook insists the aesthetic
at heart must be, without in any sense being moralizing or instrumental. Here too she seeks to reengage with the questions of justice
that animated nineteenth-century novelists but that their twentieth-
century successors have eyed with suspicion, as an assumption or
excuse, a pretext for complacency, something that needs to be upset.

Banti certainly joins in that rejection of complacency. She has every reason to: hasn't she seen a world and countless lives destroyed? She joins her twentieth-century predecessors, but she also raises them. Isn't the heroism of art itself a form of complacency? Artemisia in her pages is hardly a hero; she is a worker, trying to get things right, as is Banti, trying to catch her subject in the broken light and shadow of history, into which, in the end, she must vanish anyway. Banti the novelist writes from a destroyed world, as at the beginning of her novel Artemisia's world has been destroyed and justice has been perverted. Doesn't this make it that much more important to ask what justice is and how, in the novel, justice can be done? And so the voice saying "Don't cry" that rings throughout the opening of the book is replaced, at the end, by another that asks—about just what is left unclear: the novel, a new world—"Does it exist?"

Mrs. Dalloway and Nick Adams represented the heroic dimension of the ordinary. Now, after a new war, the thought of human potential becomes inseparable from suffering and humiliation and from the recognition that it can be altogether human to be utterly inhuman. Can the human survive? In art it takes new form as a figure stripped naked, not devoid, in its stark simplicity, of a certain classicism. Consider the figures of Giacometti, their forward steps taking us back to the monumental, imperturbable, marmoreal simplicity of the Greek kouroi who stand at the threshold of the great Western tradition of representative art, even as the modeled surface of Giacometti's sculptures is, by contrast, endlessly worried with the uncertain, shaping, and effacing touch of their maker's hand.

Outcast *Artemisia* has plenty of midcentury company, a whole gallery of look-alikes: *Native Son, Invisible Man, Dangling Man*, the junkies of *The Man with the Golden Arm, Cain's Book*, and *Naked Lunch*, the drunks of *The Power and the Glory* (a book titled with naked irony) and *Under the Volcano* ("somebody threw a dead dog after him down the ravine," it ends), the soldiers in *The Naked and the Dead*. There are Simenon's *The Man Who Watched the Trains Go By*, Sarraute's *Portrait of a Man Unknown*, Genet's *The Thief's Journal* and *Querelle*, unapologetic tales of gay desire and desperation; in Spain, Camilo José

Cela's *The Family of Pascual Duarte*, which depicts man as essentially murderous; in Switzerland, Max Frisch's *Stiller*, beginning with the protestation "I'm not Stiller," which, like Dostoevky's *Notes*—and we see the shadow of the Undergound Man lurking everywhere here—is a notebook book, a book that falls short of a book. All these figures, and Artemisia too, are summed up in Camus's *The Stranger*, internationally perhaps the single most influential book to come out during the war, the title of which should be read to refer equally and ambiguously to the protagonist, Meursault, who gratuitously murders an unknown Arab on a hot day at the beach, and to the murdered man. *If This Is a Man* is the question posed by the title of Primo Levi's account of his time in Auschwitz.

But Artemisia is not a man. She is a woman. She is something else, and though it would be misleading to suggest that women have not, as writers, readers, and characters, played a central role in the life of the novel from its beginning, a new generation of women writers, with a different sense of what it means to be a writer and a woman, does emerge from the war to energize the novel, perhaps because perceptions of women's lives are changing much more rapidly than perceptions of men's. These novelists are unwilling to cede the "extraordinary freedom" that, Banti for one says, the war had offered them—unwilling to be herded back into the home (where governments in Europe and America would soon seek to herd them). And is it a coincidence—it is striking!—how many of them come from the peripheries of Europe's crumbling empires rather than from their traditional centers? Come from elsewhere, as Jean Rhys had, to make their careers in the metropoles. Doris Lessing is from Rhodesia, where the Scottish Muriel Spark also spends formative years. The Spanish novelist Carmen Laforet comes from the Canary Islands; Marguerite Duras from French Indochina; Natalie Sarraute from Russia, as does the egregious Ayn Rand; Clarice Lispector from Ukraine. The Americans Carson McCullers, Eudora Welty, and Flannery O'Connor all hail from the Deep South. Eileen Chang, whose precocious stories and novellas of the early 1940s were written in the peculiar bubble of Japanese-occupied Shanghai and who would go on to spend her life in exile, writing both in Chinese and English, was the child of a mother who was a fanatical Anglophile (hence her daughter's English given name), modeling herself on the British New Women of the turn of the century, and a father from an old Chinese mandarin family whose views were as reactionary as his wife's were radical. Abandoned, along with Eileen, by his wife, he led a depraved life, collecting concubines and consuming opium; Chang, held captive in the family compound, ran away at eighteen. In Shanghai, her stories and essays and the clothes she designed for herself quickly found an appreciative audience who saw in them not only a beautiful new eye (newly cinematic, among other things) but also a tough, questioning worldly alertness to the ways in which men and women and families use and abuse each other.

The new presence and eminence of women in the life of the postwar novel across a variety of languages may remind us of the nineteenth century, in the course of which Mme de Staël and George Sand and George Eliot and others did so much to shape the sensibility of the times. What is in question is not the matter of some common female sensibility: many of these writers would have been quick to reject or take offense at being called women writers. Not that, then. Instead the prominence women writers attain at this postwar moment, when so much has been destroyed and left unsettled, presumably reflects the maddeningly ambiguous position of women within bourgeois society—at once central and peripheral to its routines and rituals, excluded from power, and yet proclaimed as the affective foundation of the family and civilization—and further that this ambiguous and nothing if not questionable arrangement is meant to go unquestioned. That raises questions, questions that have been coming up in novels from the start of the genre's modern emergence (and it is, as is well-known, a genre whose readership has long consisted primarily of women), but the destruction of the given social order after the war allows those questions to take the starker form they do in Banti's *Artemisia* and in the work of these other writers. Anna Wulf, the heroine of Doris Lessing's *The Golden Notebook*, is like Lessing herself a Rhodesian Jew, and her various engagements, personal, political, artistic, spiritual, with communism, with colonialism, with psychoanalysis, are chronicled in a succession of different-colored notebooks, each of which has its own style and drift, and the issue of how to combine all these disparate concerns is more and more at issue throughout. Lessing's book is a tale of freedom seized, while Lol V. Stein, in Marguerite Duras's *The Ravishing of Lol V. Stein*, is by contrast a tale of imprisonment embraced. Lol, forever marked by her fiancé's abandonment, as if she had sprung from the pages of a trashy romance, drifts listlessly around a French or French colonial suburban Nowheresville (South Tahla it is called, and almost everyone in the book has a non-French name), a cypher seeking realization in the eyes of the lover (the book's narrator) she holds at a remove. Rejected and lost to herself, she recreates herself as the other, as Duras remakes the novel as a hall of empty, agonizing mirrors, perfectly self-contained, perfectly hopeless.

These are challenging writers who show the fetters that all too many women and men all too willingly wear, and seek to imagine what it would be to cast them off in books that mix things up, whether ways of thinking or the characters in them, with abandon and a vengeance. Iris Murdoch's novels are carousels of erotic imbroglio and philosophical investigation. Lispector's *The Passion According to G.H.* is the story of a rich Rio de Janeiro socialite shut up in her apartment and transfixed by the sight of a cockroach slipping out of the cracked door of a wardrobe. In a scandalous and comical and just plain gross revision of the Christian story of the Last Supper (and Kafka's *Metamorphosis*), the protagonist is transformed—redeemed?—when she brings herself to crush and sacramentally consume the bug. G.H. becomes herself, or attains a state of mystical selflessness, by an act of sacred abjection.

How to go on, with the world destroyed around you and the book you were writing—the novel you had in mind—burnt to ash? That's the question Banti's book urgently takes up, and it is a question that would remain urgent in the early years of the Cold War, where, notwithstanding growing postwar prosperity, there was always the worry that the whole world could be obliterated. In *Artemisia*, Banti answers the question by telling an untold story from history, recognizing that history is nothing if not a repository of untold stories and implicitly proposing that in telling them, one might open a way into the future. The end of the war has brought about the collapse of European colonialism—it was hardly as quick and tidy as that, yet Indian independence and the Chinese Revolution of 1949 mark, as we can see even more clearly now, a world-historical change—opening up whole worlds of stories to the novel, stories of what has been and stories of what might be. It opens up those stories to the novel, but it also opens a wider world to the novel. In colonial sub-Saharan Africa, for example, there were oral traditions of long-form narrative, but next to no novels: the broadly literate audience with disposable income that the novel requires to flourish did not exist. The vast majority of the native African population remained economically and politically oppressed, while the minority of the settlers and the even smaller minority of the educated continued to look to Europe for cultural direction.

The war changed this, or at least began to. It had undermined the authority and the finances of the colonial powers; it had also brought many Africans, who served in colonial armies, into direct contact with other places. The Kenyan Ngũgĩ wa Thiong'o's autobiographical first novel, *Weep Not, Child* (1964) (a title that makes us think of Banti's "Don't cry"), links the hero's father's service in the British military to his realization that a black man is no different from a white man. An African could handle military equipment and could fight against white men (as indeed he had) as well as alongside them. If he did not read and write, he could learn to. His children would learn to. Ngũgĩ's novel goes on to tell the story of that education, and all the things he learned about the world and himself in the course of getting it, especially the things that needed to change.

And then there is *Things Fall Apart*, written by the young Nigerian Chinua Achebe and published in London in 1958—one of the very first African novels to emerge after the war. The book was published by the educational division of Heinemann, becoming the first in a series of books by African writers for which Achebe would come to serve as editorial adviser, and which over the coming decade would introduce a wide range of African and West Indian writers, working in a variety of languages, to the English-speaking world. It is telling that it was a pedagogic, not a literary, publisher that had the foresight and initiative to launch such a series, intent not so much on publishing great books as on providing a profitable product for former colonies in which education would be newly widespread. Heinemann published many extraordinary books, and as the struggle against apartheid in South Africa picked up in the 1960s, the books grew increasingly political. Achebe's *Things Fall Apart*, coming at the start of this remarkable literary venture, stands out by virtue of its turning, not unlike Banti in *Artemisia*, to the past the better to fashion a novel for the new postcolonial world. Achebe is consciously setting out to dramatize an episode from another, different, much bigger and longer war than the war that ended with the dropping of nuclear bombs on Hiroshima and Nagasaki. This is the world war waged for centuries by the European powers on the indigenous peoples of Africa and Asia and the Americas, a war that represented a concerted, continual effort to destroy the worlds of these other people, murdering, subjugating, and exploiting them.

Things Fall Apart finds a way to tell that story of devastation and to make us wonder if the story can ever be truly told.

Okonkwo, the hero of Achebe's novel, appears to be a man who is very much at home in his own world. His world, as far as he knows, is *the* world. In the small village deep in the great forest in a place that is not Nigeria and a time that is not, for him, a historical moment, but both the now of the living and the immemorial then of the ancestors and gods, Okonkwo is a big man. Like all the men of his village, he is a farmer, but his endeavors have prospered exceptionally, and by now he is wealthy and has several wives. A strong man—as a young man he made a name for himself as a wrestler—he is a respected voice in village councils, and he also plays important roles in the ritual dances that bind the life of the village together. Okonkwo is a successful and self-satisfied man, very different from his father, he likes to think, who was a wastrel who frittered away his life drinking and making music.

Okonkwo, in other words, knows his worth and knows himself, or so he fancies. Events, however—which is to say Achebe—soon conspire to make it clear that in fact he doesn't. Okonkwo lacks fellow

feeling, we can see, and he lacks imagination. He has will, but, forever bent on proving himself a man, he lacks wisdom and—Achebe
repeats at intervals throughout the book—especially the wisdom of
women, embodied by the sly, charming, poignant, and cryptic stories
about men and gods and beasts that women exchange together and
tell to their children, stories that to Okonkwo seem simply silly.

These deficiencies will help to destroy him. He is revealed as a
stranger to himself and a stranger to the world at large, a stranger in a
strange land. This revelation, this cataclysm, begins with two killings
that punctuate *Things Fall Apart* as unexpectedly and decisively as the
death of the Arab in Camus's *The Stranger*: unquestioningly, on mysterious orders from the village elders, Okonkwo kills a boy from another
village whom he has for some years sheltered in his own house, a boy
he had loved like a son and whom his son had come to love. The law is
the law, Okonkwo reasons inflexibly, against the advice of friends and
family, and his brutal determination to impose its sentence alienates
his son from him forever. Then, accidentally, while Okonkwo is dancing in a funeral ceremony, his gun goes off, killing another villager.
The law is the law: Okonkwo is exiled for seven years, and when he
comes back, the village he knew is gone. The white man, formerly a
weird apparition at the far edge of things, has entered his world. His
son has become a Christian. The colonial administration makes demands that Okonkwo cannot fathom. Things as he understood them
have fallen apart, reducing the strength he once boasted of to helpless violence. Destroyed by circumstances, he takes refuge at last in
self-destruction.

Okonkwo's story is a tragedy. It is, you might say, two different
tragedies. It is on the one hand the tragedy of a man of great abilities
who does not have the ability to learn from experience. The vicissi-
tudes he endures test him terribly but also in a way that might have
given rise to self-understanding, yet what makes Okonkwo formidable also makes it impossible for him to arrive at such a realization.
This, in other words, is a classic tragedy of the blindness that any and
all human beings are susceptible to, tragedy that affirms an essential
common human reality as it delineates our shared limitations.

Things Fall Apart is this kind of tragedy, but then again—and this is the really interesting thing about Achebe's book—then again it is not. It is another, much deeper tragedy, born of the absence of recognition of common humanity. In this tragedy, it makes no difference what Okonkwo does or doesn't know about himself or the world. Okonkwo, as the reader has known from the start—or, as readers of the book slowly grasp, they should have known from the start—is under siege by powers that he can neither imagine nor realistically resist. His world has been chosen for destruction, and in the world to come, Okonkwo and all that he cared for—and he is certainly a man who cares, if anything to a fault—is of no account. What seemed, in other words, like a tragedy of Okonkwo's own making is another kind of tragedy entirely, a tragedy in which he has been deprived by a strange, terrible entity called history of either the happiness or the sadness of his own making. He has been rendered null and void. He cannot— this is the bitterest thing of all—even recognize his own tragedy.

Tragedy is rare in the novel: the novel wants things to go on. Even in the saddest story, the curtain that comes down is more horizon than conclusion. The novels of Thomas Hardy are among the exceptions to the rule, and the story of Okonkwo resembles those of *The Mayor of Casterbridge* and *Jude the Obscure*, stories of men undone both by themselves and by events, men who show us how nugatory our self-importance is. But Hardy's men could at least recognize themselves in their own stories and recognize the kind of stories they are. Okonkwo by contrast is overtaken by something inconceivably alien. In a sense, even his suicide is not his own doing.

How to rescue what is beyond rescue, what is beyond the reach of justice? Achebe's predicament is of course different from Okonkwo's, but it is tricky in its own right. Achebe is writing a novel that records the downfall of a man whose world is remote from the world of the European novel, for whom the novel means nothing. He exists, in fact, in a world in which novels could not exist, since his is a world without writing. Okonkwo's world is one of living oral traditions, upheld by priests and priestesses and village councils, transmitted in common sayings, preserved in the daily and seasonal life of the village. Authority in this world is quite different from the authority of the bound sheaf of printed pages held in the hand of a solitary reader that is a novel, and it is anything but obvious that the novel is the best instrument for making sense of that altogether different, novel-free world. The novel, after all, is a form of understanding that is characteristic of the very worldview that saw fit to destroy this other worldview.

This is a problem that Achebe's book makes real, which is to say makes imaginable and inescapable, for his readers. A problem that his book discovers, you could even say. And having been brought to see that problem, we can also appreciate the art and tact with which Achebe brings it to life in his novel. There is for example his elastic handling of time, effectively bringing out the different times in which his various characters move. Especially in the first part of the book, before the intrusion of the white man, he moves freely back and forth in time, filling in past events as needs be, springing new developments on us, above all the two crucial and catastrophic killings, with peremptory aplomb. This is a world where lives unfold not according to a linear historical logic, but through ritual and revelation, where meaning is constituted by a web of associations, a web whose integrity and resilience Achebe suggests by not explaining, for example, why the village elders call for the death of the stranger boy or how it is that Okonkwo, as his best friend suggests, could have refused to do their bidding. This is a world with reasons of its own. It exists—or rather existed—in its own way.

Achebe's voice in the book is as striking as his treatment of time, as is his handling of point of view. The voice of *Things Fall Apart* is steady, subdued, muffled, born it might seem of wordless grief and tight-lipped endurance and a measured objectivity. The voice is uniform, but the point of view is multiple and equivocal. Like an ethnographer, Achebe collects and describes myths, stories, rituals, legal reckonings, magic spells, customs, and dances. Like a novelist, he explores the complications and limitations of Okonkwo's character. Turning historian, he records the arrival of missionaries and colonial administrators, and indeed, in the last line of the book—nodding at the study of the *Pacification of the Primitive Tribes of the Lower Niger* that the British district commissioner intends to write—mocks their books and claim to understanding. "There is no story that is not true," one of Achebe's characters says. "The world has no end," he continues, "and what is good among one people is an abomination with others." Ah, but worlds can end, and the truth is that all these different truths leave us in the end with no common truth—except, it seems, abomination. Achebe's novel involves an almost cubist proliferation and flattening of perspectives, while the painter's vanishing point is not an artistic convention but a matter of historical record. Every description in Achebe's book is an elegy for something lost, and "things fall apart," the stark sentence that Achebe takes from Yeats for his title, is stripped of the poet's prophetic fervor to stand in its naked finality. The center never held.

16. REFLECTIONS ON DAMAGED LIFE

VLADIMIR NABOKOV'S *LOLITA* AND
ALEJO CARPENTIER'S *THE LOST STEPS*

Reflections on Damaged Life is the subtitle of *Minima Moralia*, by the German philosopher Theodor Adorno, a set of bracingly dour fragmentary reflections on the impossibility of leading a truly reflective life in the modern world, which is to say after the outbreak of war, after the death camps, and in a newly triumphant America, where Adorno wrote the book as a refugee from the Nazis. He begins with an encomium to Proust, the independent and independently wealthy artist par excellence, and the kind of great writer that what Adorno excoriated as "the culture industry" existed, in his view, to suppress. Culture, in Adorno's mind, was what could not be reduced to product or content, but in the world of the mid-twentieth century, whether you were in Hollywood, Berlin, or Moscow, this was what the powers that be had conspired to turn it into. Official culture was designed to degrade the appetites of audiences, the better to destroy true culture and with it the freedom it grew out of and the freedoms it sustained.

Adorno—the German intellectual bitterly decrying the evils of jazz and Hollywood and astrology in a commercialized, commodified, and administered reality against which, he advises his readers, the only tonic is undiluted despair—could easily be a character in a novel by Vladimir Nabokov. He is prickly, pompous, brilliant, and in many ways not wrong, a thinker and a man whose work teeters on the verge of self-parody but never lacks daring or point. Nabokov had also fled from Europe to America and was also prickly, pompous, brilliant, and daring. And yet Nabokov's Adorno wouldn't have been a sympathetic character. Before coming to America, Nabokov had lived for years in Berlin, and he had no patience for the Teutonic. Nor does Nabokov find a place in Adorno's collected critical writings. But the writers shared a moment and a predicament, and certainly Nabokov's was a damaged life.

A life that had begun, however—on this he always insisted—as the picture of perfection. His mother, Yelena, was heir to a fortune made in gold mines; his father, after whom he was named, was the scion of an old, distinguished Russian aristocratic family, as well as a respected jurist, an amateur lepidopterist (a passion his son inherited), and, in czarist Russia, a crusading liberal politician. They lived in a palace in St. Petersburg from which they retreated at leisure to a vast country estate. Nabokov, born in 1899, was their first child, beloved, pampered, brought up to speak English and French as well as Russian, precocious: he published his first book of poems at sixteen, the same year that an uncle left him a country estate of his own, right next to that of his parents.

Then came the revolution, forcing the family to flee west, divesting them of property and wealth. Nabokov was nonetheless able to attend Cambridge, while his parents went to Berlin, where his father edited an émigré newspaper and, in 1922, was killed while shielding a political ally from assassination by Russian monarchists. In Berlin, under the pen name Sirin, Nabokov soon made himself known as a promising young poet and writer, publishing his first novel, *Mary*, in 1926. His work was well regarded, some of it even translated abroad, but he struggled to find an audience outside of the small, fractious émigré community, and he struggled to support his wife and son. His wife, Véra, was Jewish, and when the Nazis came to power, it became clear that the family could not stay in Germany. They moved to France, and in 1939, with time once again running out, Nabokov inveigled an invitation to America—and now there was the struggle to write in a new language and to make a new name as writer in the new world, while the struggle to make a living continued. Nabokov worked as an entomologist, taught at Wellesley and Cornell, published a novel—his first in English—with New Directions, the most venturesome of the American publishing houses of the time, as well as stories in *The New Yorker,* which was then beginning to figure as the beacon of American sophistication. He did well by himself—he was, all things considered, a lucky man—yet there was no denying the displacement he had suffered and endured, like the bumbling, absent-minded professor, speaking heavily accented English, who is depicted in his novel *Pnin.* In 1951 he put together the essays that comprise *Speak, Memory,* his memoir of father and mother and a fairy-tale childhood, a book full of virtuosic set pieces: "a lark ascending the curds-and-whey sky of a dull spring day, heat lightning taking pictures of a distant line of trees in the night, the palette of maple leaves on brown sand, a small bird's cuneate footprints on new snow." A born prince become an obscure American academic, a writer largely unknown in his own language and recognized only as an oddity in his adopted one, Nabokov could reasonably have thought that along with its major misdeeds, the century had consistently conspired to ruin his chances.

Then came *Lolita.*

Lolita is the story of the seduction and abduction of a pubescent American girl by a middle-aged European émigré litterateur, an elaborate story of statutory rape that Nabokov, after finishing it in 1953, sent around to various American publishers who all rejected it out of hand. In 1955, Maurice Girodias's Olympia Press, based in Paris and chiefly devoted to pornography, gave the novel a subterranean life, and it found some influential admirers (most famously Graham Greene) before being forbidden entry into Britain and banned in France (Lolita thus joining the classy company of Madame Bovary and Lady Chatterley). In 1958, the mainstream US publisher Putnam took a chance on the book, which was both a succès de scandale and a runaway bestseller, rapidly translated into all the major European languages (though unpublishable in Soviet Russia). Nabokov was now a rich man, free to return to Europe and live out his days in a fancy hotel in the Swiss Alps, where he stepped into a role that had, by mid-century, taken shape as a role, that of twentieth-century master. Who, after the war, was left to give it new life? Nabokov, hailing from Russia, the tormented empire from which the twentieth-century novel and the riven geopolitical landscape of the twentieth century had in many ways emerged, was perfect for the part, and assigned it, he played it to the hilt. When he put together a collection of his criticism in 1973, he called it *Strong Opinions*, and one of the ways he burnished his credentials as a twentieth-century master was to devote himself to denouncing the century's intellectual and ideological crazes and follies: Freud, Marx, existentialism, Dostoevsky—Nabokov reserved a special disdain for Dostoevsky, in his view a dreadful stylist and a sophomoric thinker. There were a very few other masters—Proust, Joyce, Kafka, Andrey Bely—whose merit he did recognize, and his recognition was as much to his point as their genius.

And as a literary showman, Nabokov really is unequaled, even by those precursors, none of whom wrote sentences or composed novels of such consciously licked finish. Nabokov's power of observation, his mocking humor, his gift for metaphor, his eye for color and his ear for colorful words of all sorts, his erudition and his eccentricity, the ruthlessness and tenderness of his sensibility—all these make *Lolita* a triumph of high style but also—not a quality one associates with Proust or Joyce—of pop glamour. And after all, it is an American novel—curiously all the more of an American novel for its author, and its narrator, being anything but American—coming out at the moment when American popular culture threatens to become as dominant globally as America is economically and politically. *Lolita*, whose name would become a byword, shares a decade with Marilyn Monroe, and they also share an attitude, wide-eyed and wounded, and an allure that makes us uneasy.

Supremely polished, *Lolita* is an ugly book. The narrator is the European litterateur and seducer and abductor, and he calls himself Humbert Humbert—not his real name—and he grew up in a hotel in what I have called the Hotel World of the years between the wars. As a budding boy, he fell in love with a budding girl, and ever since, his only true objects of desire are the pubescent girls he calls nymphets. Having arrived (after a failed marriage, flight to America, and a nervous breakdown for which he was institutionalized) in the provincial American town of Ramsdale with the purpose of writing a book, he takes a room in a house whose widowed owner is the mother of just such a girl, Lolita. Lolita is brimming with sexual curiosity, and Humbert cannot take his eyes off her, as Charlotte, the earnest mother, cannot take her eyes off him, tall, dark, and handsome as he often reminds us he is. To get closer to the daughter, he marries the mother, whom he intends to murder. She discovers his designs, runs distraught from the house, and is conveniently mowed down by a passing car. After that Lolita is Humbert's. He has sex with her at a motel, and after explaining to her that, with her mother dead, he is her guardian, he takes her on a road trip across America, settling down with her at last in another provincial town to oversee her education and enjoy her favors. She calls him Dad. Time passes, and Lolita wearies of the increasingly jealous Humbert; eventually she elopes with another older man, a popular playwright turned pornographic moviemaker, Clare Quilty. Humbert does not see Lolita again until she is seventeen, when she writes to tell him she is married to a mechanic (Dick) and they need money to move to Alaska to, she says in the vague American way, pursue their dream. She also tells him about Quilty, whom Humbert subsequently tracks down and shoots dead. *Lolita* is composed by Humbert on death row, a defense, a confession, a love song, written for posterity and not to be published until after Lolita dies. He does not know, as we have known from the start of the book, that Lolita has already died in childbirth.

The book, as I said, was seen as scandalous by many, and it retains the power to scandalize. In the second decade of the twenty-first century, a distinguished British editor said that were the book to come to him then, he would not—could not—have brought it out. It's worth considering why it remains controversial. It can't be because of the story itself—basically a story of an unscrupulous seducer and a wronged woman that is almost as old as story itself. Since Richardson's *Clarissa*, it has constituted one of the templates of the novel, reworked in successors such as Hawthorne's *The Scarlet Letter* and Hardy's *Tess*. It's an old story, rarely told in the twentieth-century novel because it's so old-fashioned. And because it's that kind of story, it's always been possible to say, as Nabokov himself sometimes did, that *Lolita* is the most moral of books, about a bad man and a poor, mistreated girl. It is hard, however, not to feel that such readers doth protest a little too much, and I have no doubt that Nabokov offered this defense with a wink and a smirk. Readers who recoil from the book have the merit of recognizing it for what it is, a tale told by the ravisher and ravishingly told.

Lolita's story is Humbert's story, and it shimmers throughout and especially when lust is in the air. "I lost myself in the pungent but healthy heat which like summer haze hung about little Haze," Humbert writes in an early scene, where he sits with Lolita on Charlotte's davenport, and Lolita, eating an apple, stretches out, draping her legs over his lap:

> Let her stay. Let her stay . . . as she strained to chuck her abolished apple into the fender, her young weight, her shameless, innocent shanks and round bottom, shifted in my tense, tortured, surreptitiously laboring lap, and all of a sudden a mysterious change came over my senses. I entered a plane in being where nothing mattered, save the infusion of joy brewed within my body. What had begun as a delicious distension of my innermost roots became a glowing tingle which now had reached that state of absolute security, confidence and reliance not found elsewhere in conscious life. With the deep hot sweetness thus established and well on its way to the ultimate convulsion, I felt I could slow down in order to prolong the glow. Lolita had been safely solipsized. The implied sun pulsated in the supplied poplars; we were fantastically and divinely alone . . .

To the knowing reader, Humbert is flashing his literary bona fides—Marcel with Albertine, Leopold Bloom with Molly Bloom are in the background of this masturbatory scene—while also offering excuses: it is Lolita who is making things happen, just as Eve took the first bite of the apple. Humbert deploys high art and ancient wisdom to low ends. The whole passage, which is a good deal longer and more elaborate than what I quote, is a showstopper: note, for example, how cleverly "sated" pulses in the poplars. Humbert is a master instrumentalist, we see, and Humbert is playing with his instrument, we see, and Humbert is making another person, a child, the instrument of his desire: we see that too. And we see in this at once overheated and all-too-calculated composition what a sentimentalist Humbert the connoisseur is, and what a cold-blooded one, too. "A state of absolute security . . . Lolita safely solipsized"—here we have another virtuosic pun, the *sol* of absolute and solipsized, bearing on solution and dissolution and absolution for guilty desire and the isolation of the self, while picking up a gleam of the sun that warms the scene. But it is "safely" that is the true giveaway. Humbert wants to be safe to enjoy his desires, and since he is not just a villain but also a human, there is another part of him that would like to be saved from those tormenting desires. Above all, he wants to feel he is no different from anyone else, normal.

Readers who recoil from the book realize that they are being put on the spot by it. Lolita's story is Humbert's story, and Humbert's story is Nabokov's story, because it is not just a story told from Humbert's point of view, some sort of psychological exposé, but a story told with all the brilliance its author can muster, a brilliance that can't help but bear and spread the taint of the author's sordid creation. And so, in reading it, giving it our full attention, being drawn into it, we are also implicated in it. The book blurs the difference between authorial art and its main character's arts and the reader's involvement and pleasure. It tells a sordid, heartbreaking story of a rather ordinary girl who is divinized by her despoiler, and it tells it in glorious words, glorious words in between which we get a glimpse from time to time of wretched, abandoned Lolita, who, as she says to Humbert, "If she wrote up her life, nobody would ever believe it." But the more Lolita comes to light, the more the aesthetic splendor of *Lolita*, a creation that is not only but never less than the work of Lolita's destroyer, comes to light, and if the book remains scandalous, it is because once and for all it interrupts, short-circuits, the connection between ethics and aesthetics that twentieth-century novelists like Wells and Musil, even more than their nineteenth-century forebears—who could take it for granted—were desperate to affirm. Nabokov doesn't do this out of nihilism or aestheticism; he doesn't deny that there are moral claims on us that are real, as no less real qualities set apart good art from bad. He recognizes both claims as real and both claims as bearing on our happiness (and the power of Nabokov's art is that it is rooted in the keen happiness we feel when we encounter the inspired description and the revelatory word), but he also recognizes that the claim of goodness and the claim of beauty are not at heart complementary, and, yes, in the distance that opens up between them lies a world of pain, all our damaged life. What can *Lolita* do for Lolita? Nothing. The two do not add up (even as, in the imagination, Humbert and Lolita are forever, monstrously, married); they only open a wound, and there is no reassurance for the reader in *Lolita*, which depicts a world of guilt in which the only innocence is innocence sacrificed.

Nabokov, who washed up in America nearly a half century into his life and the life of the twentieth century, faced the question that Banti faces at the start of *Artemisia*—how to go on—and also Achebe's question, how to begin. For Nabokov, however, there was also the question of how to go back, how to return to the lost paradise of childhood. "Lolita," his novel begins, as if learning its name. "Lo-lee-ta," it continues, as if reverting to preverbal infantile babble, and then the whole sad history unfolds, and as Humbert says, "you can always count on a murderer for a fancy prose style." There is no going back, in other words. All that is left is the terrible present—the vast stretch of America in the novel, both unspoiled and despoiled, like its heroine—the perversion of desire and the will to kill. How odd, too, that the story of Lolita should ultimately trace back to Nabokov's despised Dostoevsky, whose "Stavrogin's Confession," a censored chapter of *Demons* describing an aristocrat's rape of a peasant girl, it essentially reprises. It's as if Nabokov wished to confess between the lines that it was Dostoevsky who had first seen the terrible political and spiritual devastation that the twentieth-century novel was doomed to endure—isn't this all that can be said to the memory of innocence and happiness lost?— to no good end.

The Lost Steps, by the Cuban author Alejo Carpentier, also dating to 1953, features a protagonist with more than a little in common with Humbert Humbert. He isn't a pedophile or a repeat murderer, it's true, but he is a middle-aged, overeducated man from a muddle of places and is a muddle himself, his life mired in creative sterility and sexual frustration; he is vain, and he certainly has a fancy prose style. He's a composer, or was—now all he composes are commercial jingles—though it's his wife, an actress, starring in a cheesy plantation melodrama, who brings home the bacon. He solaces his self-esteem with a lover, Mouche—French for "fly," with an additional pun on English mooch—whom he despises as much as he despises himself for being with her. He lives in a big city that, like him, is unnamed but is a clearly recognizable New York, with its wartime cargo of European refugees. The book starts with the protagonist backstage at his wife's show, surrounded by the pasteboard props to which his world has been reduced, all his days running into each other, identical and without identity. For a composer, time should be the medium of the imagination, but for this composer time has run out. He is profoundly bored:

> Ascending and descending the hill of days, with the same stone on my shoulder, I was sustained by momentum, the product of fits and starts—and sooner or later, this momentum would give out, on a day that might fall even this year . . . Trying to evade this fate was as pointless as trying to relive the deeds of heroes and saints of yore. We had sunken to the era of the Wasp Man, the Nobody Man, with souls sold not to the Devil, but to the Bookkeeper or the Slave Driver.

Out on the street, however—providentially!—he runs into an old music professor of his who has a proposal to make. The old professor has a purse at his command (this is postwar America, a honeycomb already oozing institutional cash), and he has it in mind to send his sometime prize student on a musicological mission to the Amazon, where he hopes he'll be able to track down a primitive pipe that could offer a clue to the origins of music. Why not, our hero thinks. Mouche is avid for travel. He has nothing better to do. If necessary, he can

always pick up some crude whistle in a junk shop to fob off on the
old man.

That's the beginning of *The Lost Steps*, which is also like *Lolita* in
being very much set at its midcentury moment, though curiously, as
the opening of a novel, all this could easily have come from the fore-
time of the twentieth-century novel: the setup smacks of *The Time
Machine* or Jules Verne. Time and history will in any case be key in
The Lost Steps, the sections of which are assiduously dated, from the
beginning of the expedition on June 4th to the end, six months later,
on December 30th. Having flown to Latin America, the narrator finds
himself trapped in his hotel by a political coup, a spasm of pointless
bloodletting, politics at a dead end, not unlike his relationship with
Mouche. Looking to go somewhere—he is still ambivalent about even
bothering to fulfill his assignment—they take a bus over the high,
cold cordillera of the Andes to the continent's sultry hinterlands. The
bus picks up Rosario, a mestiza woman through whose mouth "the
plants spoke and boasted of their powers," fascinating to the composer, before at last arriving at a great river. Here they meet an assort-
ment of backwoods characters—a missionary to the Indians, a Greek
gold hunter never without a copy of *The Odyssey*, a collector of plants,
and the so-called Adelantado (a name formed from the Spanish for
"onward!"), who tells them about the lost steps, the entryway to an
even more remote world, that are only to be discerned when the river
is low enough. That is where he is going, and, yes, the protagonist and
Rosario—Mouche, now history, decamps for civilization—will go too.

Carpentier's worldly, hyper-cultivated, self-indulgently erudite
protagonist—a parody midcentury intellectual in midlife crisis—is
on a mythic voyage back to the origins of human consciousness,
untainted by the products of civilization, and *The Lost Steps*, again
like *Lolita* but even more like Jack Kerouac's *On the Road*, is a road
trip to the back of beyond that counts as its antecedents *Huck Finn*
and *Don Quixote* and *The Odyssey*, while additionally taking readers back to the exploratory wanderings and escapades of the young
surrealists in the streets of wartime Paris. The title *The Lost Steps* is
in fact taken from André Breton, who had given it to a collection of

his early essays. In French it also functions as a pun on "not lost," and in this book Carpentier was confident that he had found a new way to dramatize the dilemmas not only of his own life but of "our time." Carpentier, like Nabokov, had been born with the century and repeatedly displaced by its events. Raised between Cuba and Paris, he came of cosmopolitan and cultured stock (his mother, of Russian descent, was a musician, his father an architect who disappeared over the horizon before his son came of age), and Carpentier had gone on to lead a vagrant life in turn. In the late 1920s, after landing in jail for his opposition to the Cuban dictator Machado (he wrote his first novel behind bars), he fled Cuba for Paris, where he worked in radio and moved in surrealist circles before returning to the New World at the outbreak of the Second World War. There he wrote a study of Cuban popular music and a novel about the Haitian revolution, *The Kingdom of This World*, with a polemical introduction extolling the power of what Carpentier dubbed "*lo real maravilloso*" or "marvelous realism." This marvelous realism was, Carpentier argued, a New World and a Latin American thing, marked by the mingled indigenous and African and baroque Catholic currents of the Latin American popular imagination—a New World thing that Carpentier, keen in midlife to make his mark at last, saw as replacing the showy antics of Old World surrealism while bearing a political edge that, unlike the dull formulas of socialist realism, could cut home.

Marvelous realism would in time come to be known worldwide as magic realism, to a significant degree because of the example and success of *The Lost Steps*, which is both an exercise in it and an apologia for it. It is a book with something to prove, about old worlds and new, musical in character, lavish and sonorous and operatic, and employing music, too, as a metaphor to engage the question of what, especially after the Second World War, a human world can be and how art can contribute to it. A central passage of the book features the narrator listening to Beethoven's Ninth Symphony, the ultimate warhorse of the Western classical tradition, on a crackly radio in the Andean night, music that takes him back to the past. It brings thoughts of his father, a horn player in an orchestra, who fled Europe for the

States to avoid conscription in World War I, only to live long, lonely American years running a profitless music shop while missing the Europe (or call it the nineteenth century) he'd left behind, with its faith in "the relentlessness of progress, the spread of socialism, and collective culture," not to mention its "workingmen who . . . spent their leisure hours in public libraries, and on Sunday . . . took their families to hear the Ninth Symphony." The music brings thoughts of his Latin mother and his Caribbean childhood and the imaginary voyages he embarked on while she played the piano, and finally it recalls a more recent experience of his own, something that happened in Europe while he was serving as a military interpreter during the most recent war. The last movement of the Ninth begins with an eruption of "broken, lacerated, tattered, chaotically gestating" themes, becoming "a symphony . . . in ruins," and listening to it faint in the Andean night, the narrator remembers a night in defeated Germany when, camped outside a Nazi death camp now repurposed to hold German prisoners of war, he overheard the soldiers within all singing together in the shadow of "chimneys from which prayers howled in Yiddish had bellowed not long ago"—"the same words as that chorus spurred by the gestures of some distant conductor: Freude," or *joy*, the first explosive word of the great choral setting of Schiller's "Ode to Joy" with which the symphony exultantly ends.

So the great Western (nineteenth-century) tradition, pledged to progress, ends in a twentieth-century irony so devastating it is almost cheap, to which the sour, disabused knowingness the narrator displays at the start of the book is perhaps as reasonable a response as any. Is there music with the power to take us beyond such terminal irony to some marvelous reinvigoration of the sense of reality? This is the question the narrator begins to wake up to as he and Rosario and company, led by the Adelantado, enter the secret passage and pursue their way through the uncharted interior of the continent, where the Adelantado has it in mind to set up a new model community. Before they can arrive at the site of the future, however, the little band must traverse a prodigious landscape to discover a world from the primordial past, a journey the narrator describes as a "symphony we read backward . . .

returning to the measures of Genesis," arriving at last at the so-called Great Savannah and "a world anterior to man . . . the Fourth Day of Creation," beyond which lies only "the Creator's terrible solitude."

In this demi-Eden, a man from a local tribe has died—of a snake-bite. A shaman presides over the funeral rites:

> Then the Word makes its appearance . . . [a] word [that is] more than a word . . . that mimics the voice of the speaker but is equally . . . the spirit that possesses the cadaver. One comes from the enchanter's throat, the other comes from his belly; the one is grave and mingled like the subterranean roiling of lava; the other baritone and wrathful and discordant. They alternate, responding, one scolds while the other moans, the belly sarcastic, the windpipe hasty. There are guttural portamenti, stetched out into howls; syllables repeated . . . many times . . . sudden trills . . . something that lies past language and yet remains far from song; ignorant of vocalization and yet much more than words. It distends, turns horrible, bloodcurdling, this cry that echoes over the corpse surrounded by mute dogs . . .
>
> I have just witnessed the Birth of Music.

Here we have music as more than mere communication or a merely given form, at once wordless grief and pure potentiality; music as the felt possibility of going on in a world devastated not just by the wars of the twentieth century but from the start and forever.

And where does the book go from there? The plot of *The Lost Steps* stages a pratfall, bringing the action back to the modern world with a lurch and a jolt. The Adelantado is busily setting up his rustic utopia at the back of beyond, and the narrator is contemplating settling in there with Rosario as contentedly as Mr. Blanding, except that the shaman's voice has left him bitten anew by the bug (or snake) of composition, and when a search plane comes for him, he takes the ride out: he needs music paper. Up north, public scandal and divorce await him, and when he tries to return, the river has risen and the mark of the hidden passage is no longer to be seen. At the end of the story of going back, we discover there is no going back, which is, the reader is meant to wryly recognize, how stories like this always do end.

Terminal irony—and incipient despair—are once again in the air, yet the threat is averted. The first song was a song of mourning—art begins by giving form to grief, allowing us to express it and transcend it, and there is also, in any case, distinct from that, a world elsewhere: the world of the Adelantado. "Those who say a man can't escape his era are wrong," the narrator assures us. And yet "none of this is destined for me, because the only race that may not flee the clutches of chronology is the race of artists, who must hurry past the tangible testimonies of the day before and anticipate the songs and forms of those still to come, leaving new tangible testimonies in full awareness of what has been done up to the present day."

A grand affirmation—grandiloquent, and suspiciously so, as Carpentier's protagonist so often is—and at the same time a riddle. There is a world elsewhere, yes, and anyone with the will to go there can go there, except the artist cannot. As in Nabokov, the division between art and life is dogmatically absolute. History advances thanks to those like Rosario, who "know nothing of history," and the artist stands over its bier, its designated mourner and hopeless celebrant.

Nabokov and Carpentier share an unabashedly triumphalist and hopelessly conflicted sense of what they are up to as novelists. Their work is poised in an awe-inspiring defensive crouch. "My calling," Carpentier's narrator avers, was "that of compromising music," and if he is not quite as compromised as Humbert Humbert, Carpentier's book, with its digressions and allusions and high baroque rhetoric, is, like *Lolita*, a confession. It, like *Lolita*, sounds the note of grief and guilt that we have also heard in Banti and Achebe, even as, again like *Lolita*, it is a work of unfettered, almost brazen extravagance. Each book is designed as a tour de force, at once dazzling and doubt-inducing, their high flights accompanied by a sense of hokum, their narrators not to be trusted for a minute, even as these suspect narrators so manifestly exemplify their writers' gifts. Both books are self-commanded performances that at the same time glance back over their shoulders at the great performances of yore—at such precursors as Proust and Joyce and Breton—seeking to equal if not surpass them. These exuberant books in which dazzlement is inextricable from darkness are essentially excessive, largely indifferent to sturdy questions of point of view or good taste. Carpentier counterpoints Auschwitz with Beethoven; Nabokov the natural splendor of the American West with the spreading commercialized blight of the nation's highway system, as observed, with arch (and bewildered) superiority by the moral monster he plunks down at the narrative wheel. These are books in which the very idea of measure is in question, as parodic and self-parodying as they are inspired, mockingly mimicking the novel of voice that we first saw in Gide's *Immoralist*, returning to the radically unreliable voice of the Underground Man. They constitute themselves in a tradition—this too is a new thing for a twentieth-century novel to do—even as they stand out from it, their voices cracking as much as soaring. And they did stand out among their contemporaries, as they still do. If there is a great American novel of the postwar era, it is *Lolita*, and in his memoir of the so-called boom in Latin American fiction, the Chilean writer José Donoso speaks of a friend returning from a trip with Carpentier's *Lost Steps*, and "[devouring] it in one enormous bite," "able for the first time to look beyond the barriers of simplicity and realism as our literature's sole destiny." Both books are supremely cosmopolitan, troublingly suave, and of their moment. *Lolita*, as I said, has a pop sheen Lolita would have admired. It was movie-ready, as was *The Lost Steps*, even if the planned film of Carpentier's book, to feature Ava Gardner and Gina Lollobrigida, never did get made.

But then there is the darkness of both books, full of a sense of lost innocence and complicity in the loss of innocence, that marks them not only as post–World War II but also as postnuclear. Wells had characterized the Great War as the war to end all wars, and Oppenheimer briefly imagined that the bombs dropped on Hiroshima and Nagasaki at the end of the Second World War would, by their sheer destructiveness, terrify people into keeping the peace, and to a certain extent they did. World War II was followed by the Cold War, and in this new war our two authors took up seemingly distinct positions. Nabokov was fiercely anti-Communist and welcoming of the shelter of the American imperium, even if he did choose to end his days in neutral Switzerland, and *Lolita's* tragic aestheticism leaves no real room for social, much less political life, dimensions of human existence that are entirely missing from Nabokov's work as a whole. Art has no business with such things, he insisted in his criticism, but the violence of his insistence on art as a magical preserve makes us wonder. Nabokov's novels, *Lolita* most of all, depict a world of evil without consolation or redemption apart from the texture and color they provide. The books are like the butterflies that Nabokov, often posing for photographs with his net, famously hunted. In these same years, Carpentier emerged as an ardent supporter of the Cuban Revolution, and in 1966 he became Fidel Castro's ambassador to France, spending the rest of his days in Paris, at a comfortable remove from the demands of revolutionary discipline. This is entirely in tune with the conclusion of *The Lost Steps*, in which the man of action and the artist go their separate ways. Writing in a divided world under the shadow of destruction, the dogmatic division between art and life both Nabokov and Carpentier insist on remains an itch they can't stop scratching.

What is to be done? Dull, demanding Chernyshevsky's question never ceases to haunt the novel, and the most wonderful of Nabokov's Russian fictions, *The Gift*, includes an acid biography of Chernyshevsky that is also a tip of the hat to a man so absurdly unworldly that he comes to embody a hopeless, and unforgivable, innocence. Carpentier, for his part, followed *The Lost Steps* with a historical novel—an extravagant fantasia on historical fact, the magisterial *The Age of Enlightenment* (translated as *Explosion in a Cathedral*)—about the French Revolution, that bloody opening act of the modern political world, and in it he tells the story of how the revolution came to the Caribbean, first to free the slaves, then, within a few years, to enslave them anew. At the center of the book are a youthful, energetic, orphaned brother and sister (avatars of Ulrich and Agathe, you could say, or representative members of "the family of man" that Edward Steichen celebrated in a famous photography exhibition of the Cold War era), ever curious and game, around whom the smoke of history curls and clears, though there will be no escape from destruction in the end. No escape, and the book begins with an image of destiny that lingers through its pages. A ship is making its way from the Old to the New World, a ship that is bringing the new revolutionary message of a free and transfigured humanity to the world at large. On the prow of the ship is the instrument of justice by which that message will be made good, literally framing all that lies ahead: the foursquare scaffold and hanging blade of the guillotine.

17. THE WHOLE STORY OF AMERICA

RALPH ELLISON'S *INVISIBLE MAN*

"It would be hard to overestimate the amount of unhappiness in America," says Edmund, one of a crew of sad young literary men in Delmore Schwartz's *The World Is a Wedding*, a short novel about the decade before the war that came out in 1948. He adds, "The cause can't just be the depression." Yes, his interlocutor Jacob chimes in: "The depression is as much an effect as a cause." Edmund responds, "I saw the other day that 95 percent of the bathtubs in the world are in America. Now if anyone reflects sufficiently upon this interesting fact, he will conclude with the whole story of America."

The whole story of America? The whole story of Schwartz's book is that five years after graduation, these college buddies are underemployed or unemployed and generally disappointed in life. Regularly, they gather at the apartment that Rudyard, no doubt named in honor of Kipling and once deemed most likely to succeed, shares with his sister Laura. Rudyard is a playwright, but no one will perform his plays, which, he figures, means they're good. Laura wants to get married, and she is no more successful than her brother. The gang—the boys—all grew up against a background of great books, in relation to which they all feel very small. They exchange brittle repartee while condescending to one another and the rest of the world, especially America and their parents: America with its cult of success; their parents, whose only thought is money; the superficiality of it all, their own too. Laura listens from the kitchen, makes wisecracks, and drinks dismally. "All the sentences in all the books will not do away with my disappointment," she groans. Everyone is unhappy in a way that they could only be in a country dedicated to the pursuit of happiness in the form of bathtubs.

You'd imagine that in 1948, after America had scored the biggest success in its history, Schwartz's story would have seemed a bit of a period piece. Wasn't all that helplessness and hopelessness done with now? But then the point of the story, by a writer whose dazzlingly precocious career would soon take a precipitous fall into drunkenness and madness, is to lead the reader to wonder, is it?

In any case, the world of the 1930s that Schwartz depicts in his story was already in many ways the world after the war. These second-generation Jewish kids are moving on from the ghettoized life of their striving parents. Contraception is available, sexual mores are loosening, and one of the boys takes to cruising, regaling his pals with his exploits. New kinds of jobs are also opening: the story ends with Rudyard taking a position at a midwestern university, where he will teach writing. "The world is a wedding," Jacob reports excitedly to the gang, a phrase he picked up somewhere, which puts him in mind of Bruegel's great *The Peasant Wedding*, with its democratic sweep. America, this little apartment in New York, is where the great old things will—may—take on a new life, Jacob wants his audience of friends to feel. Everything is coming together in a new way; a new, roomy, festive community is taking shape. And yet it is Laura who is given the last cautionary word: "You can't fool me. The world is a funeral . . . Let your conscience be your bride."

Schwartz's small, wry, local tale sets the large terms of the postwar American novel: to be true to actual American experience, to America's peculiarly grandiose provinciality, but also to the promise of hope that America, this world apart from the world that is now on top of the world, has always claimed to present. To be as big and unbaked as the country is while being bent on bigger things yet. To have a conscience. To get out of the bathtub.

"The situation of American literature is anomalous," James Russell Lowell wrote in his 1848 essay about Edgar Allan Poe. "It has no center . . . [although] a great babble is kept up concerning a national literature." A hundred years later, the charge still held. For young American writers, many of them returning from war, the new situation presented an opportunity and a challenge; when it came to American literature, there was everything to do. The actual accomplishments of American writers, the great figures—some, like Melville, only recently canonized—had still to be properly appreciated, and the midcentury, starting before the war and then expanding wildly with the growth of the university system after, saw an explosion of critical studies of American literature, from Alfred Kazin's *On Native Grounds*, to F. O. Matthiessen's *American Renaissance*, to Perry Miller's *Errand into the Wilderness*, to Leslie Fiedler's *The End of Innocence*—titles that are suggestive in their own right of the literary claims being staked and contested. As to the novel—well, America's new position as a preeminent power made it demand a novel to match, one that looked not just to American literature but to the whole past of literature for inspiration, displaying an American vigor and individuality and variety while offering a critical check on the vulgar, sometimes vicious boosterism the country was also notorious for. It needed to be outgoing and inward-looking in equal measures, grown-up and still growing. It needed to surpass what had gone before and prove that this country without ruins, as Emerson had called it, offered a foundation for a new, liberating moral sensibility. Young writers, especially young Jewish writers like Schwartz, whose families combined dark European memories—and of course they had seen the darkness thicken unimaginably since—with new American prospects, were eager to marry the world to America and America to the world. After the bitter experiments of the twentieth century and its novel, America offered a new beginning.

You can hear that eagerness in the rousing, much celebrated beginning of Saul Bellow's *The Adventures of Augie March*:

> I am an American, Chicago born—Chicago, that somber city—and go at things as I have taught myself, freestyle, and will make the record in my own way: first to knock, first admitted . . .

—a tone of bravura that is no less present, 585 pages later, at the book's end:

> I may well be a flop . . . Columbus too thought he was a flop, probably, when they sent him back in chains. Which didn't prove there was no America.

From sea to shining sea, but especially in the great interior, where the great city of Chicago sits on the shore of the Great Lakes at the edge of the Great Plains, the great theme is trumpeted, America, but not pompously and with no trace of philistine narrowness—no, as an occasion of passionate inquiry and dazzled discovery, of adventure. Augie (his name at once absurd and august, summery and springy, and resolutely, even imperiously, on the march) has adventures that will take him up and down the length and breadth of the States, over to Europe, and even to that exciting other America, Mexico. Picaresque, picturesque, Bellow's novel looked back to fine American feats of the imagination like *Huck Finn*, while the mix of up-to-date lowlife detail and highbrow allusion, and of course the unapologetic Jewishness of the book, making nice neither to the American mainstream nor the immigrant enclave, gave the book an inclusiveness that, at this postwar, post-Holocaust moment, exemplified everything America had to offer. The book was backslapping and lyrical, street-savvy and tearstained, brainy and brawny, and it made a big, brash noise that was all its own. Bellow's style is essentially percussive—he hits on words and details with an audible glee, he wants to make an impression—get that, hear that?—and he drove it forward from the seat of a full drum kit, moving with supreme confidence from hi-hat to tom-tom to snare, from rim shot to cymbal. The book was—other defining American qualities—athletic, optimistic, and soulful. What's your game? *Augie March* allowed with every sentence. I can meet you and beat you at it, too. Bellow's novel showed power, and it showed a certain restraint. The world was wonderful but terrible too. In its way, Bellow's work caught the spirit of the new realism that America's court theologian Reinhold Niebuhr, recommending that the nation's business be conducted with the wisdom of the serpent as much as the innocence of the dove, enjoined upon the providentially appointed wielders of global power.

That was one way forward, and it was one that other rising literary celebrities of the '40s and '50s, such as Norman Mailer and the slightly younger Jack Kerouac and John Updike, also followed. These writers were writers, each and all sporting a self-conscious and highly mannered literary style and flaunting a power not only to describe but to define the latest trends in contemporary American life. On the page, none of them sounded much like the, at this point, depressed panjandrum of American letters, Hemingway, though Mailer frequently invoked him and shared his obsession with boxing and bullfighting (Bellow, in *Henderson the Rain King*, turns a Hemingway African safari story into a goofy spiritual picaresque), but they are, for all that, cut from his cloth. Hemingway's heroic ethos of individual style lies behind their self-presentation as writers, and they are similarly snakebitten by celebrity. But Hemingway was at heart an exiled spirit—he stood apart as an American because he was always an American apart—and these young writers were very much at home in their America. They projected writerly style as personality in a raft of novels that carried not only their own name on the cover but their main characters' names, characters who bear a family resemblance to Svevo's Zeno as winning avatars of the incorrigibly human. Bellow especially made a point of this—after Augie came Henderson, Herzog, Sammler, and Humboldt—but Updike had his Rabbit series, and Mailer's *The Armies of the Night*, about the 1967 anti-war March on the Pentagon, bearing the vaunting subtitle *History as the Novel, the Novel as History*, as well as subsequent books, featured an indomitable Mailer. In these books writer and character set out together as intrepid explorers of the city, suburb, self, slum, sex, politics, and the page (but hardly ever the rural sticks, a terrain left to southerners like Flannery O'Connor), gutsily determined to populate their work with striking presences from up and down the American social ladder, a mission, as Philip Roth would reveal with *Portnoy's Complaint*, that could also accommodate the most outrageous comedy. An odd thing about these imagined Americans is that they are typically and surprisingly in search of nothing less than redemption—witness Kerouac's character

Sal Paradise—and they expect to find it too, no matter that America makes the search hard.

They were prophets of the present at a time when a prosperous America seemed the future (presuming that, at that Cold War moment, America and Russia resisted the temptation to blow up the future altogether), and what they wrote was nourished by a healthy appetite for experience. They were vastly productive writers and well-known public intellectuals, and their books were very much part of the country's expanding consumer culture, which they documented and marveled at and criticized, and they sought in all earnest and in quite distinct ways to realize the lively and enlightened community that Schwartz's young men so yearned for. They began their careers in the decade after the war, lived through the threat to that community posed by the McCarthy era and the jubilant and violent expansion of it in the civil rights and anti–Vietnam War movements of the '60s; they lived on through the declining public provision and growing economic inequality of the last quarter of the century and, one and all, into the century to come, and as they did, the new America that had initially inspired them aged into what Stein had called it years before, the oldest country in the world, one in which the questing spirit of the books that had made their names had come to seem quaint and dated, if not simply alien. Augie, Rabbit: these are characters who fudge the difference between the ordinary and the extraordinary— they are the *homme moyen sensuel* as hero of our times—and the great thing about America, their authors imply, is that it makes just that fudge possible. Do such characters emerge out of a rich, new, vital, generous, worldly, fleshly, comic, and wisely sorrowful sense of common humanity? A sense of human opportunity, vulnerability, and complexity brought to life by writers whose command of their art made them as miraculously individual as they were broadly appealing? Perhaps. That was the idea.

It is striking, however, that though these American writers were translated into many languages, and Bellow won the Nobel Prize, outside the English-speaking world their work didn't have much influence on writers or find much success with readers. American genre literature, crime and science fiction and horror, had a much larger audience, sophisticated as well as popular, than did its literary fiction—and rock and roll, rhythm and blues, and soul were listened to everywhere, while Hollywood continued to lord it over the movies. These were the things that showed what America was about—forms that reflected its democratic character, its barbarism, and its riches—and the postwar picture of America that fascinated the world, and the sense of artistic and human possibility it was seen to promise, was shaped by them far more than by the writers I've been discussing. There was something insular and *retardataire* about the postwar American novel, as if it wanted to cast aside the questions and quandaries of the twentieth-century novel and retrieve and enjoy the good old authority and amplitude of the nineteenth-century novel in new and improved form. By contrast, films like *Bonnie and Clyde*, *The Last Picture Show*, *Apocalypse Now*, *Carrie*, *Nashville*, and *Blade Runner* capture the essentially fantastical and disturbed character of American reality, what Poe had seen so long ago and the very thing that continues to make it an object of outsize fascination both at home and at large. This was the world's America, and so it makes sense that the great novel of the world apart that was postwar America, of its bright blight and squandered beauty—*Lolita*—was not written by an American.

This moment of a brash, distinctive new American novel coming to light is also the moment in which the work of the much older William Faulkner finally gained recognition in his own country. Faulkner's great period as writer—the late 1920s into the middle '30s, the years of *The Sound and the Fury*, *As I Lay Dying*, *Absalom, Absalom!*, and *Light in August*—was long behind him, but it had earned him a European reputation: in France he was admired by Malraux and Sartre and translated by Jean Giono; in Italy, by Elio Vittorini and Cesare Pavese. In America, however, it took Malcolm Cowley's omnium-gatherum *The Portable Faulkner*, part of a paperback series originally designed to swell soldiers' gear with books—series that were even more in demand after the war, as the G.I. Bill swelled the ranks of college students—to gain him a real following. This was an episode in the larger paperback revolution that the war brought about, not just in America but throughout the world. (It was military consignments that made Allen Lane's Penguin Books into the powerhouse of British publishing; it was in the wake of the war that Einaudi would start a line of elegantly packaged paperbacks featuring color reproductions of masterpieces of modern art on the covers, the better that, after Mussolini, dead art should rise again.) This paperback revolution didn't simply make literature more widely available, it transformed it all around the world, not least by making literature from all over the world available all over the world, a dynamic that had been crucial to the novel's spread as a genre, but that now picked up speed.

But the deeper reason for Faulkner's new prominence at this moment of triumphant American exceptionalism is that he spoke to America about something that America, if it aspired at all seriously to its role as world leader, could no longer afford not to consider, though it had long preferred not to: American racism. Faulkner's South was a world defined not by victory, but by defeat, a world that had a history too complicated for simple reckoning, too dark to be put to rest, and as unforgivable as that of Europe. And this history was not just the history of the South—Faulkner made clear—it was America's history. It bore witness to the accommodation of slavery written into the American Constitution and to the racial and political division that had always afflicted the so-called United States, as well as to the devastation wrought by the Civil War, that first industrial war whose massive toll of death had so appalled Dostoevsky's Underground Man in faraway Russia and had so inspired the generals of the world wars to come. America was the country of the future, ostensibly, but perhaps its only future, Faulkner's work suggested, was one of degradation and destruction—this was the simple lesson of the enormously complex *Absalom, Absalom!*, in which the refusal of the self-made plantation owner Thomas Sutpen to acknowledge the darkness of his past and blackness of his progeny destroys both him and the generations to come. Perhaps the truth was that everything was already all over for the country that had dedicated itself from the start to the future; perhaps it always had been.

America, in any case, was hardly a country without ruins, ruins that even Faulkner's style, loaded with archaisms, evoked, along with the often-elusive narrative thread of his books, the story disappearing into questions about the story. Faulkner possessed a resounding, intricate, Latinate style—with James and Stein and Hemingway, he was one of the great masters of the American sentence, always driven by the outsize need to find a scale of its own. In his prose, the florid opulence of nineteenth-century public address—whether from the preacher's pulpit or the politician's podium—swells and spills into private mania and despair. Faulkner's voice is often choral, one character reporting to another what he imagines another character said to himself, and all this in an elevated tone that is at the same time uniquely authorial: the effect is like a feedback loop, overloaded, hypnotic, discordant. Murky and splendid, his sentences, as well as the plots that they circuitously unfold, are full of booby traps and swamp holes. The reader flounders and is sucked in and down into who knows what depths. This is America. It is a haunted place, a conflicted place, as is laid bare in Faulkner's 1956 "Letter to a Northern Editor," opposing the "compulsory integration" mandated by *Brown v. Board of Education* as a solution to the "compulsory segregation" he also opposed. The rediscovery of Faulkner was not only the rediscovery of a great twentieth-century novelist but a renewed recognition of the dark side of American exceptionalism that had been plain enough to the abolitionists of the antebellum Republic but had come to be seen as merely a Southern matter under Jim Crow.

The question the example of Faulkner (not so much his actual novels of the '50s) posed to American readers—and it spoke to his Latin American readers too—relates to the central question of the post–World War II twentieth-century novel: How to go on after all that has gone on? In *Invisible Man*, Ralph Ellison takes this question on with a vengeance.

A race riot breaks out at the end of *Invisible Man*. Riots and riotousness have been routine from the start of the book, which begins with a group of black high school boys—among them the book's narrator, who will remain as nameless as Carpentier's composer—who are forced to fight blindfolded for the entertainment of a drunken pack of small-town white worthies. The narrator heads to college, a southern school for blacks, but after he gets mixed up (along with a white donor to the college) in a crazy carouse of shell-shocked black vets in a road-house brothel, he is expelled and heads north to New York. There he finds work in a paint factory—Liberty Paint, it's called, and its prize product is a paint called Optic White—until an exploding boiler lays him low, the factory effectively blowing up in his face. Black and white are never simply descriptive of the look of things in Ellison's novel; they are always charged, always symbolic, as everything in the world of the book reflects the crazy set of symbols that is American racism, under which lies the everyday reality of white violence, black oppression, and suppressed black rage. It is suicidal, we understand, when, at the critical turning point of the book, a young black political organizer punches out a cop and is promptly gunned down in front of the New York Public Library. That this should happen in front of a great, resplendent but also fortresslike repository of the world's accumulated knowledge and wisdom is symbolic as well.

So the riot that breaks out at the end of the book (partly as a response to the killing) could seem like a long-awaited, necessary uprising, and yet, as it unfolds in the sweaty heat of a Harlem summer night, with the West Indian black nationalist Ras the Exhorter rallying the people from horseback and brandishing a lance like a medieval white knight, it becomes clear that even violence lacks authenticity in a world perverted through and through by racism. This is not an outbreak of restorative, revolutionary violence, but a "race riot," a newsfeed, an event strategically connived by the so-called Brotherhood, as Ellison dubs the Communist Party, bent on exploiting the grievances of black Americans for its own, different priorities, not at all unlike a plantation master. And so it is at this point, with all the fury and falsity and futility the book has testified to now come to a head, that the narrator (disappearing with comic abruptness from the scene through a coalhole in the sidewalk) discovers the new role, the new reality, which he had announced in the book's arresting first words: "I am an invisible man." Not black, not white, not to be seen, he has stepped away from all the symbolic associations and assignments he has long sought to make sense of in vain, and now, at the end of the book (which marks the moment of his sitting down to write the book), a new understanding can begin, with the rejection of given identity, with the embrace of the radical uncertainty, the amazement out of which art springs. Invisibility, Flaubert claimed, is the proper condition of the writer, who disappears behind his work. Ellison would have had this in mind, but he is also making a very different claim from Flaubert's, which is that the given identities we have, the common terms of our visibility, have made us invisible to one another and to ourselves. Invisibility is a precondition not only of good writing but also of community: you must know that you don't know me, though what exactly that might mean remains to be discovered. And if it's true that one thing an invisible man is for sure is an impossibility, perhaps, in an impossible world, only impossibility offers a new beginning.

For Ellison, as for his protagonist, finding a way to begin had been a problem from the first. Born in Oklahoma City, he lost his father to a worksite accident when he was still a child and then worked a whole slew of jobs—busboy, waiter, shoeshine boy, dental assistant—to help support his family while going to school. He developed an interest in jazz and a facility on the trumpet and saxophone, and he gained admission to Tuskegee Institute in Alabama, where he read Eliot, Joyce, Stein, and Dostoevsky. Thinking now of being a visual artist, he dropped out of college and moved to New York, where he befriended Langston Hughes and Richard Wright, both in the Communist orbit at that point, and began to write for Communist publications while also, with Wright's encouragement, trying his hand at fiction. Like Wright, Ellison came to feel betrayed by the Communists, and that sense of betrayal helped fuel *Invisible Man*, begun just after the war, though the book developed a bigger sense of purpose and range of references in the course of its long gestation. When it was published, in 1952, it was immediately recognized as having a scale and ambition of its own. There had never been anything like it in American literature, it was clear, unless it was *Moby-Dick*, and along the book's way, Ellison draws parallels between his protagonist's lurching voyage and Ishmael's on the *Pequod*. The book won the National Book Award, putting Ellison at the center of the American literary world, where he

wrote essays and delivered addresses and worked for many years on a
second novel that he was never able to finish.

"I am an invisible man." It is a very different beginning from the
"I am an American, Chicago born" of *Augie March*, published a year
later, which would also win the National Book Award. (Ellison and
Bellow became good friends.) In *Invisible Man*, the revelation of invisibility is a long time coming. For most of the book, the narrator
is hounded by nothing so much as identity, by his own admission a
prime fool, sucker punched again and again as he sets out on his obliv-
ious and merry way to make himself into a model for his people and
a spokesman for his race. Throughout the horrible (but, like so many
things in the book, horribly funny) battle royal at the start of the book,
our hero goes on hoping it's about time to deliver the uplifting speech
he has prepared for the occasion. Throughout the book, he goes on
carrying the briefcase that is his reward for being such a good high
school student, as he goes on carrying water for the powers that be,
whether college administrators or the directors of the Brotherhood.
Like a bucket, the briefcase fills up slowly and surely with symbols of
racism: among them the letter of recommendation given to him by the
president of the college on his expulsion (it is of course the opposite);
a cast-iron piggybank in the guise of a black man inscribed FEED ME; a
manacle given to him by one of the brothers; a paper puppet Sambo.
The briefcase is given not only as a reward but as symbol of a future
success, and *success* is a word that sounds throughout the book, the
rip-roaring success and self-made man that every good American is
exhorted to imagine himself as, whether in the crassly materialist gospel of Norman Vincent Peale, the transcendental one of Ralph Waldo
Emerson, or Ras the Exhorter's message of black power. Our hero is
certainly all too visibly American in wanting to live up to such expectations, and it takes him a long time, the whole book, to realize
that making a success of himself has really been all about subjecting
himself to others' wishes. He is still dragging that briefcase around in
the midst of a Harlem in flames when it comes to him at last that he,
like his forebears, is not climbing the social ladder but running for
his life. Down in the coalhole, he burns the papers in the briefcase for
the little light they will cast, before, in a nightmare vignette, envision-

ing himself caught, castrated, lynched. "And I awoke in blackness"—
a blackness that at this point I think we are to take as blackness plain
and simple, free of the false identifications and illumination of the
upper world. A primal blackness, free of identity. And here at last he
finds "I was whole."

In his letters, Ellison likes to quote Henry James's statement that
"being an American is a complex fate." A sense of irreducible complexity gathers powerfully throughout *Invisible Man*, which is all
about trying to describe what cannot be described, what cannot be
seen, and making the reader, but equally the narrator of the book,
see just that. If this is a matter of working toward a full vision of
American life in all its incoherent cruelty, it is also, for Ellison, very
much a literary matter. A good part of the work the book does involves the identification and transformation of literary forebears, a
self-conscious placing of itself within the history of the twentieth-
century novel, comparable to what goes on in *The Lost Steps* and *Lolita*. *The Invisible Man* is of course the title of one of Wells's scientific
romances, a grotesque comedy about a shameless scamp who concocts
an invisibility serum in the hopes of taking advantage of his fellow
human beings—the possibilities he supposes are endless—only to find
every humiliation a man can imagine visited upon him, and this is
much like Ellison's protagonist's brilliant career. That brilliant career
also bears comparison with that of Kafka's Karl Rossmann, who, when
we last see him, has been given the name Negro; and Ellison's hero's
stay, after the explosion in the paint factory, in a hospital, perhaps a
madhouse, under the scrutiny of a revolving array of doctors is deliberately Kafkaesque and surrealist in manner. Ellison also draws on
Faulkner—the campus of the hero's college is described with Faulk-
nerian verbal luxuriance—and Joyce, too, likewise a master of literary
pastiche. And then, explicitly, unmistakably present from the beginning of the book is that founding document of the twentieth-century
novel, Dostoevsky's *Notes from Underground*. Ellison in 1952, like
Dostoevsky in 1863, is trying to find words in which to account for
deranged and deranging social and personal realities.

This tissue of more or less visible allusions is woven into the fabric
of this novel of lost illusions in a way that reflects the hero's halting

progress toward the discovery of what the influential American literary historian Van Wyck Brooks called a usable past. He must discard the baggage that is represented by his briefcase, but this will be possible only when he has come to his own understanding of both his personal history and black American history, which is to say of American history. In a key scene in the book—a scene dead at its center—he witnesses the eviction of an elderly couple from their Harlem apartment. The eviction agents carelessly spill the contents of a bureau drawer onto the snowy street; the protagonist stops to pick up the jumble of odds and ends. They range from "a bent Masonic emblem" to "a fragile paper, coming apart with age, written in black ink grown yellow: FREE PAPERS." Black history and all the hopes and disappointments of daily life are both there. He is overwhelmed:

> I turned and stared again at the jumble, no longer looking at what was before my eyes, but inwardly-outwardly, around a corner into the dark, far-away-and-long-ago, not so much of my own memory as of remembered words, of linked verbal echoes, images, heard even when not listening at home. And it was as though I myself was being dispossessed of some painful yet precious thing which I could not bear to lose; something confounding, like a rotted tooth that one would suffer indefinitely rather than endure the short, violent eruption of pain that would mark its removal. And with this sense of dispossession came a pang of vague recognition: this junk, these shabby chairs, these heavy, old-fashioned pressing irons, zinc wash tubes with dented bottoms—all throbbed within me with more meaning than there should have been . . . Why did I see them now, as behind a veil that threatened to lift, stirred by the cold wind in the narrow street?

The passage is veiled, ambivalent and ambiguous through and through, as so much of this novel is, appalled and afraid and ashamed, words that crop up over and over in its pages, as does the image of seeing around a corner. At this point the narrator doesn't know what to make of what he sees before him, though he is stirred by the occasion to make a speech whose ferocious eloquence brings him into the orbit of the Brotherhood. Seeing these things, he thinks, reasonably enough, that things have got to change. It will take him the rest of the novel to turn away from the false promise of revolution and to find the right response, which is to say the right kind of responsibility for the jumble of forlorn articles he saw on the ground on that cold day.

About the Brotherhood, he now thinks:

> They had set themselves up to describe the world. What did they know of us? . . . And now all past humiliations became precious parts of my experience, and for the first time, leaning against that stone wall in the sweltering night, I began to accept my past and, as I accepted it, I felt memories welling up within me. It was as though I'd learned suddenly to look around corners; images of past humiliations flickered through my head and I saw that they were more than separate experiences. They were me; they defined me. I was my experiences and my experiences were me . . . And now I looked around the corner of my mind and saw . . . one single white figure . . . attempting to force his picture of reality upon me . . . I now recognized my invisibility.

Dispossessed for so long, he has at last taken possession of his past and so become his own person, just as Ellison's novel creates a literary tradition for itself, the better that it may assume its distinctive place in that tradition, putting the black novel at the center not only of the American novel but of the twentieth-century novel. Ellison's very American novel also succeeds as an ambitious international novel, marked by the disappointment with communism but also by the worldwide threat of destruction posed by the Cold War, as well as the same period's ambition—we've already seen it in Banti, Achebe, and Carpentier—to tell new stories and found a new world. In writing *Invisible Man*, Ellison was as determined to escape the political and parochial slotting by which social exclusion, even as it is documented, is maintained; he was not going to write a "black novel," much as D. H. Lawrence had no intention of being reduced to "a working-class writer." He is not going to be put in his place. Or rather, the place of his novel will be to respond in his own way to the central imperative of the American novel, the Emersonian problem of fashioning an original voice, as much as his friend Bellow. He will respond to that legacy and redefine it by speaking in a voice that is original precisely because it is the American voice, the black voice, that America for most of its history not only silenced but has been premised on silencing. It will be a true American voice, which is to say a voice that is polyphonic, provisional, in communication with all the voices of literature near and far, while haunted too by all the voices that have not come through, epitomized by those silent stray objects strewn on the tar of the street. It will be a voice that respects their silence.

The truth about America, Ellison knows, is unspeakable, which is why we need new forms of speech, new and different novels to begin to understand it, just as from its beginning the twentieth-century novel has shaped and reshaped itself in response to a world of ongoing violent change. Another word that recurs throughout *Invisible Man* is *absurd*, and in the riot at the end of the book it is none other than Ras the black nationalist who seeks to string up the protagonist from a Harlem lamppost, just another part of "the absurdity of the whole night," but equally of the absurdity of "the simple yet confoundingly complex arrangement of hope and desire, fears and hates, that had brought me here still running." Thanks to that, however, he at last knows "who I was and where I was and . . . too that I no longer had to run" from the white and black preceptors and preempters who have driven him on his way, but "only from their confusion, impatience, and refusal to recognize"—and here we come full circle—"the beautiful absurdity of their American identity and mine." *Unreal* and *real* are two other words that ricochet through *Invisible Man*, which is after all about the unreal, though all too real, phenomenon that is American racism, but the real recognition the hero arrives at is, simply enough, "it was better to live out one's own absurdity than to die for that of others." This is not much, but it is something, and having come to this realization, he turns to speak not as he has been told to speak, and not—though it is important that he has finally learned to do that—for himself alone, but to the reader. He speaks for himself and for the possibility of community, even if that possible community still lies unseen around the corner. He speaks for the necessarily invisible entity that is *us*, at home and in the world at large, beyond the visible differences we can all all too easily tot up. "Who knows," the book ends, "but that, on the lower frequencies, I speak for you?"

18. BOOM

GABRIEL GARCÍA MÁRQUEZ'S *ONE HUNDRED YEARS OF SOLITUDE*

"One day he realized that he had founded a city," we read about the Adelantado in Carpentier's *The Lost Steps*, and the mixture of the matter-of-fact and the wondrous with which the character, and the book, register that new beginning speaks for itself. Poised between history and myth, the everyday and the marvelous, it also looks forward to Gabriel García Márquez. "Many years later, as he faced the firing squad, Colonel Aureliano Buendía was to remember the distant afternoon when his father took him to discover ice," reads the famous first sentence of *One Hundred Years of Solitude*.

One Hundred Years of Solitude is also about a founding. It chronicles the life of a town, Macondo, which starts as a settlement in the middle of nowhere, and the life of the Buendía family, the founders of the town. Like the Adelantado's Santa Mónica de los Venados, Macondo originates as a refuge. To escape the ghost of a neighbor he killed in an affair of honor, José Arcadio Buendía, the feckless patriarch, leaves the no less remote village in which he and his young wife, Ursula, grew up, where their families have lived since the days of Sir Francis Drake. The couple and their companions cross forbidding mountains "to go [where] they would not leave any trace or meet any people they knew . . . an absurd journey," its desperation out of all proportion to its occasion, its difficulties inconceivable. They went, we are also told, "in search of an outlet to the sea"—they were looking, in other words, not to escape but to find a way back to the world—"but after twenty-six months they gave up the expedition and founded

Macondo, so they would not have to go back." They have been wandering for two years and are lost in the middle of an endless swamp, when José Arcadio dreams of "a noisy city having mirror walls" with "a name that he had never heard, that had no meaning at all," and so there they stop, and he lays out plans for an ideal modern village of twenty households. His first son, who bears his name, has been born on the journey. Aureliano, "the first human being to be born in Macondo," soon follows. José Arcadio is all brawn and virile appetite. Aureliano, who wept within the womb and came into the world with his eyes open, is introspective, melancholic, and angry. Colonel Aureliano Buendía will eventually lead thirty-two futile Liberal Party uprisings against the government of the unnamed country in which the story is set and sire eighteen sons, all named Aureliano, all of whom will in time be hunted down and shot.

The first half of *One Hundred Years of Solitude* describes the growing madness of the father, seized by a mania for scientific invention that will leave him tethered for his own good to a tree in the front yard, and the folly of the colonel's endless wars, which take him all over the world and finally back to Macondo. The second half of the book introduces José Arcadio the Second and Aureliano the Second (each generation reintroduces the primal fraternal pair) and describes the growing prosperity of the family and town, followed by their ultimate collapse. Ursula, the mother, lives on and on, always overseeing the house and family affairs, even when she is blind and one of her arms is frozen in a perpetual salute. It is the fate of the book's women to live on and on. Its men, by contrast, die young or exhaust themselves in pointless pursuits. Love is rare and always disastrous. What the men and women of Macondo do share is—the word tolls endlessly through the book's pages—their irreducible solitude.

One Hundred Years of Solitude is about a founding, but it is also, from that very first sentence, about the end to come. If there is any suspense of a conventional fictional sort in the book, it lies in the question of how the character introduced in the first sentence as a military officer, an erstwhile wide-eyed boy, and a man facing the firing squad will come to that death, but about a quarter of the way through the book we learn that he doesn't; the suspense is converted into how he will escape. After many years of fighting for freedom and many more years of wondering what he had fought for, the colonel dies while taking a piss by the tree his father was tied to, and his last thought is of the day he was taken to see ice. And so the book circles around and back on itself, an arabesque that encompasses both the prodigious—a plague of insomnia, biblical rains—and the historical: in the second part of the book a foreign banana company sets up outside of town, and soon the cinema, the phonograph, the telephone, the automobile all appear "as if God had decided to put to the test every capacity for surprise and was keeping the inhabitants of Macondo in a permanent alternation between excitement and disappointment, doubt and revelation, to such an extreme that nobody knew where the limits of reality lay." Eventually the local workers strike against the banana company, but the strikers and their families are machine-gunned to death, and their corpses, 3,408 of them, are taken by train to be dropped in the sea, something that everyone, except for the sole survivor of the massacre (José Arcadio Segundo), then agrees never took place at all.

Such is history, in a book where events, at first sharply delineated, blur together increasingly. Written in long, murmurous paragraphs that, like that first sentence, move back and forth freely in time (and time, never dated, figures in it only as Mondays, Tuesdays, and so on, or as the passage of years), and from a point of view so broadly distributed that it is not so much omniscient as out of sight; and deploying the accumulative narrative style of a chronicle, the book has the immediacy that a dream has for the dreamer, which is to say that it feels, like a dream, for real.

At the same time, it is very much, very self-consciously a book, like the books of the Bible or the histories of Herodotus, and then there is a book within the book, deposited in the Buendía house at the very start of the novel by the mysterious Gypsy, Melquíades. Melquíades has a room of his own in the house, one that will always remain a space apart, the room of the book, appearing miraculously untouched by time to everyone except for the colonel, who sees it as a scene of ruin and devastation. (The room of the book, like the massacre of the strikers, raises the old, inescapable question of point of view.) Melquíades's book is written in a strange, unreadable script that looks more like music or clothes on a line (it will turn out to be Sanskrit, which does look like that), and throughout the book it is periodically rediscovered by various characters and puzzled over in vain, but only in the last pages of the book is it deciphered by the last of the Aurelianos, as our wondering about what the book contains and how the novel will end come together. This book is that book, and Aureliano, the reader of the book, as impatient as we are in reading about him, skips past what we and he already know to reach the fore-told end, which can only be the destruction of Macondo, "already a fearful whirlwind of dust and rubble," even as the words unfold before him "as if he were looking into a speaking mirror." Image and real-ity, life as described and life as lived, imagined experience and actual experience all fuse miraculously, but only in the moment of ultimate destruction: this unity flares up to vanish. It is an impossible unity, but this is one of the great finales in world fiction, and the reader feels it in all its urgency, newly encountering the power of the word to conjure reality and compel belief.

Aureliano is reading out loud, chanting what are described as Melquíades's "encyclicals" (a notably strange religious word) in this final scene that takes us back to the sacred creative spoken word of God as well as to the abracadabra of *The Arabian Nights* (a book that also happens to be in Melquíades's room). But this is also very much a scene out of the twentieth-century novel. We are in Gide's abyss here, and here, too, the reader of the book and the reader in the book read in real time, and just as when we, and the student protagonist, read Sen-sei's suicide note at the end of Sōseki's *Kokoro*, we are on a collision course with the moment. However, the real antecedent here (though I am not making any claim of conscious influence in any of these cases) is Marcel emerging from the Prince de Guermantes's library at the end of *In Search of Lost Time* to confront the ghastly visages of his aged contemporaries gathered for the *bal des têtes* but with the vision of his book, the book that will contain and preserve them, at last be-fore him. Well, by now the twentieth-century novel is always coming back to the primal scene of the twentieth-century novel, shocked once again by its own creation, but something new is happening here too, and we can perhaps put our finger on what it is by contrasting Garcia Márquez's work with *The Lost Steps*.

The protagonist of *The Lost Steps*, having encountered the original and originating word, returns to daily life and the historical world, which is to say to the twentieth century. Garcia Márquez's book, by contrast, does not go back and does not go there in the first place. The world of *One Hundred Years of Solitude* remains a world unto itself, as elusive as it is inviting, and always, to echo Ellison, slipping around a corner ahead. Where and when is it set? It could not be a more American book, but *America* is a word that does not figure in its pages, and as to the time of those hundred years, they come, we know, well after Sir Francis Drake but also at a time "when the world was so recent that many things lacked names and to indicate them it was necessary to point." Yet there is a government, there are political parties, a world that includes Brussels and the West Indies, a train "like a kitchen dragging a village behind it," while by the time the hundred years are up, with the natural world invading the Buendíases' house, we have returned to a "disastrous paradise" in which the last Aureliano and his aunt Amaranta couple incestuously. We are always between first and last things, in other words, in this book of a century in which no century is named—which makes a point of not being a twentieth-century novel—a book that, as full of predestination as it is, is through and through full of the wonder of the unforeseen. Late in the twentieth century, when the twentieth century would seem to have outstripped the resources of the twentieth-century novel, the book makes present the unforeseen, not as a mere matter of surprise, but as an element in which, like fish in water, each and every one of us, historically bound as of course we are, lives: What, after all, is the present if not the unforeseen? "And there," as Wallace Stevens says, we saw ourselves "more truly and more strange."

How did García Márquez come to this strange and unexpected place? Well, he was essentially born there, at a time, as his excellent biographer, Gerald Martin, has remarked, that could just as well have been the nineteenth century. That was how cut off from the world of the day the small Colombian town of Aracataca was when García Márquez came into the world in 1927, a first child, left entirely to the care of his maternal grandparents before he was a year old. His parents moved to Barranquilla, where his father would start a pharmacy—the first of a long string of failed endeavors to get ahead—and they did not rejoin their first child until he was close to seven. He grew up in between, you could say—in between families, in between generations, and in between places—and that sense of in-betweenness is everywhere present in *One Hunded Years of Solitude*. Winning admission as a teenager to a boarding school in far-off Bogotá, García Márquez traveled upriver and overland for days, encountering a lawyer who introduced him to Dostoevsky's *The Double*, beginning what was to be a crash self-education in twentieth-century literature. In high school, then as an indifferent law student, and finally as a fledgling journalist in Barranquilla, an unusually cosmopolitan coastal town (where he roomed in a brothel named Residencia New York located in a four-story building called Skyscraper and frequented the Mundo bookstore), he devoured Faulkner, Virginia Woolf's *Mrs. Dalloway* and *Orlando* (another important precursor of his great book), Joyce, and Hemingway's *Old Man and the Sea*—and, above all, Kafka's *Metamorphosis*. Kafka, as I've said, had essentially reinvented allegory for the twentieth century by throwing away the key—everything in his work seems to mean something else, but there is no knowing just what it might be—and this was a trick García Márquez would quickly master, even as he, unusually among the many writers who have learned from Kafka, also picks up on the sheer happy weirdness that Kafka also knew how to wield. These writers, along with *The Thousand and One Nights* and *Don Quixote*, were the landmarks by which he made his way.

Latin American literature, with the important exception of Borges, was to come later, and García Márquez would not see a Latin American country other than his own until he had already toured the two sides of the divided Europe of the Cold War as a journalist working on a shoestring. In Colombia, he sold encyclopedias, wrote films reviews, and had notable success as a reporter covering sometimes politically charged cases at a moment when the country was convulsed by the

right-wing (and US-supported) government's murderous persecution
of its Liberal opponents. After years of looking in vain, he found a
publisher for his first novel, *Leaf Storm*, before being posted to Europe
as a journalist, where, in Rome, he studied at Cinecittà Studios and
encountered the great Italian neorealist movies of the 1950s, another
important early influence on his fiction. He scraped by as a bohemian
in Paris, began one novel and then another, reported from the Eastern Bloc, passed through London (Eliot's "unreal city" seeming no
less so to the young Colombian), and worked for Prensa Latina, the
news agency of Cuba's new revolutionary government, in New York.
Eventually he moved to Mexico, where, now with a wife and family
to support, he worked in film and TV and as an adman (a job Carpentier also held down). The short novels he had begun in Paris, *No
One Writes to the Colonel* and *In Evil Hour*, were published, as was a
collection of stories, *Big Mama's Funeral*, set in Macondo, and García
Márquez was just enough known to feel little-known. He was badly
blocked.

In all this, he was both inside and outside of the larger literary phenomenon that would come to be known as the Latin American Boom.
Latin American literature, as I said in my chapter about Machado,
had always been an even more anomalous entity than its counterpart
in the United States, and in the mid-twentieth century it remained
one. Spanish literature, held hostage by Franco's fascist Nationalism,
was hardly thriving—the titles of two major novels of the Francoist
'50s, *Time of Silence* and *Nada*, are telling—while in Latin America
economic underdevelopment and political and geographical division
continued to stand in the way of a common literary consciousness
or market. The Chilean José Donoso, García Márquez's contemporary and friend, describes the situation and its frustrations vividly
in his engaging *The Boom in Spanish American Literature: A Personal
History*. As an aspiring young writer, Donoso's imagination had been
stimulated and nurtured, thanks among other things to the paperback revolution and to the new work coming out of Europe and the
United States—Sartre, Camus, Salinger, Kerouac, Grass, Golding,
Pavese. By comparison, the local product looked "like statues in a
park: some with larger mustaches than others . . . but all essentially

indistinguishable and none with any power over us." And here was the vicious circle: for him to write a book that bore the mark of the mix of foreign writers he admired was to be sure to go unpublished at home, where what was valued were close studies of local matters and manners; at the same time, remaining unpublished at home would make it impossible for him to be published abroad. The young writer was condemned to sterility—and to solitude.

Other young writers all over Latin America felt this way, among them García Márquez, but immured among small circles of the like-minded in far-flung and barely communicating literary scenes, they could hardly know it. "The first active and conscious agent of the internationalization of the Spanish American novel in the 1960s" was, according to Donoso, the Mexican Carlos Fuentes, and it is to the publication in 1958 of Fuentes's ambitious first novel, *Where the Air Is Clear*, a panoramic and stylistically sophisticated picture of Mexico City and its many inhabitants, that the beginning of the Boom is conventionally dated. Donoso, like many others, sees Dos Passos behind Fuentes's book, but what really impresses him is how "language takes over the role of protagonist" as he employs "different and at times contradictory means of writing novels" in a "continual bombardment of inquiry as to other possibilities of writing." Fuentes, well-to-do, well-educated, well-connected, also served as an emissary among the young writers, linking Donoso in Chile to Mario Vargas Llosa in Peru to Julio Cortázar in Argentina to José Lezama Lima and Guillermo Cabrera Infante in Cuba—and all of them to agents and publishers in New York and Paris. International academic and cultural conferences further tightened the bonds within this unexpected band.

And then there was the Cuban Revolution, which for a time united all of them in the hope of great new things. The Cuban Revolution was one of the major events of the second half of the century, putting a scrappy island nation under youthful charismatic leadership (Castro was a José Arcadio who found his way out of the mountains) at the center of postwar politics and pitting it against the neighboring hegemon that had long treated it, along with so many of its Latin American and Caribbean neighbors, as a sugar plantation–cum–gambling den. Latin America, for so long marginalized culturally and politically by

Europe and the United States, was stepping to the front of the stage and pointing the way to the future for the postcolonial world at large, and the Cuban Missile Crisis served to make it clear just how much in question the whole world was. The writers of the Boom were one and all supportive of the Cuban Revolution, at least until the repressive, old-school communist nature of the Castro regime became, for some of them, unignorable and unforgivable, and the Boom as a whole was fueled by a mixture of revolutionary energy and resolve and market-savvy publicity. The Boom emerges at a very American anti-American moment that also sees the spread of cars and planes and television and lifestyle advertising (of which the image of the dead Che Guevara in Bolivia might be considered a perverse epitome) and, as Donoso makes a point of noting, "it was the golden age of the Beatles." It was an eclectic, mestizo phenomenon through and through, heady and unnerving, since the English word *boom*, as Donoso acknowledges, is "charged with connotations, nearly all of them pejorative or suspicious . . . Time has added to it a sense of falsity, of an eruption coming to nothing," and of course, though he does not say it, the word is more often than not followed by *bust*.

García Márquez had grown up betwixt and between, and in 1965, still blocked, he was still going nowhere. The story of how he came to write *One Hundred Years of Solitude*, a book he would later describe as an outgrowth of "the first novel I tried to write, when I was seventeen," was to become legendary. (It is a Proustian tale.) He was driving with his family from Mexico City to Acapulco for a vacation when the first sentence of the book came to him, at which point he went back home, quit his job, told his wife to look after the household, and sat down at the typewriter—"from which," he claimed, he "did not get up for another eighteen months." Bits and pieces of the book circulated among the cognoscenti, and well before the book came out, Fuentes, Cortázar, and Vargas Llosa had let it be known that a masterpiece was in the making. Published in Buenos Aires in the spring of 1967, it was an almost immediate bestseller. By the next year it began to appear in translation, and when it came out in the United States in 1970, it was reviewed on the front page of *The New York Times Book Review*, with García Márquez compared to Günter Grass and Nabokov.

"This is the great invention of our time," José Arcadio exclaims when Melquíades shows him ice. *One Hundred Years of Solitude* was received with similar wonder, and it is worth wondering why. If the Boom prepared the way for it, it was the book that made the Boom an international phenomenon, even as it would prove rather bigger than the Boom itself, and that it had this effect stems, somewhat surprisingly, from its backward-looking character, intuitively aligned as it is with the established protocols of the twentieth-century novel and the expectation, going back to Proust and *Ulysses*, that it was in the nature of the twentieth century to produce such comprehensive novels about, as the title of this one stated loud and clear, the century. It was just that sort of thing, and all the more so for being a different thing from a different part of the world—new, splendid evidence of the triumphant march of the twentieth-century novel across the whole world. *One Hundred Years of Solitude* looked back to those exemplary stand-alone novels of the early century, and it looked back farther yet to the oldest traditions of storytelling, to the premodern, and so, paradoxically, it is permeated with a piercing sense of foretold obsolescence that is entirely modern. Indeed, it was nothing if not a splendid novelty, lustrous, lambent, marked by a sure sense of design and poised exoticism that made it perfect for the psychedelic moment. The book was, all things considered, supremely timely, both a book of the Cold War years, from which it had emerged to capture the claustrophobia of a world under the threat of destruction, and a book full of the pop color of the sixties. Strikingly, it is also a book that, read in the subsequent decades, has developed a further, coincidental timeliness, as great books do. In the decline of Macondo, its history collapsing into cycles of ever more fatigued and confused commemoration, we can also now see something of the collapse of communism that was to come and of the last years of the century when, no longer in the tormenting grip of murderous ideologies, the world settled into a complacent frenzy of financial speculation encrypted in endless strings of 1s and 0s while filling up with "noisy cities full of mirror walls."

One day he must have realized he had founded a genre, perhaps the last new genre of the twentieth-century novel. Magical realism, it was called to begin with, echoing Carpentier's *lo real maravilloso*. García Márquez continued to mine this vein himself, as did other Latin American writers—some, like Isabel Allende, very popular—and it soon spread around the world and became a defining feature of what would come to be known as world literature. Salman Rushdie's *Midnight's Children* makes no bones about drawing on Grass and García Márquez in an epic of modern Indian life, and its final paragraph offers an outright, unapologetic pastiche in homage to *One Hundred Years of Solitude*. Magical realism helped Toni Morrison to broaden her range and to write the family and collective histories that are *Song of Solomon* and *Beloved*, and fabulous and folkloric and uncanny and unheard-of stories would proliferate in the work of Orhan Pamuk and José Saramago and Mo Yan, as well as in influential nonfiction (ostensibly, at least) narratives such as Kapuściński's *The Emperor*. These books spoke to and popularized local lore and history in a way that seemed "magically" designed to transcend cultural borders and to win the Nobel Prize.

The chief mark of world literature is not so much magic, however, as its being designed from the start to be translated: in that, it culminates the process by which the twentieth-century novel came into being and laid claim to the world. (García Márquez notably said that without Gregory Rabassa's English translation, as good as the book itself in his view, his novel would hardly have taken off as it did.) Of course magic may help here, flying carpets being free of the gravitational pull that makes rendering local idioms and dinner table conversations and work details such a challenging job. Woolf, as we have seen, wondered how much readers could really take away from Russian literature, which seemed to exist in a psychological gray zone with no recognizable social compass points and in the denuded language of translation. World literature of the late twentieth century, with all the amazements it described, can be seen as a utopian form of the novel, bringing new wonderful and terrible stories from all over the world that are meaningful to us all, freeing us from the limits of the lyrical and critical individual voice associated since Gide with literary fiction and ushering the reader into a new supercollectivity. Then again, it can also be seen as a homogenization of human experience and historical existence into literary formulae. The limits of the genre, for better and for worse, were all too clearly illustrated by the fate of Salman Rushdie's *The Satanic Verses*—novelistic imagination run wild running into a wall of religious proscription and enmity that it had, in a sense, completely failed to imagine.

One Hundred Years of Solitude has a purity of conception and realization that sets it apart from world literature, however, and what gives the book its continuing appeal and power (what spared it from the whimsical and fantastical into which, miraculously, it does not slip) is its extraordinary musicality, the measured flow of its sentences, the intertwining of its returning and varying themes, a musicality that the book possesses and also explores, its people and situations appearing less as individuals or discrete events and more as themes to develop. This is a book in which character matters, but not psychology, and even the characters are in some sense forms of a single man, a single woman, emerging and then sinking back down into the stream of narrative, while its voice is a strange mixture of the impersonal and the intimate, leading the reader on all the more effectively for maintaining a slight formal remove. The voice of the book is the voice of story, and really I should say voices, because the book (echoing Faulkner) is choral rather than individual. The music of the book is formal and choral and, to make mention again of the odd word *encyclical*, it is also ritual and liturgical.

With Machado, not quite a hundred years before, the Latin American novel had begun, brilliantly and improbably, as comic elegy. *One Hundred Years of Solitude* speaks for the community of the living and the dead, celebrating and mourning our common passage.

19. INTO THE ABYSS

GEORGES PEREC'S *LIFE A USER'S MANUAL*

The title, *La Vie mode d'emploi,* translated into English as *Life A User's Manual,* will puzzle the innocent reader. It doesn't sound like a novel. It sounds funny, comic but also just plain odd, not unlike Douglas Adams's *The Hitchhiker's Guide to the Galaxy,* which, before becoming a popular book, premiered as a radio show on the BBC in 1978. That was the same year that George Perec published his chef d'oeuvre in France, and the two works do share the droll stoner attitude that— after the prosperous, adventurous, and convulsive 1960s—was characteristic of the stagnant, demoralized seventies. The title puts you in mind of gadgets for the home, of diversions for the restless or weary, of the self that needs help, and it packs a little punch, like *I'm OK— You're OK,* a self-help book in vogue at the time, though it may also remind you of something much older, like *The Imitation of Christ,* promising a different solace, one that, in a world of users' manuals, people may feel they no longer need, though maybe they need it even more. Then again, *La Vie mode d'emploi* has a chilly, even scary, ring to it. If you need a user's manual to live your life, or if you treat your life as a kind of tool to make use of, well, either way you are not living life in its own right, as an end in itself. If you need a manual to live your life, could it be that you are dead?

A curious title, a tricky title, a trendy title in its way, and if it doesn't sound much like the title of a novel, that may make it the perfect title to catch the eye of the browsing book buyer all too likely to pass on a five-hundred-page brick. Especially since, when you think about it, it's a title that promises pretty much everything a good novel, a good read, is supposed to offer: life, the real; la mode (fashion), all the various and changing aspects of the modern social world, devoted as it is to change, innovation, novelty; and work—or, depending on the kind of gadget this user's manual is for, play, perhaps. Yes, everything you could ask for, except love.

The title is a puzzle—when the book came out, Perec was in fact best known as the clever crossword puzzle maker for a popular weekly magazine—and the book begins by being more puzzling yet. There's the teasing plural of the subtitle, *Novels*, before we read, "To begin with, the art of jigsaw puzzles seems of little substance, easily exhausted, wholly dealt with by a basic introduction to Gestalt," which, however, is not the beginning of the book. It is a "preamble," a puzzling disquisition on puzzle making that sorts out the typical shapes of puzzle pieces into "the little chaps, the double-crosses, and the cross-bars," after which the book proper begins with a chapter titled "On the Stairs." The book's actual subject, it now becomes clear, is an apartment building, 11 rue Simon-Crubellier in the seventeenth arrondissement of Paris. *Life A User's Manual* is a comprehensive survey of 11 rue Simon-Crubellier, systematically designed to grant us entry into every last room in the building—moving, however, not floor by floor but seemingly at random, hopscotching among stories. Breaking up the lived space of the dwelling place may seem counterintuitive, even perverse, but for the purposes of a novel, it's brilliant, a strategy designed to generate suspense, as, roving from room to room, the book continually refreshes and returns to an expanding store of stories.

The title was odd and the book is odd. How does it feel to read it? It is a book full of things, prominent among them pictures and furniture and books. (These are often described in detail: it is a book full of descriptions.) It is a book full of names, not just the names of the apartment building's past and present residents, but of places and stores and periodicals and whatnot:

Innumerable records, with and without their sleeves, are spread about the room, mostly dance records, but with a few surprising variations included, such as: *The Marches and Fanfares of the 2nd Armoured Division*; *The Ploughman and His Children, told in Cockney by Pierre Devaux*; *An Evening in Paris with Tom Lehrer*; *May '68 at the Sorbonne*; *La Tempesta di Mare, concerto in E-flat Major, Op.8, No. 5, by Antonio Vivaldi, performed on the synthesiser by Léonie Prouillot.*

It is a book full of lists like this, and at the center of its ninety-nine chapters—or rather just off center—stands a strange text resembling a poem, a list of what the reader recognizes as stories in the book, some that have been told, some presumably to come. It is above all a book full of stories, far-fetched stories of bizarre inventions and risky expeditions in the manner of Jules Verne, stories of fortunes won and lost, war stories, stories of eccentrics, stories of murder, mayhem, and patiently meditated revenge, as well as everyday stories of how people in the building got by, or didn't, over the years. Finally (though really I haven't begun to exhaust the book's multiplicity) it is a book that is various in tone—the accent can be lyrical, hyperbolic, sociological, philosophical, satirical, goofy, or prophetic—and all these tones and all those stories are mixed together in such a way that each chapter has a curious shape of its own, to which different kinds of information attach, precisely as a puzzle piece contains a mixture of hints at both the form and content of the pieces adjacent to it.

How does it feel to read this odd book? It feels both dreamy and exact, or rather dreamy, since dreams are often defined by an insistent detail, and dreams, like puzzle pieces, take funny shapes. You read it wondering at the improbability of the whole performance and wondering, as a book is supposed to make you wonder, what will come next. You read with a fascinated pleasure at getting the peculiar feel of this weird, nubbly thing. Unless of course you find you've had enough and you give up.

The variety of tone in *Life A User's Manual* is extraordinary: David Bellos, Perec's biographer and brilliant English translator, noting the number of more or less hidden allusions and quotations from other writers, ranging from Malcolm Lowry to Agatha Christie, points to the book's polyphonic character. But there is also an underlying unity of tone, comparable to what audio engineers call room tone. The tone is reserved, deadpan, poker-faced. (Perec would have enjoyed the way *poker* reshapes his name: he was not only a maker of crossword puzzles but a member of the postwar group called Oulipo, from Ouvroir de Littérature Potentielle, in which mathematicians and writers turned wordplay of all sorts into specific recipes for literary invention.) Starting with the title, the book is full of incongruous and unexplained juxtapositions, not unlike a painting by Magritte (and there is a painting by Magritte in the book), and the mixture of deliberation and lack of explanation as it goes on challenges a reader's will to make sense of the whole. What kind of book is this, you go on wondering. Perhaps a vision, disconcerting, inclusive, strangely delightful, of the common life of our times? Then again, you might say, apartments are for privacy: they are for locking things up and hiding them away. This book, segmented into so many uncommunicating chambers, could instead depict the utter atomization of our common life, perhaps as an existential statement or as a political and economic one about contemporary life as an "immense accumulation of commodities." Perhaps, but one way or another it becomes increasingly clear to the reader that this book, which is marked by a near complete absence of dialogue—the human voice is hardly heard throughout—prolific in detail and drama as it is, is also all the time witholding something from us, puzzlingly. Prompting questions, it provides no resolution to them, though of course without a solution a puzzle is not a puzzle at all.

There is an underlying uniformity of tone to the book, and there is also, among so many different stories, one altogether improbable story that is central to its action. It concerns a phlegmatic, eccentric English millionaire, Percival Bartlebooth, and it is typical of Perec that though he makes Bartlebooth's story central to the book, Bartlebooth's very name puts other stories into play: the quest for the grail;

Melville's Bartleby, who would "prefer not to"; A. O. Barnabooth, another eccentric millionaire, a character in a novel by Valery Larbaud, the early-twentieth-century poet and novelist who translated *Ulysses* into French. Percival Bartlebooth, born in 1900 (the date is not accidental), has money but no real calling in life, and to make up for that, he developed, at the age of twenty, a life plan he has done his best to follow ever since. He planned to devote ten years to learning how to paint watercolors, not to make art, but just to get the hang of it, and a further twenty years to traveling all over the world on his private ship, painting, every couple of weeks, a watercolor of a port. He would paint five hundred pictures in all, each to be sent, on completion, to Gaspard Winckler, a puzzle maker in Paris, to be mounted and turned into a puzzle. In 1950—this was the final part of the plan—Bartlebooth would return to Paris, and so he did. His subsequent years have been dedicated to putting the puzzles back together in the same order and at the same rate he produced the pictures, one every two weeks. Each puzzle, after assembly, has been stripped of its backing, returned to the scene it depicts, and destroyed: "Thus no trace would remain of an operation which would have been, throughout a period of fifty years, the sole motivation and unique activity of its author."

Bartlebooth extols the perfect modesty, perfect logic, and perfect elegance of his chosen endeavor, which is of course perfectly pointless (a reductio ad absurdum of Proust's recovery of lost time) and quite mad—and perhaps this is the point at which to say that this book, full of quirky and, as in this case, often quite unbelievable stories, is also, very often, a vision of horror. Chapter 74, "Lift Machinery," begins

> Sometimes he imagined the building as an iceberg whose visible tip included the main floors and eaves and whose submerged mass began below the first level of cellars, stairs with resounding steps going down in spirals . . .

and then proceeds to go "lower down" and "lower still" and "still further down" and "still lower" to arrive

at the very bottom, a world of caverns whose walls are black
with soot, a world of cesspools and sloughs, a world of grubs
and beasts, of eyeless beings who drag animal carcasses behind
them, of demoniacal monsters with bodies of birds, swine, and
fish, of dried-out corpses and yellow-skinned skeletons arrayed
in the attitudes of the living, of forges manned by dazed Cy-
clopses in black leather aprons, their single eyes shielded by
metal-rimmed blue glass, hammering the brazen masses into
dazzling shields.

Here we have a vision of the whole building tumbling down into
its own hell, a vision out of Bosch that belongs to Valène, a painter,
and, along with Bartlebooth—and, as we shall see, the puzzle maker
Winckler—a character of central importance to the book. Valène is
the longest-standing inhabitant of 11 rue Simon-Crubellier. It was he
who originally taught Bartlebooth to paint. This then is the action of
the book: it is the evening of June 23, 1975, and Bartlebooth, having
gone blind and fallen behind his schedule for completing puzzles, is
working on his 439th puzzle in the room of his capacious apartment
that he has dedicated to puzzle solving. A real estate agent is climbing
the stairs of the building to take a look at the apartment of the puzzle
maker Winckler—everybody involved in Bartlebooth's great plan lives
in the apartment building, we realize at a certain point—which is for
sale, Winckler having died, and also climbing the stairs is Valène, who
is thinking as he does about a picture that he has long contemplated
painting, a magnum opus depicting all the rooms in the building and
the lives of all the inhabitants he has seen come and go over the years,
himself of course included. In the book's central chapter (but one),
Valène enters his apartment, meaning to set to work on the picture; at
the end of the book (but at the very same moment), Bartlebooth dies,
with the last piece of a puzzle in hand, a final piece that the puzzle
maker, Winckler, has contrived will not fit. There were five hundred
puzzles, remember, so it is no accident that this is the five hundredth
page of the book, which describes, it would seem, nothing more than
the instant of creation of a picture that is (like the book) the spitting
image of the whole building as well as the final realization of the dead

puzzle maker's long-plotted revenge on Bartlebooth, a revenge apparently as gratuitous as Bartlebooth's own life plan. This revenge was foreshadowed in the preamble on puzzles, we now realize, which must have been composed by Winckler. It is paralleled by an epilogue, concerning Valène, who, on hearing of Bartlebooth's death, takes to his bed to die. Of his long-meditated picture, only a sketch remains.

Life A User's Manual, this mad agglomeration of descriptions, is the story of something that cannot be described: death. What has happened, once this very long and intricate book is all over, is, in a sense, nothing.

But as it happens, there is a real-life story, a real-life puzzle, behind the book. Perec's mother and father were Polish Jews, both of whom in the late twenties left Poland for Paris, where they met, married, opened a hairdressing salon, and, in 1936, had a son, Georges. When war broke out, Georges's father joined the French Foreign Legion; the following summer, caught behind the retreating French lines, he was killed. In 1941 Georges's mother sent him to live with a wealthy aunt and uncle who had found refuge in the French Alps. She herself remained in Paris until, in 1943, she was arrested and taken to the transfer camp of Drancy. A month later she was sent to Auschwitz. There is no record of her after that.

"I have no childhood memories," Perec writes in *W, or the Memory of Childhood*, the unsettling autobiographical text he composed before writing *Life A User's Manual*, though he quickly goes on to qualify this absence of memory as being as willful as actual—he wants to have no memories—and, having said that, to pick over those memories that are his, unreliable though they may be. One memory is of his mother taking him to the train station—his last memory of her. Another is of a fantasy that absorbed him during puberty, of a country in faraway Tierra del Fuego called W, whose muscular population is kept by its rulers in a state of continual murderous athletic competition. "For years," Perec writes, "I did drawings of sportsmen with stiff bodies and inhuman facial features: I described their unending combats meticulously: I listed persistently their endless titles."

Half of *W* is devoted to Perec's memories, half to a chronicle of W and its ghastly sports.

But as much as anything *W* is devoted to the question of why the land of W was called W, the question of its own title. From his time in hiding, Perec remembers happening upon an old man sawing wood on a sawhorse, called in French an *X*:

> My memory is not a memory of this scene, but a memory of the word, only a memory of the letter that has turned into a word, of that noun which is unique in the language of being made of a single letter, unique also in being the only one to have the same shape as the thing it refers to . . . but it is also the sign of a word deleted . . . the sign of multiplication and sorting . . . the sign of the mathematical unknown, and finally the starting point for a geometrical fantasy, whose basic figure is the double V, and whose complex convolutions trace out the major symbols of the story of my childhood: two Vs joined tip to tip make the shape of an X . . .

In French, a W is called a double V, and those two Vs link the two stories in Perec's book—his family story and the story of the imaginary land of W. Assembling and reassembling the lines of the Vs, Perec observes, one can compose a swastika, the lightning bolt logo of the SS, and the Star of David. Turned sideways, W becomes a Greek E, and *W* is dedicated to E, the first initial of Elsa, the aunt who served as Perec's surrogate mother, while E is also a letter that as pronounced in French is identical to the word *them*. The identity of *W* with E, and with *them*, is however something Perec does not say, as he does not say that W reversed becomes an M, the M of mother. He does not say these things, Bellos persuasively makes the case, because they are not to be said. They are too terrible, too missed, too needed to be admitted. They figure a loss that is as absolute and unrepresentable as God.

And here we come back to *Life A User's Manual*. The puzzle piece that Bartlebooth holds in his hand at the moment of his death is shaped like a W; the hole it must fill is in the form of an X. The piece doesn't fit. Then again, if you have read *W*, you know that the piece fits all too well, which is to say that the piece that solves the puzzle of *Life* is also missing from the book itself. By the time Perec wrote *Life A User's Manual*, he had come to think of all of his books as a single, comprehensive project revolving around a single, unspeakable thing that, in each book, he would find a way not to speak of—an Oulipian project in that it observes an arbitrary and impersonal verbal constraint, yet is at the same time invested with a passionate personal as well as collective and historical significance. Before *W*, Perec had written *La Disparition* ("The Disappearance"), an immense lipogram (the longest in existence) in which the letter E, the most common letter in French, does not make a single appearance—the very E that reappears as the dedicatee of *W*, his aunt's initial but also a trace of *them*, they who in the earlier book were gone. Or, equally, E, by a kind of private kabbalistic calculation, can be seen as having been set aside, having been saved. And now there is *Life*, *La Vie*, a book of death, with its terminal W/X, the signature act of the puzzle maker Winckler (who also appears in *W*, by the way). And so on and so on. X is the mark of extermination, and X marks a grave with the cross of salvation, and X is also the mark of treasure on a pirate's map in the sort of story *Life A User's Manual* abounds with (not unlike the stories Scheherazade spun out for 1001 nights to stave off death). Treasure or junk or maybe nothing at all, and here it is possible to see in 11 rue Simon-Crubellier, its rooms crammed with stuff, an image of the fortress of the grim masters of W:

> When someone gets in one day to the Fortress he will find first of all nothing but a sequence of dim, long, empty rooms. The sound of his footsteps echoing under the tall concrete roof supports will fill him with fear, but he must keep going for a long time until he discovers, deep down in the depths of the earth, the subterranean remnants of a world he will think he had forgotten: piles of gold teeth, rings and spectacles, thousands and thousands of clothes in heaps, dusty card indexes, and sticks of poor-quality soap.

He will think he had forgotten, he will think he has built an impregnable fortress against memory, but he has not forgotten, and the fortress holds what he cannot forget. It is all there in the storehouse, the indescribable death camp to which the twentieth-century novel is now condemned continually to revert. It is all there, yet these clues, these games Perec plays with the novel, meant though they are to compensate somehow for the traumatic loss of the mother they stem from, only serve to reenact and reinforce that disappearance: they are the marks that she is not and never will be there; they are marks that have no business being there themselves, marks of nothing in the end but unassuageable guilt. These crazy puzzles solve nothing; they are simply one more symptom, empty gestures, like the hole at the center of Bartlebooth's final puzzle. That hole is Winckler's fatal signature but also, it turns out, Perec's, because, as Bellos tells us, Perec derives from Peretz, and Peretz from the Hebrew word for *gap*. The X is Perec's signature, but also, I think, the X that serves as the mark of an illiterate, which is to say someone who couldn't read this book at all. Who would remain innocent of the unmentionable things that lie behind it. Someone who has been spared—and saved.

Perec means "gap," and among the countless names that litter the pages of *Life A User's Manual*, one that we hear a number of times is the title of a story by Pirandello, "In the Abyss." This is a nod to the giddy metafictional playfulness of the author of *Six Characters in Search of an Author* in whom Perec recognizes a fellow spirit, and here too we recognize the abyss of horror that Valène envisions opening up underneath 11 rue Simon-Crubellier. This is also of course an instance of the infinite self-referential spiraling action that Gide called mise en abyme. We see Perec, in other words, weaving into his own text not only a defining characteristic of the twentieth-century novel but also a historical awareness of the twentieth-century novel—and so planting the question of why it is that way right at the heart of his novel, which might be considered the most questionable twentieth-century novel of all. In this novel, one that might be said to be nothing more than one big, enormously intricate self-referential set piece, he is putting the whole question of the self-referentiality of the twentieth-century novel, as well as its relation to the history of the century, on the spot.

Because what is it about this abyss that Gide, say, finds so appealing and so revealing? Well, for Gide, it was the space that opened up between, on the one hand, his self-critical awareness—which, for this product of a rigorous Protestant formation, is a matter of interminable self-interrogation—and, on the other, imaginative possibility, the infinite riches contained in Ali Baba's cave, Scheherazade's endless fund of stories, so enchanting, so diverting, so very unbourgeois, arousing desire even as it fulfills it. Critical awareness and desire confront each other over the abyss in a heroic face-off. A fully conscious art, a truly honest art, will take account of and see through and see beyond its own effects, the better to preserve and display its freedom, the freedom to try new things, the freedom to adventure. Contrast to this attitude that of a nineteenth-century novelist like, say, George Eliot. Eliot is certainly and seriously concerned with human freedom, and as a novelist she is intensely conscious of her art, but freedom in Eliot is inconceivable apart from self-development and human well-being; freedom for her is the other face of responsibility, and at the heart of her work is an idea of the human, of the species, without which the life of the individual must be counted bereft. Gide, though, is finally, proudly, answerable only to himself and/or his art, and he would be suspicious of any given idea of the human and nothing but pessimistic about the species. Freedom is an end in itself for Gide, and all the more exhilarating if it threatens the dizzying free fall of the abyss.

Gide's introspective characters exploring their inky depths could not be less like Captain Nemo going into the depths, but they too go abroad and put themselves at peril to find themselves, much as Gide was an inveterate cruiser all his days. Perec's novel brings together both these types, until we see that the great animating force of the twentieth-century novel has been nothing so much as a craving for adventure, adventure at all costs. Everything has got to change, the young, sickly, struggling, sexually frustrated Wells felt at the start of the century. "On or about December 1910 human character changed," Virginia Woolf wrote. The outbreak of World War I was a gloriously welcome change to Thomas Mann—it would be the war to end all wars, Wells declaimed—and there is no need for me here to review all the changes that were to come, though it is important to remember that not all of them were terrible, by any means, and whether terrible or welcome, they kept everyone fixated on the fact and idea of change and in a state of anticipation that the century's novels sought in one way or another to make their own. Devoting your life to the composition of a single vast novel, as Musil and Proust did, is not the act of a professional literary man; no, it is almost Bartleboothian. Colette's Claudine is an adventuress, as are Jean Rhys's lost women. Bloom is Ulysses, the adventurer par excellence; Kipling's Kim and all the other secret agents who follow in his footsteps along the "dangerous edge of things" try to take the measure of a world that is changing around them. And these characters are not only adventurers, they are also, in one way or another, often provocatively, even incredibly, meant to be taken as heroes, which is perhaps the secret at the heart of the twentieth-century novel—that it is devoted above all to affirming and preserving an idea of the heroic, the heroic that in *Middlemarch* must be wrung out of Dorothea, but then *Middlemarch* is not an adventure.

Adventure to what end, though? Heroism in service of what cause? The answer to this question tends to be that in a century of such drastic change, it is precisely the lack of an answer that summons us to the quest for one. But that is not so much an answer as a vicious circle. It also awakens the suspicion that the venturesomeness of the twentieth-century novel reflects a certain complacency, or even an active complicity, with the century's disasters. Isn't the ideal of heroism mere fantasy, in fact vanity, George Eliot makes us ask—and Georg Lukács scoffed at Theodor Adorno and other devotees of Proust and Kafka as guests of the well-appointed Grand Hotel Abyss. And it is not as if the dangers were not evident to the writers themselves. In Gide, the freedom his protagonists seek leads again and again to murder: we saw how in *The Immoralist*, Michel thrives at the expense of Marceline, while Lafcadio, the antihero of *The Vatican Cellar*, realizes himself through an act of entirely gratuitous murder (the gratuitous murder Winckler schemes to repeat). As for Pirandello's "In the Abyss," it is a story about a man going mad.

And Perec, for all his pranks, knows very well that the abyss is neither a metaphor nor a heraldic shield. It is real and shaped like the human soul. The death camps had shown that there was nothing human beings would stop at doing, whether individually or collectively, and there was nothing that would alter that. *Life A User's Manual*, a book that can be reduced to a single mark of negation, does not shy away from either the complicity or the madness.

"All art is quite useless," Oscar Wilde famously quipped, and *Life A User's Manual* is well aware of it. The book (remember the plural subtitle, *Novels*) is among other things a repository, a dump, of all the books, all the art that went into its making, an abyss that harbors the discoverers of the abyss, Gide and Pirandello, and even a critic like Lukács; a total, or encyclopedic, novel that contains the total novels of Mann and Proust (*The Magic Mountain* is on the shelf in the room to which Bartlebooth has retreated to complete his life's work, the work of a life that begins in 1900), as well as Flaubert's *Bouvard and Pécuchet* (two clerks who set out to learn everything) and *Moby-Dick* (Bartlebooth is and isn't an Ahab), and there is even a page of *Life A User's Manual* where the little yellow flowers on Ursula Buendía's dentures bloom again. Everything and nothing are, in other words, in this book of an instant that also, of course, reflects *Ulysses*, as well as all the other books—*Mrs. Dalloway, Under the Volcano*—that also reflect *Ulysses*, even as this book of the instant of death further mirrors *The Posthumous Memoirs of Brás Cubas*. I doubt that Perec had read or even knew of Machado's work. But *Life A User's Manual*, too, makes a point of being patched together from other books—remember, Brás Cubas proudly appoints himself a plagiarist. It is designed in such a way that it contains not just certain books as ingredients, but represents, or enacts, a whole way of reading books: a way of reading that hopscotches among languages, genres high and low (between the lines you will glimpse both Lucretius and Agatha Christie), different art forms (painting, poetry, music, the movies), and all over the world and back and forth in time, a way of reading that produced the twentieth-century novel and which the twentieth-century novel trained readers in, a way of reading that at its best might be described as a heroic curiosity, but also, amidst so many changing things, such an accumulation of things, so many terrible things, a form of distraction and a measure of desperation. Perec's book models a reader's life and contains within it too the skeleton of the novel as such, because the book is also designed as an abstract, or diagram, of what the novel is. And what is the novel? A story that expands under the novelist's hand the better to come to an end, a story that the novelist must bring to an end as Bartlebooth sought to plan his life through to the end, though in the end things turned out differently, didn't they? The novel is hardly to be relied on, then (shades of the Underground Man)— a way of killing time, a killing machine; a mistake.

So there we have it at last, the book of books, a book that seeks to encompass and exhaust all the gestures of its precursors and in a sense any possible gesture a book can make. Sometimes in reading this book, which seems both so offhand and so sly, the innocent reader may suspect that it may be the product, like the serial music very much in vogue in Perec's Paris, of a certain set of procedures—that laws of a sort dictate this book of loss. And it is true that in it there is a hint of nostalgia for another book of the sort this book is not at all and could never be: scripture. This book of mad inventions, of every kind of story, is a creation that seeks to evoke creation itself. It would also, I think, like to provide consolation, yet that it cannot, even if the French word for *soul* is inscribed acrostically in the list of stories, the table of contents, that lies at the center of the book. The novel at the approaching end of the twentieth century is, however, even less like a sacred book than it is like a nineteenth-century novel like *Middlemarch*, and Perec is not pretending otherwise.

Perec's novel is a monument, an epitaph, a penance, a punishment, a joke. In 1985, nearing the end of his life, Italo Calvino prepared a series of lectures on literature that he called *Six Memos for the Next Millennium*, his message in a bottle for the century to come, in which he described *Life A User's Manual* as the only new thing in the recent history of the novel that he was aware of. What makes it new is that it is meant to be the last.

20. BEING HISTORICAL

MARGUERITE YOURCENAR'S *MEMOIRS OF HADRIAN* AND ELSA MORANTE'S *HISTORY*

But of course that is not how things end. Things end by going on and becoming, often at first imperceptibly, in time unmistakably, something else. For the novel in the latter half of the twentieth century that something else took the form of a revival of the historical novel.

A popular mainstay of nineteenth-century fiction, the historical novel fell out of favor as the twentieth-century novel came into its own. In a series of influential lectures delivered at Cambridge in the late 1920s and later published as *Aspects of the Novel*, E. M. Forster begins with a blunt attack on Sir Walter Scott, the father of the genre. Scott's plots, he says, are at once manipulative and absurd: "The reader is [made] so docile under the succession of episodes, that he just gapes, like a primitive cave-man"; his characters are as flat and flimsy as pennants. For Forster, the historical novel is itself a piece of history, and for a while it persisted chiefly as a curiosity or a piece. Think of Woolf's *Orlando*.

After the war, however, things change, slowly at first, then quickly. The genre goes back to work, and by the century's end, publishers' catalogs all over the world are packed with historical novels, many of them based on the history of the twentieth century. It seems almost predictable, as things so often do in retrospect. After World War II, the twentieth century has a history: it is not over, of course, but it certainly has a record, and how it came to have this history is a preoccupation of readers and writers. And by this time, the twentieth-century novel also has a history, a familiar repertory of themes and styles, as I have tried to show in these last chapters. In a sense, having a history and being historical is the latest news the century has brought, and the historical novel, which seemed an anachronism to Forster, looks newly serviceable as an instrument by which to gauge the situation, even as, by virtue of its long neglect, it offers a new challenge to novelists' powers of invention.

Published in 1951 to great acclaim, Marguerite Yourcenar's *Memoirs of Hadrian* is set in ancient Rome and looks in many ways like a monumental anomaly; examined closely, the book presents itself as a redeployment of the resources of the twentieth-century novel that is quite as canny and intricate as Perec's *Manual*. Elsa Morante's *History*, from 1974, also a great success, looks to the historical novel as a popular genre the better to tell a story about the countless people, lost to history, that the twentieth century destroyed.

About the time when Forster was having his fun at Sir Walter Scott's expense, a still young Marguerite de Crayencour, born into a prosperous bourgeois family in Belgium in 1903, felt a yen to write a historical novel—about the the Roman emperor Hadrian, she thought, or maybe the great Persian poet Omar Khayyam. It was the kind of idea you'd expect a brainy, bookish young person to entertain and grow out of, and in fact Yourcenar—the pen name she would fashion out of her family name—knew immediately that it was a bad idea. Like Nabokov and Carpentier, she had grown up with the century, nurtured on its art as something both to live up to and, in its own spirit, outstrip, and she was perfectly aware that much of the authority of modern literature derived from its involvement with interiority, which was hardly the stuff of history. As clearly as Forster, she saw that the novel, with its cast of little people and traffic in the ephemera of lived life, was hardly the medium in which to do justice to a great figure from the past, the kind of eminence to which, you could say, the open form and wide popularity of the novel stood as a democratic reproach. To write a novel and to write a novel about Hadrian, who (as much as Achebe's Okonkwo) came from a world before the novel, were not compatible ambitions, it seemed, and Yourcenar turned her attention to fashioning an elegant novella about homosexual desire, very much in the manner of Gide. She translated Woolf's *The Waves* and Cather's *Death Comes for the Archbishop*. She fell in love with an American woman, and when the war came, they took refuge on the other side of the Atlantic, where, after years in which her impossible project had gone on haunting her, it began to take shape. *Memoirs of Hadrian* came out in 1951. Yourcenar was almost fifty, and her subject had been been dead for nearly two millennia. The uncertain young woman who had conceived the book was nowhere to be seen in a book that is nothing if not a tour de force.

The finished composition is in fact all composure. Hadrian ruled over the Roman Empire at its apogee, but his great act as emperor was to bring an end to his predecessors' pursuit of conquest, recognizing the limits of Roman power as the condition of its continuity. He turned instead to fine-tuning the inner workings of the empire, bringing about an era of widespread peace and prosperity greater, as Edward Gibbon notes at the start of his classic history, than any known before or—Gibbon pointedly adds—since. Yourcenar's book takes the form of a letter from Hadrian to the young Marcus Aurelius, whom, with a provident eye to securing his legacy, he has already designated as the successor to his successor. In this testament Hadrian tells the story of his life and times, vaunts his achievements, and in general seeks to set an example while also setting out to show himself as he is. One of Hadrian's outstanding qualities, in Yourcenar's eyes—and as she depicts him, in his own—is his proper regard for himself, not just as a ruler, but as an individual human being, and if this necessarily entangles him in the coils of vanity and marks him as a not entirely reliable narrator, a flawed man, self-seeking, self-justifying, and plain selfish, it is also the condition of being a man at all and of ascribing a proper value to humanity. At the moment when Yourcenar writes, there cannot not be a trace of the Underground Man and *The Immoralist* in a figure like her Hadrian (asked to take him at face value, we immediately "have questions"), yet her challenge to us is to let that be. Imagine instead, imagine in its place, an emperor, an emperor as nothing more, and nothing less, than a representative human being.

Hadrian stands as a fine figure of a man, but he remains a tall order as a subject for a novel, all too likely to turn at any moment into a mere marble effigy, and this felt risk is part of the drama of the book, which, in the best tradition of the twentieth-century novel, is continually self-conscious about its own character as a book. In *Hadrian*, Yourcenar seeks to imagine the novel, and herself as novelist, out of the lonely dead end of Woolf's and Hemingway's heroic and tragic subjectivity, depicting a figure who is as public as private, as politic as passionate, who is complex and, though not uncompromised, quite unembarrassed to admit it. Along the way, the reader, echoing Shakespeare's Cleopatra, may wonder, "Think you there was, or might be, such a man / as this I dreamed of?" but that is all to the point. Yourcenar's Hadrian is a fully realized character, all the more so for his remaining before our eyes as a proposition about character, a thought experiment, you could say. He is a figure out of history and a dream figure, an enigma through and through. Yourcenar's brilliance as a novelist—parallel to the way she depicts her emperor—is resolutely to have it both ways, to strike a balance that throws us off-balance. Her whole book is set under the sign of the two-faced deity Janus, god of the turning year, of before and after, of self as other, and the Hadrian who appears in the polished, marmoreal surface of its prose—these words that are both his and hers—is at once a full-blooded presence and a spectral one.

The story is simple enough. Hadrian comes from Spain, from a provincial aristocratic family with a connection to the emperor Trajan. Summoned by the emperor to Rome, he educates himself in the ways of the capital before being given a military command, which takes him to the embattled frontiers of an empire that it was Trajan's announced aim to expand ever more. Hadrian comes to doubt this ambition as well as the conduct of Trajan, a hard campaigner and drinker who Hadrian increasingly sees as drunk on imagined glory. Trajan, having promoted Hadrian and put up with him in his feckless youth, grows suspicious in turn of his loyalty and witholds recognizing him as his successor, though on his deathbed at last he does. Or so it is reported by Hadrian and his allies. Does Hadrian in fact have Trajan murdered, as history rumors? Hadrian the memoirist deems it best to leave the question up in the air. Hadrian the emperor is, as this studied evasion suggests, a politician, but he is also a man of many talents and moods, poet, connoisseur of poetry and the arts, student of history and philosophy, military man, world traveler, lover of men and women, fickle, touchy, determined, ruthless when necessary. "I realized I was embarking on the life of a very great man," Yourcenar later wrote about the making of her book, and central to this book in six imposing and symmetrically disposed panels is a visionary scene in which the emperor, encamped in the Syrian Desert, where he contemplates the wheeling course of the stars above the turning earth, sees how the secular is enmeshed in the eternal, the eternal in our nights and days, a vision of everything that in some sense also takes in everything we cannot know. And yet, he says, "I could see myself as seconding the deity in his effort to give form and order to a world, to develop and multiply its convolutions, extensions, and complexities. I was one of the segments of the wheel . . . And it was about this time that I began to feel myself divine."

"Don't misunderstand me," he continues, "I was still . . . the same man." But the real risk here is to misunderstand just how breathtakingly audacious Yourcenar is being. How are we to take this? As purely historical? As so much old Roman-think? As a matter of personal hubris? No doubt. But also entirely seriously, as a way of imagining ourselves and our world that we may have left behind but which, in these pages of Yourcenar's, catches up with us again, so that we come to wonder at our modern selves as much as we do at Hadrian. Our estimate of humanity's place in the universe may be more modest, our sense of the universe infinitely expanded, yet less than ten years after a world war of unparalleled destructiveness, and under the shadow of nuclear war, how much weight do we give to that modesty or to that expanded view? Where at our moment of history do we stand in the universe? We could of course characterize our modern disaster as the predictable result of the imperial self-aggrandizement that is embodied in Yourcenar's Hadrian. This is what happens when a man deems himself a god, a lesson that should have long ago been learned. Then again, we might wonder whether Hadrian's influx of divinity isn't a response to and an aspiring appreciation of the great order of things of which we, branded by our latter-day skepticism and moralism, have grown incapable, and it is this failure of imagination as much as anything that has left us living in a world of ruins.

Hadrian, as I've noted, had been conceived before the war, and something of the Roman posturing of Mussolinian fascism attaches to this portrait of a great man setting things straight. Certainly the book, when it was conceived in the 1920s, partook of the yearning for a new order that marked the aftermath of World War I. Then again, the book only really took form after the Second World War and in an America that was one of the two great powers that had assured the triumph over fascism, an America that also, in the wake of war, proposed itself as the guarantor of a new international order, an empire, in effect, though one where world dominance was not a matter of claimed territory but of economic and cultural centrality—though with plenty of raw power to back it—all of which is suspiciously similar to Yourcenar's account of Hadrian's Rome. It was in America that inspiration struck—Yourcenar describes writing "until dawn, alone in an observation car of the Santa Fe limited, surrounded by the black spurs of the Colorado mountains and the eternal pattern of the stars," an experience surely reflected in her account of Hadrian's desert vision of heaven and earth—but her book, for all its triumphalism, is no less haunted by the specter of civilizational collapse, which in the end is what the ancient and modern worlds have in common for sure. Hadrian may report on his many public projects, sounding less an emperor than some high functionary of the European Union to come, and he speaks movingly of the beauty of the Pantheon, that temple to all the gods that, in its great domed space standing open to the heavens, effectively monumentalizes his desert vision. Still, at the the end of his life, he finds himself in Palestine, ill in body and soul and bent on suppressing a Jewish rebellion through "a war of extermination." And so the present ironies mount in Yourcenar's strange paean to the past, in which humanity may be linked to divinity but is never far from erasure. "Life is atrocious, we know," Hadrian remarks in passing, and even "when useless servitude has been eliminated as far as possible and unnecessary misfortune avoided, there will still remain . . . death, old age and incurable sickness, love unrequited and friendship rejected . . . all the woes caused by the divine nature of things."

Once again we hear the postwar note of mourning, which is not so much a matter of giving vent to an insuperable grief as putting it into perspective and controlling it. Perec deploys a battery of formal strictures to that end; Yourcenar adopts the archaic conventions of the historical novel, which in her hands serve to date and distance us, not only framing our historical being but putting us at a remove from the ravages of our own time. In a sense, she is revisiting the question of point of view, which, in this historical novel, is on the one hand all-encompassing, embracing as it does both past and present, and on the other a view from nowhere at all. "I begin to see the profile of my death," Yourcenar had Hadrian say in an early version of the *Memoirs*, and about this she comments, "I had at last found a point from which to view the book." In the finished book, Hadrian muses, "We are not the first to look upon an inexorable future," echoing and transforming "There is nothing new under the sun" of the Book of Ecclesiastes, while Yourcenar's own book brings its voice and us, the readers, into this cloud of witnesses. The book ends, "Let us try to enter into death with open eyes."

That is decisive and beautiful and memorable, and yet, interestingly, Yourcenar could not leave it at that. *Memoirs of Hadrian* is, as I said, a Janus-faced book, its hero both an arbiter and a breaker of boundaries, an adventurer and a pillar of the establishment, a man and a god, just as Yourcenar's novel is original, even transgressive, by virtue of appearing passé, so one might say that it was in the same spirit that, having finished it, she went on a few years later to rework it, adding a whole new section, turning this most finished of books into its opposite: a permanent work in progress. At several points I've quoted Yourcenar on the genesis of her book, comments that come from "Reflections on the Composition of *Hadrian*" that in 1958 she appended to her novel, and which she continued to include in subsequent editions, a sleight of hand by which *Memoirs of Hadrian* is transformed at the last minute into the memoirs of Yourcenar, an assemblage of fragments, a cri de coeur in which she tells the story of all her desperate blottings and jottings—a chapter from an altogether modern novel of voice coming to bookend *Hadrian*'s hard-won classical austerity—and literally has the last word. Here is her book, a monument of a sort in conception, and now, after its tremendous reception, a monument in its own right, and you could say that by adding the tale of its making, she renders the book that much more monumental. Then again, as fraught as her story is, it also undermines that monumentality. In a final, supremely equivocal gesture, the "Reflections" makes the whole story personal in a wholly different way—practically defacing the book's profile—while reminding us of Gide fitting out *The Counterfeiters* with his "Journal of the Counterfeiters." A few years later, in the American edition, Yourcenar would even throw in black-and-white photographs of classical statuary, which might be taken as a nod to the Roman practice of repurposing old pieces of sculpture (so-called spolia) in new monuments, but for a modern reader is no less suggestive of collage, travel books, newspapers. In the end, then, being historical leaves everything in suspense, or at least in pieces. What face looks out of the mirror of our death?

Memoirs of Hadrian is a novel with a pedigree, and it makes a point of it, standing at an imperial remove from the common run of novels, new and old. Elsa Morante's *History* also stands apart, but for an opposite reason. This novel of modern, not ancient Rome came out looking like the sort of great big audience-pleasing blockbuster that is meant to to take advantage of readers' gullibilities and appetites rather than challenging their preconceptions, like a good twentieth-century novel. Morante, born in Rome in 1912, her mother a Jewish schoolteacher, had spent the war hiding in the countryside with her husband, Alberto Moravia (also Jewish and already a well-known writer), before publishing a first novel, *Lies and Sorcery*, narrated by a teenage girl, in 1948 and a second, *Arturo's Island*, its protagonist an uneducated country boy, ten years later. *History* wouldn't come out until

1974, and when it did, Morante took the unusual step of pitching in to pay for publication, wanting to keep the price of the book afford-able, and let it be known that she had made every effort to keep the language of the book accessible to all. On the cover was a grisly pho-tograph, in what marketers call "action red," of a dead soldier and, under the title, not as a subtitle but as a shoutline, "A scandal that has lasted a thousand years." Pier Paolo Pasolini, a close friend of Mo-rante's, immediately denounced the book's vulgarity—the way it was published, it may as well have been *Gone with the Wind!*—and the immense success, domestic and international, that it enjoyed could be seen to corroborate the charge of opportunism. Yet for Morante, the popular form of the book was a serious matter: *History* was another of the twentieth-century novel's emergency responses, this time to the whole of the century's history and to history itself, and she fash-ioned the book to be popular in the same uncompromising spirit of literary experiment with which Joyce composed *Ulysses*. She needed, she felt, the largest audience to ask, at the end of the century, those large, urgent questions the century demanded that we—all of us— ask, about our common humanity and common life and how narra-tive sustains (or betrays) them, and if a writer wasn't asking each and all of us to ask those questions, wasn't that to fall short altogether? *La storia* means not only history but "story," and in that light you might rephrase the question the book puts to readers as how can we tell the story of the history that gets lost in works of so-called history, a story the twentieth-century novel has, even as it goes on and on, not even begun to tell? At the same time, the title makes a promise, a very an-cient one that any and all of us have hearkened to from the moment we could understand anything at all: I will tell you a story, it says. Now listen.

The title has two meanings, and the book tells two stories. One is the old story of the twentieth century, and—Morante taking a cue here from Dos Passos's *U.S.A.*—it is not so much told as outlined in the form of a chronology, starting punctually in 1900 with "the latest scientific discoveries concerning the structure of matter" that "mark the beginning of the atomic century" and going on to "three thousand six hundred and twenty-one aerial bombardments in Vietnam in a six month period, the United States declares. In Greece, army officers seize power and suspend the constitution. Mass deportations and arrests . . ." This ongoing chronology introduces each of the book's nine sections, the effect stripped down, but not a mere roll call of facts. "Instead of serving man, machines enslave him," we read. "Artificial products (plastic) alien to the biological cycle transform land and sea into a deposit of indestructible refuse . . . Popular media of communication (newspapers, magazines, radio, television) are used to spread and propagandize an inferior 'culture,' servile and degrading, which corrupts human judgement and creativity . . . and unleashing morbid collective phenomena (violence, mental illness, drugs)." These sections mix flat affect with near-incoherent outrage, and late in the book it's hinted that their tone has been set not by the narrator but by one of her characters, a troubled young man who is a drug addict, though he dies long before the dates covered by the last entries.

The other story, the story that takes up the greater part of the book, is the story of a small, poor family in Rome struggling to survive the Second World War, and what is important about the members of this family is that they are completely innocent of everything that goes on in the first story. They are innocent not only in the sense that they are free of responsibility for it but also because they simply do not comprehend it, even as they are caught in it. Innocent, yet they stand condemned for it. Morante puts it this way: her characters share "the mysterious idiocy of animals" who have "in their vulnerable bodies . . . a sense of the sacred: meaning by sacred . . . the universal power that can devour and annihilate them, for their guilt in being born." Innocent by virtue of being guilty, they are united by their creaturely vulnerability among themselves and with the birds and dogs and cats that also play a prominent part in the book. They all share a sense of shame that the self-appointed directors of History lack.

Ida Mancuso is the head of the little family, a single mother and an elementary school teacher, widowed young, whose older boy, Nino, is a rambunctious teenager, and whose baby boy, named Giuseppe but called Useppe after his baby-talk way of saying his name, was conceived when she was raped by a young German soldier, a soldier who

"knew precisely 4 words of Italian and of the world . . . little or nothing." This is the novel's long first scene: Ida returning to her apartment
from shopping; the soldier, a little drunk, wanting a place to sleep it
off and imagining that this unattractive, maternal woman will provide it for him if he carries her groceries; Ida, uncomprehending and
terrified, giving way; growing misunderstanding and the lurch into
sexual violence bringing on an epileptic fit. Ida slumps into unconsciousness and, later, on awakening, there is an awkward exchange of
courtesies, the soldier even performing a small chore and leaving his
penknife—it shows up all through the novel—as a gift. Within days,
the boy, "with his thick wrists, rough and innocent," is shot down in
an air convoy on its way to Africa. Useppe, born prematurely, will
inherit his startling blue eyes.

Why does Ida feel helpless before this German boy? Well, he is a
soldier, and she is timid, but also because she is Jewish, though all she
knows about being Jewish is that her mother told her it was a secret
she must never tell.

Ida is the head of her little family only in the sense that she is the
breadwinner and lives to keep her boys alive. Swaggering, athletic, in-
souciant Nino joins Mussolini's army and goes to war, and then, after
the dictator's fall and German occupation, returns to become a fierce
partisan. Later, the arrival of the Americans draws him into the black
market. Useppe—the story of whose conception begins the book and
who is at the center of the story it tells—is tiny, his growth retarded by
prematurity and poverty, and so he strikes his family and neighbors
as charming and even, with his curious turns of phrase and imperfect
pronunciation, precocious. He is beautiful, wonderful, and Useppe
himself approaches everything in a spirit of wonder. He doesn't just
share a sense of the sacred with animals, he understands their speech
and converses with them. After the family apartment is destroyed by
an Allied bomb, Ida and Useppe settle in a refugee camp outside of
Rome, and one day Nino shows up to take Useppe on a field trip to his
partisan outpost in the hills. The trip is the high point of Useppe's life,
and on it he hears the birds singing the song that, we are told, he goes
on singing happily to himself in later years—"it's a joke it's a joke it's a

joke"—a happy song, he thinks, one that reflects a character that is at heart festive—one of Morante's favorite words.

Useppe, in his divine simplicity so immediately engaged by the world, may seem more like Little Nell in Dickens's *The Old Curiosity Shop* than a hero of the twentieth-century novel, yet perhaps that makes him more like Hans Castorp ("nature's problem child"), Clarissa Dalloway, Bartlebooth, or, for that matter, the divinized emperor Hadrian than one might at first suppose. Could it be, Morante makes us wonder, that the twentieth-century novel has been, or could be, as she at least wishes to show us, a rearguard defense of innocence against the crushing forces of the time rather than the worldly, or innerwordly, adventure it has so often posed as? One way or another, Morante complicates our impression of the innocent Useppe by refracting his image through discrepant points of view. We see the world through Useppe's eyes, concrete, miraculous, as we all have known the world to be in childhood—and Morante writes with beautiful directness about that world—and we see Useppe too through his doting family's eyes. Then again we see him as he appears to the world at large—as nothing special, another poor kid, underdeveloped and undernourished, and this reminds us that the reason Useppe and his family are at the heart of *History* is that they are the sort of people of whom, whatever their story, history takes no notice at all.

To see through all these various eyes means that we see what goes on in the book in large part through the eyes of an omniscient narrator, and the narrator is certainly privy to all sorts of events and feelings that only a novelist could know. At the same time, the narrator has a highly personal voice. *History* is from the start very much a tale told, full of verbal tics ("in truth," "etc. etc.") and pet phrases (the "famous" day that such and such happened, and of course "festive"), and the tale is told by someone who claims not only to have looked into the story of the Ramundo family but to have seen them in passing, and as much as the story is full of things no person could know about other people, it is also full of professions of uncertainty, things the narrator admits to never having been able to nail down for sure. Who is this narrator, at times so knowing, at other times quite in the dark and yet so devoted to the novel's characters? Surely it is the author, yet we are never told that it is. We are never told who the narrator is because in the end, I think, the narrative voice is meant to stand in for us, any and all of us, observing other people and the world at large, trying to make out what is going on, and doing so by a continual, provisional comparison of how things look to us and how, we imagine, they may look to others. This narrative voice proceeds by a continual projection of the imagination, and it is this common lived world of the imagination—the reality of that, the necessity of that, our only saving truth if there is one—the book is meant to evoke in us.

Not who is the narrator, but who are we, the book wants us to ask—and what can we do for the Useppes of the world, the world being what it brutally is? Useppe's great festive outing to Nino's base camp, one of the central events of his childhood, juxtaposes two starkly different scenes. Here is Useppe returning in the company of a peasant girl called Mariulina on the back of a mule named Peppe (derived like Useppe from Giuseppe, or Joseph):

> Useppe enjoyed the journey very much. He . . . had one leg on either side of the mule's back, like a knight of olden times. He huddled against Mariulina's breast, as if against a warm pillow, and under his little behind he had Uncle Peppe's hairy withers, also warm. Before his eyes was Uncle Peppe's dark brown mane and his two erect ears . . . Around him he had the spectacle of the countryside with its lights . . . And if he turned to look up he saw Mariulina's eyes, an orange color, with black lashes and brows, and her face which, in the sunlight, was all covered with a down, as if she had a great veiled hat on her head. In Useppe's opinion, Mariulina was a universal beauty, to be gazed on with awe.

The passage glows like a Renaissance altarpiece, and it doesn't take long for us to see in it a depiction of the Holy Family on the flight into Egypt. Down the hill they go, and as they do, not far away, Nino's band ambushes a German patrol. One German is left alive:

[A partisan] burst from the brush onto the trail, saying with a
twisted laugh: "No, wait. This one's mine." . . . In determined,
raging hatred [he] aimed a terrible kick, with his heavy boot, at
the man's flung-back face. After an instant's pause, he repeated
the action, exactly the same, and again, several times, always
with the same mad violence, but with a strangely calculated
rhythm . . . [the] kicks, in their grim heaviness, following one
another at regular intervals, as if marking an incredible time
in an immense space . . . The German had reacted with a sti-
fled, rattling scream, which still sounded rebellious; but his
screams had gradually weakened until they were reduced to
a little feminine moan, like a question steeped in a nameless
shame.

And with that moan of shame we are taken back to the "guilt in
being born" of the animals, which links them to the sacred. *Sacred*
shares a root with *sacrifice*, and what we witness here, in close proxim-
ity to the little vignette of the Holy Family, is an act of human sacrifice,
the partisan seeking not only to kill the German but to kill his own
humanity, acting, we would say, like an animal, though only the human animal acts that way. And then we're reminded that, though Jesus
escapes the massacre of the innocents, his story also ends with human
sacrifice. *History* is not a religious book, but it is one in which all these
things, and all our lives, are entangled.

And no one is spared. Not Nino, not Mariulina, not the partisan (the tormented young drug addict whose later rantings echo the
novel's historical digests, Jewish like Ida, an anarchist and eventual
suicide), and certainly not Useppe, whose bright eyes will be opened
to the horrors of history and whose mind and feelings will then snap
closed. Not the narrator, whose helplessness to aid her characters will
become more and more obvious. "What is poetry which does not save
/ Nations or people?" the Polish poet Czesław Miłosz asks, and this
question haunts Morante's novel too, in which, as in *Lolita*, the only
innocence is innocence sacrificed. At the end of the book Ida is left to
live on, though the death of Useppe (who has inherited her epilepsy)

from a seizure has driven her out of her wits. Now it is suggested that it is she before whom the novel's march of history parades, in whom the voices of the characters continue to resonate. "Now in the dull and immature mind of that little woman, the scenes of the human story (History) also revolved, which she perceived as the multiple coils of an interminable murder . . . All History and all the nations of the earth had agreed on this end: the slaughter of the child Useppe Ramundo . . . Ida began moaning in a very low, bestial voice: she no longer wanted to belong to the human race." The final chronological section of the book, dated, like the first, "19—," concludes inevitably, ". . . and History continues . . ."

History is painted with such a broad brush that at times it seems almost as simpleminded as its frail little hero, but then the apparent naivete of the book, starting with its title, is part of a larger complexity. It is a total novel, like *Life A User's Manual*, that looks back at the total novels of the early century even as its sloppy amplitude and grand disunity stand as antithetical to the autonomy and self-sufficiency of the total novel. The book is openhanded and trouble-hearted and a little out of control, and it eschews the spit and polish of the Flaubertian sentence in favor of the immemorial, casual resonance of the spoken word. It is a garrulous book, pitting the human voice against human history with all its murderous excuses, and in scenes like the death of the German soldier quoted above, it also recalls *The Iliad* and the oral origins of literature. Then again, it is a great big book, a chunk of pages like the nineteenth-century novels of yore, and the Ramundo family is quite the Dickensian clan while Pyotr/Davide is straight out of Dostoevsky. At the same time, the book is, in the most literal sense imaginable, a twentieth-century novel, packed with its history like a suitcase. And as a final twist, this great big book, this book that is big with books, is about a little child, and one of the narrator's favorite words is *little* while the book as a whole brims over with the diminutives with which Italian abounds.

Written, in spite of the horror it documents, with an overflowing, even joyous, energy, *History* turns on History to offer a defense of innocence against all the odds and does it by asserting and defending the primal innocence of storytelling and make-believe. (In this, the book is the exact opposite of *Lolita*.) It is not just Useppe's innocence that Morante is standing up for, but an innocence that is common to all humanity, an innocence, a commonality, that the voice of the book continually asks us to imagine, one that the twentieth-century novel has, to its own shame, neglected. This common innocence is not to be confused with guiltlessness. Guilt is also common to humanity. This innocence of ours emerges perhaps most clearly in dreaming, dreams being both uniquely ours and out of our control. Even good men have bad dreams, Socrates says in Plato's *Republic*, but the converse is also true, and we could say that dreams are where the possibility of humanity—which is to say our sense of both guilt and innocence, of shared responsibility and love—is preserved in any of us, no matter how abused or debased. Dreams have no history.

"Now we'll try to report, at this distance, from memory, the last hours in the life of Giovannino," the narrator says at a certain point about a character, entirely peripheral to the main action of the book, who has gone off with the Italian army to Siberia. "We'll try," and the reader may wonder who is this "we" and take note too of the tentativeness of that "try," but in the meantime *History*, once again tossing aside the pretext of narrative unity, flies to his side:

> Giovannino doesn't know what's coming over him. Now he doesn't feel like doing anything but sleep . . . And, before sleeping, Giovannino would like to curl up, as he always has enjoyed doing; except that his body, because of all the cold, has become so stiff he can't bend anymore. But at the same time Giovannino realizes, as if it were a natural thing, that he also has a second body, which, unlike the first, is supple, clean, and naked. And, content, he crouches in his favorite position for lying in bed, with his knees almost touching his brow, huddled until a comfortable hole is hollowed out of his mattress beneath him . . . This is the position he has always assumed to sleep, as a baby, as a little boy, and as a grown man . . . Every

night, at the moment he curls up in this way, he feels he has
become tiny again. And indeed, little, big, young, elderly, old,
in the dark, we are all the same.

    Goodnight, Giovaninno.

    A story meant as a token of care and love, a story that rocks us to
sleep and wakens our dreams and frees us from history, Morante's
vast popular epic is at heart a lullaby.

21. THE ENIGMA OF ARRIVAL

V. S. NAIPAUL'S *THE ENIGMA OF ARRIVAL*

Back at the start of the twentieth century, between 1898 and 1904, the Danish novelist Henrik Pontoppidan—much admired by Thomas Mann and Georg Lukács, he won the Nobel Prize in 1917—wrote the vast novel that is considered his masterpiece. *Lykke-Per*, it is called, or *Lucky Per*, a title that puts its hero in the charmed company of such fairy-tale adventurers as the Grimm brothers' Clever Hans. Per is in that sense a human type and a mythic character. At the same time, he is, in the words of his wealthy Jewish fiancée, "a man for the coming century." She goes on:

> That was the precise way to put it. The precise way to illustrate his inner contradictions, excuse his failings, explain his extraordinary power. He was like the first formless template for a coming race of giants, which (as he himself had written) would finally take possession of the world as its rightful rulers and masters—a world which they would then reshape to their own liking and needs. He was a portent, cultivated in the stifling confines of domesticity and burdened with the full gamut of pettifogging timidity, superstition and subjugation and was, thus, unbending and scornful of all piety. For him there was no believing in providential powers other than those which sparked a man-made turbine into life. And who could blame him? The nineteenth-century dream of a Golden Age—its beautiful vision of building a kingdom on the twin pillars of good

fortune for all and social justice, a kingdom that would come simply by dint of the spirit of the age and the power of reasoned argument—how withered and anemic that vision looked now!

Per is a born rebel and a visionary engineer—his great ambition is to turn the remote, desolate area of Jutland, where he was born and raised as the son of a narrow-minded priest, into a center of shipping, transforming Denmark into a commercial and naval power. Per is a Nietzschean blond beast, a serial seducer, a shameless sponger, and an all-round piece of work. He is not a novelist, but he is the creation of a novelist who is as impatient as his character is with the hackneyed, small-bore character of Danish life, and Per can be said to embody the spirit of the twentieth-century novel in all its secular frenzy, consumed by a sense of momentous urgency and by the fear that its moment has past. The ambition of the twentieth-century novel, like its hunger for event, had been unlimited; abracadabra was its only prayer, and over the course of the century it would travel freely into every language and invent languages of its own, transcendent Esperantos. It set out to challenge the world and to remake the world, determined that no matter what, it would be alive, alive to what was going on, to its own shape, alive all the time. Excited by its own excitement, always going to extremes, it acknowledged and celebrated the variability and volatility of experience, no matter the consequences, without pretending, in the sanctimonious and sentimental and hypocritical manner of the fathers, that it was bent on doing good. At the same time, by going to extremes it also conjured up the utopian possibility of bridging them. Perhaps, in the end, innocence and experience would prove one.

V. S. Naipaul, born in 1932 to a family of Indian emigrants to the British island colony of Trinidad and Tobago, bears a good deal of resemblance to Pontoppidan's Per. He too came from nowhere and was determined from an early age to get away somewhere. "I was eleven, no more, when I determined to be a writer; and then very soon it was a settled ambition . . . With me, though, the ambition to be a writer was for many years a kind of sham." A sham because, though he wanted to be a novelist, he had little idea what that meant: "The novel was an imported form." If an impostor, he was a persuasive one, and from

Trinidad he went to Oxford, to the London literary world, and then, having made his name with several short and very funny novels of life on his native island, he traveled as a reporter all over the postcolonial planet. An impatient, angry, intolerant, and ungenerous man, not easy on others or himself, Naipaul (like Per) had no allegiance to anything apart from his own work. He disparaged other writers, old and new ("What," he famously asked, "was Jane Austen about?"), presenting himself as a self-made writer and a perpetual outsider. His early work was comic, but in midcareer he became celebrated for novels about the inauthenticity and inhumanity of the postcolonial world. *The Mimic Men*, one of them is called, and the writing, both fiction and nonfiction, that emerged from his travels to his native Caribbean, India (dubbed in his titles "an area of darkness," "a wounded civilization"), Africa, post-revolutionary Iran, and the Argentina of Isabel Perón depicts places and people plunged by a desperate search for certitude into ever more violent falsehoods. Naipaul's single greatest book, his warmest, funniest, and saddest, is *A House for Mr. Biswas* (1961), which tells the story of an Indian man in Trinidad, a floundering journalist, and his quixotic quest to settle his family in a place he can call his own. It is a portrait of Naipaul's own father, a tribute of sorts but also a cautionary tale. Naipaul's father also aspired to be a journalist and writer, entirely unsuccessfully. Early on, his career suffered a setback, and the man had a nervous breakdown from which in a sense he never really recovered. The adult Naipaul would ask his mother what had happened. "He looked in the mirror one day," she responded, "and couldn't see himself. And he began to scream."

In 1987, Naipaul published a novel that was very different from most of the novels he had written up to then, not least in being set in England instead of the peripheral zones of the postwar world order that his previous fiction patrolled. *The Enigma of Arrival* is the tale of a novelist told by that novelist, a novelist of Indian descent who grew up on the island of Trinidad, immediately recognizable as Naipaul himself but left nameless throughout the book. As the novel begins, the novelist has gone to live in a cottage on the grounds of a once-grand but now run-down Edwardian estate in the south of England, not far from pre-historic Stonehenge and the ancient burial grounds of Avebury and close to a big army firing range: blasting artillery rounds split the rural peace. He will stay there for ten years, courtesy of the eccentric, reclu-sive heir to the estate, who, in all those years, he sees twice.

At first the book appears to be about nothing much, about biding time, about not knowing what to do. "For the first four days it rained. I could hardly see where I was," it begins matter-of-factly, unpromis-ingly, and it will be a while before the reader realizes that this begin-ning is anything but artless, that it announces immediately what will prove to be one of the book's major themes: not seeing. The novelist is in the middle of a successful career and in the midst of a crisis. With a mixture of pride and defensiveness and resentment and dissatisfaction he looks back and considers what he has achieved and how it has been received, wanting to do something other, something new. He is impa-tient with himself. And in his bucolic English retreat, "like something out of an old novel," he also contemplates the daily rounds of a neigh-bor, Jack, a laboring man, in his small, carefully tended garden. "I saw his life as genuine, rooted, fitting: man fitting the landscape"—unlike himself:

> A man from another hemisphere, another background, com-ing to rest in middle life in the cottage of a half-neglected es-tate, an estate full of reminders of its Edwardian past, with few connections with the present. An oddity among the estates and the big houses of the valley, and I a further oddity in its grounds. I felt unanchored and strange. Everything I saw in those early days, as I took my surroundings in, everything I saw on my daily walks, beside the windbreak or along the wide grassy way, made that feeling more acute. I felt that my pres-ence in that old valley was part of something like an upheaval, a change in the course of the history of the country.

This is the tone of the book—"I felt . . . I saw . . . I saw . . . I felt"—feeling its way with cautious deliberation. A note of anxiety is never missing. The novelist's refuge from the world makes him that much more keenly aware of "that idea of ruin and dereliction, of out-of-placeness" that he has always "attached to himself." At night he dreams his head is exploding.

In the cottage, the author finds a book of paintings by de Chirico, including a picture called *The Enigma of the Arrival*. The picture depicts two figures in antique robes, one in red, tall and willowy, the other a stumpy black presence: the two of them stand at the outer limits of a stretch of checked pavement in a plaza, a certain distance from each other. The shadows in the plaza reach out, though the figures have no shadows—could they be ghosts? On the far side the plaza is walled off, and on the wall's other side there is a high, circular building girdled by an arcade: a temple, perhaps. There is the mast of a ship there too, sail billowing. It is a picture of a port, a liminal space, and is it the beginning or end of the day? Have these figures come from the ship that is now sailing away, or are they waiting for it to come in?

The novelist, intrigued by the picture, begins to imagine a story very different from the stories he has been accustomed to telling, a historical novel "set in classical times, in the Mediterranean." The narrator would tell of how he came to the port and, having arrived there, entered the busy city on some business of his own—what it was or why he had come all to be worked out. But, after a time,

> he would begin to know only that he was lost. His feeling of adventure would give way to panic. He would want to escape, to get back to the quayside and his ship. But he wouldn't know how. I imagined some religious ritual in which, led on by kindly people, he would unwittingly take part and find himself the intended victim. At the moment of crisis, he would come upon a door, open it, and find himself back on the quayside of arrival. He had been saved. The world is as he remembered it. Only one thing is missing now. Above the cutout walls and buildings there is no mast, no sail. The antique ship has gone. The traveler has lived out his life.

The novelist distracts himself with this story, and *The Enigma of Arrival* comes back to it on several occasions. It is nothing he really intends to write, however, and here again we have a case of not seeing. "It did not occur to me," he notes, "that the story that had come to me as a pleasant fantasy had already occurred, and was an aspect of my own."

The Enigma of Arrival is a novel that circles around itself, performing a slow dance of veils as it discovers its themes and develops its own distinctive character as, you could say, an end-of-the-twentieth-century novel. It is a book about how the author came to write just this book, came to feel the necessity of writing just this book, different from any of his earlier books, which means that the drama of the tale and its distinct irony arise from his not seeing his way to write the book we now see he has written. How did this happen, it implicitly asks, and Naipaul manages to invest what could easily seem an absurd authorial pretense with a sense of actual wonder and slowly spreading shock, as the story inspired by de Chirico's painting leads him to the story of his own first journey to England.

He is in Trinidad, about to fly to New York, an eighteen-year-old boy, embarrassed at the airport that his big Indian family is sending him off with half a roast chicken so that he won't have to eat the polluted food of strangers. In New York, he will board a ship to England, and his most precious possessions are the notebook and "indelible pencil" in which, determined young writer that he is, he begins to write as soon as the plane is in the air—and here, the narrator tells us, began a process of what he calls separation, between the writer and the man, he says (reminding us of the story of Naipaul's father), that would go on to afflict him for years. The boy he was knew a lot about books, at least for a boy, but nothing of the world, and what he appreciated as a fledgling writer and notebook keeper was anything that looked vaguely like what happened in the books by Waugh, Maugham, and Huxley that were his favorites. But the things that happen to him are not the things that happen in the books he's read. They are embarrassing things, compromising to his pride and personhood—cheated by a New York taxi driver, he has no money to tip the bellboy; lacking a plate, he eats his chicken with his fingers over a wastebasket in his hotel room—and these experiences, his experience, are just what he cannot find a place for in his notebook.

Racial and sexual anxiety grip him at every stage of his journey, and of this too he makes no note. However, a big mid-ocean party on the ship to England, full of recognizable characters, is stuff for a story that he will work on to no avail for years. And once in London, settled in a seedy rooming house, he sees in the bombed-out city little of the grandeur of empire and nothing of the color of Dickens, who had formed his image of it; he sees in a sense nothing, and it takes him back (or it takes the novelist writing about him many years later back) to Trinidad where, during the war, "we lived . . . among advertisements for things that were no longer made . . . or had ceased to be available . . . advertisements . . . for old fashioned remedies and 'tonics' . . . used as decoration in shops and, having no relation to the goods offered for sale." England likewise is for him a place "where signs were without meaning."

Above all, he does not see himself:

> In 1950 in London I was at the beginning of the great movement of peoples that was to take place in the second half of the twentieth century—a movement and a cultural mixing greater than the peopling of the United States . . . This was a movement between all the continents . . . Cities like London were to change. They were to cease being more or less national cities, they were to become cities of the world, modern-day Romes . . . visited . . . by all the barbarian peoples of the globe, people of forest and desert, Arabs, Africans, Malays. Two weeks away from home, when I had thought there was little for me to record as a writer, and just eighteen, I had found, if only I had eyes to see, a great subject.

Is this disingenuous? Even if the novelist missed that subject back then, the book has in fact already told us that this hapless young man did become the writer of novels about the world that produced this hapless young man. That "globalized" world, as it was not yet commonly referred to when Naipaul's novel came out, has, it's been made clear, been precisely the novelist's subject, which makes the expression

of regret here, well, enigmatic. Or is there something more to the
story not yet seen?

There is, we discover, as the novel about the novelist from Trinidad
becomes a different kind of novel. It switches genre to take the form
of "a Condition of England novel," a contemporary successor to *The
Way We Live Now* or *Bleak House.* The story now is the life of the estate and its inhabitants (that old rooming house at a new remove) over
the ten years of the novelist's stay in the cottage, the years when he
has been brooding on the inadequacies of what he has done. Mr. and
Mrs. Phillips, who have a house on the grounds, tend to the landlord
and the manor, while Pitton the gardener, always in jacket and tie,
tends to the property. Bray, the driver, grew up on the estate, a scion
of servants, but now owns a driving service of his own; in a peaked
cap, he ferries the novelist back and forth to the airport, from which
these days he departs regularly and with practiced ease. Then there is
the landlord, a bright young thing of the 1920s who was once an up-
and-coming writer himself, though for years he has been crippled by
chronic depression. Presented first as prototypes, as bits of local color
(they could be the characters from that mid-ocean party of years before), these figures are slowly revealed in their individual unease. The
enigmatic émigré novelist observing them from his cottage is also one
of them.

    The central figure, almost a tragic figure, in this later section of
the book is the gardener Pitton, in a way a counterpart to old Jack, the
man at one with the land who fascinated the writer when he first
moved to the estate. The narrator sees in him "an idea of the gardener
which I felt to be very old . . . going back to the beginning of worship
and the idea of fertility . . . the gardener as magician and herbalist,
in touch with the mystery of seed and root and graft, which . . . is one
of the earliest mysteries that a child discovers." Pitton is associated
with these mysterious regenerative powers, but he doesn't possess
them: he is an employee, paid to play the part but without the bud-
get to do anything but do it poorly, which means that he is resented

and grows resentful himself—and at last, as the inflation of the 1970s eats into the landlord's fixed income, he is given notice. "People like Pitton" were "people for whom in England, even in this well-to-do part of England, there was no longer room," the narrator reflects, as odd-jobbers are brought in to do his work: Brenda, in tight pants, her belly bared, who fools around and taunts her husband, Les, for his sexual inadequacy. "Brenda's dead," the author learns one day. "Les murdered her."

The elms on the estate die and are cut down. The rooks who nested in them circle overhead, looking for a new place to settle, rooks "whose arrival" proverbially "portended death or money." Out of money, the England that was once an empire falls to ruin, and one by one the novel's characters are picked off or dimissed or seek refuge in the part-time jobs and self-help nostrums of the new era. "I suppose they'll just sell up. In the end there'll be nothing left," Bray tells the author. Crumbling about its mysterious owner, whose one pleasure may be to watch the world he knew come to nothing, the estate that dates back to the start of the century is reverting not so much to nature as to a Hobbesian state of nature, of one against all, in which everyone is also increasingly bereft of a real sense of self. The empire is over, and is there any reason to mourn that, since its apparent order was in reality based on rapine and plunder? Then again, it did represent at least an idea of order and—to Bray, to Pitton, to the novelist, for that matter, whose presence on the estate is both a consequence of empire and of empire's end—a prospect of plenitude. In the new realm of money, by contrast, in which everything is measured and found wanting, all the world is as homeless as the rooks circling overhead, and the crumbling estate is now as much an outpost as Africa appeared to the landlord's forebears. "There was no ship of antique shape now to take us back."

"Death was the motif; it had perhaps been the motif all along. Death and the way of handling it." The author, after ten years, with age encroaching on him, too, has at last found the big story he was looking for. Death is the motif, and the book ends with an actual death—of the author's sister—and he returns to Trinidad to attend the traditional Hindu ceremony of farewell that follows the body's cremation. The estate is crumbling, but Trinidad is booming, oil having been discovered around this island at the mouth of the Orinoco, where centuries before, Sir Walter Raleigh sought gold for England in the region of Gabriel García Márquez's Macondo. Agribusiness has claimed the island's landscape, now crisscrossed with highways. "Money had touched us all . . . Money had ravaged and remade the landscape," the author reflects, and the book's final paragraph begins with the words "Our Sacred World had vanished"—though this is in fact not quite the case. Under the direction of a Hindu priest, the author and his family perform the requisite rites, and though the author remarks dispassionately on the fussy sequence of observances and the plump pandit's indifference to the family's grief, he is still moved to think of how, by ancient understanding, the burning of the body allows the spirit to reunite with the creative elements of earth and water. Our sacred world has vanished, as in the Hindu cosmogony world succeeds world in endless cycles of creation and destruction, but it remains to the living to gather and to go through the motions they have always gone through in the face of death. In this book about not seeing, these ritual observances are revealed as a form of observation. "It forced us to look on death . . . it fitted a real grief where melancholy had created a vacancy." Grief has allowed the novelist, unlike the traveler of his story, to in some sense return home, unrecognizable though that home now is, and to begin again. The book ends, "I laid aside my drafts and hesitations and began to write very fast about Jack and his garden."

The book ends with the author beginning to write the book, a motif, collapsing past and present, that we have seen in one form or another from Gide to Banti to Garcia Márquez to Yourcenar. Before that can happen, however, there has been an abrupt and bumpy descent into events of the day. Dates and datable occurrences have gone missing throughout the greater part of the book, but now the author rattles them off: the assassination of Mrs. Gandhi is mentioned; the author receives an assignment—the sort of magazine work that has kept him afloat even as he hasn't been able to write his book—to cover the Republican Convention in Dallas. It is 1984, no less. Arriving in Dallas,

the author, yet again, doesn't see what there is for him to say about
the whole business. This is a political convention, and he is looking
for political content, but the pageantry of Reaganism is as blank as
the old actor himself. But then, of course, he does see, sees that by
looking at "not the formal, staged occasion, but things around the occasion," he can write, and with a vengeance. And "it was out of that
excitement," he tells us, the excitement of "finding experience where
I thought there had been nothing, and out of that reawakened delight
in language, that I began immediately afterward to write my book."

Old Jack and Ronald Reagan! It turns out that Naipaul's book is
born out of an encounter with modern political spectacle quite as
much as it is a record of his childhood or middle years or stands as a
ceremonial reckoning with death. And to read V. S. Naipaul's magazine piece "The Air-Conditioned Bubble: The Republicans in Dallas," as the The Enigma of Arrival invites us to do, is to encounter a
prescient, even prophetic vision of that time and of the time that was
to come. "The occasion was overstaged, scripted in advance, and in
itself empty," Naipaul writes. "I was oppressed by the idea of thousands of busy journalists simply finding new words for stories that
had been already written for them." But then there are the people who
have gathered there, the evangelical minister preaching hellfire in an
air-conditioned megachurch; the repentant Black Panther Eldridge
Cleaver, "so ordinary now, so safe, this black man for whom a revolutionary's desperate death had been prophesied"; the real insurgent
power of the moment, the Republican campaign strategist Richard
Viguerie, determined to use computerized lists to foment "revolution against 'the elite establishment,'" and to advance "a new 'populist
party.'" The convention, Naipaul writes, is a religious event, "celebratory, tribal-religious," and he continues, "The scale and mood, and the
surreal setting, made me think of a Muslim missionary gathering I
had seen five years before in a vast canopied settlement of bamboo and
cotton in the Pakistan Punjab." The Republican Convention is another
dimension of a common world united, or rather, as would become
unmistakably clear in the fall of 2001, starkly divided by its hunger
for a higher meaning that the world itself seems helpless to provide,
and however much the Republican political grandees may invoke a

higher power, it is the exorbitant meaninglessness of their words that stands out above all as they deliver "The same speech . . . [in] the same language: unallusive, cleansed, sterile, nerveless and dead; computer language, programmed sometimes to rise to passion, but getting no higher than copywriter's glib." "At the climax of the great occasion, as at the center of so many of the speeches, there was nothing," Naipaul concludes. "It was 'as if' . . . 'as if inspiration had ceased, as if no vast hope, no religion, no song of joy, no wisdom, no analogy, existed anymore.'" Naipaul is quoting Emerson writing about England at the height of its power, as America may be deemed to be as he writes. "Like Emerson in England," Naipaul concludes, "I seemed in the convention hall of Dallas 'to walk on a marble floor, where nothing will grow.'"

Nineteen eighty-four: it's "Morning in America," and looking back now, we know something of what lies ahead. At the end of *The Enigma of Arrival* we have arrived in an American world (Naipaul visits a fundraiser on the ranch of Nelson Bunker Hunt, who became notorious for trying to corner the world silver market), and knowing as we do now that the 1984 convention effectively consolidated Reaganism as the century's last reigning ism, Naipaul's foresight is impressive. But Naipaul wants us to see, to read between the lines, that in rich America, as much as in impoverished Punjab, this is a world not of plenty, but of poverty and hunger, actual hunger and religious hunger—the same hunger he suffered from as a young would-be writer at large in the world he tried in vain to make sense of from the novels he had read, a deceptive scripture clutched to his heart. That endeavor, he has told us, "separated the writer from the man," and in light of that experience, *The Enigma of Arrival* shows us the world of the end of the century, the world of the Republican Convention, as—to quote Guy Debord's *Society of the Spectacle*—a world of "separation perfected." In which no one, like Naipaul's father, recognizes his face in the mirror.

What do we see at the end of this novel about a novelist in the waning years of the twentieth century that moves with the cautious slowness of a person in pain? One thing the book can be seen to be is a book about the life of the twentieth-century novel, with a young hero who, like Lucky Per, is driven to go out into the world to prove himself, driven by illusions as well as, in time, by disillusionment, eager to surmount the limitations he was born to and hungry to discover the unknown realities the world holds and that a page—written with all the wonder and perspicacity and precision the world demands— can also hold. Pontoppidan describes Per rejecting "the nineteenth-century . . . vision of building a kingdom on the twin pillars of good fortune for all and social justice," but what Per rejects, we need to bear in mind, is not the dream of progress so much as the dream of providential accommodation, that these things will just come to be, as things still tended to sort themselves out in the nineteenth-century novel because that was the way things were. That way of thinking about things was denounced by the likes of Per and by the masters of the twentieth-century novel both for complacency and hypocrisy, and was replaced by the conviction that what happens, whether on the plane of life or of art, happens by an exercise of radical will or, by contrast, by sheer contingency (Proust's Marcel stumbling over the cobblestones to discover his vision). Will and accident mark the limits of our world, where there is no order except such order as sheer will or blind chance bring about.

That is a secular vision of things, and the novelists of the early century (even if, like the great precursor Dostoevsky, they eventually turn to God) are fixated on fulfillment in time, on the adventure of getting what they want or being disappointed by what they want, much as were the politicians and celebrities of the time and the people of it as well. The imagination of the century was fixated on possibility, and though novelists tempered fixation with irony and individuality, they shared its entrancement and extremism, and they may be considered, as Mann in the excitement of the Great War, complicit in it and its mortal cost. Later they would be rueful for it, though that rue—and this is the turn Naipaul's novel represents in the form of the once-literary, now depressive, voyeuristic, and increasingly bankrupt lord of the manor—was in its way only a transformation of their original heedless enthusiasm. Through Naipaul's eyes we see that the secular frenzy of the twentieth-century novel was tantamount to a sacred horror at the bartering judiciousness of the nineteenth-century novel. When in turn the twentieth century had engendered its own horrors, its original secular urgency was transformed into a yearning to transcend its times, a renewed yearning for the sacred, though the yearning is denied: there is no going back to that antique ship.

Looking back from a historical perspective, we can see, however, that the sacred horror and hunger that fill the work of the later century are already there at the start of the century: Wells and Gide, craving worldly goods and cultivating worldly audiences, were always recoiling from the worldly accommodations of their day, imagining some larger compensation—they had wanted not the judicious, just to have it all—and over the course of the century that desired compensation has slowly been revealed to be as radically unreliable as the Underground Man. The world can never be vast enough, Baudelaire laments in his great late poem of undaunted despair "The Voyage," and at the end of the century a novelist like Naipaul can have come from one of its, as he sees it, dead ends to travel to every end of it, to find a world that, though it is interconnected in innumerable ways once inconceivable, is all the more desperate and fractured for it. A world that seeks an escape from the world it is, and if novelists like Perec and Morante and Naipaul now as openly recognize a yearning for sacred fulfillment as their precursors embarked on secular adventure, it is not obvious what their artful ministrations mean to the world's people, whether Republicans or the assembled believers in Pakistan.

The hope had been that experience and innocence would prove to be one and the same, but they were not. And what was a novelist to do about that? Pontoppidan's Per at the beginning of the century had returned to Jutland and the fold, not rejoining the community, really, but rather taking a vow of silence. Naipaul's novelist goes back to Trinidad for a family occasion and finds it in himself to write a novel. The novel at the end of the century is the most established of forms, more often than not a sentimental fixture, but Naipaul remains true to the twentieth century's extremism and intransigence: "Death is the motif."

The Enigma of Arrival is a new kind of thing, but it is also a valediction. The original adventure the twentieth-century novel had proposed—the adventure that in Naipaul's novel takes the fledgling novelist through the hotel worlds of the transatlantic ship and the London rooming house and out into the broken world—leaves him weary. The adventure has arrived at its end and is newly haunted by its beginnings. His daily walks from the manor, Naipaul tells us, always follow one of two paths—just as in Proust—and the long wait to accomplish a great work, one that threatens never to materialize; this also recalls Proust's *Recherche*. The manor is the magic mountain, too, and how far-fetched is it to see in the author of the book an unreliable narrator, ill at ease with himself and the world and his time, who descends from the Underground Man? Whether such resonances are conscious or intended is not the point. Naipaul is writing at a time when the twentieth-century novel has developed a repertory that, as is inevitable with any mature tradition, it revisits and revises while running an ever-increasing risk, like the journalist at the Republican Convention, of doing little more than "finding new words for stories that had been already written." Haunted by its precursors, haunted by itself and above all by the fear of not being itself—a fear it shares with so many of its precursors, perhaps the primal fear of the twentieth-century novel—*The Enigma of Arrival* recognizes in its own crisis of belatedness the crisis of its time. It is a story that wants to be over.

Nearing the end of the century, the narrator of *The Enigma of Arrival* walks the downs of Wiltshire, with Stonehenge on the horizon and the sound of artillery rounds in the air. He walks in silence. He lives alone. He is a lonely man, living in a place where he is not at home and with no home to go back to, and in his loneliness he makes up a story about a man just like him. Is it an accident that, as it happens, it is a variant, a reprise, an echo of another story told toward the start of the century by a lonely Franz Kafka? Kafka is the writer who captured both the euphoria and terror of the century, who saw more than anyone how it was haunted by the questions of the sacred and of justice, things it hungered after and forswore. The story I am thinking of is one of Kafka's most famous, the parable in which a man comes seeking admission to the law, only to be denied entry by a guard. The man will wait, however; the law is a secular thing, a sacred thing, and the key to everything, after all. He waits all his life and he waits in vain and only as he is dying is he struck that in all that time no one has come to keep him company. He asks the guard, How can this be? "This door was made only for you," the guard responds, "and now I will close it."

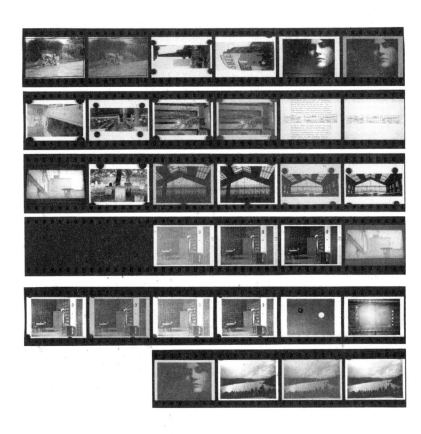

EPILOGUE

W. G. SEBALD'S *AUSTERLITZ*

Why stop there? Did 1986, the year of *The Enigma of Arrival*, constitute an appointed end? Or inaugurate a new beginning? By this time it was clear what the twentieth-century novel looked like and what it could do. It had a past: great books, great authors, great characters, great lines; it had delights, conundrums, contradictions, and limits, admirers and critics. It was a mature form. A book like this one lay in its future.

Some kind of end had been reached, and about the same time—as providentially as in a novel—one of the conflicts that had done so much to shape the novel's century also ended. In 1989, the Berlin Wall fell. In 1991, after years of stagnation, the Soviet Union collapsed. Revolutionary communism, with its great dream of social equality, its concomitant hopes and fears and staggering horrific deeds that had so convulsed the century, was over, and in the 1990s its opposites, capitalism and liberalism, enjoyed a moment of triumph. A moment—but already the post–World War II promise of widening prosperity was in question. The capitalist West faced problems of persistent injustice, deepening inequality, social decay, heedless economics, and political paralysis not unlike those forces that had undone the communist East. At the same time, there were new centers of wealth and power with quite different traditions and ideas of the good life. And fundamentalist factions, both new and atavistic—those encampments of Republicans and Islamists Naipaul had gotten an early glimpse of—were proliferating around the world.

In 2023, all this is familiar. It remains "breaking news." Plenty of novels have explored the nature of these changes and challenges, but without making any remarkable changes to the form of the novel. There have been tours de force, such as Hilary Mantel's pointillist, in-the-moment retooling of the big sweep historical novel, and some notable crazes: What was it that made autofiction, a genre that dates back to Gide, or for that matter Rousseau's *Confessions*, seem so new? Meanwhile, Sally Rooney's popular *Normal People*, in structure and conception, is indistinguishable from *Sense and Sensibility*. Novelists can now make use of a twentieth-, a nineteenth-, or an eighteenth-century playbook, and why not? Then again, a prominent critic of classical music recently said to me that in the last thirty years or so there had been to his ear no significant new developments in the music, something unheard of in all its earlier history. The same could be said of the novel.

Changes in the world at large, while the change in the novel is the lack of change. When, however, it comes to the changes in the world that have taken place since Naipaul's book, the biggest is surely the digitalization of everything and the compression of it all into ever tinier, more interactive devices. For the book, this has meant an intensification of its competition with other media—the moving image, recordings—but that's a war that's been going on in one form or another for a long time, and at the moment, at least, the book seems to be holding on. Still, will readers brought up on reading online go on reading novels? Reading online is a restless, demanding occupation—more like hunting and gathering than agriculture, and not at all like taking the time needed to absorb oneself in the great chapter in *A Portrait of a Lady* where Isabel Archer does nothing but reflect on her life. How might new reading habits change the fiction we read? You can imagine today's swelling DIY communities of writers and fans of romance, fantasy, and other forms of genre fiction continuing to grow, and perhaps something interesting will come of that. Other sources of information and entertainment have already become as central as the book, and others, unimaginable now, are likely to emerge, as may a new art form that means something like what the novel has come to mean over the last two centuries. At the same time, the information glut we now enjoy—or suffer from—has tended to reduce readers' relish in novels and their capacity to absorb them: I suspect that the emphasis on always needing to tell a story—a truism among marketers, politicians, commencement speakers, and reviewers in the last quarter century—reflects nothing so much as an increasing impatience and an inability to submit to the complex requirements of serious reading. That said, these very conditions have led other readers to relish the novel, with its many intricacies and long, rich history, that much more, precisely because it is a throwback, not just content to consume, not just a great story. The open question for people who love the novel, both readers and writers, is as always whether it is capable of transforming our attention to the page.

Questions in the message-clogged air. And then there is the looming threat of catastrophic climate change and a world of failed and barricaded states, uprooted populations, and prison camps—a world where the novel, with its expansive gaze, has no place to go or come home to, no place at all, and Prospero won't even have to bother to drown his book. But for the twentieth-century novel, that's a familiar sort of denouement. Remember the vision of the end of Wells's Time Traveller, himself a refugee, of a darkening, unpeopled world of rising waters, its shores patroled by massive predatory crabs.

Time flies; the novel hangs on. Is there a writer who captures something of this post–twentieth century mixture of blur and stasis? Perhaps W. G. Sebald, writing at the end of the last century, counts as the first writer of our digitalized and disrupted age. Sebald, born in Bavaria, the bastion of German conservatism, was educated in Germany and Switzerland and lived for most of his adult life in England, becoming a lecturer at the University of East Anglia. He was almost fifty when his first novel, *Vertigo*, came out in 1990. It was little noticed in his homeland. In the course of the ensuing decade, he published three more novels. The second, *The Emigrants*, won Sebald a passionate following in England and America, which grew with the publication of *The Rings of Saturn* and *Austerlitz*, the last in 2001, when Sebald died in an auto accident, apparently after suffering a heart attack in the driver's seat. Since then his reputation and influence on writers of fiction and nonfiction has spread from the Anglosphere to the larger world.

All four of Sebald's fictions share a common tone. Their first-person narrators exist to a large degree in the shadows, men with a distinct resemblance to the author— scholarly, bookish, hailing from one country yet living in another—who remain nameless as they recount their wanderings on earth and among strangers and through the darker passages of literature and history, all the while telling us next to nothing about their personal lives except that they are subject to depression and nervous collapse. (They remain strangers, and it is as strangers that we are drawn to them.) The Sebald narrator is especially but not exclusively haunted by the horrors of the last century, for which he shows a fascination verging on a perverse nostalgic relish, and he speaks uniformly in a voice of hushed intensity, long sentences wandering from one subject to another, so that the books come to resemble musical improvisations on a theme, like the open romantic form of the fantasia or a long, brooding jazz solo.

On the surface, these books are twentieth-century highbrow novels of voice, like Gide's, yet this comparison is deceptive. The voice is uniform, and it even speaks in something of a monotone, but this lonely, level voice becomes, as the books unfold, collective as well as individual, a sort of chorus of echoes. Nothing is more characteristic of Sebald's style than the way he peppers his pages with such turns as "He said, she continued," before the story picks up again, the narrator speaking in his own right but also channeling the voices of other people who speak to him and, on top of that, yet other people those other people have spoken to. He said, she continued: so Sebald nests story within story, a nesting that in principle could go on forever. We are dealing then not only with a variant novel of voice, but with a variant on mise en abyme, in which the narrative voice becomes at the same time the voice of narrative, the story gathering up its various narrators in the course of trying to figure out where it is going and to what end. Gathered into this a ghostly community of speakers, we wonder what holds it all together. And here the familiar question of point of view arises in a new form. What finally is the moving force behind this solitary recitation, this cloud of witnesses?

Sebald's voice has a complex literary pedigree: if it hearkens back to Gide in conception, the tone is closer to the meandering musings of Robert Walser, even as the layering of reported narratives recalls Conrad's Marlow and the novels of Faulkner (who was influenced by Conrad) and, more recently, Claude Simon (influenced by Faulkner) and Thomas Bernhard. The overall effect, however, puts me in mind of a line by the poet Paul Celan, whose work Sebald undoubtedly knew: "*Niemandes Stimme, wieder*" ("No one's voice, again"). Sebald's fiction, a chorus of voices and a compound of genres from the journal to the travelogue to the literary essay, at once fiction and nonfiction, as memory is, resembles the many messages in myriad languages that you might pick up on a shortwave radio in mid ocean. A crossed signal, charged with the lost voices of the past century and centuries past but also with intimations of the infinite memory machine that in the 1990s had begun to shape the future.

The voice of Sebald's books, as one after another they appeared, was both old and new and very striking; striking, too, was the way he incorporated visual images. Illustrations, a staple feature of the novel in the nineteenth century, had been almost banished from the twentieth-century novel, but Sebald's books were full of them, mostly photographs, even as just what they illustrate or why they are there— they certainly don't look like the illustrations of nineteenth-century fiction—is left cagily uncertain. Are they of the places and people described in the text? Could be, looks like it, but then what does it mean to present a photograph of a fictional character? The pictures and reproductions were black-and-white and generally low quality, poorly exposed or unfocused, amateurish if not incompetent, but presented as they were, they possessed the mystery of the leftover, the abandoned, the lost, the unaccounted for, precisely the subjects of the monologues the images accompany in silent counterpoint. Like the formal, reserved voice of the narrator, there was something anachronistic about these images, and photographs, unlike paintings, are images whose subjects are in their very nature already lost to the past. At the same time, these images were the most obviously innovative dimension of Sebald's work, and soon the most imitated, since old though they appeared, their presence in it was in large part due to the digitalization of typesetting, which made it easier to fold pictures freely into the pages of a book. In their mingling of image and text, Sebald's pages bear a certain resemblance to pages online, if the internet were mimeographed.

Sebald's decade was a period of waiting, and indeed the decisive turning points of *Austerlitz*, Sebald's last book and the one most like the novel as we know it, take place in the waiting rooms of train stations. *Austerlitz* is the story of Jacques Austerlitz, a lecturer in the history of architecture at the Courtauld Institute in London, whom the book's narrator, nameless as usual in Sebald, initially encounters by chance in the great nineteenth-century train station—its dome modeled on Hadrian's Pantheon—in Brussels. They meet in the so-called *salles des pas perdu* (which could be the room of lost steps or the room of those who are not lost). It is 1967. Austerlitz is dressed like a workingman, and for luggage he carries, as he does throughout the book, a simple rucksack. Immediately he begins to talk about the architecture of the train station and the Belgium of Leopold II: a fledgling nation—though lacking the unifying language of a nation—patched together from pieces of old empires in the aftermath of the Napoleonic Wars; a tiny place that soon turned into a center of capitalism, deemed at the time the America of Europe, as well as a rapacious colonialist power whose murderous exploitation of its African holdings would be exposed in Conrad's *Heart of Darkness*. The meeting place of Austerlitz and the narrator is thus historically charged, and at the time of the book's publication, history had gone on to make Brussels the capital of a new EU in which all that old bad history was at last to come to a good end. Austerlitz's scholarly interest, he tells the narrator, is the architecture of late capitalism—like the train station, devoted to the flow of people and goods. He is also interested in the architecture of public institutions—train stations, but also hospitals, libraries, museums, fortresses, prisons. After all, the flow of goods has long been lubricated by the flow of bodies and blood.

In Austerlitz, the narrator tells us, he "had found the first teacher

I could listen to since primary school." After the early '70s, the two men lose track of one another, however, not meeting again until December 1996—by chance once more, and in a train station, too, this time London's Liverpool Street. And again Austerlitz begins to talk—not about the history of architecture, but about his own history. The narrator tells us that Austerlitz now tells him that he was born in 1934 (Sebald is beginning his characteristic weaving of voices) and was a foster child, brought up by a Welsh Protestant pastor and his wife and given a Welsh name. Only at age fifteen did the school authorities inform him that he was in fact Jacques Austerlitz, a name that struck him as utterly strange, though, even so, "it never occured to me to wonder about my true origins," which seems hard to believe. But then, as Austerlitz says elsewhere, "Might it not be . . . that we also have appointments to keep in the past, in what has gone before and is for the most part extinguished, and must go there in search of places and people who have some connection to us on the far side of time, so to speak?" So it is with Austerlitz, who on retiring from his job to write a book he then finds he cannot write, begins to take long, nocturnal walks through London, one of which leads him at last to the Liverpool Street Station. There he has a vision—of a couple from the 1930s arriving at that very station accompanied by a small child with a rucksack: himself.

Where was he coming from? The year of Austerlitz's vision is 1992. The countries of Eastern Europe are open to visitors from the West. Recovering from the nervous breakdown that he suffers after his experience at the station, Austerlitz enters a shop and overhears the word Prague on the radio; immediately, without explanation, he is compelled to go there. In Prague, chance leads him to Vera (names matter in this book, and hers means truth), once, as it turns out, his nanny in the city, who tells him about his Jewish parents, the German conquest of Czechoslovakia, his father's departure for exile, his mother's deportation to Terezin, the show camp whose inhabitants were all sent off to death camps in the end. From a multivolume edition of Balzac, Vera pulls out a pair of photographs: his mother and father; a little boy in a page's costume—again, himself. And yet the strangeness that has haunted him from childhood is in no way dispelled by this discovery. He says, the narrator tells us, that at that moment he felt as utterly disconnected from this strange new image of himself as he did from his own ongoing life.

This is the core of the novel, the burden of a long, confessional monologue that unfolds not only at the train station but also at Austerlitz's house in East London, before, in the fall of 1997, arriving at a kind of conclusion in Paris, where Austerlitz has moved. The finale of his story occurs at the Gare d'Austerlitz, which Austerlitz calls "the most mysterious of all the railway terminals of Paris," where, he explains, "I spent many hours . . . during my student days, and even wrote a kind of memorandum on its layout and history." Here he feels he is coming closer to his father, whose traces he continues to pursue. Austerlitz recalls a visit to the station years earlier, when he found the huge space entirely empty except for "two tiny figures . . . moving about in ropes, carrying out repair work, like black spiders in their web." "I don't know, he continues, "what all this means." The book continues, and the reader feels its threads coming together, from the sanguinary history of modern Europe that tracks back to, though hardly begins with, the great Napoleonic triumph at the Battle of Austerlitz, a sanguinary history from which the development of the modern state and its great public institutions and facilities, among them the trains that brought the narrator to safety in Britain and his parents to death, cannot be separated. So here, at the end of the book, we encounter once again the name of Austerlitz, and as to those two spiderlike figures set against the sky—the book includes the photograph Austerlitz tells us he took of them—might they be seen now as Austerlitz and the narrator? They are a sinister duo, but they are also "carrying out repair work." Austerlitz has given the keys of his house in London to the narrator and invited him to pore over his trove of photographs. This book—*Austerlitz*—is surely the result, a true image of the man at last, though has Austerlitz lived to see it? We don't know. How his story ends we are not told.

You could call *Austerlitz* a twentieth-century novel. It is after all about the twentieth century, about the calamities it brought and about the effort, in the latter half of the century with which Austerlitz's life coincides, to bring those calamities to light. It might even be called a twentieth-century novel of record, the last. And yet it isn't that: it's something else. To return to the figure who has haunted this book from its beginning, compare the voice of Austerlitz to the voice of the Underground Man. Austerlitz is a descendant of the Underground Man, still lost in the abstract and hallucinatory city, but his voice is different. The voice of the Underground Man—angry, self-justifying, self-pitying, self-punishing, prophetic, pathetic, out of control—can't be pinned down. It snarls and squirms and slips off into the twentieth-century novel. The voice of *Austerlitz*, the voices of *Austerlitz*, are by contrast almost preternaturally level, and the story that Austerlitz tells the narrator, improbably unfolding as a series of coincidences, is to be taken entirely at face value. This man of sorrows is the ultimate reliable narrator, and listening to him, we are led to believe that the truth is at hand; maybe we are even beginning to understand. Despair, but take heart. The book's voices are desolate but hypnotic, mournful and beautiful. They echo each other and say what strike us as true things with disconsolate deliberation. We embrace them all the more at a time of "the dissolution, in line with the inexorable spread of processed data, of our capacity to remember"—such is the burden of a reported conversation late in the book between Austerlitz and yet another stray stranger in a "reading room . . . gradually emptying now" of the pharaonic new Bibliothèque Nationale in Paris. We welcome Sebald's as a voice that, by contrast, does remember, and in *Austerlitz* in particular we are further asked to welcome a sheer artificiality of fabulation that is meant to recall the nineteenth-century novel at its most far-fetched. Balzac's novels, for example, are powered by coincidence and full of long, late-night revelations and confidences of the sort that Austerlitz and the narrator engage in, and it is from the pages of a complete set of Balzac that Austerlitz's family photographs amazingly resurface.

When Austerlitz hands over his house keys to the narrator—who has been identified as German—he remarks in passing that just recently he discovered that all these years he has been living next to an old Jewish cemetery. The handing over of keys is a highly traditional symbol of the power of tradition—a power little noted by the twentieth-century novel. There is, Sebald is intimating in his soft-shoe, rather priestly way, a peaceful community of the dead that is greater than the deadly community of the living. True enough. Can the living attend to the dead or the dead to the living? No doubt we would like to believe that they do.

APPENDIX
OTHER LIVES OF THE TWENTIETH-CENTURY NOVEL

Emily Brontë. *Wuthering Heights*, 1847

Knut Hamsun. *Hunger*, 1890

Selma Lagerlöf. *The Saga of Gosta Berling*, 1891

Henry James. *The Awkward Age*, 1899

Joseph Conrad. *Heart of Darkness*, 1899; *Nostromo*, 1904; *The Secret Agent*, 1907; *Under Western Eyes*, 1911

Arthur Conan Doyle. *The Hound of the Baskervilles*, 1901

John Galsworthy. *The Man of Property*, 1906

Rainer Maria Rilke. *The Notebooks of Malte Laurids Brigge*, 1910

Raymond Roussel. *Locus Solus*, 1914

Sigrid Undset. *Kristin Lavransdatter*, 1920–22

Jaroslav Hašek. *The Good Soldier Svejk*, 1921–23

Shiga Naoya. *A Dark Night's Passing*, 1921–37

Theodore Dreiser. *An American Tragedy*, 1925

Willa Cather. *The Professor's House*, 1925

Louis Aragon. *Paris Peasant*, 1926

Evelyn Waugh. *Decline and Fall*, 1928

Mario de Andrade. *Macunaíma*, 1928

Ford Madox Ford. *Parade's End*, 1924–28

Mikhail Sholokhov. *The Quiet Don*, 1925–40

Dashiell Hammett. *Red Harvest*, 1929

Elizabeth Bowen. *The Last September*, 1929

Andrei Platonov. *The Foundation Pit*, 1930

John Dos Passos. *USA*, 1930–36

Louis-Ferdinand Céline. *Journey to the End of the Night*, 1932

Ivy Compton-Burnett. *A House and Its Head*, 1935

Georges Bernanos. *Diary of a Country Priest*, 1936

Witold Gombrowicz. *Ferdydurke*, 1937

Vladimir Nabokov. *The Gift*, 1937

Daniel O. Fagunwa. *The Forest of a Thousand Demons*, 1938

Ernst Jünger. *On the Marble Cliffs*, 1939

Nathanael West. *The Day of the Locust*, 1939

Adolfo Bioy Casares. *The Invention of Morel*, 1941

F. Scott Fitzgerald. *The Last Tycoon*, 1941

Janet Lewis. *The Wife of Martin Guerre*, 1941

Anna Seghers. *The Seventh Cross*, 1942

José Revueltas. *Human Mourning*, 1943

Charlotte Salomon. *Life? Or Theater?* 1943

Juni'chirō Tanizaki. *The Makioka Sisters*, 1943–48

Ivo Andrić. *The Bridge over the River Drina*, 1945

Gopinath Mohanty. *Paraja*, 1945

Henry Green. *Caught*, 1943; *Back*, 1946

Qian Zhongshu. *A Fortress Besieged*, 1947

Maurice Blanchot. *Death Sentence*, 1948

George Orwell. *1984*, 1949

S. Yizhar. *Khirbet Khizeh*, 1949

Jean Genet. *The Thief's Journal*, 1949

John Cowper Powys. *Porius*, 1951

Italo Calvino. *Our Ancestors*, 1952–59

Wolfgang Koeppen. *The Hothouse*, 1953

Samuel Beckett. *Watt*, 1953

J.R.R. Tolkien. *The Lord of the Rings*, 1954–55

Juan Rulfo. *Pedro Páramo*, 1955

Naguib Mahfouz. *The Cairo Trilogy*, 1956–57

Giorgio Bassani. *The Novel of Ferrara*, 1956–80

Bernard Malamud. *The Assistant*, 1957

Giuseppe Tommaso di Lampedusa. *The Leopard*, 1958

William Burroughs. *Naked Lunch*, 1959

James Baldwin. *Another Country*, 1962

Julio Cortázar. *Hopscotch*, 1963

Beppe Fenoglio. *A Private Affair*, 1963
Marguerite Duras. *The Ravishing of Lol V. Stein*, 1964
Uwe Johnson. *Anniversaries*, 1970–83
Ingeborg Bachmann. *Malina*, 1971
Thomas Pynchon. *Gravity's Rainbow*, 1973
Milan Kundera. *The Book of Laughter and Forgetting*, 1979
Shirley Hazzard. *The Transit of Venus*, 1980
Toni Morrison. *Beloved*, 1987
Penelope Fitzgerald. *The Beginning of Spring*, 1988
Yang Jiang. *Baptism*, 1988
Ibrahim al-Koni. *Gold Dust*, 1990
Philip Roth. *American Pastoral*, 1997

NOTES

These notes are limited to direct quotations from secondary sources. In the case of primary sources, I sometimes quote from several different translations of the books under discussion. Full bibliographic information appears in the bibliography.

I. THE VIVISECTOR

32 *"The girl hovers inextinguishable"*: James, *Literary Criticism*, 1079.
35 *"H. G. Wells . . . is a man of genius"*: Sherborne, *H. G. Wells*, 102.
36 *"my trump card"*: Sherborne, *H. G. Wells*, 101.
42 *"It is literally Mr. Wells's own mind"*: James, *Essays*, 137.
43 *"If the participants"*: James, *Essays*, 139.

2. THE ABYSS

47 *"Mallarmé for poetry"*: Sheridan, *André Gide*, 67.
49 *"Our child is dead"*: Sheridan, *André Gide*, 314.
51 *"Promise me one thing"*: Lestringant, *André Gide*, vol. 1, 335.
53 *"lamentable madman"*: Lestringant, *André Gide*, vol. 1, 473.
61 *"Why devote, just now, a whole book"*: Klaus Mann, *André Gide*, VIII.

3. SHUTTER TIME

70 *"an ecstasy"*: Stach, *Decisive Years*, 117.

4. YOUTH AND AGE

80 *"Imagine a whole society"*: Thurman, *Secrets of the Flesh*, 21.
90 *"knew something of the things which are underneath"*: Kipling, *Something of Myself*, xxxiv.
93 the Indian Railway Library: Gilmour, *The Long Recessional: The Imperial Life of Rudyard Kipling*, 37.

5. THE AMERICAN SENTENCE

101 *"One might enumerate"*: James, *Essays*, 351.
105 *"They are neither men nor women"*: Hobhouse, *Everybody Who Was Anybody*, 48.

6. A WORLD OF LITERATURE

119 *BB, OO, and ZZZ*: Jackson, *Machado de Assis*, 37.

130 *"the fundamental question of Sōseki's existence"*: Keene, *A History of Japanese Literature*, 325.
131 *"Evil customs of the past shall be broken off"*: Gordon, *A Modern History of Japan*, 78.
131 *"To have lived through the transition stage of modern Japan"*: Gordon, *A Modern History of Japan*, 61.
133 *"above him . . . the cracked Liberty Bell"*: Keene, *A History of Japanese Literature*, 82.
134 *"gargler of stones"*: Nathan, *Sōseki*, footnote 28.
134 *"startle westerners by producing terrific works"*: Keene, *A History of Japanese Literature*, 307.
135 *"no counterparts in the west"*: Keene, *A History of Japanese Literature*, 315.

7. HIPPE'S PENCIL
142 *"inordinately vain"*: Heilbut, *Thomas Mann*, 117.
144 *"a bourgeois book"*: Heilbut, *Thomas Mann*, 272.
144 *"the fame of the artist is a farce"*: Heilbut, *Thomas Mann*, 248.
144 *"perhaps a war is needed"*: Heilbut, *Thomas Mann*, 258.
144 *"great, fundamentally decent"*: Heilbut, *Thomas Mann*, 274.

8. WHAT DID YOU DO IN THE WAR?
166 *2,360 times*: Tadie, *Proust*, 606.
174 *"transcendental homelessness"*: Lukács, *Theory of the Novel*, 41.
179 *"They called it a ramshackle empire"*: Ellmann, *James Joyce*, 389.
179 *"supremely indifferent"*: Ellmann, *James Joyce*, 383.
179 *"As an artist . . . I am against every state"*: Ellmann, *James Joyce*, 447.
180 *"a war dodger"*: Budgen, *James Joyce and the Making of "Ulysses,"* 16.
183 *"blow the bridge sky-high"*: Ellmann, *James Joyce*, 528.
183 *"Stephen no longer interests me"*: Ellmann, *James Joyce*, 459.
184 *"I can't express myself in English"*: Ellmann, *James Joyce*, 397.
184 *"the character of Mr. Joyce's notoriety . . . is partly political"*: Ellmann, *James Joyce*, 525.
185 *a too-successful ad campaign*: Ellmann, *James Joyce*, 616, footnote.
185 *"universal gesture of the book"*: Benjamin, *One-Way Street*, 21.
186 *"a revolting record"*: Ellmann, *James Joyce*, 506.

10. NICK STANDS UP
219 *"The brutal you have surely shown the world"*: Meyers, *Hemingway*, 146.
223 *"She had an enlightened greediness"*: Forster, *Two Cheers*, 251.

12. THE HUMAN AND THE INHUMAN
242 *"end product of a century's ferment"*: Svevo, *Memoir of Italo Svevo*, 26.
242 *"the poverty of his language"*: Svevo, *Memoir of Italo Svevo*, 21.
242 *"a fashionable teacher of Trieste's rich bourgeoisie"*: Svevo, *Memoir of Italo Svevo*, 66.
242 *"Some pages of* As a Man Grows Older*"*: Svevo, *Memoir of Italo Svevo*, 67.
242 *"As far as the Italian critics are concerned"*: Svevo, *Memoir of Italo Svevo*, 82.
243 *"the Italian Proust"*: Svevo, *Memoir of Italo Svevo*, 91.

13. THE EXCEPTION
256 *"if he was really the son of a working class coal-miner"*: Maddox, *D. H. Lawrence*, 53.

256 *"incredibly plebeian, mongrel, and underbred"*: Meyers, *D. H. Lawrence*, 83.

256 *"curious, hollow, like the soft hoot of an owl"*: Maddox, *D. H. Lawrence*, 398.

256 *"I'm afraid I'm incorrigibly ill-bred"*: Maddox, *D. H. Lawrence*, 65.

14. THE END

282 *"spiritually violent for everyone alive"*: Stevens, *Collected Poetry and Prose*, 659.

287 *"When a storm or some other calamity from the heavens"*: Tatar, *The Annotated Brothers Grimm*, 401.

16. REFLECTIONS ON DAMAGED LIFE

331 *"one enormous bite"*: Donoso, *The Boom in Spanish American Literature*, 29.

17. THE WHOLE STORY OF AMERICA

335 *"The situation of American literature is anomalous"*: Wilson, vol. 1, 5.

342 *"compulsory integration"*: Faulkner, "Letter to a Northern Editor."

18. BOOM

357 *"like statues in a park"*: Donoso, *The Boom in Spanish American Literature*, 13.

358 *"the internationalization of the Spanish American novel"*: Donoso, *The Boom in Spanish American Literature*, 37.

358 *"language takes over the role of protagonist"*: Donoso, *The Boom in Spanish American Literature*, 41.

358 *"continual bombardment of inquiry"*: Donoso, *The Boom in Spanish American Literature*, 45.

359 *"the golden age of the Beatles"*: Donoso, *The Boom in Spanish American Literature*, 91.

359 *"an eruption coming to nothing"*: Donoso, *The Boom in Spanish American Literature*, 3.

359 *"the first novel I tried to write"*: Martin, *Gabriel García Márquez*, 301.

359 *"did not get up for another eighteen months"*: Martin, *Gabriel García Márquez*, 286.

20. BEING HISTORICAL

377 *"The reader is [made] so docile"*: Forster, *Aspects of the Novel*, 36.

21. THE ENIGMA OF ARRIVAL

396 *"He looked in the mirror one day"*: French, *The World Is What It Is*, 22.

BIBLIOGRAPHY

PRIMARY SOURCES

Achebe, Chinua. *Things Fall Apart*. Special Sales Edition. New York: Penguin Books in association with the Heinemann African Writers Series, 2004.

Banti, Anna. *Artemisia*. Translated by Shirley D'Ardia Caracciolo. Introduction by Susan Sontag. Lincoln: University of Nebraska Press, 2003.

Bell, Anne Olivier, ed. *The Diary of Virginia Woolf: Volume 1, 1915–1919*. New York, Harcourt, 1977.

Bell, Anne Olivier, assisted by Andrew McNeillie, eds. *The Diary of Virginia Woolf: Volume 2, 1920–1924*. New York: Harcourt, Brace, 1978.

Bellow, Saul. *The Adventures of Augie March*. Introduction by Christopher Hitchens. New York: Penguin Books, 2006.

Bernanos, Georges. *Monsieur Ouine*. Translated by William S. Bush. Lincoln: University of Nebraska Press, 2000.

Carpentier, Alejo. *Explosion in the Cathedral*. Translated by Adrian Nathan West. Introduction by Alejandro Zambra. New York: Penguin Books, 2023.

Carpentier, Alejo. *The Kingdom of This World*. Translated by Pablo Medina. New York: Farrar, Straus and Giroux, 2017.

Carpentier, Alejo. *The Lost Steps*. Translated by Adrian Nathan West. Introduction by Leonardo Padura. New York: Penguin Books, 2023.

Colette. *The Complete Claudine*. Translated by Antonia White. New York: Farrar, Straus and Giroux, 1976.

Colette. *My Apprenticeships*. Translated by Helen Beauclerk. New York: Farrar, Straus and Giroux, 1978.

Colette. *Oeuvres: Tome I*. Paris: Bibliotheque de la Pleiade, Gallimard, 1984.

Colette. *The Pure and the Impure*. Translated by Helma Briffault. New York: New York Review Books, 2000.

Cowley, Malcolm, ed. *The Portable Faulkner*. New York: Penguin Books, 2003.

Dostoevsky, Fyodor. *Notes from Underground and The Double*. Translated by Roland Wilkes. New York: Penguin Books, 2009.

Dostoevsky, Fyodor. *Memoirs from the House of the Dead*. Edited by Ronald Hingley. Translated by Jesse Coulson. Oxford, UK: Oxford World Classics, 2008.

Ellison, Ralph. *Invisible Man*. New York: Vintage Books, 1995.

García Márquez, Gabriel. *One Hundred Years of Solitude*. Translated by Gregory Rabassa. New York: Harper Perennial Classics, 1992.

Gide, André. *Fruits of the Earth*. Translated by [unidentified]. Harmondsworth, UK: Penguin Books in association with Secker and Warburg, 1970.

Gide, André. *If It Die*. Translated by Dorothy Bussy. Harmondsworth, UK: Penguin Books in association with Martin Secker and Warburg, 1977.

Gide, André. *Journals 1889–1949*. Translated, Selected, and Edited by Justin O'Brien. Harmondsworth, UK: Penguin Books, 1967.

Gide, André. *Madeleine (Et Nunc Manet in Te)*. Translated by Justin O'Brien. New York: Alfred A. Knopf, 1952.

Gide, André. *The Immoralist*. Translated by Richard Howard. New York: Vintage Books, 1996.

Gide, André. *Pretexts: Reflections on Literature and Morality*. Edited by Justin O'Brien. New York: Dell, 1964.

Grossman, Vasily. *Life and Fate*. Translated by Robert Chandler. New York: New York Review Books, 2006.

Grossman, Vasily. *Stalingrad*. Translated by Robert and Elizabeth Chandler. New York: New York Review Books, 2019.

Hemingway, Ernest. *The Garden of Eden*. New York: Scribner, 1986.

Hemingway, Ernest. *A Moveable Feast: The Restored Edition*. Edited by Sean Hemingway. New York: Scribner, 2009.

Hemingway, Ernest. *The Nick Adams Stories*. New York: Scribner, 2003.

Hemingway, Ernest. *The Sun Also Rises and Other Writings, 1918–1926*. Edited by Robert W. Trogdon. New York: Library of America, 2020.

James, Henry. *Literary Criticism: Essays on Literature, American Writers, English Writers*. Edited by Leon Edel. New York: Library of America, 1984.

James, Henry. *Literary Criticism: French Writers, Other European Writers, the Prefaces to the New York Edition*. New York: Library of America, 1984.

Joyce, James. *Ulysses*. Edited by Hans Walter Gabler with Wolfhard Steppe and Claus Melchior. New York: Random House, 1986.

Kafka, Franz. *Amerika: The Man Who Disappeared*. Translated by Michael Hofmann. New York: New Directions, 1996.

Kafka, Franz. *The Complete Stories*. Edited by Nahum H. Glatzer. Translated by Edwin and Willa Muir. New York: Schocken Books, 1971.

Kafka, Franz. *Diaries: 1910–1914*. Edited by Max Brod. Translated by Joseph Kresh. New York: Schocken, 1965.

Kafka, Franz. *Letters to Felice*. Edited by Erich Heller and Jurgen Born. Translated by James Stern and Elisabeth Duckworth. London: Martin Secker and Warburg, London, 1974.

Kipling, Rudyard. *Kim*. Edited and with an Introduction by Edward Said. London: Penguin Books, 1987.

Kipling, Rudyard. *Something of Myself and Other Autobiographical Writings*. Edited by Thomas Pinney. Cambridge, UK: Cambridge University Press, 1990.

Kubin, Alfred. *The Other Side*. Translated by Mike Mitchell. Sawtry, UK: Dedalus, 2000.

Lawrence, D. H. *Phoenix: The Posthumous Papers*. Edited with an introduction by Edward D. McDonald. New York: Viking Press, 1936.

Lawrence, D. H. *The Rainbow*. Edited by Mark Kinkead-Weekes. Introduction by James Wood. New York: Penguin Books, 2007.

Lawrence, D. H. *Sons and Lovers.* Edited by Helen Baron and Carl Baron. Introduction by Blake Morrison. New York: Penguin Books, 2006.

Lawrence, D. H. *Women in Love.* Introduction by Amit Chaudhuri. New York: Penguin Books, 2007.

Machado de Assis, Joaquim. *Epitaph of a Small Winner* [The Posthumous Memoirs of Brás Cubas]. Translated by William L. Grossman. New York: Avon Books, 1978.

Machado de Assis, Joaquim. *Helena.* Translated by Helen Caldwell. Berkeley: University of California Press, 1984.

Mann, Thomas. *Buddenbrooks: The Decline of a Family.* Translated by John Wood. New York: Vintage Books, 1994.

Mann, Thomas. *Death in Venice and Other Tales.* Translated by Joachim Neugroschel. New York: Penguin Books, 1998.

Mann, Thomas. *Diaries 1918–1939.* Edited by Hermann Kesten. Translated by Richard and Clara Winston. New York: Harry N. Abrams, 1982.

Mann, Thomas. *The Magic Mountain.* Translated by John Wood. New York: Vintage Books, 1995.

Mann, Thomas. *Reflections of a Nonpolitical Man.* Translated by Walter D. Morris. New York: Frederick Ungar, 1983.

Morante, Elsa. *History: A Novel.* Translated by William Weaver. New York: Avon Books, 1979.

Musil, Robert. *Agathe, or the Forgotten Sister.* Translated by Joel Agee. New York: New York Review Books, 2020.

Musil, Robert. *The Man Without Qualities.* Translated by Eithne Wilkins and Ernst Kaiser. New York: G. P. Putnam, 1980.

Musil, Robert. *The Man Without Qualities.*Translated by Sophie Wilkins and Burton Pike. New York: Alfred A. Knopf, 1995.

Nabokov, Vladimir. *The Gift.* New York: Vintage Books, 1993.

Nabokov, Vladimir. *Lolita.* New York: Vintage Books, 1997.

Nabokov, Vladimir. *Speak, Memory: An Autobigraphy Revisited.* Revised edition. New York: G. P. Putnam and Sons, 1966.

Ngũgĩwa Thiong'o. *Weep Not, Child.* Introduction by Ben Okri. New York: Penguin Books, 2012.

Naipaul, V. S. *The Enigma of Arrival.* New York: Alfred A. Knopf, 1986.

Nossack, Hans Erich. *The End: Hamburg 1943.* Translated by Joel Agee. Chicago: University of Chicago Press, 2004.

Perec, Georges. *Life A User's Manual.* Translated by David Bellos. Boston: David R. Godine, 1988.

Perec, Georges. *W, or the Memory of Childhood.* Translated by David Bellos. New York: Vintage Classics, 2011.

Pontopiddan, Henrik. *A Fortunate Man.* Translated by Paul Larkin. Copenhagen: Museum Tusculanum Press, 2018.

Proust, Marcel. *Against Sainte Beuve and Other Essays.* Translated by John Sturrock. New York: Penguin Books, 1994.

Proust, Marcel. *Du coté de chez Swann.* Edited by Pierre Clarac and André Ferre. Collection Folio. Paris: Gallimard, 1978.

Proust, Marcel. *In Search of Lost Time.* Translated by C. K. Scott Moncrieff and Terence Kilmartin. Three volumes. New York: Random House, 1981.

Proust, Marcel. *La Prisonnière.* Edited by Pierre-Edmond Robert. Collection Folio Classique. Paris: Gallimard, 1988.

Proust, Marcel. *Swann's Way*. Translated by James Grieve. New York: New York Review Books, 2022.

Proust, Marcel. *Le Temps retrouvé*. Edited by Perre-Edmond Robert. Collection Folio Classique. Paris: Gallimard, 1988.

Rhys, Jean. *Good Morning, Midnight*. New York: Vintage Books, 1974.

Schwartz, Delmore. *Once and for All: The Best of Delmore Schwartz*. Edited by Craig Teicher. New York: New Directions, 2016.

Sebald, W. G. *Austerlitz*. Translated by Anthea Bell. New York: Random House, 2001.

Sōseki, Natsume. *Kokoro*. Translated by Edwin McClellan. Washington, D.C.: Gateway Editions, 1996.

Sōseki, Natsume. *My Individualism and Philosophical Foundations of Literature*. Translated by Sammy I. Tsunematsu. Introduction by Inger Sigrun Brodey. Boston: Tuttle Publishing, 2004.

Stein, Gertrude. *The Autobiography of Alice B. Toklas*. New York: Vintage Books, 1990.

Stein, Gertrude. *Geography and Plays*. Introduction by Sherwood Anderson. Boston: The Four Seas, 1922.

Stein, Gertrude. *Lectures in America*. Boston: Beacon Press, 1957.

Stein, Gertrude. *The Making of Americans*. Champaign, IL: Dalkey Archive Press, 1995.

Stein, Gertrude. *Three Lives*. Introduction by Ann Charters. New York: Penguin Books, 1990.

Svevo, Italo. *The Confessions of Zeno*. Translated by Beryl de Zoete. New York: Vintage Books, 1958.

Wells, H. G. *Experiment in Autobiography: Discoveries and Conclusions of a Very Ordinary Brain (since 1866)*. New York: Macmillan, 1934.

Wells, H. G. *The Island of Doctor Moreau*. Edited by Patrick Parrinder. Introduction by Margaret Atwood. New York: Penguin Books, 2005.

Wells, H. G. *Selected Stories*. Harmondsworth, UK: Penguin Books, 1958.

Wells, H. G. *Tono-Bungay*. Edited by Patrick Parrinder. Introduction by Edward Mendelsohn. New York: Penguin Books, 2005.

Woolf, Virginia. *The Common Reader*. First and second series combined in one volume. New York: Harcourt, Brace, 1948.

Woolf, Virginia. *A Haunted House and Other Stories*. Harmondsworth, UK: Penguin Books, 1973.

Woolf, Virginia. *Mrs. Dalloway*. Introduction by Maureen Howard. Orlando, FL: Harcourt, 1981.

Yourcenar, Marguerite. *The Memoirs of Hadrian and Reflections on the Composition of Hadrian*. Translated by Grace Frick in collaboration with the author. New York: Farrar, Straus and Giroux, 2005.

OTHER SOURCES

Adorno, Theodor. *Minima Moralia*. Translated by E.F.N. Jephcott. London: Verso, 1978.

Adorno, Theodor. *Notes to Literature*. Translated by Shierry Weber Nicolson. Two volumes. New York: Columbia University Press, 1991.

Angier, Carole. *Jean Rhys: Life and Work*. Boston: Little, Brown, 1990.

Angier, Carole. *Speak Silence: In Search of W. G. Sebald*. New York: Bloomsbury, 2021.

Auden, W. H., editor. *Nineteenth Century British Minor Poets*. New York: Dell, 1966.

Baker, Carlos, ed. *Ernest Hemingway: Selected Letters: 1917–1961*. New York: Scribner, 1981.

Bakhtin, Mikhail. *Problems of Dostoevsky's Poetics*. Edited and Translated by Caryl Emerson. Minneapolis: University of Minnesota Press, 1984.

Bellos, *Georges Perec: A Life in Words*. London: Harvill, 1993.

Benjamin, Walter. *Illuminations*. Edited by Hannah Arendt. Translated by Harry Zohn. New York: Schocken, 1969.

Benjamin, Walter. *One-Way Street*. Edited by Michael W. Jennings. Translated by Edmund Jephcott. Cambridge, MA: The Belknap Press of Harvard University Press, 2016.

Borges, Jorge Luis. *Selected Non-Fictions*. Edited by Eliot Weinberger. New York: Penguin Books, 2000.

Boyd, Brian. *Vladimir Nabokov: The American Years*. Princeton, NJ: Princeton University Press, 1991.

Boyd, Brian. *Vladimir Nabokov: The Russian Years*. Princeton, NJ: Princeton University Press, 1990.

Brendon, Piers. *The Dark Valley: Panorama of the 1930s*. New York: Vintage Books, 2002.

Brown, Edward J. *Russian Literature Since the Revolution*. Revised and Enlarged Edition. Cambridge, MA: Harvard University Press, 1982.

Brown, Frederick: *The Embrace of Unreason: France 1914–1940*. New York: Alfred A. Knopf, 2014.

Budgen, Frank. *James Joyce and the Making of "Ulysses."* Bloomington: Indiana University Press, 1960.

Callahan, John F., and Conner, Mark C., eds. *The Selected Letters of Ralph Ellison*. New York: Random House, 2019.

Calvino, Italo. *Six Memos for the Next Millennium*. Translated by Geoffrey Brock. Boston: Houghton Mifflin Harcourt, 2016.

Carter, William. *Marcel Proust: A Life*. New Haven, CT: Yale University Press, 2000.

Cezar de Castro Rocha, João, ed. *The Author as Plagiarist: The Case of Machado de Assis*. Dartmouth: Center for Portuguese Studies and Culture, University of Massachusetts, 2006.

Clark, Christopher. *The Sleepwalkers: How Europe Went to War in World War I*. New York: Harper Perennial, 2014.

Clark, T. J. *Farewell to an Idea: Episodes from a History of Modernism*. New Haven: Yale University Press, 1999.

Debord, Guy. *Comments on the Society of the Spectacle*. Translated by Malcolm Imrie. London: Verso, 1998.

Debord, Guy. *The Society of the Spectacle*. Translated by Donald Nicholson Smith. New York: Zone Books, 1995.

Deleuze, Gilles, and Felix Guattari. *Kafka: Toward a Minor Literature*. Translated by Dana Polan. Minneapolis: University of Minnesota Press. 1986.

Donoso, Jose. *The Boom in Spanish American Literature: A Personal History*. Translated by Grgory Kolovakos. New York: Columbia University Press, 1977.

Easton, Laird M., ed. and trans. *Journey to the Abyss: The Diaries of Count Harry Kessler: 1880–1918*. New York: Alfred A. Knopf, 2011.

Echeverria, Roberto Gonzalez. *Alejo Carpentier: The Pilgrim at Home*. Austin: University of Texas Press, 1990.

Eliot, T. S. *The Selected Prose of T. S. Eliot*. Edited and with an introduction by Frank Kermode. New York: Harcourt Brace Jovanovich, 1975.

Ellmann, Richard. *James Joyce*. New and Revised Edition. Oxford, UK: Oxford University Press, 1982.

Faulkner, William. "Letter to a Northern Editor." March 5, 1956. http://users.soc .umn.edu/~samaha/cases/faulkner_letter_northern_ed.html.

Ferguson, Niall. *The Pity of War: Explaining World War I*. Revised ed. New York: Basic Books, 2000.

Forster, E. M. *Aspects of the Novel*. New York: Harcourt, Brace, 1927.

Forster, E. M. *Two Cheers for Democracy*. New York: Harcourt, Brace, 1951.

Frank, Joseph. *Dostoevsky: A Writer in His Time*. Princeton, NJ: Princeton University Press, 2010.

Frank, Joseph, and David Goldstein, eds. *Selected Letters of Fyodor Dostoevsky*. Translated by Andrew R. MacAndrew. New Brunswick, NJ: Rutgers University Press, 1987.

French, Patrick. *The World Is What It Is: The Authorized Biography of V. S. Naipaul*. New York: Alfred A. Knopf, 2008.

Frisé, Adolf, Mark Mirsky, and Philip Payne, eds. *Robert Musil, Diaries: 1899–1941*. Translated by Philip Payne. New York: Basic Books, 1998.

Garrard, John, and Carol Garrard. *The Bones of Berdichev: The Life and Fate of Vasily Grossman*. New York: Free Press, 1996.

Gide, André. *Dostoevsky*. Translation unattributed. London: Secker and Warburg, 1949.

Gilmour, David. *The Long Recessional: The Imperial Life of Rudyard Kipling*. New York: Farrar, Straus and Giroux, 2002.

Gordon, Andrew. *A Modern History of Japan: From Tokugawa Times to the Present*. Oxford: Oxford University Press, 2003.

Grossman, Leonid. *Dostoevsky: His Life and Work*. Translated by Mary Mackler. Indianapolis: The Bobbs-Merrill Company, 1975.

Hamilton, Nigel. *The Brothers Mann*. New Haven, CT: Yale University Press, 1979.

Harss, Luis, and Barbara Dohmann. *Into the Mainstream: Conversations with Latin American Writers*. New York: Harper and Row, 1969.

Hayman, Ronald. *K: A Biography of Kafka*. London: Weidenfeld and Nicholson, 1981.

Heilbut, Anthony. *Thomas Mann: Eros and Literature*. New York: Alfred A. Knopf, 1996.

Hobhouse, Janet. *Everybody Who Was Anybody: A Biography of Gertrude Stein*. New York: Anchor Books, 1989.

Hobsbawm, Eric. *The Age of Extremes: A History of the World 1914–1991*. New York: Vintage Books, 1996.

Jackson, K. David. *Machado de Assis: A Literary Life*. New Haven, CT: Yale University Press, 2015.

Judt, Tony. *Postwar: A History of Europe Since 1945*. New York: Penguin Books, 2006.

Keene, Donald. *A History of Japanese Literature, Volume Three: Dawn to the West: Japanese Literature of the Modern Era: Fiction*. New York: Holt, Rinehart and Winston, 1984.

Kenner, Hugh. *A Sinking Island: The Modern English Writers*. New York: Alfred A. Knopf, 1988.

Kenner, Hugh. *Joyce's Voices*. Berkeley: University of California Press, 1979.

Lee, Hermione. *Virginia Woolf*. New York: Alfred A. Knopf, 1997.

Lestringant, Frank. *André Gide l'inquieteur.* Two volumes. Paris: Flammarion, 2011.

Lukács, Georg. *Realism in Our Time: Literature and the Class Struggle.* Translated by John and Necke Mander. Introduction by George Steiner. New York: Harper and Row, 1971.

Lukács, Georg. *The Theory of the Novel.* Translated by Anna Bostock. Cambridge, MA: MIT Press, 1971.

Maddox, Brenda. *D. H. Lawrence: The Story of a Marriage.* New York: Simon and Schuster, 1994.

Mann, Klaus. *André Gide and the Crisis of Modern Thought.* New York: Octagon Books, 1978.

Martin, Gerald. *Gabriel García Márquez: A Life.* New York: Alfred A. Knopf, 2008.

Martin, Gerald. *Journeys Through the Labyrinth: Latin American Fiction in the Twentieth Century.* London: Verso, 1989.

Mazower, Mark. *Dark Continent: Europe's Twentieth Century.* New York: Alfred A. Knopf, 1999.

Meyers, Jeffrey. *D. H. Lawrence: A Biography.* New York: Alfred A. Knopf, 1990.

Meyers, Jeffrey. *Hemingway: A Biography.* New York: Harper and Row, 1985.

Millett, Kate. *Sexual Politics.* New York: Doubleday. 1970.

Moore, Harry T., ed. *The Collected Letters of D. H. Lawrence.* Two Volumes. New York: Viking Press, 1962.

Nabokov, Vladimir. *Lectures on Literature.* New York: Mariner Books, 2002.

Nabokov, Vladimir. *Lectures on Russian Literature.* New York: Mariner Books, 2002.

Nadeau, Maurice. *The History of Surrealism.* Translated by Richard Howard. Cambridge, MA: The Belknap Press of the Harvard University Press, 1989.

Naipaul, V. S. *Reading and Writing: A Personal Account.* New York: New York Review Books, 2000.

Naipaul, V. S. *The Writer and the World: Essays.* Edited by Pankaj Mishra. New York: Vintage Books, 1992.

Nathan, John. *Sōseki: Modern Japan's Greatest Novelist.* New York: Columbia University Press, 2015.

Nicolson, Nigel, and Joan Trautmann, eds. *The Letters of Virginia Woolf: 1912–22.* New York: Harcourt Brace Jovanovich, 1976.

Olson, Charles. *Collected Prose.* Edited by Donald Allen and Benjamin Friedlander. Berkeley: University of California, 1997.

Painter, George. *Marcel Proust: A Biography.* New York: Vintage Books, 1978.

Pizzichini, Lilian. *The Blue Hour: A Life of Jean Rhys.* New York: W. W. Norton, 2009.

Polizzotti, Mark. *Revolution of the Mind: The Life of André Breton.* New York: Farrar, Straus and Giroux, 1995.

Proffer, Carl R., ed. *The Unpublished Dostoevsky: Diaries and Notebooks 1860–81.* Translated by T. S. Berczynski, Barbara Heldt Monter, Arline Boyer, and Ellendea Proffer. Two volumes. Ann Arbor, MI: Ardis, 1973.

Rorty, Richard. *Contingency, Irony, and Solidarity.* Cambridge, UK: Cambridge University Press, 1989.

Ruhle, Jurgen. *A Critical Study of the Writer and Communism in the Twentieth Century.* Translated by Jean Steinberg. New York: Frederick A. Praeger, 1969.

Schwarz, Roberto. *Misplaced Ideas: Essays on Brazilian Culture.* London: Verso, 1992.

Sherborne, Michael. *H .G. Wells: Another Kind of Life.* London: Peter Owen, 2010.

Sheridan, Alan. *André Gide: A Life in the Present.* Cambridge, MA: Harvard University Press, 1999.

Showalter, Elaine. *Sexual Anarchy: Gender and Culture at the Fin de Siècle*. New York: Bloomsbury, 1991.

Stach, Reiner. *Kafka: The Decisive Years*. Princeton, NJ: Princeton University Press, 2005.

Stevens, Wallace. *Collected Poetry and Prose*. Edited by Frank Kermode and Joan Richardson. New York: Library of America, 1997.

Svevo, Livia Veneziani. *Memoir of Italo Svevo*. Translated by Isabel Quigley. London: Libris, 1989.

Tadié, Jean-Yves. *Proust: A Life*. New York: Penguin Books, 2000.

Tatar, Maria, ed. *The Annotated Brothers Grimm*. New York: W. W. Norton, 2012.

Thirlwell, Adam. *Miss Herbert*. London: Jonathan Cape, 2007.

Thurman, Judith. *Secrets of the Flesh: A Life of Colette*. New York: Alfred A. Knopf, 1999.

Tuck, Lily. *Woman of Rome: A Life of Elsa Morante*. New York: Harper, 2008.

Watt, Ian. *The Rise of the Novel*. London: Hogarth Press, 1987.

Wilson, Edmund, ed. *The Shock of Recognition: The Development of Literature in the United States Recorded by the Men Who Made It*. Two volumes. Second edition. New York: Grossett and Dunlap, 1955.

Wineapple, Brenda. *Sister Brother: Gertrude and Leo Stein*. New York: Putnam, 1996.

Winston, Richard, and Clara Winston, eds. and trans. *The Letters of Thomas Mann: 1889–1955*. London: Secker and Warburg, 1970.

ACKNOWLEDGMENTS

In the fifteen years this book has been in the making, I have incurred all sorts of debts of gratitude. First and foremost, I want to thank my editors, Alex Star and Ian Van Wye, Michal Shavit and David Milner, and my agent, Zoe Pagnamenta, for their close attention and continuing care, both encouraging and exacting, throughout the long years, and for their patience and impatience. Alex's multiple readings of the manuscript at multiple stages was especially important in giving what began as a sprawl of texts about texts the form of a book.

Along the way, Peter Ginna and Lorin Stein also provided welcome editorial advice, and Maxine Bartow brought an acute eye to copyediting. I am grateful too to Samuel Titan, for reading my pages about Machado de Assis, and to Max Lawton, who kindly contributed new translations from *Notes from Underground.*

Rea Hederman and my longtime colleagues at New York Review Books—Susan Barba, Yongsun Bark, Abigail Dunn, Nicholas During, Patrick Hederman, Linda Hollick, Evan Johnston, Sara Kramer, Alex Ransom, Diane Seltzer, and Alaina Taylor—observed this book's slow growth with interest and, no doubt, some alarm. For their goodwill, bounteous assistance, and understanding, my heartfelt thanks. To my fellow editor Alex Andriesse I am particularly obliged for his careful reading of the book in its final stages.

There really is no measuring what I owe to the biographers, critics, historians, and especially translators—so many exemplary readers, thinkers, and writers—whose labors and insights I depend on throughout this book. I am grateful to them for all that I have learned from them, and as to all those things I may have only succeeded in getting wrong, the fault is of course mine.

My thanks to the Lannan Foundation for a residency in Marfa, Texas, during which I began the book and to Beatrice Monti and the Santa Maddalena Foundation for a spell in Tuscany that moved it forward.

Many people have patiently discussed this book with me over the years, leaving me to think and think again about just what it—and I—was about; many people, dear friends and family above all, have supported me in other ways that helped me to get the work done. To attempt to list them all would only be to leave someone out: I am grateful beyond words to every one of you. I do, however, want to mention by name a few people— some no longer living—without whom the work would never have been undertaken or taken the form it has: Robert Chandler, Monroe Engel, Hardy Frank, James Frank, Jonathan Galassi, Edmund Leites, Wendy Lesser, Jill Schoolman, Lee Siegel, and Ben Sonnenberg.

Thanks, finally, to Cynthia Zarin, under whose sheltering roof this book arrived at its end.

INDEX

ILLUSTRATION CREDITS

Frontispiece: National Library of Israel.

Page 2: Photographer unknown.

Page 27: Photographer unknown.

Page 189: Houghton Library, Harvard University.

Page 299: Photograph by Gordon Parks. Courtesy of and copyright © The Gordon Parks Foundation.

Page 410: Michael Brandon-Jones, negatives for *Austerlitz* (9/2000), from *Shadows of Reality: A Catalogue of W.G. Sebald's Photographic Materials*, edited by Clive Scott and Nick Warr. Boiler House Press, 2023. Image courtesy of The University of East Anglia.

Page 420: Copyright © Woodman Family Foundation / Artists Rights Society (ARS), New York.

Edwin Frank is the editorial director of New York Review Books and the founder of the NYRB Classics series. Born in Boulder, Colorado, and educated at Harvard College and Columbia University, he has been a Wallace Stegner Fellow and a Lannan Fellow and is a member of the New York Institute for the Humanities. He has taught in the Columbia Writing Program and served on the jury of the 2015 International Booker Prize. A Chevalier de l'Ordre des Arts et des Lettres and a recipient of an Award for Distinguished Service to the Arts from the American Academy of Arts and Letters, he is the author of *Snake Train: Poems, 1984–2013*.